Planning for Retirement Needs

Huebner School Series

Gary K. Stone, Editor

Huebner School Series

Planning for Retirement Needs
Second Edition

Kenn Beam Tacchino
David A. Littell

The American College/*Bryn Mawr, Pennsylvania*

This publication is designed to provide accurate and authoritative information about the subject covered. While every precaution has been taken in the preparation of this material, the editor and The American College assume no liability for damages resulting from the use of the information contained in this publication. The American College is not engaged in rendering legal, accounting, or other professional advice. If legal or other expert advice is required, the services of an appropriate professional should be sought.

© 1997 The American College
All rights reserved

Library of Congress Catalog Card Number 96-079876
ISBN 0-943590-89-2

Printed in the United States of America

Contents

Preface

This book represents a radical departure from traditional pension literature by focusing primarily on the practical application of the retirement material in a financial services practice. To this end it includes a feature titled "Your Financial Services Practice" as well as a shorter counterpart called the "Planning Note." In addition, the book is replete with examples and case studies intended to demonstrate how the pension concepts apply in real-world situations. This new practitioner-oriented approach came about for a variety of reasons, perhaps the most important of which is that student feedback indicated a need for change in this direction.

This book is geared to those with little or no experience in the retirement field. The material focuses on the basics that a financial services professional needs to know and deals sparingly with the retirement concepts that are not germane. For example, stock plans are not discussed in great detail because they are not a part of the typical financial services professional's practice. In addition, the amount of detail on any given topic depends on the topic's relevance to our audience. Determining the appropriate plan for the small business is covered in great detail, for example, whereas the question of which funding method the actuary should choose to fund a plan is covered only briefly. In other words, areas such as funding methods and stock plans are discussed in the context of how they apply to the financial services professional. While the material is applicable to the large-, medium-, and small-plan markets, the emphasis is on the small-plan market, where the financial services professional does most of his or her business.

Almost all general statements that one can make about pension material are subject to qualification or exception. If the qualifying remark or exception is of significant magnitude, we have put it into the text as a parenthetical expression. If the qualifying statement or exception would serve to confuse the larger issue, however, we have omitted it so that you won't get caught up in the minutia and miss the major point.

It is our sincere hope that this practitioner-oriented approach will speak to your interests and provide both a practical and educational treatment of retirement planning for the business and the business owner (Book One), as well as for the individual (Book Two). For those interested in learning more about the topics discussed in other course materials and books prepared by The American College, related courses include the following:

- HS 341 Selected Retirement Planning Topics, which goes deeper into qualified and other tax-advantaged retirement plans, focusing on advanced design issues, relevant topics not discussed in depth in this book, and issues relevant to those involved in the ongoing operation of retirement plans.
- HS 336 Financial Decision Making at Retirement, which goes deeper into the topic of individual retirement planning. In addition to a discussion of determining financial needs and identifying sources of retirement income, this course provides an in-depth look at important issues facing retirees, including the taxation of pension benefits, providing for medical coverage in retirement, and housing issues facing the retiree.

The authors would like to acknowledge the help of many individuals who were instrumental in the development of this textbook.

- Current and former faculty members who participated in the drafting of Book Two of this text including William J. Ruckstuhl, Edward E. Graves, and Robert J. Doyle.
- Practitioners in the retirement planning field including Gerald Levinson, Prentice Hall, Inc.; Joseph P. Garner, Paul Paleologopoulos, and Ken Switzer, all of Massachusetts Mutual Life Insurance Company; and Gary Lyons, who acted more like a coauthor than an adviser.
- Our fellow faculty members at The American College, especially Burton T. Beam, Jr., Ted Kurlowicz, and John J. McFadden.
- Educators outside The American College including Robert W. Cooper, PhD, Drake University, and George Rejda, PhD, University of Nebraska.
- Our librarian, Judith Hill, for her help with the "other resources" section of chapter 2.
- The College's editorial staff, especially Emily Sims for manuscript editing and Suzanne Walsh Rettew for her proofreading.
- The College's production staff, especially Evelyn Rice, Jane Hassinger, and Christina Hansen for their production assistance.

About the Authors

Kenn B. Tacchino, JD, LLM, is a consultant to The American College and an associate professor of taxation at Widener University. He received his BA from Muhlenberg College, his law degree (JD) from Western New England Law School, and his LLM from Widener University School of Law. Kenn is a member of the American Bar Association and National Council on Aging. He previously worked for Massachusetts Mutual Life Insurance Company and Prentice-Hall.

David A. Littell, JD, is associate professor of taxation at The American College. A native of Chicago, David holds a BA in Psychology from Northwestern University and a JD from the Boston University School of Law. At The American College he is responsible for course development in pension and retirement planning. He is a member of the Pennsylvania Bar and the Delaware County Bar Association. He was previously an attorney with Saul, Ewing, Remick & Saul, and Paul Tanker & Associates, both Philadelphia-based firms.

Book One

Pension and Retirement Planning Overview

THE ALLURE OF THE RETIREMENT MARKET

Retirement planning continues to be an important marketplace for the financial services professional. Public consciousness regarding the need for retirement planning has never been higher. The baby boom generation is marching towards retirement age; and pension benefits are more visible to consumers as employers promote the advantages of employee involvement in 401(k) and 403(b) plans. But this is only part of the story. The retirement market is where the money is; over $4 trillion in assets is owned by private retirement plansCeven more if you add federal, state, and local government plans.[1] Also Americans are aging. As of the year 2000 one out of every eight Americans will be over age 65, and by the year 2025 that figure will increase to one out of five. Considering these demographics, the potential for the growth of the retirement market is nothing short of tremendous.

For financial services professionals the retirement market offers many attractive and lucrative opportunities to serve clients including

- setting up qualified plans or other tax-advantaged retirement plans for corporations and other for-profit business entities (chapters 3–5)
- setting up retirement programs for nonprofit organizations (chapter 6)
- modifying existing retirement programs to maximize tax-shelter potential, either by changing the existing plan or by instituting multiple plans (chapters 3–6)
- supplementing existing retirement programs with 401(k) plans (chapter 5)
- updating existing plans to conform with legislative changes (chapters 7–10)
- updating existing plans to conform with changing organizational needs (chapters 7–10)
- designing retirement programs that meet the owner-employee's tax and savings objectives (chapters 7–10)
- advising clients about investment strategies that are appropriate for retirement programs (chapters 11–12)
- selling investment products that are appropriate for retirement programs (chapters 11–12)
- planning for the purchase of life insurance in tax-sheltered plans (chapters 10 and 12)
- setting up nonqualified plans for executives (chapters 15–16)
- selling IRAs to clients (chapters 17–18)
- planning for a client's retirement (chapters 19–24)
- planning for the best disposition of a client's retirement benefits (chapters 25–26)

Many financial services professionals choose to specialize in pensions. Others, however, complement their existing practice by providing one or more of these services under the umbrella of comprehensive financial planning. Whether you choose to specialize or offer one or more of these services to clients as part of a comprehensive package, the information in this book should open up a world of opportunity.

WHAT YOU WILL FIND IN THIS BOOK

This book is intended to be an introduction to two major areas. Book 1 discusses advising businesses and nonprofit organizations regarding the choice and maintenance of the appropriate retirement plan. Book 2 provides an introduction to individual retirement planning. The marriage of these two topics reflects the current state of the pension field. As the field has matured, selling retirement plans as tax-shelters or as employee benefits is not enough. With the popularity of 401(k) and 403(b) plans, which allow for employee pretax contributions, employees are more involved than ever in ensuring their own retirement security. Employers are often looking to their pension advisers to help educate their employees about retirement planning. Employee education also helps employees better understand and appreciate the retirement benefits provided by the employer. The pension adviser helping the business owner choose an appropriate retirement plan must be able to help the owner determine his or her retirement needs.

Even the financial adviser who works as a retirement planner but not directly with pension planning must still have a great deal of knowledge of the pension area. He or she will need to be able to evaluate clients' pension benefits and understand the tax treatment of those benefits.

Book 1 begins with an overview (chapters 1–2) of the types of plans available, tax implications, and strengths and weaknesses of various choices. Chapters 3–6 discuss the various types of plans available for both for-profit businesses and nonprofit entities. Then chapters 7–10 address specific plan design issues such as designing the benefit formula, plan eligibility, vesting provisions, participant loans, and plan distributions. After that is a discussion of the funding of retirement plans (chapters 11–12) and administrative issues involved in establishing, maintaining, and terminating plans (chapters 13–14). Chapters 15 and 16 introduce nonqualified plans, which are generally used to provide additional benefits for executives. The final two chapters of book 1 discuss the one type of tax-advantaged retirement savings vehicle available for individuals—IRAs.

Book 2 begins with a discussion of the need for individual retirement planning and a review of the types of relevant issues facing various types of clients. Following that is a discussion of determining an individual's financial needs in retirement and identifying sources of retirement income. Once needs and available income are identified, the next step is determining any income shortfall and choosing an appropriate investment strategy for saving additional amounts. The final topic in book 2 relates to an important issue facing retirees: how to plan for the distribution of pension assets held in qualified plans and other tax-advantaged retirement vehicles.

THE UNIVERSE OF RETIREMENT PLANNING VEHICLES

Book 1 focuses on an introduction to the world of employer- and individually sponsored retirement vehicles. Entering this world means exposure to a whole new vocabulary. Learning and remembering this terminology is facilitated by organizing and categorizing the material. You will find that many of the plans share similar features and only occasionally have differences. Throughout the book there are charts and tables that help you remember the material.

Tax-Advantaged Plans of Private Employers

One way to organize this discussion is to look at the types of tax-advantaged retirement plans that can be sponsored by for-profit and nonprofit employers. Most of these are employer-sponsored plans that are referred to as *qualified retirement plans*. Qualified plans include defined-benefit pension plans, cash balance plans, money purchase pension plans, target benefit plans, profit-sharing plans, 401(k) plans, stock bonus plans, and ESOPs.

Universe of Qualified Plans

- Defined-benefit pension plan
- Cash balance pension plan
- Money purchase pension plan
- Target benefit pension plan
- Profit- sharing plan
- 401(k) plan
- Stock bonus plan
- ESOP (employee stock ownership plan)

All qualified plans are subject to a number of basic requirements, and each type of plan has its own special characteristics. Two other types of tax-advantaged plans available to for-profit entities are referred to as SEPs (simplified employee pensions) and SIMPLEs (savings incentive match plans for employees). These tax-advantaged plans make up the bulk of the retirement market because of their tax advantages, business applications, and special appeal to the business owner. Tax-exempt entities can also sponsor qualified plans, SEPs, and SIMPLEs. In addition, those nonprofit organizations qualifying for Code Sec. 501(c)(3) tax-exempt status can sponsor 403(b) tax-sheltered annuities.

Other Tax-Advantaged Plans Available to Private Employers

- SEPs (Simplified employee pensions)
- SIMPLEs (Savings incentive match plans for employees)
- tax-sheltered annuities (limited to 501(c)(3) organizations)

All the employer-sponsored tax-advantaged plans share some characteristics. First, all are employer-sponsored plans that provide for deferred compensation. The compensation may be part of an employee's salary that is held for retirement (as in a salary reduction 401(k) plan, SIMPLE, or 403(b) plan), a share of the profits (as in a profit-sharing plan), an employer-provided amount equal to a percentage of salary (as in a money-purchase plan), or the promise of a monthly salary substitute after retirement (as in a defined-benefit plan). In all tax-advantaged plans the sponsor is required to make contributions to a trust or an insurance contract or, the case of a SEP or SIMPLE, an IRA account. Such amounts are held and invested and distributed only at a later time according to the rules applicable to that plan.

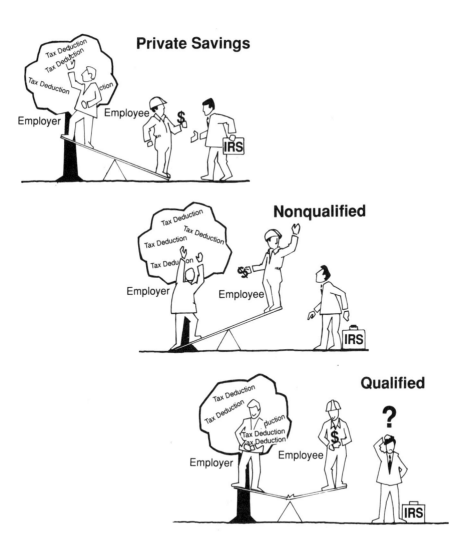

What makes tax-advantaged retirement plans special is that the employer gets to take a tax deduction at the time contributions are made to the plan, even though employees do not have to pay income tax until benefits are paid to them. Under the normal rules that apply to the taxation of compensation, the employer is eligible for a tax deduction only at the time employees are determined to have taxable income. For example, in a nonqualified plan for executives, the taxation of compensation can be deferred, but only at the cost of deferring the employer's deduction until the time taxes are paid. The normal taxation rules are like a seesaw—the employer on one end can be elevated (receive a tax deduction) only if the employee at the other end is touching the ground (paying taxes). Conversely, the employee can be elevated (avoid paying taxes) only if the employer is on the ground (not receiving a tax deduction). These "laws of tax physics" are suspended, however, if the employer is willing to satisfy the requirements of one of the tax-advantaged retirement plans.

A second unique tax advantage is that income on assets held in trust is not taxed. Retirement investments earn interest and appreciate without being subject to taxation in the year any gain occurs. (This same principle applies to the cash value buildup of life insurance.) Although such amounts are not taxed at this level, income is taxed as it is paid out as part of an employee's benefits.

A third advantage has to do with taxation of distributions. As we have discussed, benefits are not taxed until they are distributed from the plan. In addition, in most cases, distributions can be rolled over into other tax-advantaged plans, further delaying the payment of income taxes. Also death benefits paid from the proceeds of a life insurance contract are excludible from income to the extent of the pure insurance amount paid (the difference between the policy's face amount and its cash value). In addition, certain distributions from qualified plans (but not SEPs, SIMPLEs, or 403(b) plans) may be eligible for special tax treatment. Such treatment includes the following:

- *Forward averaging*—Although special averaging has generally been repealed, 10-year forward averaging continues to be available to qualified-plan participants born before January 1, 1936, and 5-year forward averaging is still available to all qualified plan participants who retire before the year 2000. Both of these methods soften the blow if the entire benefit is taken into income in one taxable year by reducing the effective tax rate.

- *Capital-gains treatment*—Another grandfathered tax rule allows individuals born before 1936 to treat the portion of a lump-sum distribution attributable to pre-1974 plan participation as capital gain subject to a grandfathered tax rate of 20 percent.

- *Deferral of gain on unrealized appreciation*—A recipient of a lump-sum distribution may elect to defer paying tax on the net unrealized appreciation in the employer securities that are distributed. If the distribution is not a lump-sum distribution, unrealized appreciation is excludible only to the extent that the appreciation is attributable to nondeductible employee contributions.

In exchange for these tax advantages, the law imposes—as you will see throughout book 1—a large number of requirements. Although the rules are different for each type of plan, there are many similarities. Before we get into the details it's helpful to get a feeling for what types of requirements are involved.

- *Broad employee participation*—In order for the owners and managers to participate in the tax benefits, the plan must cover a significant number of rank-and-file employees.
- *Vesting*—To make sure that employees who leave prior to the plan's normal retirement age receive some benefits, an employee must be vested in some benefits after he or she has reached a specified number of years of employment. Some types of plans require immediate vesting.
- *Employee communications*—All plans must describe to employees what the terms and conditions of the plan are and what benefits a participant will be entitled to.
- *Nondiscrimination*—All plans have rules regarding the relationship between the level of benefits provided for highly compensated employees and the level of benefits provided to the rank and file.
- *Prefunded*—As has already been mentioned, all plans require that assets be contributed to a funding vehicle—once assets are in the plan they are no longer owned by the employer sponsoring the plan. These assets can be used only to pay plan benefits.
- *Plan document*—Plans need to be stated clearly in writing.

Nonqualified Deferred Compensation

Another very different type of employer-sponsored retirement planning vehicle is the *nonqualified retirement plan*. Most use this term to describe deferred-compensation plans other than the tax-advantaged plans described above. Nonqualified plans differ in almost every way from their tax-advantaged counterparts. Unlike the tax-advantaged plans nonqualified plans are generally for only a few key people. There are few design restrictions regarding the benefit structure, vesting requirements, or coverage. In most cases nonqualified plans do not have separate assets. The employer either pays benefits out of general corporate assets or sets up a side account or trust.

In exchange for the added flexibility in plan design, the tax rules are not as kind to a nonqualified plan. A plan can generally be designed to defer the payment of income taxes by the employee until benefits are paid out—but the employer's tax deduction is deferred to the time of payout as well. This is a disincentive to the corporation, since cash payments or qualified plan contributions for the executive would be currently deductible. Since the loss of the tax deduction does not have an impact on nonprofit or governmental entities, Congress has established special limits on the amount of deferred compensation to employees of such entities under Code Sec. 457. Another difference between tax-advantaged and nonqualified plans is that benefits are not as secure. With a nonqualified arrangement, if the entity has financial difficulty, any money set aside to pay benefits can generally be attached by creditors.

IRAs

The final type of plan discussed in book 1 is the individual retirement arrangement (IRA). As its name implies, this type of plan is generally established not by the employer but by individuals. Although book 1 focuses mostly on employer-sponsored plans, an understanding of the IRA is crucial to this discussion. At times a business owner or employee will be faced with the choice of participating in a company-sponsored plan or establishing an IRA. Also in some cases an individual can choose to participate in both. However, today many individuals (or their spouses) who participate in an employer-sponsored retirement plan will not be able to make deductible IRA contributions. Nonetheless, IRAs are still important for the following three reasons:

1. Most working individuals may make annual nondeductible IRA contributions of up to $2,000.
2. The IRA is the funding vehicle for the employer-sponsored SEP and SIMPLE. This means that most rules applicable to IRAs will apply to those plans as well.
3. A significant portion of qualified plan and 403(b) benefits that are paid to terminated employees is rolled over into IRAs.

HOW TAX-ADVANTAGED PLANS BENEFIT EMPLOYEES

Tax-advantaged retirement plans make up the bulk of the retirement planning market because of the significant benefits to employees, employers, and business owners. Tax-sheltered plans play a significant role in the retirement security of American workers. Today, almost two-thirds of those nearing retirement age are covered by a pension plan.[2] Along with social security and individual savings, employer-provided pensions have a significant impact on the retirement security of Americans.

In addition, today employer-provided savings plans—like the 401(k) plan and the SIMPLE—help employees save additional amounts for retirement, by providing an easy payroll deduction savings vehicle with significant tax advantages for the employee. Savings plans have significantly changed the retirement planning landscape. 401(k) plans have virtually blasted their way onto the scene. Since they were established in 1978, they have grown to the extent that today one of four employees covered by a qualified plan participates in a

401(k) plan. Looking just at large and midsize employers the percentage is much higher.

Case Study: Saving on a Pretax versus an After-tax Basis

To demonstrate how saving on a tax-deferred basis affects retirement accumulations let's take the example of Bob Bluecollar and William Whitecollar. Bob Bluecollar (aged 40) earns $25,000 annually and has a 15 percent marginal federal tax rate. William Whitecollar (aged 40) earns $150,000 and has a 36 percent marginal federal tax rate. Both Bluecollar's and Whitecollar's employers offer them the opportunity to receive an additional $5,000 annually in cash or have such amount contributed to a 401(k) plan on a pretax basis. All invested money earns 10 percent interest.

Under the qualified plan both Bluecollar and Whitecollar will save $5,500 by the end of the first year:

Amount contributed	$5,000
plus 10 percent interest	500
Amount saved after one year	$5,500

If Bluecollar and Whitecollar invested the cash they received for retirement (individual savings approach), they would have less saved. The culprit would be the individual taxes that Bluecollar (15 percent) and Whitecollar (36 percent) would have to pay on the cash and interest earnings:

	Bluecollar	Whitecollar
Amount of bonus	$5,000	$5,000.00
minus individual taxes	750	1,800.00
Amount actually saved	4,250	3,200.00
plus 10 percent interest	425	320.00
Subtotal	4,675	3,520.00
minus taxes on interest earned	64	115.20
Amount saved after one year	$4,611	$3,404.80

Table 1-1 shows the growth of retirement savings for both employees from ages 40 to 65 using all methods. The figures reflect the amount of retirement savings if the funds are distributed to the employees in a lump sum at retirement. The qualified amount was calculated using 5-year forward averaging. Note that the savings for Bluecollar and Whitecollar under a qualified plan would be significant even after taxes have been paid. By age 65 Bluecollar's qualified plan would have accumulated $31,093 more than his individual savings. For Whitecollar the qualified approach would have yielded $196,178 more than individual savings. Not only is the qualified plan a more effective way to save, but also, as the figures indicate, the higher the employee's tax bracket, the greater the tax and retirement savings when a qualified plan is used. This special appeal to the highly paid employees is what fuels sales and can be considered a critical advantage of qualified plans.

TABLE 1-1
After-tax Comparison of Retirement Savings Methods*

Participant	Qualified	Individual Savings
Bluecollar at age 65	$393,850	$362,757
Whitecollar at age 65	393,850	197,672

*Certain underlying assumptions were made that may affect the actual amount received. The assumptions do not, however, significantly affect the disparity between the savings methods.

YOUR FINANCIAL SERVICES PRACTICE:
TRANSLATING TAX CONCEPTS

The extra retirement savings available under a qualified plan can perhaps best be explained to your client by using the concept of an interest-free loan. Explain to the client that by forgoing immediate taxation on amounts put into and earned by a qualified plan, the Internal Revenue Service is, in effect, making an interest-free loan to the plan participants to help them accumulate retirement savings. The amount of this "loan" for an individual in the 38 percent federal, state, and local tax bracket is 38 cents for every dollar saved and for every dollar of interest earned (in other words, the amount of the tax). To put it another way, if participants had to use after-tax dollars to save for retirement, they would have only 62 cents for every dollar saved and every dollar earned. The duration of this "interest-free loan" lasts until retirement distributions are received. For distributions paid out under a life annuity this means that the "interest-free loan" lasts in part until the employee's death. Almost everyone should understand this loan analogy—especially if they have an appreciation for time-value-of-money concepts (see below).

A Penny Saved—More Than a Penny Earned?

Another way to look at the savings opportunities in a tax-advantaged plan is simply to look at the advantages of orderly savings over a long period of time— or the time value of money. Here qualified plans don't really have an advantage over other types of savings, except for the ease of saving on a payroll deduction basis. Economists tell us that if we save over a period of time, our savings will increase due to the "opportunity cost" (that is, the gain obtained by investing as opposed to spending). In other words, by squirreling away money over time and forsaking the current use of that money we can ensure that the amount will increase through accumulated interest. Interest can be viewed as a way of quantifying the opportunity cost accruing to a person who waits to receive money. In the previous example, in the qualified plan both Bluecollar and Whitecollar accumulated after-tax earnings in the amount of $268,850.

After-tax lump sum received at age 65	$393,850
minus total amount invested	(125,000)
After-tax interest accumulation	$268,850

Note that the amount they have at age 65 is over three times the original investment. As you might expect, the combination of time value and qualified tax advantages is particularly suited to meeting the retirement-savings goal. Through the use of the qualified plan Bluecollar and Whitecollar have "purchased" some significantly enhanced retirement security.

WHY EMPLOYERS NEED TAX-ADVANTAGED RETIREMENT PLANS

Besides meeting the retirement needs of employees, what other incentives prompt employers to implement a retirement program? Unlike participation in the public retirement program—social security—participation in a tax-advantaged or nonqualified retirement program is voluntary. And administrative and funding costs represent a major expenditure (up to 10 percent of payroll for most medium-sized and large firms and even higher for firms where tax shelter is the primary objective). So what's the bottom-line payoff for these employers?

The payoff comes in the way retirement plans solve a number of operational problems. Although these solutions don't show up on the balance sheet, the following are key ingredients in a company's fiscal success:

- attraction and retention of employees
- avoidance or appeasement of unions
- employee motivation
- graceful transition in turning over the workforce
- social responsibility
- retirement saving as part of successful compensation planning

Attraction and Retention of Employees

Managers contend that the compelling reason for the salary levels and other employee benefits they offer is local and industry standards. The same logic holds true for private pension programs. In other words, if the local pay scale calls for X amount in salary to attract and retain employees, it also calls for a certain level of retirement benefits. Further, if industry standards in insurance, for example, call for a certain level of commissions, they also call for a certain level of retirement benefits. Employers who ignore what the competition is doing with their retirement programs soon become noncompetitive.

By meeting competitive standards, retirement programs play a special role in attracting and retaining key employees. An attractive retirement program has a special appeal for employees whose current income needs are being satisfied. Those employees whose skill and knowledge are at such a level as to command a high salary are particularly interested in a qualified plan as a means of sheltering their earnings from taxes. What's more, these highly compensated employees are usually desired by both an employer and a competitor, and the right retirement plan may be the deciding factor in determining which employment opportunity is best.

Retirement plans also attract older employees who are not in the relatively rare position of being highly marketable. For example, many capable employees have flocked to federal and state government jobs—even though the salary levels are not equal to those in the private sector—because of their attractive retirement benefits (for example, up to 75 percent of final salary) and their unique plan design (early retirement after 20 years of service).

Perhaps the most important role of retirement plans is not to attract but to retain employees. If they are well designed and correctly implemented, retirement plans can be a primary reason for staying with a particular company. Benefit formulas can be structured to account for service, and benefits can be vested in such a way as to make it economically desirable for employees to stay on board instead of jumping ship to a competitor. In this age of job-hopping and multiple careers, a soundly structured pension program may be the employer's best recourse against the loss of experienced personnel.

Avoidance or Appeasement of Unions

In 1948 the courts determined that pensions constitute wages and are a condition of employment and therefore are negotiable for collective-bargaining purposes (*Inland Steel Company v. National Labor Relations Board,* 170 F.2d 247). Since then retirement plans and unions have developed a special relationship.

On one hand, retirement plans have been used to stifle or limit the growth of a union movement. The implementation of a retirement system or the embellishment of an existing system is believed by some managers to be a viable method of forestalling the establishment of a union. While federal law prohibits employers from "union busting," it does not prohibit the employer from competing with unions in trying to meet employee needs. What better way to demonstrate that the employer is looking out for the best interests of the employee than to establish a system of retirement benefits?

On the other hand, in unionized companies retirement benefits and other elements of plan design are always one of the hottest bargaining chips. In these companies, private retirement plans have become a necessary way of life rather than an option. In addition, the laws for and design of some union retirement plans (collectively bargained plans in which more than one employer is required to contribute) have evolved differently from the laws for nonunion plans. These laws for the so-called *multiemployer pension plans* are beyond the scope of this book and will not be covered. (For more information see Internal Revenue Code Sec. 414(f).)

Employee Motivation

Employee motivation is another reason employers need private retirement plans. Numerous studies have shown that profit-sharing plans and stock ownership plans both increase employee identification with the corporation and provide an incentive to increase productivity. A highly visible retirement plan can do wonders for employee morale, can improve workers' attitudes toward authority in the work environment, and may be the best management tool available for turning the corner on important projects or getting through crucial times.

Graceful Transition in Turning over the Workforce

Employers face a common problem dealing with the employees who outlast their usefulness. Such employees have been there "forever" and are highly compensated, but productivity does not warrant the high salary. These employees are sometimes called *superannuated employees.* Since it is not considered valid business practice to dismiss long-time employees who are not economically productive (for whatever reason) and since personal affection and respect may keep an employer from demoting these employees, an alternative solution is necessary. The alternative is the proper use of the pension plan. With sound plan structure, early retirement can be made attractive. In addition, "golden handshakes"—special packages that make early retirement even sweeter—can be offered. If handled properly, a potentially uncomfortable situation can be turned into a mutually beneficial solution through the use of the private retirement program.

Social Responsibility

Some employers ask for private retirement programs because of their social desirability. These employers desire to provide economic security for retired workers despite the lower profit margin that will result. Traditionally the retired worker could rely on social security and private savings as well as a company pension. These employers, however, feel a need to beef up the company pension because they fear for the future existence of social security (at least in its current state), and they recognize that we have become a society of spenders and not savers. What's more, the needs of the aged are creeping more and more into the social consciousness, and these employers feel obliged to do their part by instituting forced savings through a retirement program.

Less altruistically, few employers want former employees to be destitute after retirement. Companies often go to painstaking lengths to be known as a good place to work, and fear of negative public relations stemming from the perception that the employer did not "take care of" employees can stimulate a social conscience.

Retirement Saving as Part of Successful Compensation Planning

One question often raised by clients is, Why not pay retirement benefits out as current compensation and let employees fend for themselves when it comes to saving for retirement? After all, the funds used to provide for retirement and the funds used to pay salary are both part of the same compensation package. Enlightened employers, however, feel that by committing a certain part of "salary" for retirement purposes they not only allow their employees to benefit from the aforementioned tax advantages of a qualified plan, but also provide employees with the most effective compensation package possible. In other words, they are providing a system that meets their employees' financial security needs for both today and tomorrow in the most tax-efficient manner available.

WHY BUSINESS OWNERS NEED TAX-ADVANTAGED RETIREMENT PLANS

Business owners have special needs and concerns when it comes to planning for their retirement and running their business. These include the following:

- tax sheltering as much income as possible
- solving liquidity problems that occur at retirement or death
- sheltering their assets from legal liability and bankruptcy
- avoiding taxes on excess accumulated earnings

Tax Shelter for Business Owners

Qualified plans and other tax-advantaged plans represent one of the best tax shelters available. We have already shown how much more an employee can save for retirement on a pretax versus an after-tax basis. It's important to remember that in the small business environment employers are also employees. Owners of closely held businesses, members of professional corporations, partners, and the self-employed frequently set up retirement plans with the tax sheltering of personal income as their primary motivation. These markets are comprised of upscale clients who often ask to get the most possible tax savings from the qualified-plan tax shelter (and consequently make the biggest contributions toward their retirement). Retirement plans are one of the few tax shelters still remaining today. They are also attractive because the rules are clear (making the degree of tax risk quite low) and this is one tax-shelter that is not likely to go away.

Note that when the business owner compares saving for retirement through a tax-sheltered vehicle versus after-tax savings, the comparison is not quite the same as for the average employee. The owner may look at required contributions for other employees in the qualified environment as a drain on his or her own savings account. If, for example, only 50 percent of the contribution to the plan is for the benefit of the owner, the owner may feel that he or she is better off taking the entire contribution amount, paying taxes, and saving outside the plan. This is a legitimate concern and may stop some business owners from establishing a plan. However, when working with these types of clients, be sure to fully discuss the following:

- The reality is that in almost all cases the contributions for the other employees have some value to the business. If contributions to the plan are not made, the employer may end up having to pay additional cash benefits to employees. Also, some of the other reasons for establishing a plan discussed above such as employee attraction and retention will come into play.
- If the contributions do have some value to the owner, then when making the mathematical comparison of the qualified plan versus after-tax savings, consider quantifying that value. Take, for example, the small business owner with $50,000 to save. If the amount is contributed to a qualified plan, assume that he or she will get $30,000 and other employees will get the other $20,000. If the owner feels that the contribution for the employees has a value to the business of $10,000, then compare a $40,000 contribution to the plan versus $40,000 saved in an after-tax environment.
- An experienced pension professional may be able to come up with creative ways to limit contributions for other employees. In today's pension environment there are some viable options.

Liquidity Concerns

In addition to appealing to business owners as a stable tax shelter, qualified plans are appealing because they solve liquidity problems that often occur at retirement or death. Small business owners typically have a difficult time building business or personal liquidity. They are self-achievers and feel psychologically compelled to reinvest money in their "baby." In other words, a common profile for the business owner is an individual who initially finds success by investing in himself or herself and the business and who continues to do so throughout his or her lifetime. Since his or her "money personality" tends to be more that of a spender than of a saver, the savings that occur through a qualified plan may represent the business owner's only cash available at retirement or death. Thus the qualified plan (along with, for example, a buy-sell agreement) may be essential to the continuation of the business after death or retirement.

Financial Security Concerns

A third reason that business owners are well served with a tax-advantaged retirement plan is that the plan may provide them with some financial security in the event that their business fails. Federal pension law generally forbids the assignment or alienation of pension benefits. Federal bankruptcy law, however, does not specifically exempt pension assets from the bankrupt estate. For many years the courts disagreed on this issue. The issue was finally settled by the United States Supreme Court in the case of *Patterson v. Shumate* (112 S. Ct. 1662 (1992)). The court granted extremely broad protection for assets held in retirement plans subject to the protection of ERISA—declaring that such benefits would be excluded from the bankrupt estate. *Patterson* protection seems quite secure for amounts held in qualified plans except in one case. Plans that cover only the business owner and his or her spouse are not subject to ERISA and therefore not eligible for Patterson protection. It is possible, however, for state law to expand protection to such plans. Similarly, whether IRAs are eligible for protection is a matter of state law.

Patterson protection is great news for the small business owner who can protect himself or herself from financial ruin (in case of business failure) by accumulating assets in a qualified plan. This is also good news for the financial services consultant, who now has one more reason to convince the employer to establish a retirement plan. As noted above the law is still evolving in this area and if bankruptcy protection is a critical concern for the owner, he or she should seek legal advice.

Accumulated Earnings Tax Concerns

Qualified plan contributions sometimes provide one other advantage to the small corporation—that is, lowering the business's exposure to the accumulated earnings tax. This tax is essentially a penalty tax for C corporations that attempt to reduce shareholders' tax burden by accumulating earnings instead of paying them out to shareholders. The tax rate on improper accumulations is 39.6% of accumulations that exceed $250,000 ($150,000 for a personal services corporation). Any amounts contributed to a qualified plan will reduce the exposure to the accumulated earnings tax. For a discussion of the accumulated earnings tax, see Code Secs. 531 through 537.

NOTES

1. *1995 Life Insurance Fact Book Update*, Council of Life Insurance, 1995.
2. General Accounting Office report of Aug. 5, 1996.

2

The Retirement Field

Success in finding clients, planning for clients, and servicing clients starts with an understanding of the boundaries, players, and equipment involved in the retirement field. The retirement field's boundaries are the rules set up by federal legislation and government agencies; the players include your clients, potential clients, support-service companies, and even the inner workings of your own organization; and the equipment is the information sources that are available to provide answers when experience fails to. This chapter will take you on a tour of the retirement field and introduce you to the regulatory environment, pension players, and information sources that will become an integral part of your financial services practice.

Since the multifaceted pension industry is largely an outgrowth of the regulatory process, we'll explore this complex area first (including the relationship between the financial services professional and the industry-shaping laws) and review the functions of the regulatory agencies. Then we'll discuss the pension prospects—who's involved and to what extent—and the service and financial organizations that serve them, with special emphasis on the insurance industry. We'll end by reviewing the sources for pension information—those that provide answers to a client's questions and those that analyze current trends and put pensions in perspective.

THE LEGISLATIVE ENVIRONMENT

The passage of the Employee Retirement Income Security Act (ERISA) in 1974 marked the beginning of the current retirement-plan era. ERISA represented an intensified commitment by the federal government to oversee the retirement market (especially plans that cover nonhighly compensated employees). Leery of broken retirement promises and plans being used as tax shelters for the wealthy, the federal government decided to protect the retirement interests of all plan participants and implemented ERISA to establish equitable standards and curtail perceived abuses. The text of ERISA has become the pensioner's bible. ERISA's commandments forbid discrimination in favor of the "prohibited group" (highly compensated employees), restrictive vesting schedules that keep longtime participants from receiving benefits, and inadequate plan funding, which leads to bankrupt plans. In addition, ERISA requires reporting and disclosure of information about retirement plans to the Internal Revenue Service (IRS), the Department of Labor (DOL), the Pension Benefit Guaranty Corporation (PBGC), and plan participants. In fact, ERISA forces information to be widely disseminated, thereby causing such administrative nightmares that it has become affectionately known as the "full employment in pensions act."

ERISA is composed of four sections known as titles. The purpose of the first title is to protect an employee's right to collect benefits. To accomplish this, title I requires employers to report plan information to the federal government and disclose information to participants (reporting and disclosure rules), restricts unlimited employer discretion regarding vesting and plan participation (employers cannot discriminatorily choose whom to cover), implements plan funding standards (employers must set aside sufficient assets to fulfill retirement promises), and lists fiduciary responsibilities (the responsibilities and liabilities of those in charge). Title II amends the Internal Revenue Code, setting forth the necessary requirements for special tax treatment (the plan qualification rules); these requirements are covered in detail in chapters 7 through 10. Title III creates the regulatory and administrative framework necessary for ERISA's ongoing implementation. Responsibilities are divided between the Internal Revenue Service and the Department of Labor, with the IRS having primary jurisdiction for much of the initial and operational administration of pension plans. Title IV establishes the Pension Benefit Guaranty Corporation, an agency that insures pension benefits. The PBGC collects premiums from covered plans (defined-benefit plans only; defined-contribution plans are not insured) and insures a minimum level of benefits for employees if the plan is terminated with insufficient funds.

The enforcement strategies provided by ERISA are interesting. To enforce title I of ERISA, plan participants, the Department of Labor, and plan fiduciaries can sue to force the payment of appropriate benefits and to require plan representatives to fulfill their jobs. Also, to encourage compliance, errant plan officials can be held personally liable for losses to the plan, fined for certain errors, and in some cases even held criminally liable. It is interesting to note that courts have generally interpreted the enforcement provisions of ERISA to prohibit monetary punitive damages for ERISA claims. Even though ERISA does provide for the award of attorney's fees, the inability to receive punitive damages has probably limited the number of private suits under ERISA over the years.

The strategy for encouraging compliance under the Internal Revenue Code is quite different. Here, both the plan sponsor and the plan participants enjoy special tax treatment in exchange for compliance with the law. Failure to comply can allow the IRS to take away the plan's tax-advantaged status. Since this penalty can harm participants (who are not responsible for ensuring plan compliance), plan disqualification is rarely enforced. In lieu of this terminal penalty, the IRS often negotiates a monetary penalty (payable by the sponsor) and requires that the employer fix any plan defects.[1] Disqualification is not the sole punishment contemplated under the Code. Some plan defects result, not in plan disqualification, but in a penalty tax. Examples of this will be seen throughout the text.

Unfortunately (or fortunately, depending upon your perspective) ERISA was just the beginning of what has seemed like an endless stream of legislation further regulating private pension plans. From 1974 to 1996 there have been significant law changes almost every other year. And the changes keep on coming. In 1996 Congress made sweeping pension changes in the Small Business Job Opportunities Act of 1996. For those interested in a blow-by-blow description of the changes over the years, see appendix 1. For the newcomer to the pension field the presentation in the appendix may seem overwhelming and confusing. Therefore an overview of some of the major areas of congressional involvement and a description of the legislative trends over the years appear below.

- *Taxation of pension benefits*—At the time of ERISA, pension benefits were subject to many significant income and estate tax benefits. Over the years, one by one, the special tax advantages have been repealed. For example, at one time pension benefits were not subject to estate taxes at all. Today, all pension assets that remain after the death of the participant are included in the taxable estate. Similarly, many of the special income tax rules have been repealed and in most cases pension income is treated as any other ordinary income (although some rules have been grandfathered and others have been repealed prospectively).

- *IRAs*—There has been no clear trend with regard to IRA legislation. Rule changes have swayed with the political breeze. At the time of ERISA, deductible IRA contributions were limited, then IRAs were opened up to virtually everyone, and today, once again, deductible contributions are available only to those who are either earning low incomes or who are not covered under an employer-sponsored pension plan.

- *Maximum deductible contributions*—Here there has been a fairly clear trend: to lower the maximum deductible contribution for highly compensated employees. The tax-sheltering of retirement income results in the loss of significant tax revenue—and one target for raising revenue has been to reduce deductible pension contributions, especially for the highly compensated. It seems that Congress has found every conceivable way to limit contributions, including lowering the maximum allowable amount; freezing cost-of-living adjustments on contribution limits; limiting the amount of compensation that can be taken into account; imposing limits on employee contributions; and aggregating plans. This trend has had a significant impact on executive compensation and benefit planning, making supplemental executive nonqualified deferred-compensation plans a more and more important part of the retirement planning package.

- *Limiting tax deferral*—Tax revenue is also lost the longer pension assets remain in a tax-deferred environment. To speed up the taxation of benefits, Code Section 401(a)(9) was introduced in 1986, requiring that distributions from all tax-sheltered plans begin at age 70 1/2 (or, in some cases at actual retirement, if later). These minimum distribution rules are quite complex and have an impact on any retiree receiving qualified plan, 403(b), or IRA distributions.

- *Parity*—Over the years the trend has been towards giving all types of business entities equal access to retirement plan vehicles. With a few minor exceptions, today C corporations, S corporations, sole proprietorships, partnerships, and even limited liability companies (LLCs) are all on the same footing.

- *Plans of small businesses*—Apparently, based on the perception that retirement plans of small businesses have treated rank-and-file employees unfairly, today a special set of rules, referred to as the *top-heavy requirements,* applies to the plans of many small businesses. These rules require special minimum contribution and vesting requirements for certain top-heavy plans.

- *Affiliation requirements*—To ensure that businesses cannot avoid pension coverage requirements by operating separate entities, and to eliminate "double dipping" under the maximum deduction rules, Congress has enacted over the years a series of complex rules requiring the aggregation of related employers. These rules have successfully eliminated loopholes and at the same time have complicated matters for both multinational corporations operating multiple divisions and for the small entrepreneur involved in several businesses.

- *Funding*—ERISA imposed minimum funding requirements for defined-benefit pension plans, and established the Pension Benefit Guaranty Corporation (PBGC). This organization ensures that employees in privately sponsored defined-benefit plans will receive at least some of the benefits promised by the plan. Over the years the PBGC has had to fork out large sums of money and is running a significant deficit. In response there have been numerous law changes shoring up the employer's funding requirements and the level of PBGC premiums. According to the PBGC, as of 1996 the problem of plan underfunding is improving, after the major law changes that occurred in 1994.

- *Employee Stock Ownership Plans (ESOPs)*—To encourage employee stock ownership, in 1981 the Economic Recovery Tax Act (ERTA) provided for a new type of retirement plan vehicle with numerous special tax advantages referred to as an ESOP. Today, some of these provisions have been repealed, but ESOPs still provide significant tax advantages, as well as a mechanism for a plan to purchase stock on a leveraged basis—providing a viable buyer for the small business owner looking to sell or retire. In fact, the 1996 Act now allows an S corporation the opportunity to sponsor an ESOP.

- *Simplification*—One legislative trend that had been consistent from the time of ERISA until 1996 was that each new law made the pension world more complex. Interestingly, in 1996, we had true pension simplification. The changes are modest, but hopefully future legislation will continue in this direction. Provisions include simplifying the definition of highly compensated employees, simplifying the distribution rules, and eliminating several complex aggregation requirements. This new law also introduced the SIMPLE, a savings plan alternative to the 401(k) plan with fewer administrative requirements.

REGULATORY AGENCIES

Legislation makes up only part of the regulatory picture. The other part, the administration of the qualified-plan system (and, to a lesser extent, the nonqualified-plan system), is carried out by the Internal Revenue Service, the department that is required to interpret the laws, explain legal fine points, and oversee the day-to-day operations of retirement plans.

YOUR FINANCIAL SERVICES PRACTICE:
NEW LEGISLATION AS A MARKETING OPPORTUNITY

The constant legislative changes that occur in the retirement area (some might call it overregulation) affect the financial services professional in many ways.

- Continual plan review is necessary to determine what impact the new legislation will have on corporate retirement goals.
- Plans must be serviced more frequently because new legislation requires plan amendments to be made almost annually.
- Clients rely on additional communication and explanation because pension law becomes increasingly complex and detailed.
- Continued education becomes necessary to keep up with the new laws.

One side effect of this constant federal legislation is the opportunity for financial services professionals to perform a detailed review of the plan and corporate retirement goals. Without legislative change and subsequent plan amendment employers might ignore their plans, and the plans could become stale and outdated. The financial services professional should capitalize on the opportunity created by legislative change and help the business owner evaluate new retirement goals and strategies.

A second side effect of federal legislation is the need for additional retirement coverage for highly compensated employees. The legislative trend curtailing the amount of tax-favored retirement savings for the highly paid creates an opportunity for the financial services professional to provide or recommend alternative coverage.

The Internal Revenue Service

The IRS plays the most prominent role of all the bureaucratic agencies.

- It supervises the creation of new retirement plans (in pension parlance, initial plan qualification).
- It monitors and audits the operation of existing plans.
- It interprets federal legislation, especially with regard to the tax consequences of certain pension plan designs.

Initial Plan Qualification

In order for an employer to receive favorable tax treatment the pension plan must meet the qualification requirements. Plan sponsors may, and usually do, request an IRS advance determination that the plan meets those requirements. This IRS program is handled through a number of key IRS district offices. Employers send in the plan and appropriate forms requesting IRS approval; the

IRS agent checks the plan to see if it meets the guidelines (over time the IRS has developed elaborate rules regarding which provisions may and may not be included); and, if necessary, the IRS and employer enter into negotiations over points at issue. If the plan meets IRS standards, a favorable advance-determination letter—which assures the employer that the plan is qualified and that the first year's contributions will be deductible—is issued. Although the program is voluntary, most employers take advantage of getting "preapproval" that plan contributions are eligible for special tax treatment.

Ongoing Auditing

The IRS also monitors retirement plans after they have been initially qualified by requiring many reports and statements known as the 5500 family of forms to be filed. The purpose of IRS surveillance is to make sure that changes in facts or circumstances have not affected plan qualification and that plans are used as retirement vehicles rather than as a tax shelter for the prohibited group. Information supplied in these annual filings includes the type and structure of the plan, plan assets, plan liabilities, plan income, and plan funding. In addition, information regarding plan changes, actuarial methods, and distributions to participants and their beneficiaries is required.

In recent years the IRS has developed another ongoing enforcement strategy that encourages employers to step forward voluntarily when plan problems are discovered. In exchange for voluntary compliance the employer is subject to much smaller penalties—usually a set fee—instead of the much larger penalties that could occur if the IRS found the problem upon plan audit. This program is referred to as the *voluntary compliance resolution program* or *VCR*. The IRS currently has an ongoing program for qualified plans and for 403(b) tax-sheltered annuities.

Interpretation

One of the major responsibilities of the IRS is to issue numerous communications that further explain the existing laws of the Internal Revenue Code. These communications include the following:

- *Final regulations* explain and interpret the various sections of the Internal Revenue Code and deal with legal fine points that aren't specifically addressed in the Code. Final regulations are legally enforceable, and the Internal Revenue Service is bound by them. They are originally published in the *Internal Revenue Bulletin* and the *Federal Register* and are later bound together with other regulations in a set of *Internal Revenue Regulations*. Final regulations can also be found in many of the loose-leaf services (discussed later).
- *Proposed regulations* are sometimes issued right after major legislation to give guidance to practitioners on complex provisions of new laws.

Unlike final regulations, proposed regulations will have no legal force or effect unless they specifically state that they can be relied upon. Still they are an indication of the IRS's current thinking and are widely followed. Proposed regulations can be changed before they are finalized—often as the result of negative feedback at public hearings.

- *Temporary regulations* may be issued as an alternative to final regulations, or can be issued simultaneously with proposed regulations. They are binding until they are superseded or withdrawn. This allows individual and corporate taxpayers to rely on the regulations without fear of incurring a Sec. 6661 penalty for substantially understating income tax liability, a protection that is not available to proposed regulations. A great deal of time can pass between the time a regulation is proposed and when it becomes final, and temporary regulations are relied on heavily in the interim.

- *Revenue rulings* are the IRS's interpretations of the provisions of the Internal Revenue Code and regulations as they apply to factual situations that taxpayers have presented. Revenue rulings are replete with valuable examples that clarify complex legal issues and may be used as precedents, thus giving you and your clients a sense of security if you are venturing into an area to which the rulings apply.

- *Private-letter rulings* interpret the law in light of a specific set of circumstances and indicate whether the IRS believes the action to be acceptable. Private letter rulings address only the specific facts presented to the IRS and, because of this, a taxpayer cannot rely upon guidance provided. Still, they are an important form of guidance, since they address real-life cases that might be similar to your client's situation. (*Planning Note:* If the IRS's position regarding a situation your client is entering into is unclear, you should recommend that the client consider getting a private-letter ruling. For a fee the IRS will issue a ruling that will be binding in the client's situation.)

- *Publications* include general reviews of retirement topics provided by the IRS. Using understandable terms (no legalese), these publications cover a variety of topics. (*Planning Note:* Publications are written to provide a general overview of the tax law on certain topics. The publications on Keogh plans and qualified retirement plans make good mailers for your clients.)

The Department of Labor (DOL)

Through its Office of Pension and Welfare Benefit Plans (OPWBP) the DOL is heavily involved in the pension arena.

- It ensures that plan participants are adequately informed through enforcement of some of the reporting and disclosure rules.

- It polices the investment of plan assets.
- It polices the actions of those in charge of the pension plans (fiduciaries).
- It interprets legislation.

Reporting and Disclosure Rules

Your clients are required to file descriptions of the pension plan *(summary plan descriptions)* with the DOL, as well as summaries of significant changes to the plan. The summary plan description (SPD) is intended to explain clearly the plan provisions to participants—including eligibility requirements, benefit levels, and circumstances in which benefits may be lost. Failure to comply with this or other reporting and disclosure requirements can result in fines and, in some egregious cases, imprisonment.

Prohibited Transactions

A second duty of the DOL is to oversee plan investments. To assure that no self-dealing or conflict of interest is involved, ERISA provides that plans cannot have certain dealings with parties who have close relationships with the plan or the company (referred to as parties in interest). Such behavior is referred to as a prohibited transaction. (The responsibility for overseeing prohibited transactions is shared by the IRS, and a separate but similar set of rules for prohibited transactions is also part of the tax law.). What constitutes a prohibited transaction is quite complex and will be discussed further in chapter 12. For now, understand that the goal of the rules is to keep the interests of the plan separate from the interests of the sponsoring entity, and to ensure that no persons benefit unduly because of their close relationship to the plan. Also note that the statutory scheme prohibits a broad range of behaviors and then carves out a number of statutory exemptions and gives the DOL the authority to issue others.

Fiduciaries

In conjunction with its responsibility to monitor plan investments, the DOL governs the actions of those in charge of running the retirement plans— fiduciaries. A fiduciary is a person or corporation that exercises any discretionary authority or control over the management of the plan or plan assets, renders investment advice for a fee, or has any discretionary authority or responsibility in the administration of the plan. Every plan has at least one named fiduciary who is responsible and accountable for operating the plan. Fiduciaries (named or otherwise) invest plan assets (subject to the rules on prohibited transactions), see that plan documents conform to the law, administer plans, and make major decisions regarding plan operation.

The Department of Labor has the means to ensure that fiduciaries uphold their responsibilities; it may sue plan fiduciaries and require a restitution to the plan for any losses resulting from breach of fiduciary duty. (In addition, under the tax provisions overseen by the IRS, a fiduciary may be responsible for excise taxes for violation of the prohibited-transaction provisions.) In doing its job of overseeing the fiduciary responsibility rules and the prohibited-transaction rules, the DOL (and, in a subordinate role, the IRS) acts like a police officer on the beat, carefully checking to see that the laws protecting plan participants are not broken.

Interpretation

As we have just seen, like the Internal Revenue Service, the DOL issues numerous communications that create pension rules and explain existing laws. Many of these items parallel IRS publications. The DOL issues final regulations, temporary regulations, and proposed regulations, which perform the same functions as their IRS counterparts. In addition, the DOL issues advisory opinions that are similar to the private-letter rulings issued by the IRS: As with IRS private letter rulings, your clients can inquire about the acceptability of their acts or transactions, and only the parties actually involved may safely rely on the opinion. Owing to the DOL's unique responsibilities, not all of its communications are similar to the IRS's. The DOL issues important communications called *prohibited-transaction exemptions* (PTEs). These exemptions can either be on a class basis (for example, "All banks with FDIC insurance are exempt from . . . .") or on a particular transaction basis. (*Planning Note:* The prohibited-transaction exemption is an avenue your client can travel to get approval before taking an investment action that falls into the prohibited-transaction gray area. For example, if your client is a party in interest, he or she can get an exemption from the restrictions on prohibited transactions by applying for a PTE.)

Pension Benefit Guaranty Corporation (PBGC)

The PBGC was established under title IV of ERISA as a quasi-governmental corporation. Both the IRS and the Department of Labor are involved to a certain extent with the PBGC, because the Board of Directors includes the Secretaries of Labor, Treasury, and Commerce. Even though the organization, as a quasi-governmental agency, has access to federal government resources, the federal government is not generally liable for the any of the obligations or liabilities of the Corporation. This is meaningful, since the PBGC's primary responsibility is to insure participants in and beneficiaries of employee benefit plans against the loss of benefits arising from complete or partial termination of the plan. PBGC insurance coverage applies to most defined-benefit plans of private employers (defined-benefit plans of professional services organizations such as physicians, dentists, attorneys, and accountants who have 25 or fewer active participants are exempt from PBGC coverage). The program does not apply to any defined-contribution plans.

The PBGC operates by collecting compulsory premiums, which are $19 per participant per plan year (more if the plan is underfunded). For such premiums, the PBGC guarantees to pay certain benefits promised under the plan, in the event that the plan has insufficient assets. The guaranteed benefits are subject to a specified ceiling that is adjusted annually. For 1996 the ceiling on the maximum monthly benefit guaranteed is $2,642 per month.

In conjunction with its duty to insure benefit payments, the PBGC has the power to investigate anyone who has violated or is about to violate any of the plan termination insurance provisions. It can also initiate a lawsuit in federal court for the enforcement of the provisions of title IV. To help the PBGC identify problems, certain events that would indicate that the plan is in financial difficulty must be reported to the PBGC.

TABLE 2-2		
Review of the Regulatory Environment for Qualified Plans		
IRS	DOL	PBGC
Initial plan qualification	Summary plan descriptions	Insure defined-benefit plans
Ongoing auditing through 5500 forms	Oversee fiduciaries and plan investments	Oversee plan fund solvency
Legal interpretation	Legal interpretation	Legal interpretation

The PBGC has another enforcement tool. If a PBGC investigation reveals that a plan is not funded according to legal standards or that the plan is unable to meet its benefit payments, or if there is a possible long-run loss that will get out of hand unless the plan is terminated, the PBGC may require the plan to be involuntarily terminated to help cut PBGC losses. The PBGC can also cut its losses by tapping up to 30 percent of the net worth of employers whose plans have terminated, leaving the PBGC liable for payments.

Another function of the PBGC is overseeing plan terminations initiated by the plan sponsor. Today (see chapter 14), an employer can terminate a defined-benefit plan covered by the PBGC insurance program only in limited circumstances. Essentially, the plan must either have sufficient assets to pay all benefits (referred to as a *voluntary termination*), or the company must virtually be facing liquidation (called a *distress termination*). When the employer terminates such a plan, it is required to give advance notification to employees and submit the proper forms to the PBGC.

As is the case with the IRS and the DOL's Office of Pension and Welfare Benefit Plans, the PBGC issues various communications that serve as sources of information for the financial services professional: PBGC regulations, news releases, opinion letters, publications, and multiemployer bulletins.

PENSIONS: PROFESSIONALS AND ORGANIZATIONS

While the impact of the regulatory environment on the retirement market is great, these federal laws and agencies are nonetheless only the rules and umpires. Employers sponsoring pension plans plus the expanding service and investment industry are the pension professionals and organizations. Together they are responsible for over 650,000 private pension plans covering more than 50 million participants, as well as numerous plans and participants in the public sector.

Benefit Associations and Designation Programs

In addition to The American College's CLU, ChFC, and REBC designations and the College's Master of Science in Financial Services with its pension certificate track, several other associations are prominent in the benefits community. These include the following:

- The American Society of Pension Actuaries (ASPA) is an organization for those involved with the consulting, administrative, and design aspects of pension and employee benefit plans. ASPA members include Fellows of the Society of Pension Actuaries (FSPA) and Certified Pension Consultants (CPC). ASPA can be contacted at (703) 516-9300.
- The Association of Private Pension and Welfare Plans (APPWP) is the business community's lobbying arm for pensions and employee benefit plans. APPWP can be contacted at (202) 289-6700.
- The Employee Benefits Research Institute (EBRI) is the research arm of the pension and employee benefit community. EBRI can be reached at (202) 659-0670.
- The International Foundation of Employee Benefit Plans is an organization for those involved with benefit consulting and the like. This organization is a cosponsor of the Certified Employee Benefit Specialist (CEBS) designation. The International Foundation of Employee Benefit Plans can be contacted at (414) 786-6700.
- The National Institute of Pension Administrators Educational Foundation, Inc. (NIPA) sponsors the Accredited Pension Administrator (APA) designation. NIPA can be reached at (312) 245-1085.
- The National Tax Sheltered Annuity Association (NTSAA) is a relatively new organization representing the interests of those in the 403(b) tax-sheltered annuity marketplace. They can be reached at (800) 543-0152.
- Other groups that focus in on specific portions of the pension market include the ESOP Association, (202) 293-2971, and the Profit Sharing/401(k) Council of America, (312) 441-8550.

Plan Sponsors

Retirement plan sponsors constitute one of the most important financial markets today. And since demographics indicate an aging population, which means increased savings for retirement, the plan sponsors' market is possibly *the* most important financial market of tomorrow. Currently only about 50 percent of employers have adopted retirement plans. Those who do adopt plans spend, on average, 6 percent of their payroll on qualified-plan premiums and pension payments. This figure, however, is much higher in the small plan market.

Sponsors of retirement plans include corporations, partnerships, and self-employed individuals. If a partnership or self-employed individual sponsors a qualified retirement plan, that plan is sometimes known as a Keogh plan. At one time the rules for Keogh plans and regular corporate qualified plans differed dramatically because the owner of an unincorporated business, even though he or she performs substantial services for the business, is not technically an employee of the business but is instead referred to as a self-employed person. Over time, however, the differences between corporate plans and Keogh plans have been almost eliminated. The differences that remain will be discussed in chapter 3.

Prospects—The Candidates for Pensions

Pension prospects range from business owners and professional corporations needing relief from income tax problems to larger organizations looking to satisfy organizational objectives through retirement plans. Every business owner, whether motivated by tax savings, competitiveness, or a sense of moral obligation to the employees, can be shown the need for a retirement system. The best prospects, however, will be

- businesses where the owner is an active employee interested in tax savings, such as professional corporations, sole proprietorships, and closely held businesses
- large corporations operating in a competitive labor market
- companies and service organizations—large, small, or individually run—that are just turning the corner on financial success
- institutions such as public schools, colleges, hospitals, and charitable organizations
- recently unionized employers or employers staving off union organization
- corporations with one type of retirement plan who may need a supplemental program—a 401(k) arrangement, for example

---

**YOUR FINANCIAL SERVICES PRACTICE:
RETIREMENT PROSPECTING**

Prospecting techniques in the retirement market differ from those in the personal selling market. While prospecting in the retirement market does include the traditional methods of direct mail, preapproach letters combined with phone calls for appointments, and the use of existing clients as referred leads, other unique methods are available. These include (1) developing accountants and attorneys—professionals who are in touch with the financial ability of the employers to provide retirement benefits—into centers of influence, (2) creating working relationships with banks interested in some trust business that complements pension insurance sales, (3) obtaining pension consultants or actuarial firms as referral sources, (4) working with casualty and insurance brokers in the commercial and industrial market whose clients are probably also pension prospects, and (5) purchasing the ERISA redbook that lists existing plans in your area. The redbook is published by Dunn & Bradstreet. Volumes are published for specific regions, and each volume contains information reported on the annual form 5500 reports filed by each plan sponsor in the covered area.

Service and Financial Groups

The pension market is replete with organizations offering to design and implement plans; provide consulting, record-keeping, legal, and actuarial services; furnish employee communications; and oversee plan administration. In short, those in charge of pensions can easily farm out the entire process to so-called *third-party administrators* (TPAs). The same is true regarding managing the assets of the pension plan. For those plan administrators who would rather do some or all of their work in-house, there are a variety of computer services, many of them offered by small, specialized companies.

The organizations that provide plan services include consulting houses, actuarial firms, insurance companies, administrative consultants, and software companies. In the financial market there are trust companies, commercial banks, investment houses, asset-management groups, and insurance companies. The major service and financial groups have no particular areas of concentration, but rather offer a myriad of services. For example, consulting houses don't just do consulting and plan installation and administration; they may offer computer services and investment facilities. Computer software companies may offer consulting services as well as creating software.

Studies have shown that the fewer employees an employer has, the greater the tendency there is to farm work out. Conversely, the larger firms have a tendency to do the work in-house. If your client has needs in areas you can't help with, the major consulting outfits will probably be able to provide the necessary services (table 2-3).

TABLE 2-3
Consulting Firms Operating in Most Major Cities

The Alexander Consulting Group, Inc.	KPMG Peat Marwick, L.L.P.
Buck Consultants, Inc.	William M. Mercer Companies, Inc.
Coopers & Lybrand, L.L.P.	Sedgwick Noble Lowndes
Aon Consulting	Rollins Burdick Hunter Co.
Hay/Huggins Company	The Segal Company
Hewitt Associates	Towers Perrin
A. Foster Higgins & Co., Inc.	WatsonWyatt Worldwide
Kwasha-Lipton	Numerous insurance companies

The Role of Life Insurance Companies

The insurance industry offers a complete array of plan designs, administrative services, and investment facilities. Insurance companies use a variety of methods to administer their pension services. One popular way is to divide administration between the two types of pension products: group pensions (characterized by large numbers of participants and large annual contributions) and individual pensions, a field dominated by the general agent who typically funds the plan in part or in whole with life insurance.

Group Pensions

One of the chief concerns of group pension operations is to generate assets for the division; and success in group departments depends on the ability to generate big-dollar sales. Group pension representatives—specialists in the group products—are the chief facilitators of these sales. A typical group department supports these representatives with home-office, actuarial, marketing, consulting, and administrative services (although many companies are dropping their support services in favor of strictly investment-oriented products). The actuarial components of the group division provide services such as valuation, cost projections, and, in conjunction with the company's investment department, the pricing of products. The marketing group generates employer interest in the company's investment, consulting, and administrative skills and creates the new products for sale. Generally these new products are put together jointly by the insurance company's legal department and the technical-services arm of the consulting unit. In addition, the consulting unit plays a major role in the initial design of a plan, plan qualification with the IRS, and ongoing plan design changes, as well as plan amendment to conform to changes in the law. The administrative support unit of the group division provides administrative and record-keeping functions for employers, usually with the aid of a sophisticated mainframe computer system. Record keeping includes updating employee historical data, calculating benefits, preparing statements for participants, and reporting plan and participant status to regulatory bodies. Administrative support is provided for plan administrators in the form of manuals designed to walk the administrator through his or her duties, and consulting is provided on more difficult issues.

Individual Pensions

The individual department shares all the concerns of the group department and can be similarly structured. But there are several trends—such as the tendency not to provide full service, the use of master or prototype plans, and the involvement of the general agent—that distinguish the individual department.

The Full-Service Debate. The tendency not to provide full service is probably a product of economics and expertise as they relate to general agents. In other words, some general agents don't feel that full-time involvement, including coordinating the home-office administrative support services, is cost-effective. They would rather be doing what they do best—selling the products. This may be a mistake. The combination of agency support and home-office support relieves the general agent of much of the non-cost-effective work. What's more, sales and renewals tend to come more easily when proper service is available. (Just ask any agent what happens when the home office doesn't hold up its end and fails to provide adequate services.)

Master and Prototype Plans. Master and prototype plans are standardized plans approved and qualified in concept by the Internal Revenue Service, which the insurance companies make available for their agents to sell. Although these plans must go through qualification procedures, a favorable result is more predictable. The master and prototype plans offer an employer fewer choices in plan design and thus can be installed very easily. The use of a master or prototype simplifies the task for a general agent by setting up an easily understood framework, known as the *adoption agreement,* to work with. The adoption agreement resembles a smorgasbord in many ways—for example, you choose one out of five benefit formulas, one out of three vesting tables, and so on—which simplifies the plan design process and saves time.

The Role of the Insurance Agent

The insurance agent is one of the prominent players in the pension market, particularly with respect to helping small businesses, professional corporations, and sole proprietors; setting up nonqualified plans within large organizations; and installing tax-deferred annuities for schools and charitable organizations. Agents entering the pension field reap a variety of benefits, including

- the opportunity to sell life insurance on a tax-favored basis (life insurance under a pension plan is a unique product for income tax planning)

- close contact with managers of small businesses, small-business owners, professionals, and highly paid executives (which generates opportunities for sales of other insurance products)
- the ability to demonstrate problem-solving skill in the pension arena, which may act as a corporate door opener and result in other sales
- a predictable source of renewals
- a predictable source of new business streaming from new plan entrants, plan improvements, benefit upgrades, and new business ventures of present clients
- infrequent lapses because an investment shift under qualified plans is impractical

There is a downside for agents involved in the pension market. This includes a significant lag from the time the proposal is developed until the time payment is made and difficulty in closing a sale as a result of the employer's involvement with other professional advisers. But these negatives and the fact that the pensions field is considered highly technical have not deterred many life agents from specializing in helping to design, install, and administer qualified and nonqualified plans and playing a large role in the retirement market.

INFORMATION

Where do you turn when you need to answer a client's question or find out about the latest law or idea? What sources and references offer necessary information to a pension practitioner? The resources you can call on include loose-leaf services, on-line databases, books, periodicals, primary sources, and software packages. The following is an analysis of the major items that should be considered for inclusion in your pension library.

Loose-leaf Services

Loose-leaf services are publications that describe the legal and administrative framework of pensions in an up-to-date manner. The term *loose-leaf* refers to the fact that individual pages can be constantly revised to reflect recent happenings and then mailed out to subscribers to replace current pages in a loose-leaf binder. Information about retirement plans, laws, and related areas is always available and current. The most commonly used loose-leaf services are the *BNA Pension Reporter* (published by Bureau of National Affairs, Washington, D.C.), *Pension Plan Guide* (Commerce Clearing House, Chicago, Ill.), *EBPR Research Reports* (Charles D. Spencer and Associates, Chicago, Ill.), and RIA (this service contains pension document forms from Corbel & Company, Jacksonville, Fla.). Most of these services also provide a weekly bulletin reporting the latest news about retirement plans to keep readers current and informed.

Each of the services and report bulletins mentioned above has its own special appeal: the BNA service provides a thorough and insightful weekly bulletin but lacks significant reference volumes; the CCH service provides large volumes of printed source material (revenue rulings and the like) and thorough report bulletins; the RIA service is similar to CCH, with the added strength of the Corbel plan documents; while the EBPR service provides much statistical data. Most pension practitioners have access to more than one service, and those interested in all forms of employee benefits are enthusiastic about the BNA service.

On-line Databases

There are three commonly used on-line databases that provide personal computer access to important pension libraries: ABI/INFORM, CCH Access, and Lexis/Nexis. ABI/INFORM links up with more than 660 leading business and management publications and summarizes articles for a quick reference. A controlled vocabulary lets you search for all the information on a specific pension term (for example, 401(k) plans) and lists the various article titles relating to that term. CCH Access contains the CCH tax library including texts of cases and rulings. Lexis/Nexis is basically a law library that provides considerable source material. All three databases, however, go far beyond just providing information for retirement planning. Each service is targeted for a different type of subscriber—ABI/INFORM for business and insurance, CCH Access for tax practitioners, and Lexis/Nexis for the legal profession.

Books

Several outstanding books in the pension field provide in-depth overviews of pensions and retirement plans:

- Allen, Melone, Rosenbloom, and Vanderhei, *Pension Planning* (a thorough and well-regarded treatment)
- McGill and Grubbs, *Fundamentals of Private Pensions* (a technician's delight)
- Leimberg and McFadden, *The Tools and Techniques of Employee Benefit and Retirement Planning* (a practical, "on your desk every day" tool for insurance agents)
- Beam and McFadden, *Employee Benefits* (another good overview of the employee benefits field)
- Canan, *Qualified Retirement and Other Employee Benefit Plans* (comprehensive coverage of the legal requirements)
- Bennett, et al., *Taxation of Distributions from Qualified Plans* (a comprehensive and technical treatment of the income and estate tax consequences of qualified plans)

- *The Pension Answer Book Series* (The first edition covered the whole pension field; now there is a whole series of specialty books covering such topics as 401(k) plans, 403(b) plans, plan investments, and plan distributions.)

A yearly reference book such as *Tax Facts* (published by National Underwriter, Cincinnati, Ohio) is also an important addition to any pension library.

Periodicals

There are innumerable periodicals reporting on every angle of pensions and retirement. The employee benefit side of pensions is covered in *Employee Benefits Plan Review* (which contains an excellent listing of benefit-plan service companies) and *Benefits Quarterly* (loaded with perceptive articles). From the investment side of pensions there are *Pension World* (targeted to plan sponsors and investment managers) and *Pensions and Investment Age* (the newspaper of corporate and institutional investing). The insurance side of pensions is represented by the *Journal of the American Society of CLU & ChFC* and *Life Insurance Selling* (the annual reports on pensions are chock-full of good ideas).

The World of CD-ROM

Today, many of the books, periodicals, loose-leaf services, and primary source laws mentioned above can be obtained on CD-ROM. These computer products are extremely useful since a single disk can contain a massive amount of printed materials. Another strength of CD-ROM is the ability to search through all that data for relevant information simply by typing in key words or phrases. In many cases (but not always), CD-ROM is more cost effective than receiving material in written form. Since this world is changing so fast, instead of mentioning specific products, it is better to simply give the name and telephone numbers of the major publishers in this area. Check with them to see what is currently available. Publishers include Tax Analysts (800-955-2444), BNA (800-372-0133), RIA (800-431-2057), Charles D. Spencer (800-555-5490), Warren Gorham & Lamont (800-950-1210), and Panel Publishers (800-234-1660).

Primary Sources and Other Invaluable Resources

The most reliable and important sources of information are, of course, the primary sources: texts of the laws, the Internal Revenue Code, the example-laden regulations, and many of the numerous agency interpretations discussed earlier. Unlike secondary sources such as books and periodicals, primary sources may be relied on by the practitioner as an accurate and legally enforceable representation of a situation. Primary sources can be found in most loose-leaf services and in publications such as the *Federal Register,* the *Cumulative Bulletins,* and BNA's *Daily Tax Report.* Typically the loose-leaf services publish booklets that contain the primary source material as well as an understandable explanation; these booklets are an invaluable resource.

Although not binding—like primary sources—the IRS and Department of Labor both have publications that explain, usually in plain English, the various rules and regulations. Many of these publications are well written, provide additional guidance on the agency's interpretation of the law, and, best of all, are free! The IRS has especially good publications on IRAs and the taxation of pension distributions.

A final invaluable source for learning about Congress's meaning of a particular law is to look at the law's statutory history. Generally, the most meaningful of these documents are the committee reports of the Senate, House of Representatives, and Conference Committee (where differences between provisions in the House of Representatives and Senate bills are pounded out). Also with tax legislation, oftentimes the joint committee on taxation prepares a report, which is known as the "blue book" (available from most loose-leaf services). These are highly regarded in the tax community as understandable resources explaining the legislative intent behind the law.

Surfing the Net

There is a rich array of information available on the Internet. Of interest to those in the employee benefit field are the following:

- *Department of Labor*—http://bubba.dol.gov. This site includes a summary of laws and regulations governed by the DOL. It also includes the full text of bills and statutes. It is an in-depth resource for free access to primary source materials.
- *U.S. Government Printing Office*—www.access.gpo.gov. In this site you can search the Federal Register for full text of agency regulations or the U.S. Code for laws.
- *International Foundation of Employee Benefit Plans*—www.ifebp.org. Here you will find information about the organization and available services, as well as the latest industry news.
- *Benefits Link*—www.benefitslink.com. This is another source for bills and regulations laws, as well as U.S. Supreme Court Decisions relating to employee benefits.

Every day, a massive amount of new information becomes available on the Internet. Use a search engine such as Yahoo or Altavista to locate

- web pages for the organizations and publishing companies discussed in this chapter

- news groups discussing related topics
- advertisements for other service providers in the benefits area

Software

A wide variety of software packages that enable financial services practitioners to do their jobs more efficiently are available from insurance companies and pension vendors. Software packages are available for client illustrations, pension administration, portfolio management, form preparation, and plan document preparation, as well as for number crunching in a variety of other areas.

Insurance company home offices and other financial institutions have their own software. In addition to the packages available from your own home office, there are a few vendors that you should become familiar with because of their prominence in the industry. For example, Corbel & Company is well-known for its document preparation services. For a modest fee Corbel will take the information that you've gathered on its fact finder and create plans and summary plan descriptions for your client. (*Planning Note:* For agents who do not have access to their company's prototype plans, acquaintance with Corbel's product is strongly recommended.) Another service provided by Corbel is PENTABS, which is software that completes the IRS's required 5500 family of forms.

NOTE

1. The IRS currently has a formal program for substituting plan disqualification with a monetary penalty. The program is called the "CAP" program and is applicable for certain plan defects.

3

Preliminary Concerns

Chapter Outline

One of the most promising and lucrative opportunities in the retirement market is the chance to design a client's retirement program. Financial services professionals who act as consultants in this area provide a valuable service that not only leads to the sale of retirement-plan products but also to the investment of their client's retirement assets. Furthermore, financial services professionals who bring technical expertise to the retirement-decision process gain the confidence of clients and may be entrusted with sales opportunities in other areas of the business. Conversely, financial services professionals who desire only to manage plan assets or sell investment products find themselves at a competitive disadvantage if they can't offer the technical expertise expected.

For these reasons it's essential that financial services professionals learn how to select the most appropriate retirement plan or plans for their clients. We will start our study of this process with the selection of the most appropriate tax-advantaged plan for your client (chapters 3–6). After a thorough discussion of the rules affecting plan choices, design, investment, and administration, we will discuss supplemental nonqualified plans (chapters 15 and 16) for executives.

In order to choose the best retirement plan you will need to identify your client's needs and objectives, understand the various plan options, and match the client's needs and objectives with the proper tax-advantaged retirement plan or plans.

IDENTIFYING NEEDS AND OBJECTIVES

When advising a client on retirement-plan choices, your initial step is to focus the client on the important issues he or she faces, both personally and professionally. In addition, you need to discern the organization's needs and objectives that are relevant to plan selection. The device used to accomplish these steps is a pension planning fact finder. The following seven-step fact finder gives you one perspective on this task—other choices in fact finding may work better for you. In any case, you should use this fact finder or an alternative to

- guide the client toward focusing on important issues
- gather the information necessary for you to make insightful recommendations
- provide a systematic approach for solving the client's retirement puzzle
- serve as a due diligence checklist that will ensure the selection of the most appropriate plan
- record your dealings with the client for liability protection

UNDERSTANDING THE FACT FINDER

Step 1 of the fact finder helps you to identify organizational needs, the foundation for proper plan choice. The important comparative analysis that is started in step 2 (involving the interplay between these factors) requires additional discussion with the client to establish the relative desirability of each objective. For example, when an employer has the multiple objectives of attracting and retaining key employees, avoiding an annual financial commitment to fund the plan, and providing tax shelter for top executives, you must gauge which need is most important and to what degree the other needs will have to be subordinated in order to choose the best plan for your client.

Step 3 lists the primary and secondary reasons for establishing the plan, and is a culmination of steps 1 and 2. It forces your client to set priorities on the motives for establishing the plan. Motives can be disparate even in similarly structured organizations, but several generalizations about motives can be made.

- Large organizations typically want to meet the needs of the business while getting the most for the employees out of a given expenditure.

PENSION PLANNING FACT FINDER

Client's Name _____

Address   _____

               _____

               _____

Phone Number   _____

Key Contacts   Name   _____

               Title   _____   Phone No._____

               Name   _____

               Title   _____   Phone No._____

               Name   _____

               Title   _____   Phone No._____

Client's Attorney   _____   Phone No._____

Client's Accountant   _____   Phone No._____

Employer Identification Number _____

Fiscal Year _____

Accounting Method (circle one)
    Cash
    Accrual
Business Structure (circle one)
    C Corp.
    S Corp.
    Municipal Corp.
    Partnership
    Sole Proprietorship
    Exempt Organization
    Professional Corp.
    Government Agency

State of Incorporation or Domicile   _____

Date of Incorporation or Establishment   _____

Were there any predecessor entities? (circle one)   Yes   No

Affiliated Companies

        Name   _____   Name   _____

        Address _____   Address _____

                _____   _____

    Phone No. _____   Phone No. _____

Step 1: Set retirement priorities.

Listed below are some typical concerns that organizations have when instituting a retirement program. Grade each of these concerns by scoring 1 for very valuable, 2 for valuable, 3 for moderately valuable, and 4 for least valuable.

1. To what extent is it important to use a qualified plan as a tax shelter for owner-employees and key employees? [1] [2] [3] [4]

2. To what extent is it important to maximize benefits for long-service employees by including service prior to the inception of the plan? [1] [2] [3] [4]

3. To what extent is it important to place the risk of investing plan assets with the employee? [1] [2] [3] [4]

4. To what extent is it important to institute a plan that is easily communicated to employees? [1] [2] [3] [4]

5. To what extent is it important to institute a plan that is administratively convenient? [1] [2] [3] [4]

6. To what extent is it important to institute a plan that has predictable costs? [1] [2] [3] [4]

7. To what extent is it important to avoid an annual financial commitment? [1] [2] [3] [4]

8. To what extent is it important to allow employees (including owner-employees) to withdraw funds? [1] [2] [3] [4]

9. To what extent is it important to minimize plan costs by limiting benefits for lower-paid employees? [1] [2] [3] [4]

10. To what extent is it important to create a market for employer stock? [1] [2] [3] [4]

11. To what extent is it important to leverage the purchase of employer stock? [1] [2] [3] [4]

12. To what extent is it important to attract key employees? [1] [2] [3] [4]

13. To what extent is it important to retain experienced personnel? [1] [2] [3] [4]

14. To what extent is it important to motivate the workforce? [1] [2] [3] [4]

15. To what extent is it important to deal with superannuated employees? [1] [2] [3] [4]

16. To what extent is it important to give participants the opportunity to save additional amounts on a pretax basis? [1] [2] [3] [4]

17. To what extent is it important that employer contributions be made only for employees who elect to contribute? [1] [2] [3] [4]

18. To what extent is it important that benefits for those who terminate prior to retirement be portable? [1] [2] [3] [4]

Step 2: Discuss with the client the interplay between various factors in step 1. For example:

	Yes	No
1. Does the desire to provide tax shelter for owner-employees and key employees outweigh the need to cut costs attributable to lower-paid employees?	[Y]	[N]
2. Does the desire to provide tax shelter for owner-employees and key employees outweigh the need to have an easily communicated and administratively convenient plan?	[Y]	[N]
3. Does the need to provide tax shelter for owner-employees and key employees outweigh the need to have predictable costs and payment flexibility?	[Y] [Y]	[N] [N]
4. Is it more important to retain employees than to attract employees?	[Y]	[N]
5. Is it more important to motivate employees than to attract or retain them?	[Y]	[N]
6. Is it more important to provide an adequate retirement standard of living than to cut plan costs?	[Y]	[N]
7. Is it more important to provide an adequate retirement standard of living than to have predictable costs?	[Y]	[N]
8. Is it more important to provide an adequate standard of living during retirement than to avoid an annual commitment to funding the plan?	[Y]	[N]
9. Is it more important to provide an adequate standard of living during retirement than to allow employees (including owner-employees) to withdraw funds?	[Y]	[N]
10. Is it more important to provide an adequate standard of living during retirement than to have administrative convenience and an easily communicated plan?	[Y]	[N]
11. Is it more important that contributions go only to employees to elect to participate than to provide retirement benefits to all workers?	[Y]	[N]

Additional Comments

Step 3: List the primary reason(s) for establishing the plan and the secondary reason(s) for establishing the plan.

Primary   1.

2.

3.

Secondary   1.

2.

3.

Step 4: Discuss the employer's cost objectives. Discuss the price range that is desired both now and in the future.

Step 5: (A)   What are the current and future cash-flow situations

(1) for the company

(2) for the industry in general

(B)   Attach balance sheets from the last 3 years.

(C)   Attach appropriate profit and loss statements.

principals and the organizational goals that are sought.

Step 7: Analyze the company's census (list of employees).

1. What percentage of employees can be expected to turn over before retirement?
   _____% leave before they complete one year of service
   _____% leave between their first and second years of service
   _____% leave between their second and third years of service
   _____% leave between their third and fourth years of service
   _____% leave between their fourth and fifth years of service
   _____% leave between their fifth and sixth years of service
   _____% leave between their sixth and seventh years of service
   _____% leave with more than seven years of service
   _____% are "lifers" with the company

2. What groups of employees exist?
   _____ salaried employees
   _____ hourly paid employees
   _____ collective-bargaining unit employees
   _____ leased employees

3. To what extent are part-time employees used?
   _____ part-time employees are used
   _____ no part-time employees are used
   _____ part-time employees work less than 500 hours
   _____ part-time employees work between 500 and 999 hours
   _____ part-time employees work 1000 or more hours

4. How many offices (profit centers) are there?
   _____ number of different locations

5. What benefit programs do chief competitors offer?

6. Attach employee census.

7. Attach other group benefit plans.

8. Identify other related employers and the relationship to this one. The list should include any entities with interrelated ownership and other entities that work together with this one to produce a product. Describe in detail the chain of ownership and how the entities work together.

- Small organizations, such as closely held businesses, are particularly concerned with providing tax shelter and extensive retirement benefits to owners and key employees.
- Some organizations, large and small, desire to adequately provide for rank-and-file employees; others want to favor the key employees and will only grudgingly meet the minimum statutory requirements for other employees; and still others fall somewhere between these two polar viewpoints.
- Some organizations establish plans to attract and retain key employees or to motivate employees and want the most cost-effective system to meet those goals.
- Some organizations are interested in resolving problems with older, unproductive employees and creating a graceful transition out of the workforce.
- In today's world more and more employers want to form a retirement savings partnership with employees and want employer contributions to primarily match employee contributions.

The first three steps provide some insight into the type of plan to be chosen. Steps 4 and 5 (discussing cost objectives and cash flow) are, however, perhaps the most important determinants of the type of plan the client will adopt. The price tag the client can comfortably live with is sometimes a product of the client's objectives (what he or she wants to provide) and sometimes a product of the economics of the situation (what he or she can afford). Often what clients can afford will vary according to what they want and what they consider cost-effective to pay for it. When considering cost objectives, the organization's ability to make the economic commitment year in and year out should be carefully studied. Some industries have fluctuating profits that ebb and flow with certain uncontrollable economic conditions, while others are fairly stable. In other words, it's not just a question of how much, but also how consistently a certain payment level can be maintained or how much flexibility is needed in order to meet benefit commitments. Carefully examine the following issues before deciding on a price range:

- annual variations in profits
- future cash needs for capital expansion
- potential changes in the prospect's industry over the next 5 years
- the length of time until the principals retire
- the tax-shelter needs of owner-employees

Step 6 (distinguishing between personal and organizational goals) helps you to better understand the priorities laid out in step 3 and the cost objectives laid out in step 4 by differentiating between the personal needs of the client and corporate objectives. The client's personal needs are of the utmost importance in the small-plan market and should be given every consideration. In medium-sized plans, however, equal weight should be given to the organization's goals and the needs of the principals. As a general rule, the larger the plan, the more important the organizational goals.

Step 7 (analyzing the company's census) is perhaps the most important step in the fact-finding process. A thorough understanding of the ages and salary levels of the people who will be covered by the plan is essential for making the correct plan choice and in establishing the best possible plan design. For example, if all the members of the firm are "older" (by pension standards over age 45), then it may be desirable to put in a defined-benefit plan that accounts for past service (discussed later). If, however, salary levels are low and employees are young, a more basic plan such as a simplified employee pension plan may be desirable. The last question in step 7 is also crucial. Under the plan rules, certain related employers have to be aggregated for purposes of determining whether a plan satisfies coverage requirements. The rules are quite complex; therefore it is best to simply ask some broad questions that will elicit a description about the relationships so that a qualified individual can analyze for aggregation issues.

YOUR FINANCIAL SERVICES PRACTICE: INFORMATION GATHERING

The pension planning fact finder is just the jumping-off point in your quest to identify your client's needs and objectives. The initial interview should be followed by open communication lines that allow the client's concerns to be more clearly developed over time. The following points typify what can happen in this intervening time:

- Frequently the person you speak with will not correctly represent the desires of the entire body of authority within the organization. The company will need time to sort out its collective feelings and come up with a response. Try not to get involved in the infighting that may occur, and try to remain as diplomatic and neutral as possible.
- The company's attorney or accountant should be brought into the process in the early stages. A common problem is that the attorney or accountant may resent playing the subordinate role (even though he or she may know little about pension plans). Another common problem is that the accountant or attorney may be opposed to the use of any form of life insurance in the plan. Once again the solution is diplomacy.

CHOOSING BETWEEN A QUALIFIED PLAN AND THE OTHER TAX-SHELTERED OPTIONS

Chapters 4 and 5 discuss the various types of qualified plans. Chapter 6 addresses those tax-advantaged plans that are not categorized as qualified plans. For the for-profit employer, the other types of plans available include the SEP and the SIMPLE. The nonprofit employer that is a 501(c)(3) organization also has the option to sponsor a 403(b) tax-sheltered annuity plan.

As we have already begun to discuss (and as described in detail in later chapters), establishing and maintaining a qualified plan requires a significant amount of documentation, government reporting, and employee communication. For the small business, these requirements can be quite onerous. SEPs and SIMPLEs are intended to provide the small business with some less complicated options. Plan documents are less complicated, and there are fewer IRS reporting requirements. Simplicity translates into lower administrative expenses and less time spent operating the plan. However, in exchange for simplicity is a rigidity in plan design. These plans have less flexibility than qualified plans in most regards. The important differences include:

- *Coverage*—while the qualified plan rules provide significant flexibility in the number and makeup of the employees covered by the plan, the SEP and SIMPLE eligibility requirements are set in stone.
- *Vesting*—contributions must be fully and immediately vested in the contributions to SEPs and SIMPLEs, while qualified plans can have a vesting schedule.
- *Contributions*—in some cases in a qualified plan benefits or contributions can be different for different classes of employees. This is not the case in SEPs and SIMPLEs, where all participants must receive essentially the same level of benefits.
- *Maximum contributions*—in most regards the limits are lower for SEPs and SIMPLEs than for qualified plans.

The SEP is the appropriate plan option when the employer is going to fund all the plan benefits. In a SEP, as in a profit-sharing plan, the employer can make contributions annually (or more often) on a discretionary basis. When the employer wants to allow employees the opportunity to make additional contributions on a pretax basis (making it similar to a 401(k) plan), then the SIMPLE is the appropriate choice.

The 403(b) tax-sheltered annuity is a unique retirement planning vehicle. Only tax-exempt 501(c)(3) organizations and public school systems are allowed to sponsor such plans. At one time, there were relatively few rules governing these plans. However, over time, the situation has evolved, and more and more of the rules that apply to qualified plans now apply to 403(b) plans, too. One type of plan that still operates quite differently from the way that a qualified plan does is the 403(b) plan that involves only employee pretax contributions. This type of plan will not be subject to many of the requirements of ERISA (as long as certain requirements are met). With this type of arrangement, the employer has little involvement; the service provider works directly with the employees. When the employer makes contributions to a 403(b) plan, then the plan operates very much like a qualified plan. The distinctions are covered further in chapter 6.

CHOOSING BETWEEN A DEFINED-BENEFIT AND A DEFINED-CONTRIBUTION PLAN

Assuming that the employer is going to choose from among the qualified plan options, the first consideration is whether the employer wants a plan of the: defined-benefit or defined-contribution type. All qualified plans fall into one of the two categories. Each category represents a different philosophy of retirement planning. This philosophy is reflected in the definition of each term. A *defined-benefit plan* is a plan that specifies the benefits each employee receives at retirement. In most plans the benefit is stated as a percentage of preretirement salary, which is payable for the participant's remaining life. Under a defined-benefit plan the contributions required by the employer vary depending upon what is needed to pay the promised benefit, and the amount of annual funding is determined each year by the plan's actuary. Under current law, the maximum yearly benefit allowed is the lesser of 100 percent of the highest 3-year average compensation or $125,000 (in 1997, and subject to cost-of-living increases).

In many ways the defined-benefit plan looks like an insurance solution to the retirement problem. The risk being insured is the loss of income due to the inability to work any longer. Another risk here is that an individual will outlive his or her money in retirement. The traditional defined-benefit plan addresses both of these issues. The amount of the benefit is tied to what will be lost— employment income. To address the issue of longevity, in the traditional plan, the benefit is payable for the retired employee's entire life. It is interesting to note that this plan design is due in part to the fact that the first defined-benefit plans were funded with insurance products—although today many "self-fund" the promised benefits.

A *defined-contribution plan,* on the other hand, is a type of plan in which employer contributions are allocated to the account of individual employees. This approach is similar to a personal savings approach in which an individual opens up a bank account and makes regular contributions, and the account grows based on the rate of investment return. Because of this approach, defined-contribution plans are sometimes called *individual account plans.* The maximum contribution that can be made for any participant for the year (called *annual additions*) is the lesser of 25 percent of salary or $30,000. (This figure will be indexed for inflation.) One way to look at these dissimilar approaches is to say that defined-benefit plans provide a fixed predetermined benefit that has an uncertain cost to the employer, whereas defined-contribution plans have a predetermined cost to the employer and provide a variable benefit to employees (based upon the rate of return).

So where does the philosophy differ? Defined-benefit plans are designed purely as retirement plans. Stated benefits are intended to replace a specified portion of lost employment income for long-service employees. Such plans reward those employees who continue employment until retirement, since benefits are usually tied to both length of service and final income. In defined-benefit plans, the burden of providing an adequate retirement income is placed solely on the employer, since the employer promises to fund the plan sufficiently to pay promised benefits.

Plans in the defined-contribution category are different. From the perspective of both the employer and the employee, such plans look and feel more like deferred-compensation plans. A specified amount is set aside for the employee's benefit, which is paid out at termination of employment (as long as the participant is "vested") or, in some cases, even earlier. Here the employee can have a clearer feeling for how much he or she is being paid, since the cost to the employer is clear. On the other hand, such plans do not provide a retirement benefit that is closely tied to the individual's retirement needs—as in a defined-benefit plan. It's not to say that defined-contribution plans will not provide adequate retirement income; it's just that it's much harder to pinpoint the benefit. Also, in a very real way, the employee is at more risk, because the benefit is tied to the plan's investment return. In other words, if stock market prices fall drastically, it is the employee who must worry in a defined-contribution plan and the employer who must worry in a defined-benefit plan.

All qualified plans fall into either the defined-benefit or the defined-contribution category. The names of the various qualified plans and the categories into which they fall are listed below. Note, however, that two types of plans are referred to as *hybrid* plans. First is the *cash-balance plan*, which is a defined-benefit plan that has some of the characteristics of a plan using the defined-contribution approach. Second is the *target-benefit plan*, which is a defined-contribution plan that has some of the characteristics of a defined-benefit plan. These distinctions will become more clear in the next two chapters, where the plans are discussed in more detail. Also note that the SEP, the SIMPLE, and the 403(b) tax-sheltered annuity plan all use a defined-contribution approach and share the same strengths and limitations of other defined-contribution plans (in comparison to the defined-benefit approach).

Qualified Plan Categories

Defined-Benefit Plans	Defined-Contribution Plans
• Defined-benefit pension plan	• Money-purchase pension plan
• Cash-balance pension plan	• Target-benefit pension plan
	• Profit-sharing plan
	• 401(k) plan
	• Stock bonus plan
	• ESOP

Structural Differences

Plans from the defined-benefit category can often provide more retirement income for employees (especially older workers) than plans from the defined-contribution category can. This is partly due to the fact that defined-benefit plans can provide benefits based on past service (that is, years worked before the plan was initiated), while defined-contribution plans cannot. Also, defined-benefit plans can gear benefit payments to salary levels received just prior to retirement—meaning that benefits increase automatically for increases in salary that are due to inflation. In this way, it is appropriate to characterize benefits as providing a "preretirement" inflation factor. Defined-benefit plan benefits generally do not increase automatically for inflation occurring after retirement—although it is not unusual for an employer to provide periodic ad hoc benefit increases for retirees. This inflation protection cannot be provided by a defined-contribution plan. Since contributions are made annually based on that year's compensation, the benefit builds steadily over the employee's career. Because the benefit is tied to each year's salary-based contribution, the benefit will not increase dramatically if inflation is high near retirement and salaries rise dramatically. Employers looking to maximize benefits, employers who want employees (including key people) to enjoy a standard of living after retirement comparable to the standard of living prior to retirement, and employers whose financial position and competitive posture oblige them to satisfy these retirement needs will usually choose a defined-benefit plan.

Defined-contribution plans are quite different. Here the employer's cost is determinable—and will not vary with the plan's investment return. Also these plans cost less to administer. Employees can more easily follow the growth of their benefits and can more readily appreciate the value of the cost of the plan to the employer. Defined-contribution plans may also allow employees to direct the investments in their individual accounts. As well, the participant's benefit is stated as a single account balance and lump-sum distributions are generally allowed—which is not always the case in a defined-benefit plan. Also, with defined-contribution plans, benefits are portable should an employee switch jobs.

Easily determinable costs appeal to employers whose financial positions dictate caution (typically organizations with volatile cash flow). What's more, key employees tend to feel more comfortable about individual accounts that they invest, portable benefits, and the lump-sum distributions traditionally offered under defined-contribution plans. As a result of this employer and key-employee appeal, defined-contribution plans have become a hot ticket for financial services professionals in the pension field.

Choosing between a Defined-Benefit and a Defined-Contribution Retirement Approach

The choice between the defined-contribution and the defined-benefit approach is often difficult given the variety of employer needs. As a general rule, if the employer's primary concern is a stable retirement benefit for employees that reflects a standard of living comparable to that enjoyed prior to retirement, a plan from the defined-benefit category should be chosen. If the employer perceives the retirement needs of employees differently, however, or does not feel responsible for satisfying the needs of postretirement income adequacy, then

TABLE 3-1
Types of Plans Compared

Defined-Benefit	Defined-Contribution
Specifies the benefit an employee receives	Specifies employer contributions made on behalf of employee
Law specifies the maximum allowable benefit payable from the plan—lesser of 100% of salary or $125,000 per year	Law specifies the maximum allowable annual contributions—the lesser of 25 percent of salary or $30,000
Contributions not attributed to specified employees	All contributions allocated to individual employee accounts
Assigns the risk of preretirement inflation, investment performance, and adequacy of retirement income to the employer	Assigns the risk of preretirement inflation, investment performance, and adequacy of retirement income to the employee
Can provide benefits based on past service	Cannot provide benefits for past service
Is relatively costly to administer	Has lower administrative costs
Can be difficult to communicate both the amount of benefits and the value of the benefit (amount it costs the employer)	Easy to communicate the amount of employer contributions and the "bank-account" type benefit.
Has less predictable costs	Has predictable costs

a plan from the defined-contribution category may be desirable. Factors such as financial position, cash flow, tax implications, corporate objectives, and competitive posture tend to militate against any easy formula for making a decision. It is very important for an employer to correctly identify and prioritize needs before a decision can be reached. In fact, since employers generally desire features of both plans, it may be appropriate to suggest *both* a defined-benefit and a defined-contribution plan.

The Realities of the Marketplace Today

A look at the contrast between the defined-benefit and the defined-contribution approach would not be complete without a discussion of the realities of today's marketplace. Even though the defined-benefit approach still has the strengths that have been mentioned, very few small businesses today are interested in establishing or maintaining this type of plan. Back in the mid-1980s, defined-benefit plans were quite popular in the small plan market, since often the maximum contribution to the defined-benefit plan (on behalf of the business owner) was substantially larger than to a defined-contribution plan. This afforded the middle-aged business owner the opportunity to both save on taxes and quickly accumulate a significant retirement benefit.

However, the trend began to change with the Tax Reform Act of 1986. This act made changes that lowered maximum contributions and increased the complexities of maintaining a defined-benefit plan. Many small plans were terminated and few new ones were established. For example, in 1991, 10,064 defined-benefit plans were terminated and only 370 new plans were started. Another change in 1994 has meant even more trouble for the small plan. Under current law, the amount of benefit that can be paid out (in a single sum) to the business owner fluctuates with changes in interest rates. This could be the death knell for the small defined-benefit plan, because plans can be left with significant assets that cannot be paid out as benefits to the business owner. What this means for us in the mid-1990s is that the defined-benefit plan for the small business has become relatively rare. The only remaining viable candidate is the older, self-employed person with no employees who has a high income and who needs a significant tax-shelter.

This does not mean, however, that defined-benefit plans are not an important part of the retirement planning landscape. Many midsize and large companies still maintain defined-benefit plans and, overall, defined-benefit plans still cover a larger percentage of the workforce than defined-contribution plans do. In fact, for the first time in years, 1995 saw the number of new defined-benefit plans increase, with 9 percent of all new plans being defined-benefit plans, as compared with 6 percent in the previous year. Also, defined-benefit plan terminations are down; defined-benefit plans constituted only 36 percent of the plan terminations in 1995—compared to 45 percent the year before. Also, a Kwasha-Lipton study showed that the percentage of businesses sponsoring defined-benefit plans in the state of Illinois in 1995 was 56 percent, up from 44 percent in 1994.

Nevertheless, defined-contribution products have become the bread-and-butter sale for those who deal in qualified deferred compensation. While larger companies still have defined-benefit plans, these plans are serviced by providers that are generally well established and firmly entrenched. The more available market consists of new small to medium-sized firms, and these firms are clearly looking for defined-contribution plans. For example, in 1995, 40,271 of the 44,389 new plans that were issued IRS determination letters were defined-contribution plans. The defined-contribution approach appears to appeal both to senior managers—who are looking for simplicity and contribution certainty—and to employees—who like that they can more easily understand the plan and appreciate that benefits are more portable.

Multiple Plans—Combining Defined-Benefit and Defined-Contribution Plans

As mentioned, defined-benefit plans and defined-contribution plans are not mutually exclusive, and two or more plans can be set up for any one employer. If defined-benefit and defined-contribution plans are used together, restrictions apply to the overall deduction limits and, more important, to the maximum benefits that can be provided for individual participants.

Today, a combination defined-benefit and defined-contribution plan is typically used in a larger company to provide a comprehensive benefits package. As discussed earlier, an individual participating in a defined-contribution plan (or plans) may receive an allocation of the lesser of 25 percent of pay or $30,000 (in all plans). And an individual participating in a defined-benefit plan (or plans) may receive a maximum annual benefit of the lesser of 100 percent of salary or $125,000. Historically, there has been an overall limit for individuals who participate in both types of plans. However, effective for plan years beginning in year 2000, this combined limit will no longer apply. Note that the only persons still affected by the combined limit will be those individuals who begin to receive benefits from a defined-benefit plan before the year 2000.

CHOOSING BETWEEN A PENSION PLAN AND A PROFIT-SHARING PLAN

All qualified plans fall into either the defined-benefit or defined-contribution categories. Similarly, all plans are also classified as either pension plans or profit-sharing plans. As you can see in the chart below, both types of defined-benefit plans, along with target-benefit and money-purchase plans, are categorized as pension plans. All other defined-contribution plans are profit-sharing plans.

Qualified Plan Categories

Pension Plans	Profit-Sharing Plans
• Defined-benefit pension plan	• Profit-sharing plan
• Cash-balance pension plan	• 401(k) plan
• Money-purchase pension plan	• Stock bonus plan
• Target-benefit pension plan	• ESOP

The most important difference between a plan in the pension category and one in the profit-sharing category concerns the employer's commitment to the plan. Under a pension plan, the organization is legally required to make annual payments to the plan, since the main purpose of the plan is to provide a retirement benefit. Under a profit-sharing-type plan, however, an organization is not required to make annual contributions. The reasoning here seems to be that profit-sharing plans aren't necessarily intended to provide retirement benefits as much as to provide a sharing of profits on a tax-deferred basis.

Consistent with this rationale, the law generally provides that profit-sharing-type plans may be written to allow distributions during employment, while pension plans cannot make distributions until the participant terminates employment. The law allows a profit-sharing-type plan to make in-service distributions on amounts that have accumulated in the plan for a stated number of years. The IRS has interpreted this to mean that distributions can be made on contributions that were made to the plan 2 or more years ago. Also, anyone who has 5 years of plan participation can receive a distribution of his or her entire account balance. In-service distributions can also be made after a stated event, such as a financial hardship. Note that one type of profit-sharing plan, the 401(k) plan, is subject to special, more restrictive in-service withdrawal constraints (discussed in chapter 5).

Another distinction between plans in the pension category and plans in the profit-sharing category is the maximum tax-deductible contribution. Here the distinctions are broken down by defined-benefit and defined-contribution as well. For a pension plan in the defined-contribution category, the maximum deductible contribution is 25 percent of aggregate participant payroll. If the pension plan is of the defined-benefit type, the maximum deductible contribution is based on actuarial cost calculations, which may exceed 25 percent of aggregate participant payroll. In a profit-sharing plan the organization's deduction is limited to 15 percent of aggregate participant payroll.

A final distinction between pension and profit-sharing plans concerns the ability of these plans to invest in company stock. Plans in the pension category can invest only up to 10 percent of plan assets in employer stock. Plans in the profit-sharing category, on the other hand, have no restrictions; all plan assets can be used to purchase employer stock (although this is seldom the case). See table 3-2 for a summary of plan differences.

TABLE 3-2
Differences between Pension and Profit-Sharing Plans

Characteristic	Pension Plan	Profit-Sharing Plan
Employer commitment to annual funding	Yes	No
Withdrawal flexibility for employees	None	After 2 years
Employer deduction	25% (or more)	15%
Investment in company stock	Limited to 10%	Unlimited

KEOGH PLANS

In addition to categorizing plans either as defined-benefit or defined-contribution or as pension or profit-sharing, qualified plans are categorized by the type of business organization they serve. Today, all types of businesses choose from among the same group of qualified plans. Historically, that was not always true. At one time plans for partnerships and self-employeds were governed by separate statutory provisions, and plans for such organizations were referred to as Keogh plans. Unfortunately, the name still sticks—generally creating more confusion than information. Today, a sole proprietor does not establish a Keogh plan; he or she establishes a profit-sharing, defined-benefit, or other plan from the array of tax-advantaged retirement plans. And, except as described below, the rules for sole proprietorships and partnerships are entirely the same as for corporate entities, and the same considerations regarding plan choice and plan design apply.

There are, however, two important distinctions between plans of sole proprietorships and partnerships[1] and corporate plans: (1) Such plans are not permitted to have loan provisions for owner-employees, while corporate plans can generally allow plan loans (the rules for plan loans are discussed in chapter 9) and (2) the self-employed person's contribution or benefit is based on net earnings instead of salary. This creates some complications because net earnings can be determined only after taking into account all appropriate business deductions, including the deduction for the retirement contribution—thus the amount of net earnings and the amount of the deduction are dependent on each other.

If a defined-benefit plan is used, an actuary is needed to straighten out this mess and to determine the plan contribution amount itself. However, if a defined-contribution plan is used, you will need to calculate the maximum deduction for your client (see the work sheet in table 3-3).

Traditionally this has meant that a sole proprietor or partner with a profit-sharing plan could contribute only a maximum of 13.0435 percent of net earnings (not 15 percent of salary, as in a corporate plan) to the plan. A sole proprietor or partner in a pension plan was limited to a maximum plan contribution of 20 percent of net earnings (not 25 percent of salary). Further complicating matters is the fact that self-employed individuals get a deduction for income tax purposes equal to one-half of their social security self-employment tax on their federal tax return. In addition, when calculating the contribution the maximum compensation that can be used is $160,000 (in 1997) (see chapter 8 for a discussion of the compensation cap). Fortunately, these complications can be eliminated if you follow the formula below.

Example: Julie is a sole proprietor. Her qualified profit-sharing plan provides that she contribute 15 percent of earned income. Julie's self-employment contribution rate is 13.0435 percent (see example in rate work sheet). Julie's net earnings from Schedule C are $150,000. Julie's deduction for self-employment tax (Form 1040) is $6,062.40. Julie's deduction for the 1996 tax year will be determined as follows:

(1) Enter self-employment rate from Line 3 above   <u>.130435</u>

(2) Enter the amount of net earnings from Schedule C (Form 1040) or from Schedule F (Form 1040)   <u>$150,000</u>

(3) Enter the deduction for self-employment tax from Line 25, Form 1040 (for 1996).   <u>$6,062.40</u>

(4) Subtract Step 3 from Step 2 and enter the amount.   <u>$143,937.60</u>

(5) Multiply Step 4 by Step 1 and enter the amount. This is the amount that may be deducted by the business owner.   <u>$18,774.50</u>

TABLE 3-3 **Keogh Deduction Work Sheet**	
Step I: Self-employed person's work sheet	
1. Plan contribution as a decimal (for example, 15% would be 0.15)	_____
2. Rate in Line 1 plus 1, shown as a decimal (for example, 0.15 plus 1 would be 1.15)	_____
3. Divide Line 1 by Line 2. This is the self-employed contribution rate. (For example, 0.15 ÷ 1.15 = .130435)	_____
Step II: Figure the deduction	
1. Enter the self-employed contribution rate from Line 3 of Step I.	_____
2. Enter the amount of net earnings that the business owner has from Schedule C (Form 1040) or Schedule F (Form 1040).	$_____
3. Enter the deduction for self-employment tax from the front page of Form 1040.	$_____
4. Subtract Line 3 from Line 2 and enter the amount.	$_____
5. Multiply Line 4 by Line 1. This is the amount that may be deducted by the business owner.*	$_____
*Note that this amount cannot exceed $30,000.	

ADDITIONAL PRELIMINARY CONCERNS

Before we study the menu of qualified plans, it should be noted that choosing the best retirement plan is not as simple as picking one type of plan from the menu. The design of the plan must also be considered in order to make the proper plan choice. This is because qualified plans are principally differentiated by only one design feature—their benefit formulas. The many other design choices, however, also affect your plan choice. To put it another way, plan choice is a function of plan design, and plan design is a function of plan choice.

> *Example:* The professional corporation of Davis and Wickstrom is primarily interested in providing tax-sheltered savings for key employees and minimizing costs attributable to rank-and-file employees. Davis and Wickstrom ask you to help choose the best retirement plan for them. A defined-benefit plan designed with a benefit formula that is integrated with social security, and with restrictive eligibility and vesting provisions, is most probably the preferable choice. But if you had only considered the menu of retirement plans without considering the design features, you might have chosen a 401(k) plan instead. At first blush the 401(k) sounds like a likely fit because it allows tax-sheltered savings for key employees and minimizes costs attributable to the rank and file. On closer inspection, however, you'll see that 401(k) plans may not provide enough tax shelter for the principals because such plans must be designed to meet a special nondiscrimination test known as the *actual deferral percentage test.*

The plan-design details that help you to make a more informed decision are presented in chapters 7 through 10.

A second consideration when choosing a qualified plan is the makeup of the entire benefits package. For example, if there is a nonqualified plan for key employees, the choice of a qualified plan for all employees should be dovetailed with the nonqualified plan to reach the desired result. When group life and group disability plans are involved, other considerations arise. As a general rule, the choice of a retirement plan should reflect the fact that it is only one part of a benefits package. Special care should be taken to ensure that benefits are not duplicated under the different employee benefit plans.

NOTE

1. Note that limited-liability companies that are taxed as partnerships will be subject to the same limitations as those that apply to partnerships.

4

Defined-Benefit, Cash-Balance, Target-Benefit, and Money-Purchase Pension Plans

Chapter Outline

In order to help your client choose the best retirement plan, you first need to examine the menu of tax-advantaged plans. In the next two chapters we will preview the full range of qualified plans, and in chapter 6 we will discuss SEPs, SIMPLEs, and 403(b) plans. We will assess each plan's strengths and weaknesses, focus on the objectives that each plan serves for your client, and discuss the typical candidates for each type of plan.

The various types of qualified plans are in part explained by the characteristics of the categories they fall under (defined-benefit versus defined-contribution, and pension versus profit-sharing) and in part by their benefit or contribution formula. In chapter 3 you learned a significant amount about each type of category, as you learned how each plan was categorized. The one remaining piece of the puzzle is the plan's benefit or contribution formula. Let's take a closer look at the various types of retirement plans and their benefit (contribution) formulas.

DEFINED-BENEFIT PENSION PLANS

A defined-benefit pension plan falls within both the defined-benefit and pension categories. Knowing this means you already know that defined-benefit plans have the following characteristics:

- The maximum benefit that a person can receive each year is $125,000, as indexed.
- Assets are *not* allocated to individual accounts.
- The employer assumes responsibility for preretirement inflation, income adequacy, and investment results.
- The benefit formula can be designed to consider past service.
- The older business owner can provide the maximum tax-shelter potential available under a qualified plan.
- They are more costly to administer than defined-contribution plans, because, among other things, they require the services of an actuary.
- The benefit formula and value of the benefit may be more difficult to communicate than in defined-contribution plans.
- The employer's future costs are not precisely known.
- Annual employer contributions are required.
- Participants may not take in-service withdrawals.
- Investment in the sponsoring company's stock is limited to 10 percent of the plan's assets.

Let's take a closer look at defined-benefit pension plans from a design standpoint by examining the various types of benefit formulas that are used.

The Unit-Benefit Formula

The most frequently used defined-benefit formula is the *unit-benefit formula* (also known as the percentage-of-earnings-per-year-of-service formula). This formula uses both service and salary in determining the participant's pension benefit. A unit-benefit formula might read this way: "Each plan participant will receive a monthly pension commencing at normal retirement date and paid in the form of a life annuity equal to 1.5 percent of final-average monthly salary multiplied by years of service. Service is limited to a maximum of 30 years."

Example: Larry Novenstern is retiring after 25 years of service with his employer. Larry's final-average monthly salary is $5,000. To determine Larry's benefit, multiply 1.5 percent by the $5,000 final-average monthly salary by 25 (the number of years of service). Larry's monthly retirement benefit will be equal to $1,875 paid in the form of a life annuity. (Note that a life annuity need not be the actual form of benefit. If a different annuity form is chosen, an actuarial adjustment is made to the benefit amount to account for any survivor benefits provided under the different annuity form.)

The unit-benefit formula is the most frequently used benefit formula because it best serves a variety of employer goals:

- The goal of retaining and rewarding experienced personnel is achieved because the pension benefit is based in part on the years of service an employee works for the employer.
- The goal of rewarding owner-employees and key employees is achieved because the pension benefit is based in part on salary, which is higher for owner-employees and key employees.
- The goal of providing the desired income-replacement ratio can be achieved through proper design of the benefit formula. The *income-replacement ratio* represents the amount of an employee's gross income that will be replaced under the retirement plan. Employers believe that there is no need to replace 100 percent of an employee's final-average salary in order to provide the desired standard of living at retirement for several reasons:

  - Social security benefits and private savings will fund part of the needed retirement benefit.
  - The preretirement standard of living can be maintained at retirement on a lower income because the employee pays less in taxes in the retirement years (for example, no social security taxes).
  - The preretirement standard of living can be maintained at retirement on a lower income because the employee has reduced living expenses (no work-related expenses such as transportation and clothing; self-supporting children; paid-up home mortgage; and so on).

For these reasons, employers generally choose an income replacement of between 40 and 60 percent of final-average salary for employees who have spent their career with the employer, and something less for employees who have not spent as long with the employer.

Example: The Cooper Corporation would like to provide a 60 percent income-replacement ratio for long-service employees and would like to provide a proportionately reduced income-replacement ratio for shorter-service employees. In order to accomplish these goals the Cooper Corporation should choose a benefit formula that reads, "Each plan participant will receive a monthly pension commencing at normal retirement date and paid in the form of a life annuity equal to 2 percent of final-average monthly salary multiplied by years of service. Service is limited to a maximum of 30 years."

Under this benefit formula, the long-service employees will be provided with a 60 percent income-replacement ratio, and employees with fewer than 30 years of service will be provided with an equitably reduced income-replacement ratio. What's more, by placing the years-of-service cap at 30 years, the Cooper Corporation will never have to fund for benefits higher than 60 percent of average monthly salary.

- The goal of providing for a graceful transition in the workforce is achieved because the use of a years-of-service cap (in the example above, 30 years) discourages employment beyond the stated period. If the employer desires a more rapid turnover of older employees, a lower service cap can be used. If the employer wants to retain experienced personnel, however, a longer service cap may be used, or the employer may choose not to cap service at all.
- The goal of providing the most cost-effective defined-benefit plan possible is achieved because the unit-benefit formula is more cost-effective than other types of defined-benefit formulas. Cost-effectiveness can be defined in this case as getting the most value for each pension dollar by achieving employer goals at the least possible cost. To the extent permitted by law, the employer can reward employees with long service and/or high compensation and avoid paying disproportionate benefits for other employees.

The reason that unit-benefit formulas are the most cost-effective means of spending defined-benefit dollars can be best understood by examining the alternative defined-benefit formulas.

Other Defined-Benefit Formulas

Under an alternative defined-benefit formula called the *flat-percentage-of-earnings formula* (on IRS forms, called a *fixed-benefit formula*), the benefit is related solely to salary and does not reflect an employee's service. A flat-percentage-of-earnings formula might read, "Each plan participant will receive a monthly pension benefit commencing at normal retirement date and paid in the form of a life annuity equal to 40 percent of the final-average monthly salary the participant was paid."

This formula is not cost-effective, however, because it provides a disproportionate benefit to employees hired later in their careers, which is costly to fund.

Example: Patty Brown has worked for your client for 30 years and has final-average earnings of $60,000. Debbie Green has worked for the same client for only 10 years and her final-average earnings figure is $50,000. If a 50 percent flat-percentage-of-earning formula is used, Patty's pension would be $30,000 a year and Debbie's pension would be $25,000 a year. Probably the employer would have preferred both a fairer system (one that rewarded Patty's long service proportionately greater than Debbie's service) and a more cost-effective system (one that didn't provide such an extravagant benefit for an employee who had been with the organization for only 10 years).

For the reasons illustrated in the example, historically this formula has been used rarely except in church plans and in certain tax-shelter-type plans. Churches have used this formula because the parish goal is to provide a livable benefit, not a benefit based on cost-effectiveness. In the past, this type of formula was also common in a small businesses when the owner was significantly older than the rank-and-file employees. The owner could accrue a full benefit over a short period of time (as Debbie does in the above example) while benefits for other employees accrued over a much longer period of time. Realizing that this was discriminatory, the IRS passed regulations that now require a flat percentage of earnings formula to have a 25-year minimum period of service in order for the participants to receive the full benefits promised. For those with less than 25 years of service the benefit will be proportionately reduced. If this had been the case in the example above, Patty would receive the full benefit of $30,000 and Debbie would receive only ten twenty-fifths (10/25) of her $25,000 benefit (or $10,000).

A second alternative to the unit-benefit formula is a formula that relates the pension benefit solely to service but does not reflect an employee's salary. This type of formula, called a *flat-amount-per-year-of-service* formula, might read, "Each plan participant will receive a monthly pension benefit commencing at normal retirement date and paid in the form of a life annuity equal to $10 for every year worked."

Employers seldom choose the flat-amount-per-year-of-service formula because it, too, is not cost-effective. The lack of cost-effectiveness stems from the fact that the flat-amount-per-year-of-service formula will not simultaneously provide the proper income replacement for both highly paid employees and rank-and-file employees.

Flat-amount-per-year-of-service formulas are, however, popular in union-negotiated plans. When used in union plans a flat-amount-per-year-of-service formula may relate the benefit to the actual hours a participant worked. For example, participants working 1,000 hours might receive half as much as participants working 2,000 hours. For more on union plans, see the books listed in the additional reading in appendix 1.

A third alternative to the unit-benefit formula is the *flat-amount* formula (on IRS forms the flat-amount formula is called a *flat-benefit* formula). The flat-amount formula provides the same monthly benefit for each participant. This type of formula treats all employees alike and does not account for differences in earnings and service. A flat-amount formula might read: "Each plan participant will receive a $200 a month pension benefit commencing at normal retirement date and paid in the form of a life annuity."

As with the flat-amount-per-year-of-service formula the flat-amount formula is not cost-effective. Once again you will find this formula primarily in union plans.

Mixing Formulas

In addition to using the benefit formulas by themselves, the financial services professional can design the plan to mix benefit formulas. For example, the flat-amount formula can be used in conjunction with the unit-benefit formula to provide a base of coverage. This base of coverage can meet your client's goal of providing a floor of benefits that enables retirees to meet minimum living standards. In addition, the other benefit formulas described can be mixed to achieve your client's goals or to fund for past service (see below). Finally, it is worth noting that law changes, corporate goal changes, or business ownership changes may invoke a situation where a plan has several pieces of different (amended) formulas. For example, a plan may provide

	1 percent x years of service x final average salary from 1980–1985
plus	1.5 percent x years of service x final average salary from 1985 to the present
plus	a flat benefit of $500

Elements of the Benefit Formula

Now let's turn our attention from the defined-benefit formulas themselves to the major elements that constitute them. If a plan has a unit-benefit formula, that formula commonly will read as follows:

A participant will be entitled to a life annuity beginning at the normal retirement age in the amount of 1.5 percent of final average compensation times years of service. Normal retirement age is the later of age 65 or 5 years of plan participation.

Each of the factors in this benefit formula affects the ultimate value of the benefit. The factors include the definition of compensation under the plan, the definition of years of service, the form of benefit, and the age at which benefits can begin. Each of these factors is discussed more fully below.

The Definition of Compensation

One of the most important elements of the defined-benefit formula is the amount of compensation used in the benefit formula. This is a function of both the definition of compensation and the definition of "average" (or final-average) compensation. The most comprehensive definition of compensation includes all wages that are included in taxable income, plus any pretax salary deferrals under a 401(k) plan (or 403(b) or SIMPLE). A less comprehensive definition can be selected but must undergo scrutiny under rules that prohibit discrimination in favor of the highly compensated employees. As a way to keep plan costs both predictable and under control, many employers will choose base salary as the definition of compensation—*excluding* any extra pay such as bonuses, overtime, or commissions. Under the nondiscrimination rules, this definition would be a problem only if the rank-and file-employees received significant additional pay while the highly compensated did not.

Just as meaningful is how "final-average compensation" is defined. Benefits could simply be based on the participant's final year (or highest year) of compensation—but this, too, could result in both higher and more unpredictable plan costs. It is more common to choose a definition such as the average of the final 3 (or 5) years' salary, or the average of the highest 3 (or 5) years' consecutive salary. Averaging the highest few years of salary serves the dual purpose of leveling off any abnormal years of compensation while providing a benefit that is tied to the individual's highest salary (providing preretirement inflation protection).

In the past, plans sometimes based benefits on the individual's entire salary history. This type of formula is referred to as a *career-average* benefit formula. This formula worked in one of two ways. One way was to have the benefit based on average compensation—looking at the individual's entire salary history. The other way was to have the formula provide a benefit such as one percent of the current year's salary plus one percent of the next year's salary, and so on. In this way, the benefit was an accumulation of the benefits earned for each year of service. Today, this type of formula is rare. If the employer really wants a plan that provides benefits based on career average salary, a defined-contribution plan is generally chosen.

Service

Another important element of the defined-benefit formula is the definition of service. What's unique to the defined-benefit approach is the ability to account for past service—service with the employer prior to the inception of the plan. Providing for past service is particularly important to clients who are setting up a new plan for the benefit of long-service employees. If past service is not accounted for, these employees will find that their retirement benefits are inadequate. Another important reason to account for past service is to maximize the tax-shelter potential of the plan for owner-employees and key employees. A benefit formula that fully accounts for past service provides a bias toward these employees because they frequently are the ones who have the most past service.

Past service can be accounted for wholly or partially. In other words, the plan can provide for all service prior to the inception of the plan (for example, 2 percent x final 3 years' average salary x *all* service with the employer) or can provide a downgraded benefit (or no benefit) for service prior to the inception of the plan. A benefit formula with a downgraded past-service benefit might read, "Two percent x final 3 years' average salary x all service with the employer after the plan's inception date *plus one percent* x final 3 years' average salary x all service with the employer prior to the plan's inception date."

Form of Benefit

In a defined-benefit plan, the *normal form* of benefit payment is an essential characteristic of the plan benefit. The most common normal form of payment is a life annuity (meaning that payments continue only for as long as the participant lives). However, some plans will use a different normal form, such as a life annuity with a certain period of payments (typically 5 to 10 years)—meaning that the benefit will be payable for the longer of life or the specified time period.

The normal form of payment has a direct impact on the value of the benefit. For example, a life annuity with 10-year certain payments of $1,000 a month is more valuable than a straight life annuity of $1,000 a month. This is significant when participants have the option to receive the benefit in other forms, since the optional forms of payment are almost always the actuarial equivalent of the normal form of payment. For example, if the life annuity with 10-year certain payments were converted to a single-sum benefit, the participant would receive more than if the conversion were based on the straight life annuity. If this concept seems confusing, the discussion in chapter 25 regarding forms of payment should help to clarify.

Finally, note that providing a benefit as a life annuity is very different from a defined-contribution plan, where the benefit is based on the account balance. With a defined-contribution plan, if the participant elects to receive a life annuity, the amount of the benefit payment will be based on the annuity that can be "purchased" with the single-sum amount. Another way of saying this is that in the defined-contribution plan, the normal form of payment is a single-sum amount.

Normal Retirement Age

Since defined-benefit plans generally provide benefits in the form of a life annuity, another factor that directly affects the value of the benefit is the date at which benefits can begin. The earlier the retirement age, the longer the payout period and the more valuable (and costly) the benefit. This subject is discussed more in chapter 9.

Candidates for This Type of Plan

Defined-benefit plans can be thought of as the Cadillacs of the retirement fleet because they can be designed to ensure that benefits replace a specified portion of the participant's preretirement income. But this type of plan comes with a fairly high price tag. Although there may be mitigating factors such as integration of the plans with social security (see integration, chapter 8) and lower costs owing to better-than-expected investment return, defined-benefit plans remain expensive to fund. Also the actuarial calculations involved make them costly to administer.

For the older business owner, the defined-benefit pension plan is a way to shelter larger amounts than can generally be contributed to a defined-contribution plan. This is because the time to fund for the benefit is short and the annual contributions required to fund the plan will be more significant. At the same time the older business owner can create a significant retirement benefit over a short period of time. This is because past service can be factored into the retirement computation.

The Fact Finder

Candidates for defined-benefit pension plans fill out step 1 of the fact finder by grading as "very valuable" the following:

- using a qualified plan as a tax shelter for owner-employees and key employees
- maximizing benefits for long-service employees by including service prior to the inception of the plan

Candidates for a defined-benefit pension plan frequently grade as "least valuable" these goals:

- placing the investment risk with the employee
- avoiding an annual financial commitment
- instituting a plan that has predictable costs
- instituting a plan that is administratively convenient
- instituting a plan that is easily communicated to employees

In addition, defined-benefit pension plan candidates fill out step 2 of the fact finder by answering yes to these questions: Is it more important to provide an adequate retirement standard of living than to cut plan costs? Is it more important to provide an adequate retirement standard of living than to have predictable costs? Is it more important to provide an adequate standard of living during retirement than to have administrative convenience and an easily communicated plan?

YOUR FINANCIAL SERVICES PRACTICE: GETTING MORE OUT OF DEFINED-BENEFIT PLANS FOR LITTLE OR NO COST

Surprisingly, in large and medium-sized organizations, employee enthusiasm about defined-benefit plans is generally low. This is especially true for younger employees. Improved relations in this area could generate a high employee morale, but few employers pick up on this oversight. Several cost-effective solutions are available. Suggest that the employer

- issue more frequent and more informative benefit statements
- periodically rework the summary plan description (see chapter 13)
- set up periodic meetings to review all employee benefits
- demonstrate how favorably an employee's defined-benefit plan compares with other retirement plans
- publicize the amount and percentage of employee payroll used to fund the defined-benefit plan each year

---

CASH-BALANCE PENSION PLANS

The cash-balance concept is a relatively new idea in pension plan design, with the first plan introduced in 1984. In its short history, it has been used primarily by midsize and larger corporations as an alternative to the traditional defined-benefit plan. In fact, most of the cash-balance plans in existence today started as traditional plans that were later amended. As of August 1995, approximately 200 cash-balance plans had been established, several by large employers including BankAmerica Corp., RJR Nabisco, and IBM. The cash-balance plan is generally motivated by two factors: selecting a benefit design that employees can more easily understand and appreciate, and as a cost-savings measure.

The cash-balance plan is a defined-benefit plan that is designed to look like a defined-contribution plan. As a defined-benefit plan, it has some level of funding flexibility and is subject to minimum funding requirements and the PBGC insurance program. At the same time, the defined-contribution-like design means that it is easier to explain the benefit formula and that the plan will provide a more portable benefit for today's mobile workforce.

The heart of the cash-balance plan is the benefit structure. As in the defined-contribution plan, the benefit is stated as an account balance that increases with contributions and investment experience. However, in a cash-balance plan the account is fictitious. Contributions are a bookkeeping credit only—no actual contributions are allocated to participants' accounts. Investment credits are also hypothetical and are based either upon a rate specified in the plan or on an external index. To the participants, however, this plan looks like a traditional defined-contribution "account balance" plan. And when an employee terminates, the benefit payout is based upon the value of the participant's account.

The cash-balance benefit can be used as the sole benefit structure under the plan, or as an add-on to a preexisting, more traditional defined-benefit plan formula. The sponsor can design any contribution credit formula that will meet its goals, as long as it is clearly defined in the plan document and satisfies nondiscrimination rules and other legal requirements. Most typically, the contribution credit is stated as a percentage of the individual's current year's pay (for example, 5 percent of salary) or as a formula that considers both salary and years of service to reward those with longer service. For example, a formula can assign credits of 3 percent of salary for those with less than 5 years of service, 6 percent for those with 10 or more years of service, and 9 percent for 20-year veterans. Credits given for investment experience can be stated as a fixed, predetermined rate; a floating rate (based on some external index outside the control of the employer), or a combination of a fixed and floating rate, such as the rate of one-year Treasury bills. The contribution and interest credits can be treated as made annually or more often, if the employer prefers. Also, since this is a defined-benefit plan, contribution and interest credits can be made for past years of service.

From the employer's perspective, this plan is still a defined-benefit plan. Contributions are required in the amount necessary to satisfy the minimum funding requirements. Under these rules, the employer has a degree of flexibility in determining the required contribution. Also, as in any defined-benefit plan, the employer is ultimately responsible for making contributions necessary to pay promised benefits—meaning that the sponsor is "on the hook" for the plan's investment experience. If trust assets earn a higher rate of return, then expected future contributions are reduced, and vice versa.

From the employee's perspective, the cash-balance design looks mostly like a defined-contribution plan. The only similarity to the defined-benefit approach is that benefits are guaranteed by the PBGC and are not affected adversely by downturns in the market. In all other ways, the cash-balance plan mirrors the strengths and weaknesses of the defined-contribution plan. Benefits accrue (depending upon the formula) more evenly over the participant's career, meaning that benefits are not lost if the employee decides to change jobs. A cash-balance plan, like a defined-contribution plan, is easy to communicate. The contribution and interest credits are both easy to follow and may be more appreciated than a traditional defined-benefit plan. Similarly, the cash balance plan does not have many of the strengths of the traditional defined-benefit approach. Benefits do not replace a specified percentage of preretirement income, and since benefits are not based on final salary, the benefit is not inflation-adjusted up to the time benefits begin.

Advantages and Disadvantages

The fact that the cash-balance plan looks like a defined-contribution plan makes the plan easier for participants to understand. But the more interesting question is, looking at the plan as a defined-contribution substitute, does it offer anything that a defined-contribution plan does not? The answer is yes. A cash-balance plan formula can establish credits for past service; in some circumstances this is a big advantage over the defined-contribution plan. However, looking at the plan from the participant's perspective, the real thing (a true defined-contribution plan) is probably better than the imitation. In an account plan, assets are generally invested with a long-term investment horizon. Participants sharing in the investment experience of a long-term stock-oriented portfolio will generally be better off than if they are credited with a small but steady rate of return. Also, the PBGC guarantee is not really meaningful. The PBGC does not guarantee all benefits, and an employee could lose out if the company folds at a time when the plan has insufficient assets. On the other hand, in a defined-contribution plan, benefits are fully funded at all times and are outside the reach of the employer's creditors.

But this leads us to the real point of the cash-balance concept: It is not driven solely by employee concerns but in conjunction with the employer's needs and objectives. At least up to this point in time, almost all cash-balance plans in existence today are converted traditional defined-benefit plans. There are two main driving forces: cost savings and a decision that the defined-contribution philosophy makes more sense for the company. The employer may feel that the defined-benefit plan is underappreciated and that the defined-contribution approach will be better received by the employees.

Candidates for This Type of Plan

As described above, so far, the typical candidate for the cash-balance plan is the midsize or large company that has a well-funded defined-benefit plan and that is looking to both save on benefit costs into the future and change to a defined-contribution approach. Prior to the cash-balance concept, the employer looking to save on costs would amend the traditional benefit formula—either lowering or freezing future benefit accruals. However, this would alarm plan participants as they saw their benefits being reduced. Under the cash-balance alternative, the old defined-benefit promise is frozen at the current accrued benefit level and the benefit is stated as its single-sum equivalent. Benefits accruing after the change simply increase the total account balance. With the right cash-balance formula, employees might actually welcome the change in benefit structure, while the employer saves money.

However, this is not magic. The new benefit structure cannot be cheaper and be just as good. Generally, older, long-service employees are hurt the most in the transition. To protect this group, some employers grandfather the old benefit formula for older employees or give them a larger annual credit under the new formula. The employer could also decide to put some of the savings into another plan, such as making a matching contribution to a 401(k) plan. In this way the employer sends the message that retirement security is now going to be a joint effort between the employer and employees.

This same employer with the overfunded defined-benefit plan could instead terminate the plan and establish a true defined-contribution plan. However, there are several reasons that amending the plan into a cash-balance plan is more appealing:

- While the employer would not be able to effectively use any excess in the defined-benefit plan to fund the defined-contribution plan, this can be accomplished seamlessly with the cash-balance approach.
- In the future, benefits in the cash-balance plan could be increased both for current and past service. This would be prohibited in a defined-contribution plan.
- The defined-contribution plan lacks the funding flexibility of the cash-balance plan.
- Unlike the cash-balance plan, in a defined-contribution plan, future employer contributions are not reduced by stronger-than-expected investment performance.

For all these reasons, the cash-balance plan is a terrific solution to this one specific situation. Expect more large and midsize companies to continue to explore the possibility of changing to the cash-balance approach.

Finally, it is not yet clear whether cash-balance plans will become popular as a new plan alternative. For the smaller employer looking for a new retirement plan, the cash-balance approach has all the headaches of a defined-benefit plan: PBGC premiums, large administrative costs, and an annual required contribution. The cash-balance option has more funding flexibility than a traditional money-purchase or target-benefit plan, but it also has much less flexibility than the discretionary profit-sharing or profit-sharing 401(k) plan. It is unlikely that the cash-balance approach will become popular as a new plan alternative.

MONEY-PURCHASE PENSION PLANS

A money-purchase plan falls within both the defined-contribution and pension categories. Knowing this means you already know that money-purchase pension plans have the following characteristics:

- The maximum annual contribution that an employee can receive is the lesser of 25 percent of salary or $30,000.
- Participants in the plan have individual accounts that are similar to bank accounts
- The employee assumes the risk of preretirement inflation, investment performance, and adequacy of retirement income.
- The plan cannot provide for past service.
- Administrative costs are relatively low.

- The plan is easily communicated to employees.
- The plan has predictable employer costs.
- The employer is required to fund the plan annually.
- Employees are restricted from having in-service withdrawals.
- The employer can deduct up to the full amount available under the Sec. 415 limits.
- Investments in company stock are limited to 10 percent of the plan's assets.

**YOUR FINANCIAL SERVICES PRACTICE:
SWITCHING INVESTMENT CARRIERS**

More often than not, when you are prospecting in the retirement field you will encounter the existence of an established plan that's invested with a competitor. The emergence of new types of plans can be a useful weapon in fighting the uphill battle of converting already-spoken-for assets. Prospective clients can be made aware of new types of plans, such as cash-balance plans, and this contact can be the proverbial foot in the door that may lead to a new client. For example, likely candidates who might consider switching to cash-balance plans include companies interested in providing something more than their current defined-contribution plan without the total commitment of a defined-benefit pension plan approach, and companies seeking to reduce or modify their defined-benefit pension plan obligations. Even if the cash-balance plan doesn't fit the needs of these prospective clients, at the very least you will be regarded as someone who is in touch with current trends and who is on the cutting edge of your profession. Future dealings may stem from this favorable impression.

Under a money-purchase plan, the company's annual contributions are based on a percentage of each participant's compensation. For example, the money-purchase contribution formula may provide that annual contributions will equal 10 percent of compensation for each participant (if Karen Lamb earns $40,000, the annual contribution placed in her account is $4,000). Money-purchase plan benefits for each employee are the amounts that can be provided by the sums contributed to the employee's individual account plus investment earnings. For example, if Karen Lamb worked for 20 years and her salary remained at $40,000, at retirement she would have $80,000 plus accumulated interest of $58,876 (assuming a 5 percent annual rate) in her account. The term *money-purchase* arose because the participant's account is traditionally used to purchase an annuity that provides monthly retirement benefits.

The maximum annual limit that can be tax sheltered under a money-purchase plan is 25 percent of total covered compensation. This deduction limit is higher than for profit-sharing plans. However, because of the fixed annual contribution, money-purchase plans are rarely used on their own to maximize tax-shelter. More often they are used when the employer wants to provide a plan that has a fixed contribution—and therefore gives the sense to employees that it is a substantial and permanent retirement plan. Typically these organizations provide between 3 and 12 percent of compensation as the annual contribution.

Self-employed people provide another market for money-purchase plans (they like the money-purchase plan's simplicity). For example, a self-employed person may express a desire to tax-shelter 15 percent of his or her earned income for retirement. Also, self-employed persons and small businesses looking to maximize tax shelter will often adopt both a profit-sharing plan (with a maximum contribution of 15 percent of participant's compensation), and a money-purchase pension plan with a 10-percent-of-compensation formula. In this way the employer can limit the required contribution to 10 percent and make the additional 15 percent contribution (totaling the maximum of 25 percent of compensation) if and only if sufficient assets are available.

Money-purchase pension plans can be likened to the station wagons of the retirement fleet because of their dependable annual contributions and simple, basic design. The major advantages of money-purchase pension plans are the predictable costs for the employer (since contributions are based on employee compensation, the employer contribution is basically a percentage of payroll), administrative ease, and understandability for the employees. Corporate objectives such as competitiveness and attraction and retention of key employees can be met within the money-purchase framework without being prohibitively expensive for the employer.

Advantages and Disadvantages

One major drawback of a money-purchase plan is that it is a career-average plan. Contributions are based on the participant's salary for each year of his or her career, rather than on the salary at retirement. Given a stable inflationary environment, this may not have a negative impact on the adequacy of retirement income. If inflation spirals in the years prior to retirement, however, the chances of achieving an adequate income-replacement ratio are diminished. Take, for example, someone who earned an average middle-class income and whose career spanned the 1950s, 1960s, and 1970s. In 1950 this person earned $2,000 and received a 10 percent money-purchase contribution of $200. In 1960 the employee earned $12,000 and received a 10 percent money-purchase contribution of $1,200. In 1970 the employee earned $24,000 and received a $2,400 contribution. During the 1970s, double-digit inflation hit, and salary levels increased to account for the increased cost of living. If the participant retired in 1980, he or she would be at a disadvantage because only part of the plan contributions would account for the inflationary period right before retirement. What's more, most of the annual contributions would be based on deflated salaries that accrued before the inflationary spiral. In other words, if a final-average defined-benefit plan were used, the employer would have to make significant contributions to account for an increased final-average salary assumption owing to higher inflation.

A second drawback is the inability to provide an adequate retirement program for older participants. Participants who enter money-purchase pension plans later in their careers have less time to accumulate sufficient assets.

Example: New employee Bill Nelson is 55 years old and has no other retirement funds except social security. Nelson earns $50,000 annually and plans to retire at age 65. The money-purchase pension formula calls for 10 percent of salary to be deposited in Nelson's account each year. The account earns 10 percent interest. Under this accumulation scheme, Nelson will have $79,687 at age 65. Even after combining this with social security, Nelson's income will not be adequate to continue his preretirement standard of living.

Money-purchase pension plans can work, however, given the right set of circumstances.

Example: New employee Gloria Benson is 35 years old and has no other retirement funds except social security. Benson earns $50,000 annually and plans to retire at age 65. The money-purchase formula calls for 10 percent of salary to be deposited in Benson's account each year. The account earns 10 percent interest. Under this accumulation scheme, $1,355,122 will be amassed at retirement. Combined with social security, Benson's income will be adequate during the retirement years to maintain the proper standard of living.

Candidates for This Type of Plan

Candidates for money-purchase plans are businesses with

- a steady cash flow
- young, well-paid key employees
- a stable workforce (low turnover)
- the need for easily communicated employee benefits

Money-purchase candidates disclose on the fact finder that it is less important to provide an adequate retirement standard of living than to have predictable costs, and that it is more important to have administrative convenience and an easily communicated plan than to provide an adequate retirement standard of living.

TARGET-BENEFIT PENSION PLANS

A cousin to the money-purchase pension plan, the target-benefit plan falls within both the defined-contribution and pension categories. Because of this, it shares many of the characteristics of the money-purchase pension plan, including the following:

- The maximum annual contribution that an employee can receive is the lesser of 25 percent of salary or $30,000.
- Participants in the plan have individual accounts that are similar to bank accounts.
- The employee assumes the risk of preretirement inflation, investment performance, and adequacy of retirement income.
- Administrative costs are relatively low.
- It has predictable employer costs.
- The employer is required to fund the plan annually.
- Employees are restricted from having in-service withdrawals.
- The employer can deduct up to the full amount available under the Sec. 415 limits.
- Investments in company stock are limited to 10 percent of the plan's assets.

Target-benefit pension plans are, however, a unique form of defined-contribution plan because they include some of the features associated with traditional defined-benefit plans. One of these features is that a defined-benefit formula is used to determine the annual contribution. An actuary determines the amount of funds needed for a level annual contribution by using actuarial and interest assumptions in conjunction with the benefit formula. The organization's level annual contribution will not change in subsequent years except to reflect new plan participants and increases in the compensation of existing plan participants. For the sake of convenience and simplicity the plan is often equipped with a chart indicating contribution levels, and the further use of an actuary after the plan's inception is seldom needed (see figure 4-1).

Once the plan has been established, the employer hopes to provide a specific benefit (the target) at retirement. However, the employer does not guarantee that the targeted benefit will be paid. The investment risk falls on the participants, and an amount less than or greater than the target may be available, depending on the actual interest. (*Planning Note:* Under most target-benefit plans, the employee directly participates in the investment return on his or her account balance. If your client desires, however, you can structure the plan to provide a floor of benefits for participants regardless of poor investment return.)

Example: The Ma and Pa Diner has a target-benefit plan for its five employees, Ma Kettle (aged 58), Pa Kettle (aged 60), Sam Chef (aged 47), Wanda Waitress (aged 28), and Wendy Waitress (aged 26). The benefit formula in the plan provides for 3 percent of final-average salary multiplied by years of service. At the inception of the plan the actuary takes into account final-average salary assumptions, age, mortality, interest earnings, and other assumptions in order to project the annual level contribution for each participant. Because of the comparatively advanced ages of Ma and Pa Kettle, their annual contribution is likely to be very high (particularly since the plan was just recently adopted). But because Wanda and Wendy Waitress are relatively young, and there are many years to accumulate interest and to fund for the benefit, their annual contributions will be relatively low. At retirement the benefits for any employee may be lower or higher than the targeted amount, due in part to the investment performance of the employee's account.

FIGURE 4-1

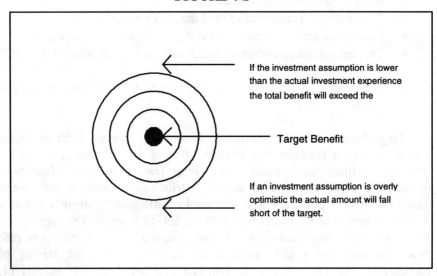

Employers that are good candidates for target-benefit plans are businesses that have

- an employee census that shows a mix of employees that includes older owners and younger rank-and-file employees
- recent economic success and the likelihood that the success will continue
- older, well-paid owner-employees and key employees
- a desire to have a defined-benefit plan without a pocketbook to match their desire

Advantages and Disadvantages

Target-benefit pension plans are uniquely suited for older owner-employees who are initiating a retirement program. Typically these types of owner-employees have put off retirement programs because in the early years money was tight. They have now reached a stage of fiscal maturity, and the 50- to 55-year-old owner-employee has started to think about tax shelters and retirement. The benefit formula in a target-benefit pension plan requires contributions for older employees that will be larger because there is less time to fund for the target benefit.

Target-benefit pension plans can be thought of as the sports cars of the retirement fleet: They provide for the speedy accumulation of substantial retirement benefits for older employees. They also offer the added inducement of big tax deductions just when they are needed for the owner-employer. While target-benefit plans may be slightly more expensive to administer than other types of defined-contribution plans, generally the tax shelter, and not the higher cost, is the client's chief concern.

Target-benefit plans have several disadvantages, as well. They do not provide the same level of security as the defined-benefit plan and at the same time lose some of the simplicity of the defined-contribution approach. More specifically, the disadvantages include the following:

- Unlike the defined-benefit plan, the participant is not promised a specified benefit. Even though the plan can target a benefit, the actual benefit will be more or less, depending upon the performance of plan assets.

- The benefit formula is more difficult to understand than in a traditional money-purchase pension plan. The annual contribution is based on the amount needed under an actuarial cost method to fund a targeted benefit amount. This is a difficult concept to communicate.

- Rank-and-file employees may have difficulty understanding why two workers with the same wages and years of service but who are of different ages will be entitled to different contributions under the plan.

- In most cases the plan is established with the goal of allocating the lion's share of the contribution to the business owner. The contribution for even one older nonhighly compensated employee can be so high that it can defeat this goal. Therefore this plan design is not appropriate when either the owner is young, or the company has one or more older rank-and-file employees.

Target-Benefit Plans in the Marketplace Today

Currently the target-benefit plan is somewhat out of vogue. Enthusiasm for this type of plan has waned with the advent of age-weighted and cross-tested profit-sharing plans (discussed in the next chapter). The primary reason for this waning interest is that almost the same objectives can be met with those plans without the employer having to commit to annual required contributions. As you will understand better after reading about those plans, the age-weighted plan is really quite similar to the target-benefit concept, while the cross-tested plan is even more flexible.

5

Profit-Sharing Plans, 401(k) Plans, Stock Bonus Plans, and ESOPs

Chapter Outline

Let's turn our attention to some qualified plans that aren't necessarily intended to provide a pension at retirement. Unlike the pension plans discussed in chapter 4, profit-sharing plans, 401(k) plans, stock bonus plans, and employee stock ownership plans (ESOPs) are often designed to distribute organizational earnings on a tax-sheltered basis with only a partial regard to meeting retirement needs. Historically these plans have been considered more of a tax shelter for deferred income than a retirement system that will provide an adequate pension in the retirement years. More recently, however, these plans have become intimately involved with the employer's decision to meet the need for an adequate pension in the following ways:

- They have become part of a comprehensive retirement package that combines these plans with other plans to fund for retirement needs.
- They have become "pensionlike" in their actual application. (For example, some profit-sharing plans are designed to provide adequate retirement benefits even if the employer has no profits.)

PROFIT-SHARING PLANS IN GENERAL

Beggar:	Alms for the poor, alms for the poor.
Merchant:	Here you go; here's one kopeck.
Beggar:	One kopeck? Last week you gave me two kopecks!
Merchant:	I know, but last week vandals destroyed my store and floods wiped out my supplies.
Beggar:	Just because you had a bad week, why should I suffer?

As its name implies, a profit-sharing plan falls into the profit-sharing category. (*Planning Note:* Don't be confused by the fact that profit sharing is both a category of plan and a type of plan.) In addition, a profit-sharing plan falls under the defined-contribution category and shares all the defined-contribution characteristics that have been previously discussed. Also recall that a profit-sharing plan is generally not structured to provide a monthly pension benefit at retirement. Instead it is usually intended to offer employee participation in company profits. For this reason, like the beggar, participants in a profit-sharing plan are in a precarious position when it comes to retirement income.

Advantages of a Profit-Sharing Plan to the Business and Business Owner

Even though profit-sharing plans do not provide the most secure benefit to employees, they can serve a number of the company's interests. For this reason they are a popular choice in today's business environment. Here are some of the organizational objectives these plans serve:

- *allowing discretionary contributions*—The plan can be designed with no predetermined formula so that the employer has the option of not making contributions in a given year (for example, the plan may provide that contributions, if any, will be determined annually by the board of directors). One caveat, however: the client who chooses to have no predetermined formula may run the risk of not motivating employees because the promise of a benefit is too tentative. What's more, the employer must make substantial and recurring contributions over the years, or else the IRS will retroactively disqualify deductions because it believes the plan was set up as a sham.

- *permitting withdrawal flexibility*—Plans can be designed to allow employees to withdraw funds from participant accounts as early as 2 years after they were contributed by the employer. If the plan allows withdrawal flexibility for key employees, it cannot discriminate and restrict withdrawal flexibility for rank-and-file employees.

- *controlling benefit costs*—Organizations find that adopting a profit-sharing plan is a fiscally responsible move. The organization won't be saddled with cash-flow problems caused by mandatory contributions. Flexibility is especially important for employers with fluctuating profits. Another cost advantage is profit sharing's correlation to productivity. Many believe these plans help to increase employee identification with the employer and provide an incentive to employees. This increased productivity can be viewed as a way to maximize the cost-effectiveness of the employer's contributions. The old saying "You have to spend more to get more" applies here, however. In order to provide an incentive for *all* employees to increase output and reduce operating costs, profit-sharing plans are generally designed with less restrictive (or unrestricted) eligibility and coverage requirements and vesting schedules. This will increase employer costs.

- *providing legal discrimination in favor of older owner-employees*—The profit-sharing plan can be set up to give (allocate) the majority of the profits to older, high-salaried owner-employees. When used in this manner, the profit-sharing plan makes an excellent tax shelter for the older business owner. This approach also lowers contributions for rank-and-file employees (see chapter 8).

- *providing built-in safeguards*—The employee's benefit is usually based on the contingency that the employer has profits. Some plans are set up so that a certain level of profits must be achieved before contributions to participant accounts will be made (for example, the plan's contribution formula might read, "Contributions will be made from profits in excess of $50,000."). What's more, employers can set a cap on the amount of profits that will be contributed (for example, the plan's contribution formula might read, "Contributions will be made from the first $100,000 of profits only.").

Disadvantages of a Profit-Sharing Plan to the Business and Business Owner

As we have seen, profit-sharing plans have their limitations. One disadvantage is that rank-and-file employees might perceive the plan as a hollow benefit if discretionary contributions are not made or if the lion's share of profits

goes to the business owner. Another disadvantage of profit-sharing plans is that
the organization's deduction for contributions to the plan is limited to 15 percent
of aggregate participant payroll. *Aggregate participant payroll* is the total
salaries of all employees eligible to participate in the plan. Many get confused by
this limit, thinking that contributions for any one participant cannot exceed 15
percent of compensation. This is not true, unless the plan covers only one
participant.

YOUR FINANCIAL SERVICE PRACTICE:
WHAT CAN YOU DO IF THE EMPLOYER CONTRIBUTES TOO MUCH?

Even though the profit-sharing plan limits the business deduction to 15 percent
of aggregate participant payroll, any single participant is eligible to receive a
contribution up to the defined-contribution limit of 25 percent of salary or $30,000.
Therefore contributions for some participants may be under the 15 percent
threshold, while contributions for others may be over 15 percent. This frequently
occurs in two types of situations—age-weighted profit-sharing plans (discussed
later) and integrated profit-sharing plans.

Because of the complexity of such allocation formulas, the employer might
accidentally contribute more than the maximum deductible amount of 15 percent of
aggregate payroll. If the employer does so, any nondeductible amounts will be
subject to a 10 percent excise tax (Sec. 4972). However, these nondeductible
contributions may be "carried forward" and deducted in the next year to the extent
that the carryover and next year's contribution do not exceed the 15 percent limit.
This is known as a *contribution carryover.*

Contribution Carryover

Example: The Burns Corporation has three employees. In 1995 the
corporation contributed $20,000 to the profit-sharing plan ($12,000 to the
business owner and $4,000 to each of the other 2 participants). They complied
with individual participant contribution limits as well as the other qualification
requirements but forgot that the maximum deductible contribution was limited to
15 percent of the corporation's $100,000 payroll ($15,000). Since they
contributed $20,000, they contributed $5,000 too much. After discovering this in
early 1996, they ask you how to solve the problem. The corporation tells you
that the payroll for 1996 will remain at $100,000. First, you remind them that
they are required to pay a $500 excise tax ($5,000 multiplied by 10 percent).
Then you indicate that the problem may be resolved this year by limiting the
contribution to $10,000. Since the maximum deductible contribution is once
again $15,000, the company can now deduct the $5,000 carryover as well as
the $10,000 contribution. At the end of the year, no excess will remain.

TYPES OF PROFIT-SHARING PLANS

There are two parts to the contribution formula in a profit-sharing plan. One
relates to how much the company contributes to the plan and the other relates to
how the contribution is allocated among the participants. Let's take a closer look.

Required Contributions

By far the most common type of profit-sharing plan is one that provides for employer contributions on a discretionary basis. When this is the case, the employer (or whoever is designated in the plan document) decides whether a contribution will be made and how much that contribution will be. Typically, contributions are geared to profits, although the employer can make contributions even if there are no profits. (Since 1987, profits are no longer required in order to make profit-sharing contributions.) What's more, even in a profitable year an employer may keep contributions low in order to use company assets for other reasons such as a distribution of dividends or a capital expansion.

However, a profit-sharing plan can also be written to require a specified contribution. This is typically done in one of two ways. One way is to state the required contribution as a specified percentage of profits or some other objective formula stated in the plan. This approach is appropriate when the employer wants employees to feel that they have a clear and determinable stake in the performance of the company. Another way is to stipulate that a certain percentage of each participant's salary will be contributed each year. For example, the company will contribute 10 percent of a participant's compensation. This type of contribution requirement allows the employer to use the profit-sharing plan in the same manner as a money-purchase pension plan, in which the corporate goal is typically to provide an adequate pension benefit, not to provide a vehicle for employees to share in company profits.

Allocation Formulas

The heart of a profit-sharing plan is the method of allocating the employer contribution among the participants. This formula must be definite and predetermined. Historically, the most common allocation formula has been one that allocates the total contribution so that each participant receives a contribution that is the same percentage of compensation, for example, 3 percent or 5 percent. This allocation formula would read in the plan document something like this:

> "Employer contributions made for the year will be allocated, as of the last day of each plan year, to each participant's account in the proportion which that participant's compensation bears to the total compensation of all eligible participants for the plan year."

Under this type of allocation formula, if, for example, the employer contributed $10,000, total payroll was $100,000, and Alexander earned $25,000, he would have an allocation of $2,500 ($10,000 x $25,000/$100,000). If Barbara earned $30,000, her allocation would be $3,000 ($10,000 x $30,000/$100,000). As you can see, the employer contributed 10 percent of payroll and each participant receives an allocation of 10 percent of his or her compensation.

Another common method has been to allocate contributions based on a combination of both salary and service. Let's look at an example:

Example: Peggy, Arthur, and Kim are three owners of a shoe store. The store makes a profit-sharing contribution of $2,000 for 1996. Its allocation formula stipulates that profits shall be allocated to participants by the ratio that the units allocated to a participant bear to the total of units allocated to all participants, with one unit allocated for each $100 of compensation and two units allocated for each year of service. Peggy has 10 years of service and earns $20,000 (220 units), Arthur has 8 years of service and earns $15,000 (166 units), and Kim has 5 years of service and earns $10,000 (110 units). The total of the units for all participants is 496. To determine Peggy's benefit multiply her units (220) over the total units by the $2,000 profit ([220/496] x 2,000). The contribution to Peggy's account will be $887. Arthur's contribution will be $669. And Kim's contribution will be $444.

These allocation formulas have been popular, in part because it is clear that they satisfy the requirement of Code Sec. 401(a)(4), which requires that contributions or benefits cannot discriminate in favor of the highly compensated employees. Other ways to allocate contributions include integration with social security and newer methods such as age-weighting and cross-testing. All of these allocation methods are discussed fully in chapter 8. As you will see, these allocation formulas add a whole new dimension to the profit-sharing plan, allowing this simple, versatile plan to be used to skew the contributions to older (and, not coincidentally, more highly compensated) business owners. As well, allocation formulas can be designed to meet any number of other compensation objectives.

Special Use of Profit-Sharing Plans

Because they may not provide an adequate retirement benefit for employees, profit-sharing plans are frequently piggybacked with other plans (defined-benefit or money-purchase plans). Piggybacking allows the employer to maintain contribution discretion for the profit-sharing part of the plan and still maximize tax deductibility in the second plan. For example, if your client wants to maximize tax-shelter potential and retain contribution discretion, he or she may want to consider instituting a 15 percent profit-sharing plan and a 10 percent money-purchase plan.

Candidates for Profit-Sharing Plans

With the incredible versatility of the profit-sharing plan, a large number of companies are candidates for profit-sharing plans. These include businesses with

- cash-flow problems
- less economic stability (for example, new businesses and capital-intensive businesses)
- young, well-paid key employees
- a desire to contribute not more than 15 percent of compensation (Note, however, that if tax-shelter maximization is sought, the profit-sharing plan should be designed to piggyback with a money-purchase plan.)
- no desire to ensure the adequacy of an employee's retirement income

Candidates for profit-sharing plans fill out the fact finder by typically grading as "very valuable" the following:

- placing the investment risk on the employee
- avoiding an annual financial commitment (If this is the case, design the plan with no predetermined formula so that the employer has the discretion not to make contributions in a given year.)
- allowing employees (including owner-employees) to withdraw funds (If this is the case, design the plan to allow withdrawals after 2 years; if this is not the case, a profit-sharing plan may still be desired but withdrawal restrictions should be incorporated.)
- motivating the workforce

Candidates for a profit-sharing plan typically grade these goals as "least valuable":

- maximizing benefits for long-service employees by accounting for past service
- providing a specified replacement ratio

Profit-sharing candidates typically answer yes to the fact finder question: Is it more important to motivate employees than to attract or retain them? And they typically answer no to these fact finder questions: Is it more important to provide an adequate retirement standard of living than to allow employees (including owner-employees) to withdraw funds? Is it more important to provide an adequate retirement standard of living than to have predictable costs?

Candidates for a profit-sharing plan usually put contribution flexibility at the head of their priority list, usually opt for a low income-replacement ratio, and typically come from an organization or industry with an unstable cash-flow history.

With the flexibility in allocation formulas available today, profit-sharing candidates also include those businesses interested in providing a lion's share of the benefits for the key employees while minimizing the cost of benefits for the rank-and-file employee. This can be done quite effectively using the age-weighted and cross-tested allocation formulas discussed briefly above and in more depth in chapter 7. At one time, employers with this goal looked either to the defined-benefit plan or the target-benefit plan. Today, the profit-sharing plan allows for similar skewing of the contribution to the targeted group while maintaining the flexibility of the profit-sharing plan.

YOUR FINANCIAL SERVICES PRACTICE:
LIFE INSURANCE AND PROFIT-SHARING PLANS

Profit-sharing plans have a unique need that can be met through the purchase of life insurance. In addition to using life insurance to fund participants' accounts (discussed in chapter 12), life insurance can be purchased on the client's key people (owner-employees, key employees, and officers) as a general asset of the profit-sharing trust. The profit-sharing trust is permitted to make this purchase because it has an insurable interest in the client's key people. This insurable interest stems from the fact that company profits are generally required to fund the profit-sharing trust and that these people are primarily responsible for these company profits. Here's how it works:

- Insurance contracts are purchased out of unallocated assets given to the trust by the organization.
- The insurance contracts are owned by the trust, which pays the premiums and is also the named beneficiary.
- Since the contracts are not allocated to participant accounts, the percentage limitation applied under the incidental death benefit rules (see chapter 10) is not applicable.
- Upon the death of the insured, the insurance proceeds are paid to the trust and are then typically allocated among participants on the basis of the account balance of each participant.

CASH OR DEFERRED ARRANGEMENTS—401(k) PLANS

An option that is available under a profit-sharing plan (or a stock bonus plan, which is discussed next) is the cash or deferred arrangement (CODA). When the CODA option is part of a profit-sharing or stock bonus plan, that plan is usually referred to as a 401(k) plan. (401(k) is the section number in the Internal Revenue Code that outlines CODAs.) A 401(k) plan allows plan participants the opportunity to defer taxation on a portion of regular salary or bonuses simply by electing to have such amounts contributed to the plan instead of receiving them in cash. Participants enjoy abundant tax savings. For example, if Simms is in the 28 percent marginal tax bracket and elects to reduce his salary by $6,000, he will save $1,680 in taxes. That's like having Uncle Sam as a contributing partner in Simms's retirement savings. What's more, the money Simms puts in the plan earns tax-deferred interest until retirement. If Simms encounters financial problems, he may decrease his future contributions or discontinue contributions altogether simply by changing his salary reduction agreement (the form that authorizes the employer to reduce the salary and make plan contributions in the amount of the reduction).

In order to understand the popularity of 401(k) plans, it's important to look at their history. For many years employers who felt they could not adequately fund their employees' (and their own) retirement needs provided thrift plans (also called savings plans or thrift and savings plans) in addition to other qualified plans. Under thrift plans, employees become partners of the employer in providing for their own retirement needs. A thrift plan calls for employees to contribute a fixed percentage of salary to the plan and for the employer to make a contribution in the same amount or in a reduced amount (these are known as matching contributions). Thrift plans, however, are not tax efficient because the employee's contribution is made with after-tax dollars. The Revenue Act of 1978 included provisions allowing employees to make before-tax thrift contributions to qualified plans, but the provisions under which plans qualified were unclear. In November 1981 the IRS issued proposed regulations covering these statutory provisions, and plan sponsors began to adopt the new 401(k) plans.

At first the 401(k) plan could be structured to allow an individual participant to reduce his or her salary by an amount equal to the defined-contribution limit of the lesser of 25 percent of salary or $30,000. In time, however, the legislature realized that (1) salary reductions were siphoning off much-needed tax revenue and (2) employers were shifting too much of the retirement burden to employees by using 401(k) plans in lieu of, rather than in addition to, other qualified plans. To rectify this, Congress enacted a $7,000 annual limit (which is indexed annually; in 1997 the figure is $9,500) on the amount of salary reductions.

Even with the $9,500 limit, the 401(k) plan has taken the marketplace by storm. Today almost all large private employers and many midsize companies sponsor such plans (often in addition to sponsoring more traditional plans such as a defined-benefit or money-purchase pension plan). The plan is starting to expand into the small plan market, as well. Into the mid-1990s, the most popular new plan to install has been the 401(k) plan. In fact, in 1995 almost 70 percent of the new plans receiving determination letters from the IRS were 401(k) plans. Also, beginning in 1997 nonprofit organizations will be able to establish 401(k) plans. This opens up a whole new market. Nonprofits that are 501(c)(3) organizations have the 403(b) plan as an option (see chapter 6), but other nonprofit organizations have not had the opportunity to sponsor any tax-advantaged plan that allows for pretax salary deferrals. This means that these employers should be very interested in exploring the opportunity to establish a 401(k) plan.

401(k) Plan Design

Remember that a 401(k) plan is a profit-sharing (or occasionally a stock bonus) plan that contains a salary deferral (401(k)) feature. This means that in addition to the salary deferral feature, the plan can contain a traditional profit-sharing feature, an employer matching contribution feature, or both. The plan may even allow for employee after-tax contributions. This means that the plan can be as simple as a stand-alone salary deferral plan, or as complex as a plan that allows pretax and after-tax employee contributions, employer matching contributions, and employer profit-sharing contributions.

YOUR FINANCIAL SERVICES PRACTICE:
401(k) PLANS

Even with the popularity of 401(k) plans, only 11 percent of small businesses sponsor them—meaning that there is still lots of opportunity for the financial services professional. Open doors to new clients with the following approaches:

- One method of retirement prospecting is to send a letter that inquires whether the prospect has a 401(k) plan. The letter should explain that 401(k) plans can (1) save taxes for the owner-employee, (2) encourage employees to become partners in their retirement savings and consequently lower employer retirement costs, and (3) attract key employees to the firm.
- The 401(k) plan can be marketed as an IRA substitute. You can point out that while the Congress has shut the $2,000-deductible-IRA door to highly paid persons, it left open a $9,500 401(k) window.
- The 401(k) plan can be marketed as a way to beef up an existing retirement system by adding the state-of-the-art 401(k) feature.
- Combined with matching and profit-sharing contributions, the 401(k) plan can serve as an effective stand-alone retirement plan for the small business.

A stand-alone plan (a plan allowing only pre-tax salary deferrals) can be used by an organization that cannot afford a comprehensive retirement program. The stand-alone plan can be expanded and enhanced in the future as the financial strength of the sponsor grows. It can also be established as a supplement to other retirement plans.

The employer that wants to combine salary deferrals with additional employer contributions to the same plan can choose how to spend those dollars—as matching or as profit-sharing contributions. A common practice today is to choose a matching contribution feature in which the plan sponsor agrees to match employee savings to a certain extent; for example, the sponsor might agree to contribute fifty cents to the plan for each dollar that the employee saves, up to the first 6 percent of compensation that the participant saves. In this example, the maximum employer match is 3 percent of compensation.

Both the matching percentage and the maximum match must be carefully chosen to meet the employer's objectives and budget. The primary reason for the match is to stimulate plan participation through the offer of an instant return on the participant's savings. Another goal is to create a retirement planning partnership between the employer and the participants. Under this philosophy, an employer is committed to contribute toward an employee's funds for retirement, but only if the employee is willing to save for retirement. Finally, the feature can act as a profit-sharing incentive.

To meet specific employer objectives, the design of the matching contribution can be as straightforward as described above, or more complex—such as a graded formula in which the matching contribution rate varies for different levels of salary deferrals. Under a typical graded formula the employer contributes fifty cents for each dollar saved by the plan participant, up to 4 percent of covered earnings, plus twenty-five cents for each dollar saved over 4 percent, but not more than 6 percent of covered earnings. Matching contributions can also be made on a discretionary basis, like a profit-sharing plan. Under this approach, the plan sponsor sets a rate of matching contributions at year-end, based on the operating results of the organization. Since the uncertainty of the employer contribution might discourage plan participation, it is more common to provide a small, guaranteed matching contribution, which can be made larger at the discretion of the employer.

A profit-sharing feature in a 401(k) plan works the same way as in a traditional profit-sharing plan. Contributions are made for eligible participants, regardless of whether they make salary deferral contributions. When the 401(k) plan is the only plan sponsored by the employer, it is not uncommon—in a good year—for the sponsor to make both matching contributions and profit-sharing-type contributions.

Also note that a 401(k) plan can include employee after-tax contributions in addition to employee pretax salary deferrals. This feature is not that common, but is occasionally included—primarily because employees like the withdrawal flexibility of after-tax contributions. These contributions do not have to be subject to the withdrawal restrictions that apply to pretax contributions (as discussed below). This feature is common in older plans that were converted from after-tax thrift plans. In this case, some employees are more secure with the old way of doing things.

Note that when a plan has more than just salary deferrals, it must have separate bookkeeping accounts for each type of contribution. This requirement is due, in part, to the fact that the accounts attributable to employer matching and profit-sharing contributions are subject to the same rules that apply to a traditional profit-sharing plan, while the salary deferral account is subject to the special rules described below.

Special Rules That Apply to 401(k) Salary Deferrals

The 401(k) salary deferral part of the profit-sharing plan is subject to a number of special rules:

- 401(k) salary reductions are immediately 100 percent vested and cannot be forfeited.

- Withdrawals under 401(k) plans are different from those under profit-sharing plans.
- An extra nondiscrimination test called the *actual deferral percentage test* applies to salary deferral amounts.

Vesting

Technically, amounts contributed to the plan under a salary deferral election are considered employer contributions—even though they are made at the election of the participant. Still, such amounts are treated somewhat differently the way that other employer contributions are. Normally, employer contributions can be subject to a vesting schedule, meaning that if the employee leaves before working for a designated period of time, some or all benefits are forfeited (as discussed further in chapter 9). In fact, if a 401(k) plan has employer profit-sharing or employer matching contribution accounts, such accounts can be subject to a vesting schedule under the normal rules. The portion of the participant's account that is made up of employee salary deferrals (and investment experience thereon) must be nonforfeitable at all times. In other words, employee salary deferral contributions to a 401(k) plan are always 100 percent vested. This makes sense, since participants were entitled to receive such amounts at the time they elected to make the salary deferral.

Withdrawals

A regular profit-sharing plan can allow employees the option of withdrawing the entire account upon 5 years of plan participation or withdrawing contributions 2 years after they are made. However, under a 401(k) plan, withdrawals from the salary deferral election account are restricted.[1] The plan must provide that no distributions from the salary deferral account will be made for any reason other than one of the following:

- retirement
- death
- disability
- separation from service
- attainment of age 59 1/2
- hardship

Out of the six opportunities to receive withdrawals under a 401(k) plan, the only one that allows something of an escape from strict withdrawal limitations is the hardship distribution. Hardship has been defined as anything that is "necessary in light of immediate and heavy financial needs of an employee." In addition, no other resources can be reasonably available to meet this need.

So that plan administrators do not have to make difficult hardship determinations on a case-by-case basis, the regulations provide a safe harbor method for determining hardship. Under the safe harbor rules, the following specific circumstances constitute hardships, per se:

*   medical expenses
*   purchase of a principal residence for the participant
*   payment of tuition for postsecondary education for a participant or his or her spouse, children, or dependents
*   payment of amounts necessary to prevent the eviction of the participant from his or her principal residence or from foreclosure on his or her mortgage

The rules also provide a safe harbor method for determining whether "other resources are reasonably available to meet the need." An employee will be deemed to lack "other reasonable resources" if the following conditions are met:

*   The employee must obtain all distributions other than hardship distributions and all nontaxable loans available under all plans maintained by the employer.
*   The plan must provide that the employee's elective deferral contributions and nondeductible contributions will be suspended for 12 months after the distribution and that the maximum contribution in the year following the suspension is reduced by amounts contributed in the prior year.

Example: Employee Adams makes elective contributions totaling $3,500 to his 401(k) plan from January 1996 to July 1996. In July 1996 Adams takes a hardship distribution from the plan. Adams cannot contribute to his 401(k) plan, nor can he make elective deferrals, until August 1997 (the 12-month waiting period). At that time he may make only a limited number of contributions for the remainder of the year. His maximum contribution would be determined by subtracting the amount of contributions made in 1996 ($3,500) from the maximum elective deferral possible. Since the 1997 limit was $9,500, Adams could make only $6,000 in elective deferrals from August 1997 to December 1997.

Actual Deferral Percentage Test

401(k) plans are subject to a special nondiscrimination test known as the *actual deferral percentage test,* which

*   ensures that higher-paid employees don't use the 401(k) plan to stockpile contributions that otherwise would have produced needed tax revenue

- forces employers to design the 401(k) plan so that it attracts participation by lower-paid employees by making the amount that higher-paid people can tax-shelter conditional on the amount that the lower-paid employees actually tax-shelter

In order to pass the actual deferral percentage (ADP) test, one of two requirements must be satisfied:

- *the 125 percent requirement*—Under this requirement the average of the *actual deferral percentages* (ADPs) for highly compensated employees for the current year cannot be more than 125 percent of the average ADPs for nonhighly compensated employees in the previous year.
- *the 200 percent/2 percent difference requirement*—Under this requirement the average of the ADPs for highly compensated employees for the current year cannot be more than 200 percent of the average ADPs for nonhighly compensated employees in the previous year and the difference between the deferral percentages for the two groups cannot be more than 2 percent.

The first step in performing the ADP test is determining who a highly compensated employee is. The Small Business Job Protection Act of 1996 simplified the definition of *highly compensated employee*. For years beginning in 1997 highly compensated employees include

- individuals who are 5 percent owners during the current or previous year and
- individuals who earned $80,000 (as indexed in 1997) in the preceding year (The employer can elect to limit this group to employees whose compensation puts them in the top 20 percent of payroll.)

The second step is determining the ADP for each employee eligible to participate in the plan. The ADP is simply the individual's salary deferral amounts for the year divided by compensation earned for the year. The final step is determining the average for the nonhighly compensated group for the previous year. Remember that all participants eligible to make salary deferrals are included, meaning that those who do not make salary deferrals have ADPs of zero.

Once the average of the ADPs for the nonhighly compensated employees for the prior year is determined, the maximum average of the ADPs for the highly compensated employees for the current year can be determined. In general, if the ADP for the nonhighly compensated group is less than 2 percent, the 200 percent limit applies. If the ADP for the nonhighly compensated group is at least 2 percent and not more than 8 percent, the 2 percent spread limit applies. If the

ADP for the nonhighly compensated group is 9 percent or more, the 125 percent limit applies (see table 5-1).

TABLE 5-1	
Maximum ADP Limits for Highly Compensated Employees	
ADP of Nonhighly Compensated Group	ADP Limit
1%	2%
2%	4%
3%	5%
4%	6%
5%	7%
6%	8%
7%	9%
8%	10%
9%	11.25%
10%	12.50%
11%	13.75%
12%	15%
13%	16.25%
14%	17.50%
15%	18.75%
16%	20%

Case Study: Medical Group Professional Corporation

Now that we have laid out the rules, let's examine the application of the ADP test in a case. The Medical Group Professional Corporation has a 401(k) plan and wants to know what the maximum deferral percentage for the highly compensated employees will be for 1998. At the end of 1997 the census data are as follows:

	Salary	Percentage Contributed
Dr. Ben Casey (CEO/75% owner)	$60,000	8%
Dr. Roberta Stone (V.P./25% owner)	60,000	8%
Dr. Mel Practice	99,000	6%
Dr. Frank Burns (treasurer)	20,000	5%
Dr. Ruth Rosenhauser	86,000	8%
Dr. Julius Miller	40,000	8%
Nancy Doe	40,000	5%
Joe Jones	25,000	5%
Sally Crowe	25,000	5%
Jack Dixon	20,000	5%

The first step in the ADP test is to determine who falls into the highly compensated group and who is not a member of that group:

- Dr. Ben Casey and Dr. Roberta Stone are highly compensated employees because they are more-than-5-percent owners.
- Dr. Mel Practice and Dr. Ruth Rosenhauser are highly compensated employees because they receive annual compensation in excess of $80,000 and are members of the top-paid group (the top 20 percent of the employer's payroll).
- Dr. Frank Burns, Dr. Julius Miller, Nancy Doe, Joe Jones, Sally Crowe, and Jack Dixon are not highly compensated employees.

The second step necessary to perform the ADP test is to determine the deferral percentage for the nonhighly compensated group.

Nonhighly Compensated	
Dr. Frank Burns	5.0%
Dr. Julius Miller	8.0%
Nancy Doe	5.0%
Joe Jones	5.0%
Sally Crowe	5.0%
Jack Dixon	5.0%
Average % Deferred	5.5%

This means that in 1998, the maximum average ADP for the highly compensated group will be 7.5 percent. (As discussed above, if the deferral percentage for the nonhighly compensated employee group is between 2 and 8 percent, the allowable spread is 2 percent.) Looking at the 1997 data, the average of the ADPs for the highly compensated is on track.

Highly Compensated	
Dr. Ben Casey	8.0%
Dr. Roberta Stone	8.0%
Dr. Mel Practice	6.0%
Dr. Ruth Rosenhauser	8.0%
Average % Deferred	7.5%

Satisfying the ADP Test

A common fear among clients is that they will not be able to pass the actual deferral percentage test because the lower-paid employees will not contribute. And up until 1997 this has been a serious concern for the prospective plan sponsor. The changes made in the Small Business Job Protection Act of 1996 did a lot to help the situation. The changes that affect testing include the following:

- *Last year's ADP*—The new rules allow the deferral percentage for highly compensated employees to be tied to the average ADP for the nonhighly compensated group for the previous year. This change means that the employer will now know the maximum deferral percentage for the highly compensated group at the beginning of the plan year, meaning that contributions can be appropriately limited.

- *401(k) SIMPLE*—As described more fully in chapter 6, an employer can establish a plan called a SIMPLE. This plan can be designed using IRAs as the funding vehicle or using the traditional 401(k) plan arrangement. Using the 401(k) SIMPLE approach means that the employer can avoid the ADP test by satisfying a number of plan design requirements. As you will see, the SIMPLE approach is quite rigid. Strict employer contribution limits apply, and the maximum salary deferral amount is reduced to $6,000. Appropriate situations for using this plan will be discussed further in chapter 6.

- *401(k) Safe harbor*—Under another, less restrictive and more useful design safe harbor approach, the ADP test will be deemed satisfied if an employer safe harbor contribution is satisfied. With this rule the employer must make at least a 100 percent matching contribution on the first 3 percent of salary deferred and 50 percent of the next 2 percent of salary deferred[2]. In the alternative, the employer can make a nonelective contribution of 3 percent of compensation. In addition, contributions must be fully vested and subject to the hardship withdrawal restrictions. Under the rules, it is even possible to satisfy the safe harbor contribution with contributions to another plan. The design safe harbor 401(k) plan may turn out to be quite useful to the 401(k) sponsor. The rules do not put a maximum on employer contributions. The biggest drawback at this time is that the safe harbor cannot be used until 1999. Once available, the decision to elect the safe harbor also can be made on a year-to-year basis. The major considerations for the 401(k) sponsor considering the safe harbor will be the following:

  - Is the sponsor willing to make contributions that are 100 percent vested at all times?
  - How does the safe harbor contribution compare to the current level of employer contributions?
  - Are the goals of the highly compensated employees being thwarted by failure to satisfy the ADP and ACP tests?

Besides the new rules, note that under the old rules (which still apply), a plan that fails the ADP test has a period of time after the end of the year to correct the situation in a number of ways.

401(k) Plans and Other Employee Benefits

Cafeteria Plans

A popular use of 401(k) plans is to include them as one of the benefits available under a cafeteria plan. The 401(k) plan is the only type of qualified plan that can be part of a cafeteria plan. The term *cafeteria plan* stems from the fact that these plans allow employees to pick from a menu of benefit choices. More specifically, the benefit dollars in a cafeteria plan are flexible, which means that employees can take them in cash; or allocate them to pay for certain welfare benefits (such as life insurance, health insurance, or child care); place them in a 401(k) plan; or do a combination of any of these three. To the extent that an employee elects to spend benefit dollars on tax-advantaged benefits like a 401(k) plan, there is no current taxation. For this reason, employees may wish to contribute to 401(k) plans in lieu of other benefits available in the cafeteria plan (such as group life insurance in excess of $50,000) that are taxable.

The Salary Reduction Impact

Many employee benefit plans (including pension plans, group life insurance, and disability insurance) calculate benefits based upon the participant's compensation. For example, in a group life insurance plan, the employee's beneficiaries may be entitled to a benefit of two times compensation. When an employer installs a 401(k) plan, benefits under other plans may be reduced if salary reduction elections reduce the definition of compensation under those plans. Unless the employer is exceptionally concerned about costs, it will not want to reduce the definition of compensation, since this indirectly penalizes employees for making salary deferrals. Sometimes the employer forgets to review the impact of the salary deferrals on other employee benefits, and benefits are accidentally reduced. The adviser should be sure to discuss this issue with the employer at the time the plan is installed.

Note that salary deferral elections do not adversely affect social security benefits. Salary deferrals are considered wages for calculating benefits (as well as for determining social security taxes).

Plans with Matching Contributions

If a 401(k) plan has matching contributions or after-tax employee contributions (or both), the plan generally must satisfy another nondiscrimination test referred to as the *actual contribution percentage test* or ACP test. This test is discussed in detail in chapter 8. Note that the ACP test will not have to be performed beginning in 1997 if the plan adopts the 401(k) SIMPLE approach (see chapter 6) or the 401(k) safe harbor design discussed above.

STOCK BONUS PLANS AND EMPLOYEE STOCK OWNERSHIP PLANS (ESOPS)

Stock bonus plans and ESOPs are variations of profit-sharing plans and are therefore similar in many ways:

- Stock bonus plans, ESOPs, and profit-sharing plans are all defined-contribution plans and all fall into the profit-sharing (not pension) category.
- Contributions need not be fixed and need not be made every year.
- The allocation formulas used under a profit-sharing plan may be used under either a stock bonus plan or an ESOP.
- The amount of deductible employer contributions allowed (15 percent) is the same for all three types of plans.
- Contributions for all three types of plans are usually based on profits but are not legally required to be.

Stock bonus plans and ESOPs differ from profit-sharing plans, however, in three important ways:

- Both stock bonus plans and ESOPs typically invest plan assets primarily in the employer's stock (in fact, an ESOP is required to invest primarily in employer stock). Profit-sharing plans, on the other hand, are usually structured to diversify investments and do not concentrate investments in employer stock (even though they are legally permitted to).
- Both stock bonus plans and ESOPs are chosen because they provide a market for employer stock. This in turn generates capital for the corporation and is a method to finance a company's growth. Profit-sharing plans, however, are not viewed as a way to finance company operations and are more concerned with providing tax-favored deferred compensation that can be used for retirement purposes.
- Stock bonus plans and ESOPs allow distributions to participants in the form of employer stock. Profit-sharing plans generally do not do so. This creates a distinct advantage for participants in a stock bonus plan or an ESOP because they receive a tax break inasmuch as the unrealized appreciation (gain in value) is not taxed until the stock is sold. In other words, when the stock is distributed at retirement, the employee's tax liability is limited to the value of the stock when it was placed in the plan (the cost basis) and not on any growth (the capital gains).

Example: In 1995 Steve Gilchrist receives 10 shares of his company's stock valued at $10 a share. In 1996, when Steve retires, the stock is worth $12 a share. Steve elects to take the ESOP distribution in stock. Steve's tax liability will be determined on the cost basis of $100

(10 shares x $10 per share), not on the actual value of $120. When Steve sells the stock in 1997 at $12 a share, he will then pay taxes on the $20 appreciation ($2 a share x 10 shares). By taking the distribution in employer stock Steve acquired a valuable tax-timing strategy that could effectively lower the actual amount paid in taxes.

Stock Bonus Plans

Stock bonus plans traditionally have been a favorite alternative to profit-sharing plans. Stock bonus plans have recently given way in popularity to ESOPs, however, because ESOPs offer several additional advantages that stock bonus plans do not have. Let's take a closer look at ESOPs.

Employee Stock Ownership Plans

ESOPs enjoy the same advantages as stock bonus plans and offer an extra advantage to your clients. ESOPs can be used to allow the employer to borrow in order to provide contributions. (When an ESOP is used for this function it is also known as a *leveraged ESOP,* or LESOP.) Under this technique, known as leveraging, the plan trustee acquires a loan from the bank and uses the borrowed funds to purchase employer stock. Generally the employer guarantees repayment of the loan, and the purchased stock is held as collateral. The result is that the plan receives the full proceeds of the bank loan immediately and pays the loan off with the employer's tax-deductible contributions to the ESOP. The collateralized stock is placed in a suspense account. The employer makes annual (deductible) contributions to the plan, which are used to pay back the bank. As the loan is paid off, the stock is released from the suspense account.

Reasons Candidates Choose Stock Bonus Plans and ESOPs

One major advantage of stock bonus plans and ESOPs is that they give employees a stake in the company through stock ownership. This neatly fits most employers' goals of employee motivation and retention. A second major advantage is the previously mentioned delayed taxation of gain on stock distributions. Enhanced cash flow is a third advantage. Cash flow is enhanced because the employer makes a cashless contribution to the retirement plan. A fourth—and perhaps most important—advantage of stock ownership plans is that they help to create a market for employer stock. This is especially important if the organization's stock is not publicly traded. What's more, the leveraging advantage associated with ESOPs is also enticing for organizations.

The major disadvantage of stock ownership plans is the possibility of the employer's stock falling drastically in value and therefore cutting the availability of retirement funds. Without any diversity of investment, participants are exposed to potential disaster. There is, however, some relief available for ESOP participants. The law requires that once an ESOP participant attains age 55 and completes at least 10 years of participation, the participant may elect (between the ages of 55 and 60) to diversify the retirement benefit by moving up to 50 percent of his or her account balance into other investments. (For more information, see Code Sec. 401 (a)(28).)

A second disadvantage of stock ownership plans is that if the stock is not readily tradable on an established market, the employer is required to offer a repurchase option (also known as a put option). This option must be available for a minimum of 60 days following the distribution of the stock and, if the option is not exercised in that period, for an additional 60-day period in the following year. The repurchase option creates an administrative and cash-flow problem for employers.

Candidates for ESOPs and stock bonus plans are similar to candidates for profit-sharing plans and generally fill out the fact finder in a similar manner. But unlike the typical profit-sharing candidate, ESOP and stock bonus plan candidates rate as "very valuable" fact finder item 10—creating a market for employer stock. What's more, ESOP candidates rate as "very valuable" fact finder item 11—leveraging the purchase of employer stock.

YOUR FINANCIAL SERVICES PRACTICE:
LIFE INSURANCE AND ESOPs

Special arrangements must be made in advance in order for the corporation to buy back stock from a terminated employee or from a deceased employee's estate without creating a cash-flow crunch. Typically this is accomplished through the sale of life insurance to the ESOP. For example, the ESOP could purchase life insurance on the lives of its principal employees. At the death of these employees the life insurance proceeds are used to buy back the stock transferred from the deceased employee's estate.

CASE STUDY: BAKER MANUFACTURING, INC.

Bill Baker is the president of Baker Manufacturing, Inc., a firm that produces parts for personal computers. Baker Manufacturing has a defined-benefit pension plan for its 40 employees. Bill is concerned with improving rank-and-file productivity and morale. Business is excellent, but to meet increased sales orders, Bill needs to get more out of his employees. What's worse, two of Bill's experienced line workers have just left to work for a competitor. In addition, several of Bill's people have approached him regarding tax-sheltering part of their salary (Bill himself is also interested in this). Bill would like to do something extra, but cash flow is a problem. Bill feels he may need to hold onto profits in case the never-ending "new generations" of computers require different manufacturing equipment. How would an ESOP help to solve Bill's problems? Would a 401(k) plan offer a solution?

TABLE 5-2
Qualified-Plan Scorecard

PENSION	**PROFIT-SHARING**
Defined-benefit	Profit-sharing
Cash-balance	Stock bonus
Target-benefit	ESOP
Money-purchase	401(k)
DEFINED-BENEFIT	**DEFINED-CONTRIBUTION**
Defined-benefit	Target-benefit
Cash-balance	Money-purchase
	Profit-sharing
	Stock bonus
	ESOP
	401(k)
CORPORATE	**KEOGH**
Defined-benefit	Defined-benefit
Cash-balance	Cash-balance
Target-benefit	Target-benefit
Money-purchase	Money-purchase
Profit-sharing	Profit-sharing
Stock bonus	401(k)
ESOP	
401(k)	

An employee stock ownership plan (ESOP) would be helpful in solving Bill's problems because it would allow Bill to do something extra without creating cash-flow problems. Reason: Bill's ESOP will be leveraged. What's more, employee morale will be improved by the extra benefit provided, and employees will be encouraged not to jump ship because of their ties to the company's fortunes through the stock itself and the amount of stock contributions, which are based on company profits. And since company profits are more important to the employees than ever, productivity is likely to increase. Bill and his executives will also enjoy the tax advantages of taking distributions of highly productive company stock when they terminate.

A cash or deferred arrangement (401(k) plan) would also be helpful because it would provide something extra for only a minor cost. The executives who wanted to shelter income from taxes would have the opportunity to convert some of their salary into pretax savings (up to the $9,500 maximum). If Bill provides a matching contribution, the organization's cost would rise slightly, but the paybacks would be increased productivity, better morale, and retention of employees.

NOTES

1. Note that, similar to the vesting rules, the participant's profit-sharing and matching contribution accounts can be subject to the normal withdrawal rules that apply to profit-sharing plans.
2. The rules actually allow the matching formula to be stated in a different way as long as resulting contributions equal the contributions under the basic matching formula. Also the rate of matching contribution for any highly compensated employee cannot exceed the rate for any nonhighly compensated employee. This provision would prohibit a formula that gave a larger match for individuals with long service if even one highly compensated employee received the larger contribution.

6

SEPs, SIMPLEs, and 403(b) Plans

Chapter Outline

In this chapter we explore three types of tax-advantaged retirement plans that are not qualified plans covered under Code Sec. 401(a). What is meaningful about these plans is that each has its own set of rules, unique to it. How much can be contributed, who must participate, vesting provisions, and how contributions are allocated are different from these aspects of qualified plans—and different from each other. You will also see that in some instances, some of the qualified plan rules do apply.

In order to determine whether the SEP, the SIMPLE, or the 403(b) plan is more appropriate for your client than any of the qualified plan alternatives, this chapter fully explores each type of plan, and also compares these plans to qualified plans. At times, the comparisons might be somewhat confusing since at this point in the book you are not yet familiar with all the rules that apply to qualified plans. Previous chapters have introduced you to the types of qualified plans available, and chapters 7 through 9 will flesh out eligibility, vesting, and limits on contribution formulas, as well as other issues. You may find it helpful to review this chapter for a second time after finishing chapter 9.

SEPs

A simplified employee pension (SEP) is a retirement plan that uses an individual retirement account (IRA) or an individual retirement annuity (IRA annuity) as the receptacle for contributions. As its name implies, this type of plan is simpler than a qualified retirement plan, making it in many cases attractive to the small business owner.

The documentation, reporting, and disclosure requirements are less cumbersome than for a qualified plan. Trust accounting is also eliminated, because separate IRAs are established for each participant and all contributions are made directly to each participant's IRA. Since contributions must be nonforfeitable, the participant's benefit at any time is simply the IRA account balance.

The SEP is often a good choice for the small business because of the reduced administrative tasks and expenses. However, the SEP still has its complications, and the prospective sponsor needs to go in with a clear understanding of the ongoing responsibilities of maintaining such a plan. Also note that there is a tradeoff under the tax rules: in exchange for simplicity is the loss of flexibility. For example, under a SEP, all employees meeting specified requirements must be covered under the plan; the allocation formula may not contain an age-weighting factor (unlike the profit-sharing plans, discussed in chapter 5); and benefits must be fully vested at all times. These requirements are reviewed in more depth below.

Characteristics of the SEP

From a design perspective, the SEP is quite similar to the profit-sharing plan. The employer may, on a discretionary basis, make contributions, which are allocated to participants accounts. The plan may also allow employees to make pretax salary deferrals, like in a 401(k) plan—except that the nondiscrimination requirements are even stricter than for a 401(k) plan.

Technically, SEPs are subject to the rules contained in IRC Sec. 408(k)—in contrast to qualified plans, which are subject to IRC Sec. 401(a) and related provisions. IRC 408(k) provides some requirements that are unique to SEPs, borrows some of the qualified plan requirements, and states that the investment and distribution provisions for IRAs also apply to SEPs. To learn these rules, it is helpful to group them in these categories.

Requirements Unique to SEPs

Coverage Requirements. SEPs are subject to a very different set of participation requirements from those for qualified retirement plans. The rules require that contributions be made for all employees who have met all three of the following requirements:

- attained age 21
- performed services for the employer for at least 3 of the immediately preceding 5 years
- received a minimum of $400 of compensation for the year (This is the 1997 limit, which is adjusted for cost-of-living increases.)

From a planning perspective, this set of requirements means that the employer can exclude employees with less than 3 years of service but must cover all employees—including part-time employees earning more than $400—who have 3 or more years of service. For the employer with numerous short-term employees, this requirement is significantly preferable to the qualified plan rules. On the other hand, the employer with a number of long-term part-time employees may not be satisfied with the coverage provisions of the SEP.

The 3-year requirement can also cause problems for companies with related subsidiary companies and for small groups of individuals who own two or more companies. If, in either case, the affiliation constitutes a "controlled group of corporations,"[1] the employees of all the related companies must all be covered under the same plan. This rule generally eliminates the SEP as a viable alternative in the larger corporate setting. The most dangerous problem is that a small employer who is not aware of this rule will establish a plan for one company and forget to cover employees in related companies.

Contribution and Allocation Formula. The SEP is generally designed to mirror a profit-sharing plan—that is, company contributions are made on a discretionary basis, although the plan can require specified employer contributions. What makes the SEP different from the profit-sharing plan is that contributions *must* be allocated to participants in such a way as to provide a benefit as a level percentage of compensation. (For example, all employees receive an allocation of 5 percent of compensation.) This limits the use of the SEP in two regards. First, if the plan has employee pretax contributions (SARSEP), the employer may not encourage employee contributions by providing matching contributions. Second, the allocation formula cannot use cross-testing (discussed in chapter 8) to skew contributions to the older employees. The only exception to the level percentage of compensation rule is that the allocation formula may be integrated with social security in the same manner as in other defined-contribution plans. This provides highly compensated employees with contributions that are slightly larger (as a percentage of pay) than those for the rank-and-file employees.

Vesting. All contributions to a SEP, either by the employer directly or as an employee contribution (by deferral election), must be immediately and 100 percent vested. From the employer's perspective, this requirement is more onerous than for qualified plans, but remember that employees can be excluded from the plan until they have completed 3 years of employment.

Employee Elective Deferrals. Before 1997 an employer could establish a SEP that allowed employees the opportunity to make pretax contributions in the same way as in a 401(k) plan. This type of salary reduction SEP is often referred to as a SARSEP. Under the Small Business Job Protection Act of 1996, the SARSEP was replaced with a new type of salary reduction plan referred to as the SIMPLE (discussed in the next section). The new law permits employers to sponsor SIMPLEs in 1997, and no new SARSEPs can be established after December 31, 1996. Still, SARSEPs in existence on that date can continue indefinitely. Therefore it is important to understand how they work.

In a SARSEP, the maximum employee contribution is the same as in the 401(k)—$9,500 for 1997—and this amount can be contributed as long as the maximum deductible contribution and maximum allocation rules described below are satisfied. The SARSEP salary deferral feature is subject to several requirements that do not apply to 401(k) plans, each of which makes the plan less attractive than a 401(k) plan:

- Only an employer with 25 or fewer employees can sponsor a SARSEP.
- At least 50 percent of all eligible employees must participate in the SARSEP.
- The employer may not make matching contributions to encourage employees to contribute to the plan.

Like the 401(k) plan, the SARSEP must satisfy a mathematical nondiscrimination test. The test is similar to, but more stringent than, the 401(k) test. Under this test, the deferral percentage for *any* highly compensated employee (HCE) cannot exceed 125 percent of the average deferral percentage of the nonhighly compensated group. For example, if the average deferral for the nonhighly compensated group is 5 percent, no HCE can contribute more than 6.25 percent of compensation.

Timing of Distribution. Participants must be given the opportunity to withdraw the account balance at any time. This is entirely different from the situation with qualified pension plans, which do not allow distributions until termination of employment, and from qualified profit-sharing plans, in which the employer can choose whether or not to allow in-service withdrawals.

Documentation and Reporting. The supporting plan document is much simpler than with a qualified plan. The IRS supplies a form document—Form 5305(SEP) for plans with employer contributions only and Form 5305A(SEP) for plans that allow employee pretax contributions. Service providers, such as banks and insurance companies, may also sponsor a SEP prototype document and receive IRS approval. If the IRS form or the prototype document is used, the plan does not have to file Form 5500 annually as long as participants receive (1) either a copy of the plan or a summary of the plan, (2) some general information about SEPs, and (3) annual notice of contributions made on their behalf. When working with SEPs, note that these alternative document and disclosure requirements must be followed exactly or the plan sponsor will be required to file annual Form 5500 reports and meet all other ERISA disclosure requirements.

Qualified Plan Rules That Apply to SEPs

Maximum Contribution and Allocation Limits. The maximum employer contribution to the SEP is the same as for a profit-sharing plan, that is, 15 percent of the compensation of all employees eligible to participate in the plan. Note that pretax employee contributions count toward this 15 percent limit. All profit-sharing plans and SEPs sponsored by the same company are aggregated under this rule. The maximum amount that can be allocated to each participant from employer and employee contributions is the lesser of 25 percent of compensation or $30,000—the same as for other defined-contribution-type plans. Similarly, the $150,000 compensation cap that applies to qualified plans also applies to SEPs.

Top-heavy Rules. The same rules that apply to qualified plans apply to SEPs. Although most SEPs will be top-heavy (benefits for key employees will generally equal or exceed 60 percent of total benefits), the top-heavy rules do not have much effect on the SEP. SEPs are already required to have 100 percent immediate vesting, and the minimum contribution requirement for nonkey employees does not have much effect because of the special nondiscrimination rules that apply to SEPs.

IRA Rules That Apply to SEPs

Investment Restrictions. Since contributions are held in IRA accounts, the limitations that apply to individually sponsored IRAs also apply to SEPs. These rules prohibit investment in life insurance and in collectibles (except for U.S. government gold coins). Similarly, loans cannot be made from a SEP.

Taxation of Distributions. Distributions are taxed in the same way as distributions from IRAs. Distributions are treated as ordinary income and are not eligible for special lump-sum averaging. The penalties for early withdrawals and large distributions apply (as they do with qualified plans). Most distributions can also be rolled over to avoid current taxation, but only to other IRAs.[2]

SEP Candidates

Candidates for SEPs fill out the pension planning fact finder by grading as "very valuable" the items about avoiding an annual financial commitment and instituting a plan that is administratively convenient. SEP candidates say "no" to the following questions in step 2 of the fact finder: Is it more important to provide an adequate retirement standard of living than to avoid an annual commitment? Is it more important to provide an adequate retirement standard of living than to have administrative convenience and an easily communicated plan?

The SEP is a good choice for the small employer with these goals in mind. The coverage rules are easier to work with than those for a qualified plan; shorter-term employees (less than 3 years) can be excluded from the plan, eliminating cost and administrative burdens. However, the SEP is not the right approach when the employer has many long-term part-time employees, since they will have to be covered under the plan. The lack of flexibility in the coverage and vesting requirements also eliminates larger employers as SEP candidates.

Any employer considering a profit-sharing plan should also consider a SEP, because the maximum deduction limits (15 percent of compensation) and the ability to make discretionary employer contributions are the same. Assuming the coverage requirements discussed above do not cause any problems, the SEP is usually the better choice. However, the profit-sharing plan should be chosen when the employer wants a more aggressive, age-weighted or cross-tested allocation formula that skews contributions to the older, more highly compensated employees.

YOUR FINANCIAL SERVICES PRACTICE:
OPPORTUNITIES IN THE SEP MARKETPLACE

The financial services professional who can offer the employer a SEP in addition to offering investment services has a real business opportunity. Take, for example, the business owner who has been frustrated by the complexity and expense of maintaining a qualified plan. He or she may be swayed to change vendors if you can offer a superior investment product and at the same time reduce headaches and administrative expense with the SEP approach.

The SARSEP (which cannot be adopted after 1996) was a great idea, but it was burdened with a number of difficult requirements that limited its usefulness. The stringent nondiscrimination test, the inability to make matching contributions, the 50 percent participation requirement, the top-heavy test, and the 25 employee rule kept most employers away from adopting SARSEPs. The SIMPLE is Congress's next attempt at a more useful 401(k) look-alike that will be appealing to small businesses. As discussed below, the SIMPLE may have its own set of problems.

The employer that had a SARSEP before 1997 will have the option to switch to the SIMPLE or retain the SARSEP. There are two major reasons for an employer to keep the SARSEP. First, if the employer wants to have a salary reduction only plan, it may want to retain the SARSEP. As long as the SARSEP is not top-heavy (discussed further in chapter 10), no employer contributions are required. If the plan is top-heavy, then the employer's required contribution is actually lower in the SIMPLE. Second, the employer contribution to the SARSEP is more flexible than in the SIMPLE. The allocation formula can be integrated with social security, and the maximum contribution amount is higher than in the SIMPLE. These choices should seem clearer after reading the next section.

SIMPLEs

Beginning in 1997, the new law eliminates SARSEPs and replaces them with a similar plan referred to as the Savings Incentive Match Plan for Employees (SIMPLE).

Plan Requirements

Like SEPs and SARSEPs, the SIMPLE plan is funded with individual retirement accounts, which means that the following requirements apply to the SIMPLE:

- Participants must be fully vested in all benefits at all times.
- Assets cannot be invested in life insurance or collectibles.
- No participant loans are allowed.

Eligible Employers

Any type of business entity can establish a SIMPLE; however, the business cannot have more than 100 employees (only counting those employees who earned $5,000 or more of compensation). If the employer grows beyond the 100-employee limit, the law does allow the employer to sponsor the plan for an additional 2-year grace period. Also note that to be eligible, the sponsoring employer cannot maintain any other qualified plan, 403(b), or SEP at the same time it maintains the SIMPLE.

Contributions

In a SIMPLE, all eligible employees have the opportunity to make elective pretax contribution of up to $6,000 (subject to cost-of-living adjustments). Unlike the 401(k) plan (or the old SARSEP), there is no nondiscrimination testing, meaning that highly compensated employees can make contributions without regard to the salary deferral elections of the nonhighly compensated employees.

However, in exchange, the SIMPLE has a mandatory employer contribution requirement. This contribution can be made in one of two ways:

- The employer can make a dollar-for-dollar matching contribution on the first 3 percent of compensation that the individual elects to defer, or
- The employer can make a 2 percent nonelective contribution for all eligible employees.

If the employer elects the matching contribution, it has one other option. Periodically the employer can elect a lower match as long as

- the matching contribution is not less than one percent of compensation
- participants are notified of the lower contribution within a reasonable time before the 60-day election period before the beginning of the year

The employer can elect the lower percentage for up to 2 years in any 5-year period, which can even include the first 2 years that the plan is in force.

The employer contribution amount just described is both the minimum required and the maximum employer contribution allowed. In other words, if the employer elects the matching contribution, 3 percent is the maximum match, and nonelective contributions are not allowed. If the employer elects the nonelective contributions, then the 2 percent contribution is the maximum, and matching contributions are not allowed. This means that the maximum amount that can be contributed for the owner or other highly compensated employee in a SIMPLE is $12,000 (table 6-1). This amount includes the $6,000 salary deferral and $6,000 for the dollar-for-dollar match, up to 3 percent of compensation. To contribute the full $12,000, the employee must earn $200,000 of compensation or more (3 percent of $200,000 equals $6,000[3]). For the individual earning less, the maximum matching contribution is limited by the 3 percent rule (see table 6-1).

Eligibility Requirements

The SIMPLE has eligibility requirements that are different from both the SEP and the qualified plan. The plan must cover any employee who earned $5,000 in any two previous years and is reasonably expected to earn $5,000 again in the current year. Employees subject to a collectively bargained agreement can be excluded. Eligible employees must be given the right to make the salary deferral and receive either an employer matching or nonelective contribution. For determining eligibility, compensation is essentially taxable income plus pretax salary deferrals. For a self-employed person, compensation is net earnings (not reduced by salary deferral elections). SIMPLEs can be maintained only on a calendar-year basis. And all employees become eligible to participate as of January 1.

Table 6-1 Maximum SIMPLE Contribution			
Salary	Maximum Salary Deferral	Matching Contribution	Total Contribution
$ 50,000	$ 6,000	$ 1,500	$ 7,500
$ 75,000	$ 6,000	$ 2,250	$ 8,250
$ 100,000	$ 6,000	$ 3,000	$ 9,000
$ 125,000	$ 6,000	$ 3,750	$ 9,750
$ 150,000	$ 6,000	$ 4,500	$ 10,500
$ 175,000	$ 6,000	$ 5,250	$ 11,250
$ 200,000 or more	$ 6,000	$ 6,000	$ 12,000

Plan Operations

The sponsoring employer must notify participants that they have the 60-day election period just prior to the calendar year to make a salary deferral election or modify a previous election for the following year. The employee who does make a salary deferral election must be given the option to stop making deferrals at any time during the year. The sponsor can require that the participant wait until the following year to elect back in, or may have a more liberal election modification provision—for example, allowing participants to modify their election at any time.

Every year, prior to the 60-day election period, the trustee must prepare and the employer must distribute a summary plan description (SPD) that includes employer-identifying data, a description of eligibility under the plan, benefits provided, terms of the salary election, and description of the procedures for and effects (tax results) of making a withdrawal. Also, 30 days after the calendar year ends, the trustee must give participants a statement of the year's activity and the closing account balance.[4]

The clear and precise disclosure requirements are accompanied by clear penalties for failure to comply. The trustee is fined $50 a day for late distribution of participant statements or the annual summary plan description. The employer is fined $50 a day for late notification to participants of their right to make salary deferral elections.[5] The disclosure requirements and penalty system were probably deemed necessary, since there is no direct incentive for the employer to encourage SIMPLE participation (unlike the 401(k) plan, in which highly compensated contribution levels are tied to nonhighly compensated contributions under the ADP nondiscrimination test).

Like SEPs, the plan cannot put any limitations on participant withdrawals. This means that participants have access to funds at any time to spend them or roll them over into another IRA. To discourage participants from spending their SIMPLE accounts, a special new tax rule assesses a 25 percent penalty tax (in addition to ordinary income taxes) for amounts withdrawn within 2 years of the date of participation. Other early withdrawals may be subject to the special 10 percent excise tax discussed in chapter 23.

Administrative costs for a SIMPLE should be quite low. At the present time, no annual reporting with the IRS or DOL is required. Also, unlike the 401(k) plan, no ADP test or other nondiscrimination tests must be performed.

Candidates for the SIMPLE

The candidate for the SIMPLE will be the employer looking for a plan that allows participants the right to make pretax contributions and who wants to create a plan that creates a retirement planning partnership between the employer and employee. The candidate must have 100 or fewer employers and also be looking for a plan with the lowest possible administrative hassle and cost.

The employer considering the SIMPLE will be choosing between the 401(k) plan and the SIMPLE. After analyzing and comparing these two plans, it is difficult to see why small employers would establish a SIMPLE. The plan design is so rigid that it severely limits its usefulness.

Feature by feature, the advantage almost always goes to the 401(k) plan. 401(k) plans are better for maximizing contributions and skewing employer contributions to a targeted group of employees—which are typically two common goals of small plan sponsors. In addition, a 401(k) plan is much more flexible. The plan can be limited to part of the workforce as long as the minimum coverage requirements are met, and matching and profit-sharing contributions can be designed to meet a variety of goals. Finally, employer contributions can increase or decrease over time. The features that make the 401(k) plan the more useful retirement planning vehicle are described briefly below:

- *Salary deferrals*—The maximum salary deferral amount of $9,500 is substantially higher than in the SIMPLE.
- *Maximum tax shelter*—The total maximum contribution on behalf of a highly compensated employee is $12,000 in a SIMPLE and as high as $30,000 in a 401(k) plan.
- *Matching contributions*—The matching contribution in a 401(k) plan can match both the employer's goals and budget. Matching contributions can be subject to a vesting schedule and may even be made on a discretionary basis.
- *Profit-sharing contributions*—Nonelective contributions can be allocated using a cross-testing method in which the lion's share of the contribution is on behalf of the highly compensated employees.
- *Coverage*—The qualified plan coverage requirements are more flexible and allow the employer to keep part-time employees out of the plan.

There are few reasons, however, that a small business would choose the SIMPLE over the 401(k) plan:
- The employer wants to spend the fewest dollars and the least amount of administrative effort on a plan.

- A 401(k) plan would be top-heavy, and the employer's goal is to minimize employer contributions (*see chapter 10*).
- The employer contribution constraints under a SIMPLE still allow the employer to meet its goals.
- The employer is attracted to the withdrawal flexibility of the SIMPLE.

403(b) PLANS

The plans we've studied up to this point are not limited to any particular type of industry; for the most part, they're available to any organization. In contrast to other retirement plans, a 403(b) plan can be sold only to tax-exempt organizations and public schools. Despite these limitations, 403(b) plans represent a separate and lucrative opportunity for financial services professionals, particularly those who sell annuity products. A 403(b) plan, which is also referred to as a tax-sheltered annuity (TSA) or a tax-deferred annuity (TDA), is similar to a 401(k) plan. Like the 401(k) plan, the 403(b) plan

- permits an employee to defer tax on income by allowing before-tax contributions to be made to the employee's individual account
- allows deferrals in the form of a salary reduction that is chosen by the employee or a retirement payment that is made by the employer
- can be used in conjunction with, or in lieu of, most other retirement plans

However, 403(b) plans are distinguishable from 401(k) plans both in the market they serve and in their makeup. In this section we will discuss the distinct market that 403(b) plans serve and analyze the fundamental makeup of a 403(b) plan.

The historical development of 403(b) plans has a direct bearing on understanding their use today. The 403(b) plan was originally used as a special lure to entice tax-exempt organizations and public schools into providing for the retirement needs of their employees. Qualified plans—which offer tax incentives—didn't motivate these organizations to cover employees because the organizations don't pay taxes. It was decided that a plan that was not qualified (and therefore not subject to all the qualification hurdles) might provide an incentive for coverage, and 403(b) plans were born. Originally these plans were distinct from regular qualified plans in two important ways: employers could discriminate with regard to employee coverage, and employees were free to make unrestricted withdrawals from the plan. Subsequent legislative changes, however, which restricted withdrawals from 403(b) plans and subjected them to the nondiscrimination rules applicable to qualified plans, have taken away some of the luster. Nevertheless, today's 403(b) plans remain a viable retirement planning tool.

The 403(b) Market

While the 403(b) market is generally composed of tax-exempt organizations and public schools, there are restrictions placed on these organizations. If the employer is not a "qualified employer," the use of a 403(b) plan will be prohibited.

Qualified Tax-Exempt Organizations

In order to qualify for a 403(b) plan, a tax-exempt organization must be a so-called 501(c)(3) organization. (501(c)(3) refers to the Internal Revenue Code section that specifies certain tax-exempt organizations.) If a corporation, community chest, fund, or foundation is organized and operated exclusively for religious, charitable, scientific, testing for public safety, literary, or educational purposes; to foster national or international amateur sports competition; or for the prevention of cruelty to children or animals, then it will probably qualify for 501(c)(3) status. For example, hospitals, humane societies, charities, private schools, and churches are typically 501(c)(3) organizations. Not all organizations created for these purposes, however, will be judged by the IRS as qualifying under Sec. 501(c)(3); for example, organizations that engage in political activity will not be granted 501(c)(3) status even if set up for charitable purposes. The only way to know for certain is to see the sponsoring employer's IRS determination letter granting that organization 501(c)(3) status.

In order to be a qualified public school an organization must meet two requirements:

- The employer must be an educational organization that maintains a faculty and curriculum and has an enrolled body of students in attendance at the place where its educational activities are carried on.
- The organization must be a state, a political subdivision of a state, or an instrumentality of a state or political subdivision.

In general, this encompasses almost all public school systems and state university systems. In addition, since private schools and colleges usually qualify for a 403(b) plan if they are 501(c)(3) organizations, they, too, are ripe markets for this kind of plan.

Eligible Employees

In addition to being restricted to qualified employers, the 403(b) market is restricted to eligible employees. Not all members of qualified tax-exempt organizations and public schools are considered eligible. Full-time and part-time employees of a qualified employer will be eligible employees if they are so-called common-law employees (their work, both what they do and how they do it, is subject to the control and direction of the employer). If they are not common-law employees, however, but instead are independent contractors (because their work is subject to the control or direction of the employer regarding the result only and not how they do the work), they cannot be covered by the 403(b) plan. If the employer is required to withhold federal taxes and social security, the employee is a common-law employee. If no federal taxes are withheld and no social security is paid, the employee is an independent contractor.

Examples of employees who are typically considered eligible employees include

- public school teachers
- teachers in private and parochial schools
- school superintendents
- college professors
- members of the clergy
- social workers
- part-time and full-time custodial workers for eligible schools
- doctors who work for a hospital (and are under the hospital's supervision and control)

Examples of employees who are not entitled to be covered include

- persons working with the organization in a self-employed capacity
- doctors who are not hospital employees even though they have significant contact with the hospital

Invariably some employees will fall into the gray area. No clear-cut rule is issued in advance; instead, the IRS will look at the surrounding facts and circumstances to determine if these employees are eligible.

Ground Rules

The 403(b) plan can be distinguished from the 401(k) plan (and all qualified plans) in several ways: by the way it is funded, by the legal requirements that are applicable, and by an individual's contribution limit.

Funding

There are basically two varieties of 403(b) plans: the pure annuity type and the mutual fund type. The pure annuity type is funded with an annuity contract. The annuity can be either an individual or group annuity contract, with either fixed or variable terms and either level or flexible premiums. The mutual fund type is funded by mutual fund shares held in a custodial account. In either case "incidental" life insurance protection can be provided. Contributions to annuity contracts can be used to provide insurance protection as long as the insurance protection is incidental and the value of the insurance is taxable to the employee each year (see chapter 10). Contributions to mutual fund custodial accounts can be used to purchase insurance if (1) the insurance has no cash value (unless the contract is distributed within 30 days), (2) the insurance is incidental (the cost of the insurance cannot exceed 25 percent of the employee contribution to the account), and (3) the cost of the insurance is included in the employee's gross income.

General Legal Requirements

Sec. 403(b) of the Internal Revenue Code contains some specific rules and restrictions that govern both the design and operation of a 403(b) plan. Here are the most important ones:

- Until 1997, only one salary deferral election could be made each year. Beginning in 1997, 403(b) plans can allow participants to change salary reduction agreements any number of times during the year.
- Premiums to a 403(b) annuity can be paid on a single-premium, annual-premium, or monthly-premium basis. Some companies provide a flexible-premium arrangement to accommodate nonuniform payments.
- The 403(b) annuity is not transferable or assignable to another party. However, the participant can exercise all other ownership rights, including electing to take a reduced paid-up annuity or borrowing against the cash value of the annuity.
- The 403(b) plan can be designed to permit loans.
- In general, the nondiscrimination rules that apply to qualified plans apply to 403(b) plans (except church plans).
- Certain rules regarding distributions from a 403(b) plan apply. In general, funds can be withdrawn by an employee (or an employee's beneficiary) only if the employee dies, is aged 59 1/2, separates from service, becomes disabled, or encounters financial hardship. (Exception: 403(b) contributions not made pursuant to a salary reduction agreement [for example, employer retirement payments] may be distributed at any time.) In addition, amounts withdrawn are includible in gross income, and most hardship withdrawals prior to age 59 1/2 are subject to a 10 percent penalty.
- Unlike qualified plans, no 5-year or 10-year forward averaging is available for distributions from 403(b) plans.

Contribution Limits

There are special rules that restrict the amount that an employee can put into a 403(b) plan (in the case of the salary reduction 403(b)) or that can be put in on behalf of an employee (in the case of nonelective employer contribution 403(b)). The maximum limit is the lesser of two amounts: (1) the exclusion allowance for a given year and (2) the $30,000-or-25-percent-of-income defined-contribution limit. Moreover, a $9,500 limit generally applies to the amount of salary reduction that an employee can take.

Exclusion Allowance

The annual exclusion allowance (table 6-2) is calculated by multiplying 20 percent of the employee's *includible compensation* (excluding 403(b) contributions) by the total *number years of service* the employee has and then by subtracting *contributions made in prior years*.

TABLE 6-2
Steps in Determining the Exclusion Allowance

(1) Determine annual includible
     compensation.   _____

(2) Determine years of service.   _____

(3) Multiply (1) x (2) x 20%.   _____

(4) Subtract the total contributions   _____
     made in prior years.

(5) The result is the exclusion   _____
     allowance.

- *Includible compensation* is generally the salary for the current taxable year (for full-time employees) or a combination of aggregate earnings of fractional periods that constitute a full year's earnings (for part-time employees). For example, assume that at the end of 1996 an employee has worked 2 years half-time and earned $9,000 in 1995 and $10,000 in 1996. When computing the exclusion allowance for 1996, includible compensation would be $19,000 ($9,000 + $10,000).

  Generally, includible compensation does not encompass amounts that are not includible in an employee's gross income. So if an employee takes a reduction in salary to finance the 403(b) plan, the exclusion allowance is based on the reduced salary. In addition, if employer contributions are made to a supplemental qualified retirement plan, these contributions are not includible contributions. What's more, the cost of incidental life insurance provided under the 403(b) plan is not includible compensation even though this cost is taxable as gross income.

- *Years of service* will be calculated differently, depending on whether the employee was employed full-time or part-time. For a full-time employee, *years of service* is defined as the actual number of years worked. For a part-time employee the number of years of service is determined by adding fractional years. For example, an employee who has worked one-third of a year for 9 years will have 3 years of service. Every employee, however, will be considered to have at least one year of service even if their months of service don't add up to twelve. For both a full-time and part-time employee the number of years of service will be counted at the close of the taxable year for which the exclusion allowance is determined.

- *Contributions made in prior years* refers to the total amount of employer contributions made on an employee's behalf (employee salary reductions are considered employer contributions for these purposes) to (1) the 403(b) plan, (2) all other qualified plans, or (3) 457 plans (plans used by some state and local governments). Under some plans a question may arise as to what the value of the employer contributions will be—if, for example, a defined-benefit plan exists. The answer is derived from actuarial calculations and IRS-supplied formulas (see IRS Regulations). Contributions made in prior years will generally not include amounts that were not excludible from gross income. For example, employee after-tax voluntary contributions or PS 58 costs (see chapter 10) will not count in the calculation of the prior years' contributions. What's more, rollover contributions are also not used in figuring the prior years' contributions.

Example 1: Karen Lee is in her first year of service and earns $24,000; Karen can contribute $4,000. The $4,000 is equal to 20 percent of her $24,000 gross pay after netting out her 403(b) contribution (20 percent of $20,000). Note that the $4,000 contribution is also equal to 16 2/3 percent of gross pay ($24,000 x 16 2/3 percent = $4,000). The figure 16 2/3 percent can be used as a rule of thumb when determining the maximum 403(b) contribution. The reason is that one-sixth (16 2/3 percent) of a person's gross income is equal to 20 percent of a person's net taxable income.

Example 2: At the end of 1996 Arthur Power has a $35,000 salary and 6 years of service. Arthur would like to make a 10 percent salary reduction contribution to his 403(b) plan. In addition to his 10 percent contribution, Arthur will receive a $1,050 employer contribution to his 403(b) plan (3 percent match) and a $1,750 contribution made to his money-purchase plan by his employer (5 percent of salary). Over his years of service, Arthur has made a 3 percent contribution to his 403(b) plan each year and has received the 3 percent employer match, and his employer has also made a 5 percent money-purchase plan contribution in every year but the first, when Arthur was not eligible to be a plan participant.

Arthur's includible compensation is $31,500 ($35,000 salary minus the $3,500 projected contribution). Note that the money-purchase contribution does not count as compensation. Arthur's contributions for the 6 years noted are $17,740, determined as follows:

Year	Salary	403(b) Salary Reduction	403(b) Employer Match	Money-Purchase Contribution	Total
1996	$35,000	$1,050	$1,050	$1,750	$ 3,850
1995	$33,000	$ 990	$ 990	$1,650	$ 3,630
1994	$31,000	$ 930	$ 930	$1,550	$ 3,410
1993	$26,000	$ 780	$ 780	$1,300	$ 2,860
1992	$24,000	$ 720	$ 720	$1,200	$ 2,640
1991	$22,500	$ 675	$ 675	0	$ 1,350
					$17,740

Arthur's Exclusion Allowance for 1996

(1)	Includible compensation	$31,500
(2)	Years of service	6
(3)	(1) x (2) x 20%	$37,800
(4)	Minus contributions made in prior years	$17,740
(5)	Exclusion allowance	$20,060

Since the 10 percent contribution of $3,500 plus the $1,050 employer match is less than the $20,060 allowance, Arthur can make the contribution.

Financial Services Professionals and the Exclusion Allowance

Financial services professionals who are asked to calculate the exclusion allowance for an individual client or for an organization should be aware that there are many pitfalls awaiting them; it might therefore be a good idea to have an actuary, the home office, or an employee benefits consulting firm with the proper software make the calculations for these reasons:

- A new calculation must be done for each employee every year. This can be time-consuming and prevent the financial services professional from taking advantage of more appropriate opportunities.
- There are special rules dealing with service with prior employers.

- Determining the projected amount of pension benefits from a defined-benefit plan may be difficult for anyone who is not familiar with actuarial computations.

- There are limitations on the percentage of total employer contributions that can interfere with a contribution made by, or for, an individual.

- There are special catch-up provisions that allow employees of hospitals, home health service agencies, and educational institutions to make larger contributions. One catch-up provision permits a once-in-a-lifetime election of up to $30,000 (and ignores the 25-percent-of-income limit placed on defined-contribution plans). The actual amount represents the unmade contributions in the 10-year period prior to separation from service. The second special limit (the $15,000 maximum rule) allows annual contributions to be made up to the 25 percent of includible compensation plus $4,000 (with a $15,000 maximum). The third election permits an employee to exclude contributions up to 25 percent of salary or $30,000 without regard to the exclusion allowance. Under this election, includible compensation does not include the amount contributed during the year, whether or not it is includible in gross income.

- Past service may be used to provide a larger exclusion allowance by being prorated over future years of service. In other words, the maximum-level premium annuity may be increased if past-service years were without compensation or if the plan didn't exist during years when past service was performed.

- The $9,500 salary reduction limit is subject to an exception that allows certain employees with at least 15 years of service to qualify for up to a $12,500 salary reduction.

- If an employee participates in a 401(k) plan or a SEP, elective contributions under those plans are aggregated with 403(b) deferrals when applying the $9,500 limit on salary deferrals.

NOTES

1. The determination of whether a controlled group of corporations exists is governed by IRC Secs. 414(b) and (c). The area is quite complex, but as a rule of thumb, a controlled group exists when one company owns 80 percent or more of another corporation or the same five or fewer individuals have controlling interest in two or more businesses. The rules also apply to partnerships and sole proprietorships. In the small business setting, a common example would be one individual owning two separate businesses.

2. Only installment payments or a part of a minimum required distribution may not be rolled over.

3. Note that 408(p)(2)(iii) does not apply the $150,000 compensation cap for purposes of determining the 3 percent matching contribution. However, for the employer that elects the 2 percent nonelective contribution in lieu of the match, the $150,000 compensation cap does

apply. This means that the maximum nonelective contribution would be $3,000 (2 percent of $150,000).

4. Code Sec. 408(l).
5. Code Sec. 6693(c)(1).

7

Coverage, Eligibility, and Participation Rules

Chapter Outline

Perhaps the most challenging assignment in the retirement field is advising a client about how his or her plan should be designed. In order to design a plan effectively the financial services professional must

- acquire an expertise about the qualification rules
- ascertain the client's objectives
- choose plan provisions that meet the qualification rules and accomplish employer objectives

In addition, both the client's objectives and the qualification rules are constantly evolving and require financial services professionals to monitor client needs and know the latest laws and regulations. In this chapter and the next three chapters we will define and explore the various plan-design features. The emphasis will be on the qualification rules that apply to qualified plans and the ways plan design can be used to meet your client's objectives. The last part of the chapter will review the different rules that apply to other tax-sheltered plans. Let's start out, however, with a brief overview of the plan-design process.

THE PLAN-DESIGN PROCESS

The first step toward effective plan design has already been taken. The fact finder that you set up to choose the best retirement plan can also be used to help you design the plan properly. However, designing a plan is dictated not only by the client's objectives but also by the laws and regulations regarding plan qualification. In other words, picking the specific provisions that will constitute the client's plan consists of weighing what the Internal Revenue Code permits against the client's objectives and pocketbook. Take as an example the first design feature we consider below—which employees should be eligible for the plan. The coverage rules are really quite complex. In this case, complexity allows a great deal of freedom in plan design, but also requires intimate knowledge of the boundaries of the law.

The plan-design process is simplified for insurance agents and other financial services professionals by the use of master and prototype plan documents. With these documents most of the plan language is standardized, and the employer has limited design alternatives, which are contained in a document referred to as the *adoption agreement*. The adoption agreement approach helps the adviser by organizing the design process. The document is relatively simple to follow, since it lists the various design features and provides several alternatives under each one (for example, the various vesting schedules and the alternative design choices available for early, normal, and deferred retirement). Employers (with your help) then pick from the menu of options that are provided.

The adoption agreement simplifies plan design by directing and limiting available design options, but it also locks out from consideration some important but nonstandard design choices that might meet a unique employer need. Generally if employers desire this specialized treatment they should pay the additional fees to have an attorney, consulting firm, or insurance company home office design the plan (called an individually designed plan). On the other hand, employers willing to buy an "off-the-rack" plan probably can save on fees and yet meet their goals and objectives through the use of the standard design options contained in your company's adoption agreement.

You can see that to properly advise the client, the adviser needs to have an in-depth understanding of the rules. Knowing the options in the adoption agreement is not enough. The adviser must be able to know the limits of the law, so that the client will be able to decide when it is time to establish a plan that does not fall within the prototype options.

**YOUR FINANCIAL SERVICES PRACTICE:
EFFECTIVE PLAN DESIGN**

As a rule of thumb, any design decision you make in one area of the adoption agreement should be consistent with design decisions you make in other areas of the adoption agreement. In other words, one strategy in designing an effective plan is to ask yourself, Does each design decision consistently support the employer's objectives? For example, if the desire to limit costs attributable to short-service employees motivated the employer to choose the most restrictive age and service requirements offered in the adoption agreement, the same employer objective should also generate a restrictive vesting schedule and a benefit formula that rewards service. This approach to plan design will ensure a design that's correct and complete. However, remember the words of Alfred North Whitehead: "Seek simplicity and distrust it." There may be reasons to stray from design consistency to meet a unique employer objective.

COVERAGE REQUIREMENTS

The first major design decision facing you and your client is deciding which employees to cover under the retirement plan. This decision is directed by extensive and complicated laws and regulations. As a payback for providing valuable tax advantages for qualified plans (and consequently losing revenue), the legislature requires that retirement plans must cover a broad spectrum of employees and not just a group of highly compensated employees (who are defined by statute).

The Definition of a Highly Compensated Employee

Understanding the coverage requirements begins with identifying which employees are considered *highly compensated employees.* We first encountered the highly compensated group when discussing the 401(k) actual deferral percentage test. As you may recall highly compensated employees include individuals who are 5 percent owners during the current or previous year and individuals who earned $80,000 (as indexed in 1997) in the preceding year. Under the second category the employer can elect to limit the group to only those individuals whose earnings put them in the top 20 percent of all employees.

The 410(b) Rule

Sec. 410(b) of the Internal Revenue Code specifies who must be covered under a qualified plan. The rules are meaningful any time that the employer decides not to cover all employees under the plan. The employer may want to exclude one class of workers, such as hourly employees, or employees who are part-time or have short-service. In other cases, the employer will want to set up two or more plans, each covering a different group of employees. Essentially the a plan can cover any portion of the workforce, as long as it satisfies one of three tests under Sec. 410(b)—the percentage test, the ratio test, or the average-benefit-percentage test.

When performing any of these tests, note that certain classes of employees can always be excluded from testing. These include collectively bargained employees, employees who have worked less than one year, certain part-time employees (working less than 1,000 hours per year), and employees younger than age 21 (discussed in more detail later in this chapter). These employees will be referred to as *excludable employees*. Essentially this means a plan can always exclude those employees defined as excludable, as well as any additional employees as allowed under one of the three coverage tests.

Also be aware that when testing a 401(k) plan, an individual eligible to make a salary deferral election will be considered a participant in the plan, regardless of whether he or she makes the election to make a salary deferral. For other plans this is not the case. Subject to several exceptions, a participant must actually receive a contribution (or benefit accrual in a defined-benefit plan) in order to be considered a participant for that year.

The Percentage Test

A plan will satisfy Sec. 410(b) if it benefits at least 70 percent of employees who are not highly compensated employees. As just described, employees who are not eligible for participation in the plan because they don't meet the age and service requirements or who are covered by a collective-bargaining agreement (discussed later in the chapter) are not counted for purposes of this test.

> *Example:* The law firm of Block, Meyers, and Andrews has 24 employees. Since 4 of these employees work part-time and have not met the minimum-service requirements for participation in the plan (discussed later in the chapter), the percentage test would apply only to the remaining 20 employees. Of these employees, 12 fall within the statutory definition of highly compensated and 8 do not. Six of the 8 employees who are not highly compensated belong to the Manhattan office (the one covered by the plan) and 2 belong to the Teaneck, New Jersey, office (which does not have a plan). Under the percentage test the plan must benefit at least 70 percent of the 8 employees who are not highly compensated (note that employees from both offices are counted).

That is, 6 employees (6 out of 8 is 75 percent) must be benefited. Since the law firm's Manhattan plan benefits 6 of the nonhighly compensated employees, the plan passes the percentage test.

The Ratio Test

The ratio test requires a plan to benefit a percentage of nonhighly compensated employees equal to 70 percent of the percentage of highly compensated employees benefited under the plan. Again, employees who are not eligible for participation in the plan because they don't meet the age and service requirements or are covered by a collective-bargaining agreement are not counted for purposes of the ratio test.

> *Example:* The Thunder Company has 120 employees on its payroll. Since 20 of these have not yet met the minimum age and service requirements of the plan, the ratio test would apply to only 100 employees. Thirty of the remaining employees are highly compensated, and 15 of 30 highly compensated employees actually participate in the plan (the additional 15 are part of a separate group that does not have a plan). Seventy of the remaining employees are nonhighly compensated, and 40 of 70 nonhighly compensated employees participate in the plan (the additional 30 are part of the separate group that does not have a plan).
>
> Since 50 percent (15 out of 30) of the highly compensated employees participate in the plan, the ratio test requires that at least 35 percent of the nonhighly compensated employees (70% x 50% = 35%) must benefit under the plan. In other words, at least 25 (35% x 70 = 24.5) nonhighly compensated employees must benefit under the plan. Since Thunder Company has 40 nonhighly compensated employees benefiting under the plan, the plan satisfies the ratio test.

Average-Benefit Test

Another way to satisfy the minimum coverage requirements is to satisfy the average-benefits test. This is actually a very complex analysis that has three separate parts. Here we will summarize these rules and when they are generally applied, but will not get into all the details..

The first requirement under the average-benefits test is that the plan has to cover employees who represent a *reasonable classification of employees*—which means that the eligibility requirements (specifying who qualifies for participation and who does not) must use some objective means of classification, such as job classification, nature of compensation (salaried or hourly), or geographic location. The second part of the test is a very complex percentage test. Suffice it to say that the percentage of nonhighly compensated employees required to be covered under this section will generally be quite small. The third part of the test is the average-benefit-percentage test. This portion is satisfied if the average-benefit percentage for nonhighly compensated employees is at least 70 percent of the average-benefit percentage of the highly compensated employees. This requirement is different from the others in that it counts benefits earned in any qualified plan sponsored by the employer.

In operation, note that the administrator will test the plan under the less complicated percentage and ratio tests before tackling the more complex average percentage test. Understand that the reason for this test is to provide relief for the larger employer that wants to cover most employees under some qualified plan, but chooses to cover them under two or more separate plans. The employer might want to do this because it has different geographic locations or has workers with very different types of jobs. Although the math is complex, the bottom line is that the employer can generally have such an arrangement as long as, overall, the benefits for nonhighly compensated employees under all the plans are at least 70 percent of the benefits provided to the highly compensated under all the plans.

For the small employer sponsoring one plan, the average-benefit test will not result in lower required participation than the ratio test. All the nonhighly compensated employees who are excluded from the plan are counted as having zero benefits when determining whether the average percentage test has been satisfied. In other words, the small employer sponsoring one plan will have to satisfy the percentage or ratio test. The average-benefits test will be of no help.

Separate Lines of Business

If an employer has separate lines of business, the 410(b) tests may be applied separately in each line of business. In order to qualify for this favorable treatment the separate lines of business must be operated for bona fide business reasons and must have at least 50 employees. The IRS has issued complex regulations for determining whether a separate line of business exists. Because of the difficulty of demonstrating compliance, most employers will look to the separate line of business rules only as a last resort—when looking for ways to ensure that each plan meets the coverage requirements.

The 401(a)(26) Rule

Up until 1997, in addition to satisfying the Code Sec. 410(b)(1) requirement, *all qualified plans* had to satisfy a second coverage requirement under Code Sec. 401(a)(26). The pension simplification provisions of the Small Business Jobs Protection Act of 1996 made a significant change. Under the new rules, now only defined-benefit—and not defined-contribution—type plans must satisfy Code Sec. 401(a)(26).

Under the 401(a)(26) rule, an employer's plan will not be qualified unless it covers (1) 50 employees (2) 40 percent of the employer's employees, *whichever is lesser.* However, a special rule applies when there are two employees; in this case, both employees must be covered.

This rule does not count employees who are not eligible because of the age and service requirements or who are part of a group covered by a collective-bargaining agreement. The effect of this rule is that employers with more than 125 employees cannot maintain a plan covering fewer than 50 participants, and if the employer has fewer than 125 employees, then the 40 percent limit applies. What this boils down to is that smaller employers will be limited to a maximum of two separate plans (in order to meet the 40 percent rule).

Aggregation Rules

To avoid the coverage requirements, some employers try to segregate their management employees from the rank-and-file employees by creating a related or subsidiary corporation. To close this loophole, the Code contains what are referred to as the *controlled group rules* that require aggregation of employers that have a sufficient amount of common ownership, and the *affiliated service groups rules* for other situations in which related businesses work together to provide goods or services to the public. When either aggregation rule applies, the employers are treated as one employer for virtually all the qualified plan rules. Both rules apply to both corporations and "trades and businesses," including partnerships, proprietorships, estates, and trusts. Regulations provide guidance for determining ownership interests in these kinds of entities.

A third type of affiliation relates to situations where individuals are "leased" on a long-term, full-time basis. In some cases, such individuals will be treated as working for the recipient for purposes of the coverage requirements. Each of these rules is covered more fully below.

Controlled Group Rules

There are three types of controlled groups: parent-subsidiary, brother-sister, and combined groups. A parent-subsidiary controlled group exists whenever one entity (referred to as the *parent company*) owns at least 80 percent of one (or more) of the other entities. Additional entities may be brought into the group if a chain of common ownership exists. Other entities included in the chain must be at least 80 percent owned by one or more (in combination) of the other entities within the chain.

> *Example:* Corporation A owns 80 percent of Corporations B and C, and Corporations B and C each own 40 percent of Corporation D. Because Corporation D is 80 percent owned by entities within the group, Corporation D is part of the parent-subsidiary controlled group that includes all four corporations.

A brother-sister controlled group exists whenever the same five (or fewer) owners of two or more entities own 80 percent or more of each entity, and more than 50 percent of each entity when counting only *identical ownership*. Identical ownership is tested by counting each person's ownership to the extent that it is identical in each entity. For example, if an individual owns 10 percent of Corporation A and 20 percent of Corporation B, he or she has a 10 percent identical ownership interest with respect to each corporation. The identical ownership interests of each of the five (or fewer) individuals is added together to determine whether the 50 percent test has been satisfied, as shown for these shareholders:

Shareholder	Corporation X	Corporation Y	Identical Ownership
Joe	20%	12%	12%
Sally	60	14	14
Ralph	20	74	20
Total	100%	100%	46%

Under these assumed facts, the 80 percent ownership test has been met, because three individuals who have ownership in each entity own 100 percent of both businesses. However, the 50 percent identical ownership interest test has not been satisfied (only 46 percent identical ownership). Therefore this group does not constitute a controlled group.

When determining an individual's ownership interest under the brother-sister controlled group rules, attribution rules require that stock owned by spouses (with one narrow exception) and children under age 21 must be treated as owned by the individual. When a person owns more than 50 percent of an entity, he or she is deemed to own any interest owned in that entity by his or her adult children, grandchildren, parents, and grandparents, as well.

The last type of controlled group is the combined group under common control. A combined group exists if an entity is both a common parent in a parent-subsidiary group and a member of a brother-sister group. If this is the case, than the two related controlled groups are treated as one controlled group.

Affiliated Service Group Rules

In 1980, Congress enacted the first affiliated service group rules. Small business corporations had managed to divide management and the rank and file into separate entities and avoid the controlled group rules. The rules have been expanded several times over the years to address new avoidance schemes. Today, the law is quite complex, and the details are beyond the scope of this book. However, when working with clients, there are several threshold issues that help advisers to identify when affiliation problems might be present. Except for management services affiliation, discussed below, affiliated groups exist only when all three of the following elements are present:

- Two or more business entities work together to provide one service or product to the public.
- At least one of the entities is a service organization, which is an organization for which capital is not a material income-producing factor. Organizations in the fields of health, law, engineering, actuarial science, consulting, and insurance are automatically deemed service organizations.
- There must be at least some common ownership between the two entities.

**YOUR FINANCIAL SERVICES PRACTICE:
AVOIDING HIDDEN AGGREGATION PROBLEMS**

One common problem the financial services professional faces when setting up a retirement plan is finding out important information at the last minute or after the fact. For example, an employer who is interested in setting up a plan for the ABC Company may also own the XYZ Company but fail to give you this important information. Since it's possible that the employees of both ABC and XYZ must be considered for the purposes of the coverage requirements, it's important to question the employer about additional holdings, other key employees' additional holdings, and the corporation's additional holdings. (See question 8 in Step 7 in the fact finder in chapter 3.) In the small-company context, the minimum coverage rules are unforgiving, and an employer who misses a controlled group issue may very well end up with one or more disqualified plans. This is a complex area of the law, and the role of the pension advisor should be to identify affiliation issues and then encourage the client to pursue a final determination from a qualified tax attorney.

The affiliation rules come into play regularly in the medical world, where there are partnerships between doctors and hospitals providing services in outpatient clinics, MRI testing centers, and other cooperative medical centers. In these cases, there must be a careful analysis to see if the MRI testing center, for example, is affiliated with the doctor's medical practice or with the hospital.

Management services affiliation is defined by a much broader rule, which essentially prohibits an executive of any size company from separating himself or herself from the company for the purpose of establishing his or her own retirement plan.

The Leasing of Employees

Instead of hiring employees directly, a business may lease employees from a third party for a number of legitimate reasons. Unfortunately, at one time, leasing of employees was also used as a way to circumvent the minimum coverage requirements. The employer would lease rank-and-file employees and then exclude them from plan eligibility. Code Sec. 414 (n) was enacted to eliminate such practices by requiring that individuals leased on a full-time, ongoing basis would be treated as employees for purposes of the coverage requirements.

A leased employee is a person who provides services to the recipient and meets all three of the following requirements:

- The services are provided pursuant to an agreement between the recipient and a leasing organization.
- The services are provided on a substantially full-time basis for a period of at least one year.
- The individual's services are performed under the primary direction or control of the service recipient.

Under the regulations, an individual need not be an employee of a leasing organization. The leasing relationship can exist directly with the leased employee, which means that a self-employed individual can be treated as a leased employee. Services are deemed to be substantially full-time for a year if the individual is credited with 1,500 or more hours of services (this number is reduced if employees generally work fewer than 40 hours a week). Legislative history indicates that the "primary direction or control" test is determined considering whether the recipient of the leased employee's services has control of where, when, and how services are performed; the order in which they are performed; who performs them; and whether the leased employee is directly supervised. This same legislative history indicates that clerical workers are generally considered within primary direction and control, while self-employed professionals such as attorneys, accountants, computer programmers, and the like are not.

Even if an individual is a leased employee under the above conditions, he or she will not be treated as an employee of the recipient if leased employees constitute no more than 20 percent of the recipient's nonhighly compensated workforce and the leasing entity maintains a safe harbor plan. A safe harbor plan must be a money-purchase plan with a nonintegrated contribution rate of at least 10 percent of compensation, and must provide for immediate eligibility and 100 percent immediate vesting.

The objective of the leased employee rule is to ensure that a company cannot avoid covering a large number of employees by leasing them versus hiring them directly. On the other hand, if the employer leases only a few individuals, the minimum coverage rules have enough latitude to allow the leased employees to be excluded from the qualified plan—or, in the alternative, the leased individuals can be ignored if the leasing organization maintains a safe harbor qualified plan. In this way, the leased employee rules work fairly well to eliminate abusive situations without penalizing the average employer. In general, the most annoying requirement for employers is that businesses that receive nonemployee services are required to keep records to demonstrate whether individuals are technically considered leased employees. An employer may be exempted from the record-keeping requirement, but only if all three of the following conditions are satisfied:

- All of the recipient's qualified plans must specifically state that leased employees are not eligible to participate.
- No qualified plan of the recipient can be top-heavy.
- The number of leased persons providing services to the recipient during the plan year must be less than 5 percent of the number of employees (excluding leased persons and HCEs) covered by the recipient's qualified plans.

One final note: the controlled group rules, affiliated service rules, and leased employee rules have been written to eliminate most situations where entities were artificially separated so that a qualified plan would cover only some of the employees. Be careful when looking at any arrangement that "smells bad." The rules are fairly comprehensive—most such schemes are prohibited. This is one area of the law where if it looks too good to be true, it probably is!

WHICH EMPLOYEES THE PLAN SHOULD COVER

We have just touched on some of the key rules that dictate whom a plan *must* cover.

- Plans cannot be used exclusively to tax-shelter income for highly compensated employees.
- To discourage this use, and to encourage a national policy of private retirement coverage, the coverage tests ensure that rank-and-file employees are sufficiently included.

But beyond this lies the question of whom the plan *should* cover. While it's true that most clients with smaller organizations will be trying to maximize tax advantages for themselves as opposed to providing coverage for rank-and-file employees, there is a case to be made for covering these employees. It's not an idealistic plea for the underdog or merely an opportunity to increase commissions; it's plain common sense that employers in small firms often overlook. First, an employee who is not covered by the plan resents second-class status and will eventually seek employment elsewhere. Even if the employer spent only 40 work-hours training that individual, 80 work-hours have been lost since the training process must be repeated with the new replacement. The cycle is also apt to repeat itself several times. What's more, the most important asset a small business can have is the experienced rank-and-file employee. There's little room for inexperienced and unproductive or counterproductive people in any organization, and—especially in small businesses—retirement plans go a long way toward coaxing employees to remain long enough to become experienced, productive workers. The second reason to cover the rank and file in a small business is to encourage loyalty and team spirit. For small businesses it's crucial that their employees not only be experienced but also committed to the business's welfare. What it boils down to is that the principal reason to encourage a retirement umbrella covering all employees is that the business is best served by this arrangement and that it *is* cost-effective to include nonkey employees.

OPTIONS AVAILABLE UNDER THE PLAN COVERAGE RULES

In spite of such legislative roadblocks as Secs. 410(b)(1) and 401(a)(26), as well as the aggregation rules and your good advice, many employers (especially small employers) still desire to provide retirement benefits for owners and key employees only, and to avoid the expense of providing benefits for the rank-and-file employees. If this is how your clients feel, relief is available in the following forms:

- gaps under the coverage requirements
- coverage of employees in comparable plans
- certain plan-design features to delay the participation of employees for as long as possible (discussed later in this chapter)
- nonqualified deferred compensation (discussed in chapters 15 and 16)

Gaps in the Coverage Requirements

The coverage rules allow the employer to save costs by excluding a portion of the workforce. To summarize, the rules allow the following employees to be excluded:

- All employees who have not satisfied minimum age and service requirements or are subject to a collective bargaining agreement (often referred to as "excludables") can be excluded without issue.
- If the plan covers all of the highly compensated employees, an additional 30 percent of the (nonexcludable) nonhighly compensated employees can be excluded.
- Any HCE can be excluded from coverage.

In addition, if the plan does exclude some of the highly compensated, fewer nonhighly compensated employees have to be covered under the plan.

Example: Loophole, Inc. has 10 employees (who are not excludables). Two are highly compensated and 8 are not. If the employer establishes a defined-contribution plan that covers one highly compensated employee, only 35 percent, or 3, of the nonhighly compensated employees have to be covered. This is because under the ratio test, 70 percent of the percentage of highly compensated employees covered (50 percent), equals 35 percent.

As you can see, the ratio test allows the exclusion of a significant number of rank-and-file employees when some of the highly compensated employees are excluded from the plan. This rule can be effective for small businesses when some of the highly compensated are not interested in participating in the plan because they are very young, very old, or not interested for other reasons.

One important limitation applies to the rules described above. The Age Discrimination in Employment Act (ADEA) prohibits discrimination against individuals aged 40 and older. To avoid problems under this act (and possibly other, state laws) a plan provision excluding a group of employees from a qualified plan should be based on a reasonable (and real) job classification. For example, the plan may exclude hourly employees, secretaries, associate attorneys, or other job classification. It is a good idea to seek the advice of a labor or employment lawyer when addressing this specific issue.

Coverage of Employees in Comparable Plans

As described above, each plan sponsored by the employer must satisfy the Sec. 410(b) minimum coverage requirements. Also defined-benefit plans must satisfy the requirements of Sec. 401(a)(26). There are several meaningful exceptions to these rules. First, if the employer excludes all highly compensated employees the plan can cover any group of nonhighly compensated employees, without regard to either coverage rule. This rule allows for tremendous design freedom. This approach could be used by an employer that decided to provide retirement benefits for executives through a nonqualified arrangement, and wanted a qualified plan for only a small portion of the nonhighly compensated workforce.

Another option under Sec. 410(b) is to aggregate two plans for purposes of testing whether the coverage requirements are met. Under this option, if the employer wishes to establish two plans for separate groups of employees, and the plans will not meet the coverage requirements on their own, they can generally be aggregated and tested together, as long as the total benefits provided (looking at the plans as one) do not discriminate in favor of the highly compensated. How this works will be clearer after reading the next chapter, which explains the nondiscrimination requirements. Note, however, that the aggregation rules do not apply to the Sec. 401(a)(26) minimum participation rule. In other words, a defined-benefit plan (that covers at least one highly compensated employee) will always have to cover the lesser of 50 employees or 40 percent of the workforce.

In total, you can see that the coverage rules are really quite flexible, especially in the case of an employer that wishes to have numerous plans that cover different groups of employees. There are a number of ways to demonstrate compliance with the coverage rules in this case. And as described above, even the employer that wants to have a single plan that excludes some employees will have more freedom to do so than you might first suspect.

WHEN SHOULD PARTICIPATION BEGIN?

Once you and your client have decided which employees should and must be covered, the next step is to decide when an employee's participation should begin. In general, participation can be delayed for certain employees on the basis of their ages and their years of service with the company.

There are several reasons to delay participation as long as legally possible. For one thing, employees don't start earning benefits until they become plan participants (except in defined-benefit plans, which may count service with the employer prior to the participation date for benefit purposes), and by delaying participation the client's organization can save retirement dollars attributable to turnover. A second cost-saving feature of delayed participation involves the administrative and record-keeping duties associated with tracking employees who leave. Since turnover is highest for employees in their first few years of employment and for younger employees, it makes sense from an administrative standpoint to delay their participation in the plan. Besides, if the retirement plan is funded with individual insurance policies, the employer loses out on funds that provided death benefits and the commissions paid for benefits for employees who leave (the front-end load).

There are, on the other hand, some good reasons to begin participation immediately. These include maximizing contributions for employees by not delaying coverage and attracting specialized employees by making the plan highly competitive. These specialized employees (such as a computer whiz or high-powered salesperson) usually possess highly desired skills or profit-making ability, and any delay in participation may make the plan's benefit package less desirable to them.

If your client's circumstances warrant immediate participation, then the plan should be designed appropriately. But even under such circumstances, the client must still adhere to the statutory participation rules. In general, any employee who is not excluded from the plan based upon employment classification must become a participant no later than the first entry date after the employee meets the age and service requirements of the plan. The maximum age and service requirements are age 21 and one year of service (commonly referred to as the 21-and-one rule), so after an employee becomes 21 and has garnered one year of service, he or she will be entitled to join the plan on the next plan entry date.

The 2-Year/100 Percent Rule

One exception applies to the general 21-and-one rule—a special provision that allows up to a 2-year service requirement if the employee is immediately 100 percent vested upon becoming a participant (called the 2-year/100 percent rule). This method is desirable if the company's vesting schedules are already as liberal as the 2-year/100 percent schedule and your client desires to delay participation as long as possible. If your client wants a more restrictive vesting schedule and also desires to delay participation, however, you will have to determine which carries more weight—the maximum-service requirement or the restrictive vesting schedules.

Entry Date

The last choice associated with when plan participation must and should begin is the selection of an entry date for employees to become participants in the plan. An employee who meets the minimum age and service requirements of the plan, and who is otherwise eligible to participate in the plan, must be allowed to participate no later than the earlier of (1) the first day of the first plan year beginning after the date the employee met the age and service requirements or (2) the date 6 months after these conditions are met. In other words, entry dates can delay participation up to 6 months after the 21-and-one or 2-year/100 percent hurdles are jumped. For clients who desire to delay participation as long as possible, semiannual entry dates should be set up, typically January 1 and July 1. This way the employer will stretch out the preparticipation period as long as possible. Other typical entry dates include the anniversary date of the plan (this can be used only if the age requirement is not more than 20 1/2 and the service requirement is 6 months or less), quarterly entry dates, monthly entry dates, and daily entry dates.

Determining Service

The term *year of service* has a special meaning for purposes of meeting the one-year-of-service or 2-years-of-service eligibility requirements. An employee who works 1,000 hours during the initial 12-month period after being employed will earn a year of service. For example, Larry is hired on October 5, 1996. If Larry has worked at least 1,000 hours or more by October 4, 1997, he has acquired a year of service. Note that Larry does not receive a year of service after he worked his 1,000th hour but on his first anniversary of employment.

The phrase *an hour of service* also has a special meaning; it includes not only the hours an employee works, but also any hours an employee is entitled to be paid for, such as vacations, holidays, and illness time. One way to compute the hours for purposes of the 1,000-hour requirement is to count each hour an employee works for which he or she is entitled to be paid (the standard-hours counting method).

**YOUR FINANCIAL SERVICES PRACTICE:
THE ELIGIBILITY AND PARTICIPATION RULES IN A SAMPLE
ADOPTION AGREEMENT**

The following sample illustrates how the rules might appear in a typical adoption agreement (note that terms whose first letter is capitalized are defined in the plan):

Section B: Eligibility (refers to Section 2 of the plan)

(1) The Age and Service requirements for participation in the Plan are

    (a) Attainment of age ___ (not to exceed 21)

    (b) Completion of ___ Year(s) of Service (not to exceed one year, unless the Plan provides Full and Immediate Vesting (Section G). (If the Plan provides for Full and Immediate Vesting, it is not to exceed 2 years.)

(2) The Plan's Entry Date will be (check one)

    ( ) daily
    ( ) the Friday in any calendar week
    ( ) the first day of any calendar month
    ( ) quarterly (Jan. 1, April 1, July 1, Oct. 1)
    ( ) semiannually (Jan. 1, July 1)
    ( ) annually (Jan. 1) (Note: If the entry date is annually then the Age requirement in Section B(1)(a) cannot exceed 20 1/2 and the Service requirement in Section B(1)(b) cannot be more than 6 months.)

(3) Hours of Service shall be determined on the basis of the method selected below. The method selected shall be applied to all Employees covered under the Plan. (Check one)

    ( ) On the basis of actual hours for which an Employee is paid or entitled to payment.

    ( ) On the basis of days worked. An Employee shall be credited with 10 Hours of Service if under Section 19 of the Plan such Employee would be credited with at least one Hour of Service during the day.

    ( ) On the basis of weeks worked. An Employee shall be credited with 45 Hours of Service if under Section 19 of the Plan such Employee would be credited with at least one Hour of Service during the week.

    ( ) On the basis of semimonthly payroll periods. An Employee shall be credited with 95 Hours of Service if under Section 19 of the Plan such Employee would be credited with at least one Hour of Service during the semimonthly payroll period.

    ( ) On the basis of months worked. An Employee shall be credited with 190 Hours of Service if under Section 19 of the Plan such Employee would be credited with at least one Hour of Service during the month.

Since the standard-hours counting method can be administratively cumbersome, the IRC permits some alternative counting methods—called equivalencies—to be used. However, in choosing an equivalency the employer will pay a premium of extra hours for using this administratively convenient system. Therefore another aspect of plan design is helping your client choose the best alternative. The equivalencies include the following:

- The elapsed-time method, which does not look at the hours of service worked because service is measured from date of employment to date of severance. For example, if Barbara starts working on January 18, she would have one year of service on the following January 18 regardless of how many hours she actually worked.

- The hours-worked-including-overtime method, which looks at the actual hours worked including overtime but excluding nonworked hours such as vacation, holidays, and sick time. If this test is used, an employee needs to work only 870 hours to earn a year of service.

- The hours-worked-excluding-overtime method, which looks at the actual hours worked excluding overtime, vacations, holidays, and sick time. If this is used, an employee needs only 750 hours for a year of service.

- The time-period or pay-period method, which looks at the days, weeks, semimonthly pay periods, months, or shifts actually worked by the employee and applies the following equivalencies:

  - a credit of 10 hours of service per day if the employee worked one hour in any day
  - a credit of 45 hours of service per week if the employee worked one hour in any week
  - a credit of 95 hours of service for semimonthly pay period if the employee worked one hour in any pay period
  - a credit of 190 hours per month if the employee worked one hour in any month
  - a credit of the number of hours per shift if the employee worked one hour in any shift

- The equivalencies-based-on-earnings method, which calculates the hours worked on the basis of the employee's earnings. For example, if the employee is paid hourly, the equivalency can be determined by dividing the employee's total earnings by the hourly wage. (If the hourly wage changed over a period, the employer should look at the actual hourly wage, or the lowest hourly wage during the period, or the lowest hourly wage paid to employees in the same or similar job classification during that period.) If the employee's earnings are not based on hourly rates, the hourly rate is calculated by translating the employee's salary into an hourly rate—for example, by dividing annual salary by a 40-hour week or 8-hour day.

The choice of an equivalency boils down to two disparate considerations. The first is administrative convenience. By coordinating the hours of service with payroll's records the employer may be able to use an existing computer or accounting system and eliminate duplication of work efforts. The second and more important concern when choosing an hour-of-service definition is to permanently exclude part-time employees from the plan. This can result in substantial savings for your client and, what's more, it will not prejudice your client when the coverage rules are applied because part-time employees (with less than 1,000 hours of service) are generally not counted for purposes of the 401(a)(4), 410(b)(1), or 401(a)(26) tests. If your client's desire is to exclude part-time employees, as is usually the case, then it is likely that the standard-hours counting method should be used in lieu of any equivalency (note that all equivalency methods generously define the hours used). To make sure that part-time employees don't slip in under these rules—complicating administration of the plan—the employer may want to establish a policy limiting the number of hours part-time employees can work.

CASE STUDY:
THE MATTHEW MATT MANUFACTURING COMPANY

The Matthew Matt Manufacturing Company, makers of wrestling mats, employs 75 full-time employees and 15 part-time employees. Matthew Matt is establishing a qualified plan and is trying to determine the appropriate eligibility and participation provisions. He desires to minimize costs, encourage rank-and-file employees to stay (experienced mat makers are hard to find), and exclude the part-time employees from the plan. In addition, Matthew tells you that a competitive wrestling mat company is forming in the area. The relevant questions the financial services professional must address are these:

- Should participation be delayed and, if so, for how long?
- What definition of hour of service should be used?
- What entry date should be used?

In answer to the first question, Matthew Matt should delay participation as a cost-saving measure. When a plan is installed in an existing business, however, the employer must take into account the service already acquired (preplan service) for eligibility purposes. In this case, to placate employees who might jump to the competitor, the plan will count preplan service.

How long Matthew delays participation—which could be for one or 2 years, the statutory maximums—would depend on his decision about vesting and his perception of the competitive threat.

Since Matthew wants to exclude part-time employees to the full extent possible, the company will choose the most restrictive method for determining whether the 1,000-hours-of-service requirement has been met. This is generally the standard-hours counting method. However, if Matthew uses his part-time employees seasonally (for 2 months during wrestling season) and needs them for overtime during that period, then the most restrictive method might be the hours-worked-excluding-overtime method. This method looks at the actual hours worked and excludes overtime, the Christmas holidays (which fall in wrestling season), sick time, and the like.

When choosing an entry date, considerations such as administrative convenience and employee morale also come into play. Since employee morale is most important in light of the threat of competition, it will probably be desirable to choose a less restrictive entry date that matches administrative pay practices—monthly, for example.

OTHER TAX-SHELTERED RETIREMENT PLANS

While the eligibility and participation requirements for qualified plans are quite flexible, this is not the case for SEPs and SIMPLEs. The rules here are quite rigid. The same eligibility requirements that apply to qualified plans apply to 403(b) plans, as well as an additional requirement that applies to salary deferral elections. Also note that the aggregation rules discussed in this chapter apply when performing the coverage tests for 403(b) plans, SEPs, and SIMPLEs.

SEPs

As described in chapter 6, any individual (not subject to a collective bargaining agreement) who is aged 21 and has earned $400 (1997 indexed amount) in three of the five previous plan years must be a participant as of the first day of the following plan year. Take, for example, an individual who meets the $400 requirement in 1994, 1995, and 1996 and works for a company that maintains a SEP on a calendar-year basis. That person must become a participant as of January 1, 1997.

Under these inflexible requirements, all long-term employees—even part-timers—must be covered under the plan. This causes problems for larger employers that may want to establish separate plans for different groups of employees and employers with a significant number of part-time employees. Finally, note that nothing in the SEP rules stops an employer from establishing less restrictive eligibility requirements.

SIMPLEs

Similar to the SEP, SIMPLEs have totally inflexible coverage requirements. The rules, however, are different from both the qualified plan and the SEP requirements. Under the new statute, it does not appear that the SIMPLE can exclude employees under the age of 21. The SIMPLE must cover any employee who earned $5,000 in two previous calendar years and is reasonably expected to earn $5,000 again in current year. Employees subject to a collectively bargained agreement can be excluded. SIMPLEs can be maintained only on a calendar-year basis. And all employees become eligible to participate as of the January 1 after they have earned $5,000 in two prior years. Essentially, SEPs have a 3-year wait, while SIMPLEs have a 2 year waiting period.

403(b) Plans

If a 403(b) plan includes employer contributions (that are not related to a salary reduction agreement), the plan must satisfy the 410(b) requirement discussed earlier in this chapter. An additional coverage rule applies to 403(b) plan salary deferral elections. Essentially any employee who can contribute $200 or more must be given the option to make a salary deferral election. Exceptions are made for employees who normally work fewer than 20 hours per week and employees eligible to make salary deferral elections to other types of plans, including 401(k) and 457 plans.

8

Designing Benefit Formulas and Employee Contributions

Chapter Outline

PRELIMINARY CONCERNS

When designing the benefit structure in a qualified plan or 403(b) plan, the rules provide for a substantial degree of discretion. The primary limitation is Code Sec. 401(a)(4), which provides that benefits cannot discriminate in favor of highly compensated employees. In this context the definition of highly compensated is the same as described in previous chapters. In this chapter we will review the nondiscrimination rules and explore its boundaries.

First, we will give an overview of the nondiscrimination rules. Next we will review some concepts relevant to a discussion of nondiscrimination, and then discuss the specific impact on defined-contribution and defined-benefit plans. Finally, we will compare these rules to the allocation rules that apply to SEPs and SIMPLEs.

Nondiscrimination Rules

All qualified plans (and 403(b) plans) must be designed to satisfy the rule that a plan cannot discriminate in favor of highly compensated employees (HCEs) with regard to benefits or contributions. The requirements are satisfied if either the contributions or the benefits are nondiscriminatory. Under the statutory language contained in IRC Sec. 401(a)(4), a plan will be deemed nondiscriminatory if contributions or benefits bear a uniform relationship to compensation. For instance, if in a defined-contribution plan, contributions are allocated so that all participants receive a contribution of 3 percent of the current year's total compensation, the plan is not discriminatory. If the plan is a defined-benefit plan, and each participant earns an accrued benefit of 2 percent of compensation for the current year of service, the plan will also be deemed nondiscriminatory.

The more interesting question is to what extent the plan can deviate from the uniform percentage of compensation rule without being considered discriminatory. Ever since the enactment of ERISA, one form of discrimination has been allowed: the plan can have benefits that integrate with social security. Essentially this allows a plan to discriminate in favor of the highly compensated employees to make up for the fact that the social security system discriminates against them. However, for many years it was unclear what else could be done, since no regulations clarified the general statutory language. Due to the lack of guidance, designing any other type of formula was risky. Since 1993, when the IRS issued almost 200 pages of final regulations, the situation has changed drastically. The regulations were quite helpful, since they

- establish objective criteria for determining whether a plan violates the nondiscrimination requirement
- clarify that a plan can demonstrate that it is not discriminatory by showing that its contributions or benefits are not discriminatory
- establish several safe harbor methods for determining whether the plan satisfies the nondiscrimination standards
- create general tests for testing a plan that chooses not to adopt one of the design safe harbors

Now, with regulations that contain clear, objective, rules, a plan can determine at any time whether or not it is in compliance with the nondiscrimination standards, and if the employer is willing to do some testing, the plan design can really be quite creative.

After reviewing some preliminary issues, we will more fully discuss just what these regulations allow defined-contribution and defined-benefit plans to do.

Accrued Benefits

One key concept under the nondiscrimination rules is that discrimination is tested based on the benefit provided for that year, not the overall benefit provided under the plan. When discussing the total benefit that a participant has earned under a plan up to the present time, this amount is referred to as the participant's *accrued benefit.* This is in contrast to the benefit that will be provided at retirement ,which is referred to (at any time prior to retirement) as the *projected benefit.* The amount earned for the current year is simply referred to as the accrued benefit for the year.

In a defined-contribution plan, the participant's accrued benefit at any point is the participant's present account balance. The accrual for the specific year is the amount contributed to the plan on the employee's behalf for that year.

In a defined-benefit plan, the concept is the same. The accrued benefit is the benefit earned to date, using current salary and years of service. The accrued benefit earned for the year is the additional benefit that has been earned based upon the current year's salary and service.

A number of complex rules apply to the way benefits accrue under a plan. This is due to the fact that before ERISA was enacted, a participant would often be entitled to no benefit until he or she hit normal retirement age after, say, 30 years of employment. In this case, the entire benefit was essentially earned in the final year. This was called backloading the benefit. ERISA imposed rules to prohibit backloading. For example, under the rules, a plan's benefit formula could not be written to say that an individual earns a benefit of one percent of final average compensation times years of service for the first 10 years of service and 2 percent of final average compensation for service in excess of 10 years. This would be a prohibited backloading.

Permissible methods of determining a participant's accrued benefit are complex, and are well understood by pension actuaries working with defined-benefit plans. At the same time, most plans accrue benefits using one of two permissible accrual methods. Therefore, instead of going through the rules, the material below briefly discusses the two common accrual methods. If you were to see a benefit accrual method that was different, you might want to discuss the issue with the plan's actuary.

As discussed in chapter 4, the most common benefit formula in a defined-benefit plan today is the unit benefit formula. In most cases, under this formula, the accrued benefit is determined by applying the formula based on the current salary and service.

Example: The Average Corporation has a retirement benefit formula of 1.5 percent of final average compensation times years of service.

Normal retirement age is 65. Joe started employment at age 30. At age 40, after 10 years of service, Joe's accrued benefit is 15 percent of his final average compensation—based on his salary history to date. He has accrued a benefit of 1.5 percent of final average compensation for the current year. His projected retirement benefit is 45 percent of final average compensation, since he will have earned 30 years of service if he continues working until normal retirement age.

The second method of accruing benefits is referred to as the fractional method. This approach is generally used when the plan's benefit formula is a flat percentage of final average compensation (for example, 40 percent of final average compensation). Under this rule, you divide the participant's years of participation in the plan by the total number of years of participation until normal retirement age, and then multiply that by the employee's projected monthly retirement benefit:

$$\frac{\text{years of participation}}{\substack{\text{years of participation to} \\ \text{normal retirement age}}} \times \substack{\text{projected monthly} \\ \text{benefit at normal} \\ \text{retirement aage}} = \text{accrued benefit}$$

Example: Leo DiVinci, who joined the firm at age 25, is now 35 and has worked 10 years under the plan; he can retire at age 65 after 40 years of plan participation. Leo's accrued benefit is 1/4 (10 years of actual participation over 40 years of projected participation) of his monthly retirement benefit at normal retirement age, which is projected to be $800. Therefore Leo's accrued benefit is $200 a month at age 65, or its actuarial equivalent in a lump sum.

$$\frac{10}{40} \times \$800 = \$200$$

Calculating Service

In chapter 4, we began to discuss the implications of the definition of service for purposes of determining the participant's benefit in a defined-benefit plan. There is one additional concern that is important to consider. Similar to the eligibility and vesting rules, there are minimum service requirements for determining whether the participant is entitled to earn a year of service under the plan. In a defined-benefit plan a participant is not typically credited with a year of service if he or she has 1,000 hours of service (as is the requirement with the eligibility and vesting rules). In a defined-benefit plan a year of service can be defined for benefit purposes in a variety of ways, as long as the definition of a year of service

- is applied on a reasonable and consistent basis
- does not require more hours of service than are customarily rendered during a work year in the industry involved
- accrues benefits for less than full-time service on at least a pro rata basis
- gives participants with 1,000 hours at least a partial year of service (For certain industries that customarily work for seasonal or nontraditional years, 1,000 hours must garner a full year of service.)

This last requirement means that unlike the rules that apply to eligibility and vesting, the plan can actually require up to 2,000 hours of service before a full benefit is accrued.

Example: The ABC Corporation is in an industry that typically works a 2,000-hour year. The ABC Corporation can meet the benefit service requirements if it provides

- no years of service for participants with less than 1,000 hours of service
- a full year of service for participants with 2,000 hours of service
- a partial year of service (decided on a pro rata basis) for participants with 1,000–1,999 hours of service (For example, if James has 1,000 hours of service, he shall be credited with half a year's service—2,000 maximum hours divided by 1,000 actual hours.)

By designing the benefit formula to give no benefit credit to participants with less than 1,000 hours of service and only a partial year's credit to participants with under 2,000 hours of service, the employer has saved benefits costs that would have otherwise provided a full benefit for a part-time employee. On the other hand, if part-time employees are a valuable commodity, the employer may want to change the benefit formula to give a year of service for all employees, regardless of hours of service.

In a defined-contribution plan, contributions must be made for participants who earn 1,000 hours of service for the year. This means that an individual can become eligible to participate, receive an allocation for one year, and, if he or she then goes part-time, may not be eligible for contributions in subsequent years. There is an exception. Participants who terminate employment before the last day of the year can be excluded from receiving a contribution for the year, even if they have earned 1,000 hours of service. However, if such persons are excluded, they are also not considered participants under the minimum coverage requirements. Therefore having a last-day requirement means that the employer could have trouble passing the coverage tests if a significant number of employees terminate employment before the end of the year.

In either a defined-contribution or a defined-benefit plan, hours of service may be determined by using the standard-hours counting method (each hour actually worked is counted, plus hours for which the employee is entitled to be paid, such as vacations and holidays) or by using one of the equivalency methods discussed earlier. The definition of hour of service for contribution or benefit purposes can be different from the definitions used for eligibility or vesting purposes.

Compensation for Benefit-Formula Purposes

When looking at the plan's benefit or contribution formula, benefits are based, in part, on how compensation is defined in the plan. The definition of compensation can include or exclude overtime, bonuses, and other nonrecurring compensation. In the small-plan market, the plan should be designed with a liberal definition of compensation in order to maximize the amount of contributions or benefits (tax shelter) that can be made. In larger, nonintegrated plans, employers typically ask you to use the definition of compensation that best suits the company's goals. One caveat, however: the IRS will monitor the compensation that's being considered and will not permit discrimination to occur. For example, if executives are the only employees who receive bonuses and rank-and-file employees are the only ones who work overtime, a definition of compensation that includes bonuses but not overtime will be considered discriminatory. Within the nondiscriminatory limits, however, there is some room to design your definition of compensation to provide for the objectives of your client. As you will see when we begin discussing some of the safe harbor design alternatives, the IRS requires an inclusive definition of compensation. Choosing another definition may be legal but could require that the sponsor perform annual nondiscrimination testing.

Compensation Cap

A second rule relating to compensation is that the annual compensation considered in the benefit or contribution formula is limited to a maximum amount. In 1993 the amount was limited to $235,840 for any participant. The law was changed, however, for plan years beginning in 1994. The limit was lowered to $150,000. To show the impact of the lower cap, take, for example, a money-purchase plan that provided annual employer contributions of 10 percent of compensation. In 1993, under that plan, an employee earning $400,000 would receive an annual contribution of $23,584, because only the first $235,840 of compensation could be considered for benefit-formula purposes. In 1994, the same participant only received $15,000, with the lower compensation cap.

As you can see, this limit has a major impact on the benefits of employees earning more than the cap. Note that the cap applies both for determining contributions or benefits and for performing the nondiscrimination test. The cap is raised for cost-of-living increases; and as of 1997 the cap is $160,000. The impact of the cap will be discussed more fully below.

Amending Benefit Formulas

The process of plan amendment is typically thought of in conjunction with changes mandated by legislative reform and changes necessitated by unforeseen business developments. There is, however, a plan-design strategy that works just the opposite way and anticipates the periodic upgrading of the benefit formula. The technique used to accomplish this strategy is sometimes known as *updating*. Clients may desire the updating technique for a variety of reasons, including the following:

- A gradual benefit upgrade may satisfy the employer's benefit objective of consistently improving the employee benefits package. Some employers feel that periodic movement in the employee benefits package is necessary in order to retain employees.
- Employers may be skeptical of funding unknown plan costs and may desire to ease into the plan commitment slowly.
- An employer with erratic cash flow may set up a manageable benefit formula that will gradually be increased as cash flow stabilizes, as opposed to adopting a discretionary profit-sharing plan.

There are many ways to upgrade the benefit formula, ranging from increasing contributions in a money-purchase plan from 5 to 7 percent, to the complex procedure of setting up a career-average defined-benefit formula and then, after the plan has been in existence for awhile, doing a cost calculation that funds for past service (service from the inception of the plan, not service prior to the inception of the plan). When the latter method is used, your client has the advantage of funding a known amount. (*Planning Note:* Keep the updating techniques in mind, not only for your existing clients, but also for use as an excellent prospecting tool.)

The primary legal restriction on plan amendments is the anti-cutback rule. Essentially, the rule provides that benefits that already accrued cannot be taken away from the participant. Several years ago the anti-cutback rules were expanded to include other aspects of the participant's benefit, such as the form of benefit payment. Congress considered the form of payment to be an essential part of the benefit promise. For example, if the plan allows benefits to be paid as a life annuity or as a single sum, the plan cannot be amended to take away the single-sum form of payment.

The anti-cutback rules do not, however, prohibit amending the benefit formula on a prospective basis. This applies both to the actual benefit formula and the form of payments.

DEFINED-CONTRIBUTION PLANS

The nondiscrimination rules apply (with the exception of the target benefit plan) in essentially the same manner for all types of defined-contribution plans. First we will discuss three major allocation approaches that are used today: contributions as a level percentage of compensation, integration with social security, and cross-testing. Then we will apply these concepts to specific types of plans.

Level Percentage of Compensation

As mentioned above, the nondiscrimination regulations offer several methods for determining whether the plan satisfies the nondiscrimination rules. One method is to satisfy a safe harbor test that is completely design based. That is, if the plan design fits within the specified safe harbor design, the plan will be deemed to satisfy the nondiscrimination test. To satisfy the basic defined-contribution plan design safe harbor, the plan must

- have a uniform normal retirement age and vesting schedule applicable to all employees, and
- group all employer contributions and forfeitures for the plan year under a single, uniform formula that allocates the same percentage of compensation or the same dollar amount to every participant

This formula is often chosen. In larger companies, a plan that provides the same benefits to everyone is easy to administer and explain. If larger benefits are to be provided for the executives, they are provided in a nonqualified environment. Small employers also choose this approach, sometimes for the same reason and other times because simply because this allocation formula is offered as an option in a prototype plan, and the owner (and unfortunately sometimes the adviser) does not fully understand other options. In today's qualified plan environment, the small employer should, even in a simple profit-sharing plan, be making an informed choice between the level percentage of pay, integration with social security, and cross-testing methods.

Integration with Social Security

Before discussing any of the newer, more exotic methods of skewing contributions in favor of the highly compensated employees, let's review an older, basic one: developing a plan that integrates with social security. Under this approach, the employer essentially gets to make larger contributions for those individuals who earn more than the taxable wage base. This is allowed because under the social security system, the employer does not make contributions (pay taxes) on earnings in excess of the wage base. In this way, social security actually discriminates against the highly compensated. This disparity can be made up to a certain extent under a qualified plan using the methods described below.

Both money-purchase and profit-sharing plans can use this method, although if an employer sponsors both types of plans only one plan can have a fully integrated formula. If a defined-contribution plan formula is integrated with social security, contributions may be higher (as a percentage of compensation) for those employees who earn more than a specified integration level. If the integration level is set at the current taxable wage base ($65,400 for 1997), HCEs may receive up to 5.7 percent of compensation in excess of the taxable wage base, as long as the employer makes contributions equaling at least 5.7 percent of total compensation.

> *Example:* Justin, Inc., establishes a money-purchase pension plan that provides for a contribution of 5.7 percent of compensation plus 5.7 percent of compensation in excess of the taxable wage base. Justin, the owner, earns $200,000. The contribution made on his behalf is $14,512. This is 5.7 percent of $160,000 (the maximum allowable compensation) ($9,120) plus 5.7 percent of $160,000 minus $65,400, which equals $5,392.

If the employer cannot afford to contribute at least 5.7 percent of compensation across the board, the maximum disparity will be reduced. Under the rules, the integrated portion cannot exceed the contribution that is based on total compensation. This means that if 4 percent is contributed based on total salary, an additional 4 percent can be contributed based on compensation in excess of the integration level.

Under the rules, the integration level cannot exceed the taxable wage base. The integration level can be lower, but this generally reduces the maximum disparity allowed. Table 8-1 below shows the required reductions. The reason for the reduction is to take away the advantage of setting the integration level just above the compensation level of the highest rank-and-file employee.

> *Example*: Bakery, Inc., rank-and-file workers earn a maximum of $30,000. The owner, Mr. Crueler, earns more than $160,000. He might want to consider setting the level at $30,000 (instead of the taxable wage base—$65,400 in 1997) to maximize the integrated contribution on his own behalf.

Even though the required reductions are supposed to take away the advantage of lowering the integration level, it may be worth running the numbers to see what happens in a particular situation. Let's look at our example above. Since $30,000 is between 20 percent and 80 percent of the 1997 taxable wage base, the maximum disparity is reduced to 4.3 percent. Comparing the two integration levels, the maximum integrated portion using the $30,000 integration level is $5,590 ($160,000 − $30,000 x 4.3 percent) while the maximum integrated portion using the taxable wage base (in 1997) is $ $5,392 ($160,000 – $65,400 x 5.7 percent). In this case there is a slight, but not significant, benefit for setting the integration level at $30,000. However, next year, rank-and-file employees' salaries might go up and the integration level would need to be changed. In most cases the "game is not worth the hunt," and the integration level should simply be set at the then-current taxable wage base.

TABLE 8-1	
Maximum Integration Disparity Using Different Integration Levels	
Integration Level	Maximum Disparity Allowed
Taxable Wage Base (TWB)	5.7%
Below the TWB but at least 80% of the TWB	5.4%
Below 80% of the TWB but at least 20% of the TWB.	4.3%
Below 20% of the TWB	5.7%*

*Note that the maximum disparity bounces back to 5.7% with a very low integration level. This is because at very low levels the rank-file employees will also be receiving a contribution based on salary above the integration level.

Choosing the Integrated Formula

Before 1994, integrated plans worked quite well as a method of skewing contributions toward the highly compensated employees. Unfortunately, the Omnibus Budget Reconciliation Act of 1993, which reduced the compensation cap from $235,840 to $150,000, effective for plan years beginning in 1994, drastically limited the effectiveness of the integrated plan. For example, in 1993, when the cap on compensation was $235,840 the maximum integrated portion for an individual earning that amount was $10,160 (5.7 percent of $178,240, which is $235,840 minus the 1993 taxable wage base of $57,600). In 1994 the maximum integrated portion for the same person dropped to $5,096 (5.7 percent of $89,400, which is $150,000 minus $60,600, the 1994 taxable wage base). One result of this change was that in 1993, a plan could be designed that allocated $30,000 to the business owner (earning at least $235,840) while allocating just 8.4 percent of compensation for all employees earning less than the taxable wage base ($57,600 in 1993). With the $150,000 compensation cap, allocating $30,000 to that same business owner in 1994 required a contribution of 16.6 percent of compensation for the rank and file—double the 1993 amount! As of 1997, the situation is essentially the same as in 1994. Even though the compensation cap went up to $160,000 in 1997, the taxable wage base has moved up as well, offsetting any advantage of the higher compensation cap.

Today, if the business owner's goal is maximizing disparity, he or she should consider the cross-tested allocation formula described below. However, as you will see, these are complex plans that have some extra administrative costs. As an alternative, the integrated plan provides some disparity without much complication. A plan may be adopted using a standardized prototype plan document. This means that the inexpensive standardized plans sponsored by many insurance companies and other service providers can be adopted at little expense. Also, a plan can be designed to fit within the safe harbor, ensuring ongoing satisfaction of the nondiscrimination regulations without annual testing.

The compensation cap has created another reason for using an integrated formula. Some small business owners are perfectly happy to establish a plan that allocates the same percentage of compensation for each participant (such as 3, 4, or 5 percent of compensation). However, today, if the owner earns more than $160,000, the contribution on behalf of the owner with this type of formula will actually result in a smaller amount (as a percentage of pay) than for other employees.

> *Example*: Mr. Nice Guy wants to contribute 5 percent of compensation for each employee. If he earns $250,000, the contribution on his behalf will actually be 3.65 percent of compensation! That is because 5 percent of $160,000 equals a contribution of only $9,120 for the owner. A $9,120 contribution is only 3.65 percent of $250,000.

For this reason, today the same business owner might consider the integrated formula simply to make up for the loss associated with the $160,000 compensation cap.

Cross-testing

If the employer does not want to use a contribution or allocation formula that fits within one of the design safe harbors, virtually any other formula can be adopted as long as, on an annual basis, the plan can demonstrate compliance with the general nondiscrimination test. This can be done in one of two ways— either by testing contributions made to the plan on behalf of each participant, or testing benefits that can be provided from contributions and forfeitures made for the year. Testing benefits in a defined-contribution plan is referred to as *cross-testing*. It requires converting allocations into equivalent life annuity benefit amounts using the methodology described in the regulations. Once these allocations have been converted, the general test is then performed, using benefit accrual rates based on those annuity amounts expressed as a percentage of compensation.

In the most practical terms the regulations allow discrimination in favor of older workers since it takes a larger contribution to buy a specific benefit for an older worker than it does to buy the same benefit for a younger worker. This is a powerful concept, and the regulations are really quite flexible. An employer that decides to go the cross-testing route must understand the following:

- *Mathematical test*—On an annual basis the administrator must perform a test to demonstrate compliance with the nondiscrimination rules.
- *Retroactive compliance*—Even if the test is not satisfied, the plan can be amended—increasing benefits for the nonhighly compensated employees—to the extent necessary to satisfy the test.
- *Additional expense*—Plan documents, IRS determination letters, and annual administration will be somewhat higher for a cross-tested plan.

The simplest method to satisfy the general test is to allocate the contributions and forfeitures in such a way that, after conversion to a defined-benefit accrual, the rate of accrual is the same for each participant. In this way, the general nondiscrimination test will always be satisfied, without further testing. This type of allocation formula is referred to as an *age-weighted formula.*

Example: Consider a plan with three participants. Susan is aged 50 and earns $150,000 a year. Her employees, Ralph and Paula, ages 35 and 28 respectively, each earn $30,000 per year. Also assume that the employer wants to contribute the maximum deductible contribution of $31,500 (15 percent of $210,000 total compensation). In order to determine the appropriate allocation formula that will result in a uniform benefit accrual for each participant, take the following steps:

- The first step is to determine how much would have to be contributed for the year in order to provide a monthly benefit at age 65 equal to 1 percent of each participant's compensation. One percent of Susan's $150,000 annual (or $12,500 monthly) compensation is $125. One percent of Ralph's and Paula's $30,000 annual (or $2,500 monthly) compensation is $25.
- Next, assume it costs $95.38 (see table 8-2) at age 65 to provide a benefit of $1 per month payable for life. Susan would then need $125 x $95.38 = $11,922, and Ralph and Paula each would need $25 x $95.38 = $2,384 at age 65 to provide a benefit of one percent of their pay.
- Assuming plan assets earn 8.5 percent, a single contribution of $3,506 today would accumulate after 15 years to the $11,922 that Susan would need at age 65 ($11,922 x .2941; see table 8-3). Similarly, a single contribution of $206 today would accumulate after 30 years to the $2,384 that Ralph will need at age 65, and a single contribution of $117 today would accumulate after 37 years to the $2,384 that Paula will need at age 65.
- Under the age-weighted profit-sharing plan, the actual contribution is discretionary. However much is contributed will be allocated to participants in proportion to the $3,506, $206, and $117 amounts calculated above. Susan receives 91.82 percent of the total contribution, Ralph receives 5.40 percent of the contribution, and Paula receives the remaining 2.78 percent of the contribution.

- In this example, if an age-weighted allocation method was adopted, the maximum deductible contribution would be $31,500 (15 percent of the $210,000 covered payroll). Table 8-4 shows how this $31,500 contribution is allocated under an age-weighted profit-sharing plan.

Table 8-2
Annuity Purchase Factors

1984 UP Mortality Table 8.5% Interest

Age	Amount to Purchase $1 Monthly Annuity	Age	Amount to Purchase $1 Monthly Annuity
55	115.0104	63	99.7222
56	113.3069	64	97.5720
57	111.5413	65	95.3829
58	109.7158	66	93.1640
59	107.8336	67	90.9263
60	105.8896	68	88.6669
61	103.8869	69	86.3737
62	101.8294	70	84.0346

Table 8-3
Discount Factor

8.5% Interest

Years before Retirement Age	Discount Factor	Years before Retirement Age	Discount Factor
1	0.921659	23	0.153150
2	0.849455	24	0.141152
3	0.782908	25	0.130094
4	0.721574	26	0.119902
5	0.665045	27	0.110509
6	0.612945	28	0.101851
7	0.564926	29	0.093872
8	0.520669	30	0.086518
9	0.479880	31	0.079740
10	0.442285	32	0.073493
11	0.407636	33	0.067736
12	0.375702	34	0.062429
13	0.346269	35	0.057539
14	0.319142	36	0.053031
15	0.294140	37	0.048876
16	0.271097	38	0.045047
17	0.249859	39	0.041518
18	0.230285	40	0.038266
19	0.212244	41	0.035268
20	0.195616	42	0.032505
21	0.180292	43	0.029959
22	0.166167	44	0.027612

TABLE 8-4
Age-Weighted Allocation Method

Name	Age	Monthly Earnings	1% Monthly Annuity	Single Sum at 65	Present Value	Allocation Percentage	Allocation of $31,500
Susan	50	$12,500	$125	$11,922	$3,506	91.57%	$28,844
Ralph	35	2,500	25	2,384	206	5.39	1,697
Paula	28	2,500	25	2,384	117	3.04	959

As you can see in the example, with the right census and appropriate employee communications, the age-weighted profit-sharing plan can be an excellent choice. It has all the advantages of the profit-sharing plan, and can result in substantial skewing of the employer's contribution to the key employee(s). In most cases, the plan will pass the annual nondiscrimination test without actual testing, although the plan design will not technically satisfy one of the design safe harbors.

The major problem with the age-weighted formula is that it is contingent upon having the perfect employee census. In the above example, the approach works because the NHCEs are substantially younger than the HCE. Even a single older employee may destroy the intended result. In addition, age weighting is hard to explain, and might cause employee dissatisfaction. In the example above, Paula might have difficulty understanding why Ralph is entitled to a $1,697 allocation, while she receives only $959, since they each earn the same salary.

For these reasons the age-weighted allocation has not become that popular. Also, the more the pension industry has grown to understand the general nondiscrimination test, the opportunities that it provides have become clearer. When working with the general nondiscrimination test, the employer can essentially start with any plan allocation formula—which is then tested against the general nondiscrimination test. This design approach is much more satisfying, since the employer can first create a design that meets its goals, and then analyze whether the design satisfies the test.

For the small employer, this might mean allocating $30,000 (the maximum allocation under the 415 limits) to the highly compensated, and 3 percent of compensation to all other employees (the top-heavy minimum allocation described further in chapter 10). Once the objective has been determined, projected contributions are then translated into an accrued benefit for each employee, which is tested under the general nondiscrimination test. If the plan passes, then the design can be adopted. If not, then the contribution level for the nonhighly compensated can be raised or the contribution for the owners can be lowered until the test is satisfied.

Unfortunately, the actual mechanics of cross-testing are quite complex, and are beyond the scope of this book. However, note that the following objectives can generally be accomplished with a cross-tested plan:

- *Skewing contributions*—When the average age of the businesses owners is 10 years or more older than the nonhighly compensated employees, cross-testing will allow the plan to establish an allocation formula in which the owners receive the maximum allocation allowable under IRC Sec. 415 (the lesser of 25 percent of compensation or $30,000), while the rank-and-file employees receive substantially less—typically 4 or 5 percent of compensation.

- *Older nonhighly compensated employees*—Unlike age-weighting, cross-testing works even with several older nonhighly compensated employees—as long as the average age of the owners is somewhat greater than the average age of the nonhighly compensated.

- *Design flexibility*—One other substantial advantage is the incredible design flexibility allowed under the general test. Often an employer will want to make a larger contribution for a specific group of employees (for example, longer service employees or salespersons). Before these regulations, an employer had little flexibility. Now the opportunities for creative plan designs that meet a number of planning objectives are almost limitless. For example, the employer may decide to contribute 3 percent of pay for new employees, 4 percent for employees with 5 or more years of service, and 5 percent for employees with 10 or more years of service.

Any employer considering a plan with a cross-tested allocation formula must be advised of certain disadvantages. The plan will need to be tested for discrimination on an annual basis. Gathering accurate employee data, especially age information, may be a daunting task. Preliminary testing (at the beginning of the year) and final testing will have to be performed. The plan design may have to change on an annual basis if census data or employee salaries change. For example, the plan may satisfy the rules in year one with a 3 percent allocation for NHCEs, while the next year a 4 percent allocation may be required. A design change must be accompanied by a properly timed plan amendment. A plan sponsor will need to adopt an individually designed plan and will have to request an IRS determination letter under the general nondiscrimination test with a minimum $1,250 filing fee.

Each of these disadvantages ultimately relates to one element: additional cost. The prospective client should be given a clear picture of just what to expect in additional fees. The additional costs will not stop the employer if the savings under the cross-tested plan (compared to an age-weighted or integrated plan) are substantial.

Types of Plans and Nondiscrimination Approaches

Now that we have looked at the nondiscrimination rules in general, let's take a look at the types of choices employers commonly make with specific types of plans.

Profit-Sharing Plans

Profit-sharing plans are designed using all three approaches. Today, almost all employers that have been interested in age-weighting or cross-testing have chosen the versatile profit-sharing plan. Discretionary contributions, in-service withdrawals, and the ability to circumvent the qualified joint and survivor annuity rules (see chapter 10) are meaningful qualities for the small business owner in today's business environment. The major limitation of the profit-sharing plan is its lower contribution limit. The limit is 15 percent of covered payroll as compared to 25 percent for pension plans. However, this limit generally does not get in the way in a cross-tested plan. Even though the plan might allocate the maximum $30,000 to the owner, contributions for other participants will generally be well under 15 percent. In most cases the employer will be able to meet the plan's objectives without running up against the 15 percent limit.

401(k) Plans

Remember that 401(k) plans are profit-sharing plans. If the 401(k) plan has a profit-sharing type contribution, an allocation could be designed that takes advantage of the cross-testing flexibility. Nondiscrimination testing can be confusing in a 401(k) plan because of the different types of contributions allowed and the nondiscrimination rules that apply to different types of contributions. Let's review:

- *Employee salary deferral contributions*—Nondiscrimination is tested solely through the ADP test (see chapter 5). The 401(a)(4) rules do not apply.
- *Employer matching contributions*—Nondiscrimination is tested solely through the ACP test (which is discussed later in this chapter). The 401(a)(4) rules do not apply.
- *Employee after-tax contributions*—Nondiscrimination is tested solely by the ACP test.
- *Employer profit-sharing contributions*—Only these types of contributions must satisfy the nondiscrimination rules of 401(a)(4) discussed in this section.

403(b) Plans

403(b) plans, like 401(k) plans, must be analyzed feature by feature. 403(b) plans are subject to the following discrimination requirements:

- *Employee salary deferral contributions*—Unlike in the 401(k) plan, salary deferrals in a 403(b) plan are not subject to any nondiscrimination requirements.
- *Employer matching contributions*—If the 403(b) plan has a matching contribution, these contributions *do* have to satisfy the ACP test (which is discussed later in this chapter). The 401(a)(4) rules do not apply.
- *Employer nonelective contributions*—If the 403(b) plan has an employer contribution for all eligible employees, these types of contributions must satisfy the nondiscrimination rules of 401(a)(4) discussed in this section. Like profit-sharing plans, the 403(b) plan can use either of the design safe harbors—level percentage of compensation or integrated with social security. The allocation formula also can take advantage of the cross-testing or age-weighted approaches.

Money-Purchase Pension Plans

Even though money-purchase pension plans can take advantage of cross-testing, most employers choosing this allocation approach have chosen profit-sharing plans—where contributions are discretionary. Money-purchase plans more typically contain contributions that are a level percentage of compensation or that are integrated with social security.

Target-Benefit Pension Plans

The contribution formula established under a target-benefit plan could be tested under the general nondiscrimination test. However, the regulations provide a separate design safe harbor for such plans, and employers establishing such a plan will probably want to take advantage of the design safe harbor.

Several threshold issues determine whether a target plan is suited for a particular employer. First, a target plan, like the age-weighted profit-sharing plan, will not work with even a single older NHCE. Second, since the target plan is a pension plan, the employer must be willing to commit to a timely annual contribution. And unlike a defined-benefit plan, the annual contribution is a fixed amount. Finally, the employer must be willing to live with pension plan requirements (including no in-service distributions and the qualified joint and survivor annuity requirements).

Since today an age-weighted profit-sharing plan could be designed to give similar results as in the target-benefit plan, the employer is more likely to choose either the age-weighted or more flexible cross-tested profit-sharing plan. Most employers today are simply not willing to make a commitment to a fixed annual contribution. And for those few who are willing to commit to annual contributions, a defined-benefit plan is often the better choice, due to the flexibility of annual contributions and the ability (in the right circumstances) for the employer to contribute more on the key employee's behalf than in a defined-contribution plan.

SEPs

As you learned in chapter 6, the contribution to a SEP must either be allocated as a level percentage of compensation or integrated with social security (in the manner described above). The SEP cannot use a cross-tested or age-weighted allocation formula.

SIMPLEs

Contributions to a SIMPLE are subject to even more rigid rules. If the employer makes a profit-sharing type contribution, all eligible participants must receive 2 percent of compensation. If instead the employer makes a matching contribution, the match is fixed as a dollar-for-dollar match, up to the first 3 percent of compensation deferred.

DEFINED-BENEFIT PLANS

The nondiscrimination rules provide design safe harbors for plans that provide level benefits and those that integrate with social security. Again, if the employer wants to establish a plan that does not fit within the safe harbor, the formula can be defined in any way, as long as the plan can demonstrate nondiscrimination on an annual basis. Each of these three alternatives is discussed below.

Uniform Percentage of Compensation

There are actually three design-based safe harbors under the regulations. For all three, the plan must have the same benefit formula (and form of payment) for all participants and a uniform retirement age. Most important, the benefit formula must provide at the normal retirement age—for all participants with the same years of service—either the same dollar benefit or the same percentage of average annual compensation. Also the plan cannot require mandatory employee contributions.

All the following designs can satisfy the safe harbors:

- *Unit credit plans*—As long as the above requirements are met, the plan can use a standard unit credit plan that accrues the benefit each year based on the plan's benefit formula.

- *Fractional accruals*—A unit benefit formula or a flat percentage of pay (with a 25-years-of-service requirement) that accrues benefits using the fractional accrual method can also satisfy the design safe harbor.
- *Fully insured plans*—As long as the above requirements are met and the plan satisfies the definition of a fully insured plan under Code Sec. 412(I), the plan satisfies the nondiscrimination requirements.

In addition, any of these approaches will still satisfy the design safe harbor if the plan is integrated with social security as described below.

Integration with Social Security

Similar to the defined-contribution plan, the defined-benefit formula can be designed to provide a greater percentage of benefits for highly paid employees than for rank-and-file employees. Even though the rules are conceptually similar to defined-contribution plans, the integration-level approach for defined-benefit plans applies somewhat differently.

The rules also allow for an integration approach in which a benefit is described and then a portion of an individual's social security benefit is subtracted from the total (referred to as *offset integration*). At one time this was the most common integration approach in defined-benefit plans. However, under current law, this approach rarely works as well as the integration approach and is therefore not used very often. This approach, therefore, will not be discussed here.

Defined-benefit plans that use the integration-level approach are called *excess plans* (or *stepped-up plans*). Here's how an excess plan works:

- The plan has a specified integration level, which is tied to compensation.
- The benefit formula can provide the participant a higher rate of benefits for compensation above the integration level.
- The benefit that can be provided based on compensation in excess of the integration level cannot exceed either of the following limits:

  - For each year of service, the excess benefit percentage cannot be more than 0.75 percent of compensation. Looking at the total benefit, this disparity can be provided only on the first 35 years of service, meaning that the maximum disparity cannot exceed 26.25 percent.
  - In no case can the additional benefit provided based on compensation in excess of the integration level exceed the benefit provided based on total compensation.

The integration level is most plans is defined as "covered compensation." This is a term of art used in the regulations that describes the average of the taxable wages for the individual participant using the 35-year period ending with the year that the employee reaches the social security retirement age. This means two things. First, the covered compensation level is different for participants of different ages, because the average of taxable wage bases depends on the years worked. Older workers will have lower covered compensation levels than younger workers, since the taxable wage bases over their final 35 years of work are lower than those for younger workers using more current years. Second, every year the table for covered compensation changes as cost-of-living increases change the taxable wage base. Therefore covered compensation keeps increasing as the current year is adjusted for inflation—as are all future years.

If the integration level is something other than covered compensation, adjustments must be made in the maximum disparity. Most plans use the covered compensation integration level. A final concern is that under the integration rules, the plan must define final average compensation as at least the 3 highest years of compensation.

Other Plan-Design Alternatives

If the employer with a defined-benefit plan wants to establish a benefit formula that does not satisfy any of the safe harbor designs, the plan will have to satisfy the general nondiscrimination tests. Two types of plans are likely to have plan designs that do not satisfy the safe harbors. The first group includes plans that historically have had nonconforming benefit formulas. In other words, the sponsor adopted a formula in the past, that does not today satisfy the nondiscrimination safe harbors. If the plan is still meeting the objectives of both the employer and employees, the sponsor may choose not to bring the formula into compliance, but instead to go through the testing process.

The second group will be employers that choose to provide different benefit levels for different groups of employees in one plan. The employer might, for example, want to provide different benefit levels for employees of certain classes, in different geographic locations, or in different subsidiaries. The employer here has two choices: either establish one plan with different benefit levels and go through annual testing, or establish separate plans for each group. Here, each plan will have to satisfy the minimum coverage requirements of Code Sec. 410(b). Under the law, either approach will generally work, meaning that the employer will make the decision based upon its own goals and objectives and not on the legal limitations.

EMPLOYEE CONTRIBUTIONS

In addition to the benefit formula, another major plan-design question is whether employee contributions should be allowed. Discussed below are the three types of employee contributions: mandatory, thrift arrangements with an employer match, and nondeductible voluntary; these options should be considered in conjunction with the employer's plan choice and benefit formula, since they have a direct bearing on employer cost. Note that most of these types of employee contributions have been supplanted with pretax salary deferrals in 401(k) plans and SIMPLEs, discussed in chapters 5 and 6. Even though these types of contributions are rare today, they have historical significance and are important to a full understanding of the current state of pension planning.

Mandatory Employee Contributions

The employer may choose to require employees wishing to be covered by the plan to pay for part of their benefit. Mandatory contributions are sometimes a feature of defined-benefit plans but rarely of defined-contribution plans. The employee contribution typically ranges between 2 and 6 percent of *after-tax* pay—that is, the employee must pay taxes on his or her compensation before the plan contribution is made.

The primary reason for making the employee bear part of the plan's cost is that it reduces costs for the employer (or conversely, raises retirement benefits to an adequate level with the same employer expenditure). Having the employee provide part of the funding may enable the employer to meet the organizational goals that spurred the retirement plan. If, for example, the underlying reason the employer adopted the plan was to avoid or appease unions or to provide for the retirement needs of the rank and file, yet the employer's price range is limited, a contributory plan may be a good idea. What's more, one school of thought claims that if employees are forced to make contributions, they will better appreciate the benefit they are receiving.

The problem with mandatory employee contribution defined-benefit plans is that employee contributions are on an after-tax basis. These plans were more common in the past, when employers could not sponsor 401(k) plans. Today, the employer that wants to use this approach will generally choose the 401(k). Few mandatory employee contribution plans exist today in the private sector, although this approach is used more often in government plans (where in certain cases the contributions can be made on a pretax basis). However, a few of these plans still exist, most likely in the union context.

Thrift Arrangements with an Employer Match

Even before employees could make pretax contributions to a 401(k) plan, employees appreciated the ability to save through an employer-sponsored retirement vehicle. These plans, referred to as thrift plans, were profit-sharing plans in which employees made voluntary contributions with after-tax dollars. In thrift plans, like in 401(k) plans today, savings was commonly encouraged through an employer matching contribution. Thrift plans looked very much like today's 401(k) plans, and were used for many of the same reasons. The only real difference was that employee contributions were made on an after-tax basis. Since 1978, when 401(k) plans were first allowed, most thrift plans were amended into to 401(k) plans., so that employees can take advantage of pretax savings. In fact, employers with thrift plans often have the most successful 401(k) plans, since employees have a long history with the salary savings option. The only remnant of the thrift plan is the name. You will still see a number of 401(k) plans referred to as thrift plans.

Nondeductible Voluntary Employee Contributions

Another type of contribution that was once quite popular was the nondeductible employee contribution. These type of contributions could, and technically can still, be a feature that is part of any type of qualified retirement plan. After-tax contributions were quite popular with the business owner since, before 1987, up to 10 percent of compensation could be contributed by any employee without have to consider any of the other contribution limits, and without regard to which employees elected to make contributions. For these reasons this was a common feature in the small employer plan, and in many cases the feature was used primarily by the highly compensated.

Beginning in 1987, however, many of these provisions were eliminated due to new nondiscrimination requirements (discussed in the next section) and a new rule requiring that all such contributions count against the maximum annual contribution limit (the lesser of 25 percent or $30,000) for defined-contribution plans. Because of this most plans eliminated contributions after 1986, however, many plans still have older contributions. This is important to note when dealing with a client receiving a pension distribution. The principal amount of employee contributions is treated as basis, and is not subject to income tax. Earnings are subject to the same taxation rules that apply to other pension distributions.

The only place where after-tax contributions are still found is in 401(k) plans, where employees are sometimes given the opportunity to make contributions on a pretax or after-tax basis. This is generally left over from the thrift plan days. Some employees prefer the after-tax contributions because they can be withdrawn more easily than pretax contributions, which are subject to the special withdrawal requirements discussed in chapter 5.

Nondiscrimination Requirements for Employer Matching Contributions and Employee Contributions: The 401(m) Test

Plans that provide for employer matching contributions and/or employee contributions (either voluntary or mandatory) are subject to a nondiscrimination test that is similar to the actual deferral percentage (ADP) test called the 401(m) or ACP test. Under the 401(m) test instead of comparing the salary deferrals—as a percentage of compensation—we are comparing the matching and after-tax contributions as a percentage of compensation.

In operation the test is virtually the same as the ADP test. In order to pass the 401(m) nondiscrimination test for employer matching contributions and employee contributions, one of two requirements must be satisfied:

- *The 1.25 requirement.* Under this requirement the contribution percentage for all highly compensated employees for the current year can't be more than 125 percent of the contribution percentage for nonhighly compensated employees for the previous year.
- *The 200 percent/2 percent difference requirement.* Under this requirement the contribution percentage for highly compensated employees for the current year can't be more than 200 percent of the contribution percentage (in the previous year) for nonhighly compensated employees, and the difference between the two groups must be 2 percent or less.

For purposes of these nondiscrimination tests the term *highly compensated employee* is defined as described under the ADP test in chapter 5.

Table 5-1 (see chapter 5) can be used to determine the maximum contribution percentage limits for highly compensated employees. For example, if the contribution percentage is 6 percent of compensation for nonhighly compensated employees, then the highly compensated employees can have an 8 percent contribution percentage.

9

Helping Clients Choose the Best Loan, Vesting, and Retirement-Age Provisions

Three of the most important decisions in designing a plan are

- deciding whether the plan should permit loans
- choosing the plan's vesting schedules
- choosing the plan's retirement-age provisions

Decisions in these areas significantly affect the makeup of the plan's participants, the makeup of the employer's work force, and the employer's costs.

PLAN LOANS

Most types of retirement plans may have provisions that allow participants the opportunity to borrow from the plan. Loans allow participants the ability to access funds without tax consequences. However, loans also add administrative expense and may undermine retirement planning objectives. The decision whether or not to have a loan provision depends upon the type of plan, plan objectives, and the legal restrictions upon plan loans. An informed decision must address the following two important concerns:

- Are plan loans appropriate?
- What legal restrictions will apply?

Are Plan Loans Appropriate for Your Clients?

The Advantages and Disadvantages of Plan Loans

The primary reason to include a loan provision in the plan is so that employees (including executives and business owners to the extent legally permitted) can enjoy the current beneficial use of their retirement savings. In other words, a loan provision in a qualified plan provides the best of both worlds—tax shelter for plan contributions and access to sheltered funds when the need arises without causing a taxable distribution.

There is another side to the story, however. Several good reasons for *not* allowing plan loans also exist. First, a loan provision in the plan may be inconsistent with the employer's objective of providing retirement security. Funds used to repay plan loans are often taken from funds that would have been retirement savings. This might create an unwanted dependence on the employer's plan as the sole source of retirement funds, especially when loans are taken by employees who are close to retirement. Second, loan provisions are labor-intensive and costly to administer. Especially troublesome from an administrative point of view is dealing with the default of a loan. Employers typically do not relish being put in the untenable position of being a credit agency or hounding their employees for payment. What's more, if a loan is defaulted, serious consequences abound, such as the following:

- There is an immediate tax liability to the participant, since the defaulted loan is treated as a current distribution.
- The participant may incur a 10 percent penalty if the distribution occurs prior to age 59 1/2.

A third reason loan provisions are forsaken is that in partnerships, sole proprietorships, and S Corporations the very people who decide whether a provision should be included in the plan are not permitted to receive loans. Specifically, owner-employees (that is, more-than-10-percent owners of an unincorporated business) and more-than-5-percent shareholder-employees of an S corporation are prohibited from taking loans.

Despite their pitfalls, loan provisions are very popular for the following reasons:

- Business owners in a C corporation are eligible for plan loans.
- Administrative problems with plan loans can be minimized by using a program that would only permit loans under a stipulated number of circumstances, such as for college education payments, purchase of a home, or demonstrated financial hardship.
- Administrative problems can also be mitigated by placing a $1,000 minimum on the amount of any loan, thus eliminating pesky small loans.
- Problems with loan defaults can be eliminated if the employer requires payroll deduction for loan repayments and requires complete repayment upon termination of employment. If the participant defaults, benefits payable are reduced by the outstanding balance (resulting in a taxable distribution of the amount of default).

Types of Plans

The degree to which a loan provision is considered desirable depends on part on the type of plan involved. Clients who have a 401(k) plan or 403(b) plan should strongly consider a loan provision. In these plans it can be difficult to get the enrollment necessary to pass the actual deferral percentage test, if participants are concerned that elective deferrals will be locked up until retirement However, by "unlocking" plan funds through a loan provision an employer may be able to entice the required participation to satisfy the applicable tests.

Sometimes loan provisions are considered for pension plans of the defined-contribution type. Since pension plans are prohibited from making in-service withdrawals—that is, distributing funds prior to death, disability, termination of employment, or retirement—a loan provision allows "use" of plan assets during employment. However, pension plans of the defined-benefit type seldom contain a loan provision. First, calculating the maximum loan amount requires an actuarial calculation, increasing administrative expenses. Second, a loan provision undermines the concern for retirement security, usually the number one reason for adopting the plan.

For profit-sharing plans the consideration is somewhat different. Since a profit-sharing plan may be designed to allow in-service withdrawals, a loan provision is not necessary to provide employees access to plan benefits during employment. However, loans do provide for the use of funds on a tax-free basis.

Employee stock ownership plans (ESOPs) generally do not have loan provisions since plan assets are required to be "primarily invested in employer securities" meaning that the plan will not have sufficient cash investments to support a loan provision. For the same reason, stock bonus plans that are heavily invested in employer securities should not have a loan provision.

Finally, note that plan loans are prohibited in SEPs, SIMPLEs, and IRAs. Table 9-1 summarizes the applicable rules.

TABLE 9-1
Desirability of Plan Loans

Plan	Consideration
401(k) plan	A loan provision entices participation so that the actual deferral percentage test can be passed.
403(b) plan	A loan provision entices participation so that the 401(m) test can be passed.
Contributory plan	A loan provision entices participation so that the 401(m) test and 410(b) nondiscrimination tests can be passed.
Pension plans (money-purchase, target-benefit, cash-balance, and defined-benefit plans)	A loan provision can get around the restriction against in-service withdrawals.
Profit-sharing plan	A loan provision is less crucial, since in-service withdrawals are allowed. However, the loan does provide for tax-free access.
Defined-benefit plan	Although a loan provision can be useful (see pension plan), it is often forsaken because of administrative problems.
ESOP	A loan provision is seldom used because of the requirement that the plan be invested primarily in employer stock and because the plan often lacks the cash to loan to participants.
Stock bonus plan	A loan provision is a problem if the plan lacks cash to support the program.
SEP	No loans are permitted.
SIMPLE	No loans are permitted.
IRA	No loans are permitted.

YOUR FINANCIAL SERVICES PRACTICE: PLAN LOANS

Some financial services professionals use loan provisions to overcome the employer's common objection about locking up retirement funds. In some cases this may eliminate the final hurdle to a sale. On the other hand, some financial services professionals are not fond of plan loans because loans take potential investment funds away from the asset pool. The decision is, of course, up to the plan sponsor, who will probably not be as concerned with depleting the asset pool.

Legal Parameters for Plan Loans

Plans designed to permit loans must adhere to certain requirements that govern the availability, amount, duration, interest, security, and repayment of the loan.

Loan Availability

As was previously stated, your client can choose to include the option for plan loans or to exclude the option altogether. If plan loans are made available, however, they must be available to all participants on a reasonably equivalent basis and must not be available to highly compensated employees in an amount greater than the amount made available to other employees. In addition, loans must

- be adequately secured
- be made in accordance with specific plan provisions
- bear a reasonable (market) rate of interest

Almost all plans use the participant's accrued benefit as security. Other security can be appropriate, but most plans will not want to get into this because of the administrative complexities. If the participant defaults on the loan, the benefit will be reduced in the amount of the outstanding principle (and accrued interest). If this happens, the participant now has a taxable distribution subject to ordinary income tax and the 10 percent early distribution excise tax, if the participant has not attained age 59 1/2 (see chapter 26).

Another issue that comes up with loans is that in plans subject to the qualified joint and survivor annuity requirements (see chapter 10), both spouses must sign off on the loan. This is because a loan default can reduce the participant's benefit, which affects the spousal rights to that benefit as well.

Restrictions on Amounts and Repayments

In addition to rules on loan availability, there are limits on the amount each participant can borrow. The limit is $50,000 or one-half of the vested account balance, whichever is less. Under the tax rules, a participant may borrow up to $10,000 even if this amount is more than one-half of the vested benefit. For example, a person having a vested benefit of $13,000 could still borrow up to $10,000. However, in practice, employers do not allow loans in excess of the 50 percent limit, since DOL regulations would require security other than the participant's vested account balance—which would be complex to administer.

A participant's loan must be repayable by its terms within 5 years. The one exception to the 5-year rule is if a loan is used to acquire a participant's principal residence. In this case a reasonable repayment schedule (presumably over the life of any mortgage involved) will suffice. Another important factor concerning the 5-year rule is that "sham" repayments are not allowed. Before 1987 the 5-year rule was subject to frequent abuse. Participants would repay the loan on the last possible date and take out the loan again immediately after repayment. For this reason the rules were designed so that $50,000 limit is reduced by the highest outstanding loan balance during the one-year period ending the day before the loan date. The rules were also changed to add a restriction that requires level amortization of loan repayments of principal and interest being made at least quarterly.

> *Example:* Bill Smith borrows $50,000 from his qualified plan and pays off the loan on a level amortization basis over 5 years ($10,000 annually). At the end of 5 years when the loan is repaid, Bill wants to take out another loan. The maximum amount available for this second loan is $40,000 ($50,000 limit minus $10,000 paid back in the prior year).

Interest on a plan loan will be treated as consumer interest that is not deductible by the employee as an itemized deduction unless the loan is secured by a principal residence. Since plans generally do not want to make loans on this basis, the tax deduction is rarely available. Note that even if a plan wanted to allow them, such loans are specifically prohibited in situations where the loan is (1) made to a key employee, as defined by the Code's rules for top-heavy plans (see chapter 10), or (2) made in a 401(k) or 403(b) plan.

VESTING

Determining a plan's "vesting schedule" is another important and difficult planning decision. This is partly because of the common misconception that retirement benefits are a form of deferred wages owned by the employee. This misconception is fostered by the fact that benefits are usually related to salary levels. The fact is, however, that retirement benefits are not a deferred wage but rather a wage-related benefit that is contingent on the employee's ability to meet the requirements of the vesting schedule.

Understanding the Vesting System

The vesting concept is perhaps best understood in light of its history. Before the passage of the Employee Retirement Income Security Act (ERISA) in 1974, it was accepted practice in some companies to offer retirement benefits only to employees who retired from the company after completing long periods of service (for example, 30 years). The result was a system that ignored the retirement needs of many, bound others in an unwanted fashion to their company, and shortchanged employees whose service was long but not long enough. Partly as a result of a television documentary and subsequent congressional hearings that publicized horror stories of long-service employees left penniless during retirement, Congress recognized the injustices of this situation and enacted ERISA, which ensured that employees would receive some retirement benefits if they terminated employment prior reaching normal retirement age. ERISA established rules for determining how much service is required before benefits become nonforfeitable. Subsequent to ERISA the rules have been changed several times, each law providing less and less required service before full vesting occurs.

Vesting Schedules

An employer is required to choose a vesting schedule that is at least as favorable as one of two statutory schedules: the 5-year cliff vesting or the 3-through-7-year graded vesting. Note, as described further in chapter 10, that a plan that is considered top-heavy must actually adopt a vesting schedule that meets even more rigid requirements.

The 5-year cliff vesting is a schedule under which an employee who terminates employment prior to the completion of 5 years of service will be entitled to no benefit (zero percent vested). After 5 years of service the employee becomes fully entitled to (100 percent vested in) the benefit that has accrued on his or her behalf. Five-year cliff vesting is easy to remember if you visualize an employee climbing a cliff for 5 years and finally becoming entitled to the benefits upon reaching the top. The cliff vesting schedule is as follows:

5-Year Cliff Vesting

Years of Service	Percentage Vested
0–4	0
5 or more	100

The other statutory vesting schedule, known as the 3-through-7-year graded schedule, requires no vesting until the third year of service has been completed;

at that point the vested portion of the accrued benefit increases 20 percent for each year served.

3-through-7-Year Graded Vesting

Years of Service	Percentage Vested
0–2	0
3	20
4	40
5	60
6	80
7 or more	100

While these two schedules constitute the legally mandated requirements, more liberal vesting schedules can be employed if desired. For example, an employer could establish a 2-year cliff vesting schedule or a 4-year graded schedule, where the participant earned an additional 25 percent vesting for each year of service.

When examining the issue of vesting it is important to note that the vesting schedules just described apply primarily in the case of an individual who terminates employment (on a voluntary or involuntary basis) prior to reaching a plan's normal retirement age—or some other stated event that triggers a benefit under the plan. Under the law, an individual who reaches the plan's normal retirement age must become 100 percent vested regardless of the number of years of service earned. For example, if Don Fields starts working for the Bonanza Company at age 62 and the Bonanza plan has 5-year cliff vesting and a normal retirement age of 65, Don must be 100 percent vested at the plan's normal retirement age of 65 in spite of the fact that he is not entitled to anything under the vesting schedule. Also it is typical for a plan to fully vest participants—regardless of the years of service performed—at attainment of an early retirement age, upon disability, or at death. These decisions are voluntary, and are based on the plan's objectives (discussed in chapter 10).

Another important consideration is that the participant's benefit attributable to employee after-tax contributions or employee pretax salary deferral elections in a 401(k) plan must be 100 percent vested at all times. This rule applies both to contributions and to investment experience thereon. For this reason, any plan that has either type of employee contributions must keep separate accounts for employer and such employee contributions.

In today's pension environment, there are numerous other exceptions to the normal vesting rules—which are described more fully elsewhere in this book. All of them are summarized below. As you can see, Congress keeps whittling away at the vesting restrictions. This is probably because anything less than full and immediate vesting limits benefit "portability"—an important concern to a mobile workforce that changes jobs frequently.

- *SEPs and SIMPLEs*—Contributions to a SEP or SIMPLE must be fully vested at all times (chapter 6).
- *403(b) plans*—Employer contributions to a 403(b) plan are generally fully vested. Such amounts could technically be subject to a vesting schedule, but because of the operation of the exclusion ratio, it is impractical to do so (chapter 6).
- *Plan termination*—Benefits must become fully vested upon a full or partial plan termination (chapter 14).
- *Safe harbor 401(k) plans*—Contributions to a 401(k) SIMPLE and contributions made to satisfy the 401(k) safe harbor provisions must be fully vested (chapter 5).
- *Two-year eligibility rule*—In exchange for the ability to exclude employees for 2 years (instead of one), contributions must be fully vested (chapter 7).
- *Top-heavy vesting*—Small employers with top-heavy plans are subject to more restrictive vesting schedules (chapter 10).

Choosing the Most Appropriate Vesting Schedule

The various vesting schedule choices and their exceptions obviously have design implications you must consider in helping your clients make the best choice. The most important vesting design question is whether an employer should choose a restrictive schedule (using the maximum wait allowed) or liberal vesting schedule.

To the employer, the major advantage of choosing a restrictive vesting schedule is that it may be able to cut costs attributable to employee turnover. When employees terminate employment prior to being fully vested, the nonvested portion of the accrued benefit (referred to as a *forfeiture*) can be used to reduce future employer contributions. For example, if five employees terminate employment with the National Furniture Company, each with a $4,000 forfeited benefit, National's contribution for next year is reduced by $20,000. The employer also has the choice in any defined-contribution plan to use forfeitures as an additional contribution for remaining employees (in pension parlance, this is referred to as *reallocating forfeitures*). Reallocated forfeitures do not result in a direct cost savings, but they do allow the employer the opportunity to provide bigger benefits for long-term highly compensated employees—at no extra cost. (*Planning Note:* Forfeitures that are reallocated to employees are added to other contributions, and the aggregate amount cannot exceed the 25 percent or $30,000 limit. If the plan's benefit formula is already designed to reach this limit, then forfeitures should not be reallocated.)

Another advantage of choosing a restrictive vesting schedule is that it helps retain employees. Many employees are convinced that it is economically desirable to delay a job change until they become fully vested (this may not always be the case in reality, but many employees believe it to be true) and consequently stick it out at a company until the vesting requirements are fulfilled. When employers have spent time training employees and having them become acclimated, a restrictive vesting schedule that encourages employees to stay around after they have reached a productive level may pay back the organization for the time it invested.

In contrast to these reasons for adopting a restrictive schedule, there are some good reasons to adopt a more liberal schedule or to have immediate and full vesting:

- to foster employee morale
- to remain competitive in attracting employees
- to meet the design needs of the small employer who desires few encumbrances to participation for the "employee family"

YOUR FINANCIAL SERVICES PRACTICE:
CUTTING COSTS FOR CLIENTS THROUGH PRUDENT
VESTING DESIGN

More often then not, clients in the small-plan market are concerned about lowering plan costs attributable to rank-and-file employees. One way to painlessly accomplish this objective is to carefully consider the clients turnover pattern before setting a vesting schedule. The fact finder (chapter 3) provides a series of questions addressing employee turnover (or expected turnover). For example, if a high employee turnover is expected between 5 and 7 years of service, then a graded schedule (as opposed to a cliff schedule) may save the employer money. Conversely, if turnover is expected to occur between 3 and 5 years of service, then a 5-year-cliff schedule is preferable to a graded schedule which begins partially vesting people after 3 years of service. In any case it is prudent to look closely at the pattern of turnover that exists and design the vesting schedule accordingly.

Additional Vesting Rules

The choice of a vesting schedule is only the first in a series of vesting-design choices. The vesting schedule raises several questions that need to be answered through plan design:

- Does the adoption of one of the legally required vesting schedules (or a less restrictive version) guarantee that the plan does not discriminate in the vesting area?

- What years of service must be counted for vesting-schedule purposes?
- What happens if an employee leaves employment and then returns?

Vesting and Discrimination

Usually the inclusion of one of the required vesting schedules (or a less restrictive schedule) guarantees that the plan will meet IRS standards. There is, however, an exception: a plan cannot in practice have a pattern of abuse that discriminates in favor of highly compensated employees. For example, a plan could have a discriminatory turnover rate if the company made a practice of firing employees before their benefits were vested. If this happened, the IRS would disqualify the plan because of its discriminatory vesting application. As a planner you should advise the employer to use self-restraint in its personnel practices—in other words, make sure the company polices itself before the IRS has to.

Vesting-Service Considerations

As we've seen, vesting schedules rely exclusively on years of service to determine an employee's vested benefit. The years of service that are counted for vesting purposes include years in which the employee has 1,000 or more hours of service. Hours of service may be determined by using the standard-hours counting method (each hour actually worked is counted plus hours for which an employee is entitled to be paid, such as vacations and holidays) or by using any one of the equivalency methods discussed in chapter 7. If this sounds familiar, it should; the 1,000-hour rule and definition for years of service were used for eligibility purposes and in the benefit formula, and many of the same issues (exclusion of part-time employees, administrative convenience) discussed under eligibility and benefit formulas arise here too.

It would seem likely that the same methods of counting years and hours of service should be used for eligibility, benefits, and vesting, but this is not always the case. In other words, the plan's definition section can be designed to include different definitions for years of service and hours of service. One instance when this would be appropriate is if the employer desires immediate eligibility (to make the plan competitive) but restrictive vesting (to cut costs and to encourage employee retention). Under this circumstance a liberal definition for year of service and hour of service may be employed for eligibility purposes, while a restrictive definition is used for vesting purposes.

If the employer's goal is to delay an employee's receipt of benefits for cost or other reasons, the definitions of year of service and hour of service should be appropriately restrictive (use the full 1,000 hours and the most restrictive definition for hour of service, which is typically the standard-hours counting method). One other difference between counting service for eligibility and vesting is that vesting service can be measured for all years based on the plan year. Remember that the first year of eligibility service must be measured from the hire date. Many plans will choose the plan year definition for administrative simplicity. Also, for the individual hired in the second half of the plan year, it could mean one less year of service.

In addition to designing these definitions, you can design the plan to exclude certain years of service:

- Years of service earned prior to age 18 can be excluded. Generally it's a good idea to exclude vesting service prior to age 18, since turnover is higher among younger employees, and the employer could save on future expenditures because of forfeitures.

    > *Example:* Checkout clerk Alice White has a year of service for each year from age 16 through age 21, at which time she terminates. If the employer's plan is designed to count vesting service prior to age 18, Alice meets the plan's 5-year cliff vesting schedule, having had 6 years of service (16, 17, 18, 19, 20, 21). But if the plan is designed so that only service after age 18 is counted, Alice is not vested because she has only 4 years of service (18, 19, 20, 21). (Note that Alice meets the definition for eligibility most commonly used: one year of service and attainment of age 21.)

- Years of service before the plan went into effect can be excluded.
- Certain years of service prior to a break in service can be excluded (discussed below).

There are, however, circumstances where the plan cannot be designed to cut service for vesting purposes:

- Service prior to eligibility (past age 18) will be counted even if the employee was not a participant in the plan.
- Service for a different component of the employer (such as a subsidiary), even though the employee was not covered by the plan, must be counted. For example, Sally Jerkins is a 15-year member of the Oakland office, which does not have a pension plan. Her company transfers her to the San Diego office, which does have one. Sally will be 100 percent vested when she transfers to San Diego under the plan's cliff vesting schedule because of her 15 years of service.
- Service with any member of a controlled group of corporations, with a commonly controlled business, or with an affiliated service group must be counted for vesting purposes. For example, George Gray is a 15-year employee of Modern Kitchens, which is under a controlled group with Total Home Concepts. Modern Kitchens has no plan; Total Home has

one. When George is hired by Total Home, his years of service from Modern Kitchens will apply for vesting purposes.

- Service with a predecessor employer if the successor employer maintains the predecessor's plan must be counted. In other words, if an employee's company changes hands and the new owners maintain the same plan, service with the old owner counts for vesting purposes.

Breaks in Service

In some limited circumstances the rules allow a plan to disregard certain years of vesting service during which a participant has had sporadic employment. The employer establishing the plan can take advantage of these rules or choose to disregard them.

For any of the rules to apply, the participant must first incur a break in service. A break in service is a year (using the same measuring period used for determining vesting) in which the individual does not complete more than 500 hours of service. If there is a break-in-service there are three rules that may be applicable. Under the first rule, prebreak service may be disregarded until an individual is reemployed and completes a full year of service. For administrative purposes, this is probably a good idea, in case the reemployment does not last.

The second and most useful rule applies only to defined-contribution plans. Under this rule, if an individual has five consecutive breaks in service, the nonvested portion of the benefit earned prior to the break can be permanently forfeited.

YOUR FINANCIAL SERVICES PRACTICE:
WHEN TO REALLOCATE FORFEITURES

If a defined-contribution plan is drafted to reallocate forfeitures to the remaining employees, a decision has to be made as to when the forfeitures will occur. One option is to wait until the participant has been gone for 5 years (five one-year breaks in service). This option ensures that the contributions are still available if a terminated employee returns to service and earns the right to such amounts. When the plan does not allow the distribution of benefits before the normal retirement date, the employer should always elect this option. However, if the employer allows immediate payment at termination of employment, the employer may wish to allocate forfeitures on the valuation date immediately following termination. This eliminates both the administrative expense and the confusion involved in maintaining many small accounts for terminated employees. This option makes sense if terminated employees generally do not return to service. If this option is elected, the employer must understand that additional contributions might have to be made when terminees return to service within 5 years.

Example: Ralph terminates employment with a $2,000 account balance. He is 50 percent vested and so he is eligible to receive a benefit of $1,000. He returns to the same employer 7 years later. Regardless of how much postbreak service he earns, Ralph cannot earn back the $1,000 benefit that he forfeited.

Most defined-contribution plans should consider adopting this provision. Otherwise, it is possible to have to make up contributions (or hold the forfeitures in a separate account) virtually forever.

Under the third rule, prebreak and postbreak service do not have to be aggregated for an individual who is zero percent vested and who then incurs five consecutive one-year breaks in service. This rule is not adopted as regularly as the others because it adds administrative complexity and rarely applies. The employer who has a revolving workforce might want to consider adopting this vesting requirement.

RETIREMENT AGES

Choosing the plan's retirement age should be motivated primarily by business reasons, not tax or plan cost considerations. The employer should carefully consider at what age it wants to encourage employees to retire. The employer has to be concerned about the orderly retirement of older, highly compensated employees, while it does not want to inadvertently encourage its older, more experienced employees to leave and go to competitors. Such issues determine the success or failure of an organization and are much more important than plan cost or tax considerations.

Effective plan design concerning retirement age boils down to the following four questions:

- What should the normal retirement age be?
- Should there be early retirement, and if so, when should it start?
- Should early retirement be subsidized?
- What provisions should be made for deferred retirement?

Normal Retirement Age

When you are designing the retirement plan, you typically define a normal retirement age—that is, the age specified in the plan at which the employee has the right to retire. The term *right to retire* means that the employee can retire without the employer's consent and will receive his or her full benefit under the plan. In general an employer and his or her adviser can choose any age up to 65 as the normal retirement age. Age 65 is typically chosen as the plan's normal retirement age because that's the age at which a retiree (currently) can receive unreduced social security benefits. Age 62 is another common choice for normal retirement because that's the earliest age at which a retiring worker can receive reduced social security benefits. In addition, some retirement ages are set by industry standards. For example, a relatively young age can be chosen if it is the age at which employees customarily retire, such as in professional sports. Finally, some government plans don't link normal retirement to any particular age but take into account only years of service. For example, a plan can be structured to have the normal retirement age after 25 years of service.

Under certain circumstances the normal retirement age can be greater than 65. This usually occurs in new defined-benefit plans that have a number of older employees, which makes the start-up funding cost prohibitive, or in existing plans that frequently hire people 55 or older. In these cases the employer should take advantage of an exception to the general rule: For an employee who commences participation in the plan within 5 years of the plan's normal retirement age, the plan can delay actual retirement until the employee's fifth anniversary. For example, a 62-year-old hiree can have a normal retirement age of 67, not 65 as is the case for other employees in the plan.

(*Planning Note:* If life insurance is used in part or in whole to fund the plan, then this post-65 normal-retirement-age provision should be strongly considered. In effect, it takes time for cash values to accumulate in the policies, and these exceptions stall retirement so that accumulation can occur.)

Early Retirement

An employer can choose to provide retirement benefits earlier than normal retirement age. As with the choice of normal retirement age, the pension tail should not wag the business dog when the employer makes this decision. Typical early retirement ages are 55, 60, and 62. Effective design of a plan offering early retirement should take into account the practices of the employer's competitors.

Sometimes (especially in defined-benefit plans) age is not the only determinant of early retirement; rather, both age and service dictate the early retirement age. One typical early-retirement provision requires age 55 and 10 years of service (in pension parlance, this is known as 55 and 10). The service requirement is valuable for employers who would like to assure themselves of enough time to fund the benefit (for example, when life insurance is used to fund the plan). So if cash flow is a problem, a years-of-service requirement is desirable.

If the employer's industry is prone to have superannuated employees or if the industry requires certain physical skills that employees may lack later in their careers, an early-retirement option is probably a good idea. What's more, the early-retirement option serves the business purposes of allowing for a graceful change in management and attracting key employees who consider early retirement a valuable lifestyle choice. Under certain circumstances early retirement may not be a desirable option. If the employer fears that certain key employees will take a job with a competitor so as to acquire a second pension check or if a majority of the organization's business skills and knowledge are centered in a few key people whose loss would devastate the organization, early retirement is probably not a good idea.

The early-retirement benefit can either be subsidized or nonsubsidized. If it is subsidized, the actuarial reductions for early retirement (that is, the percentage reductions taken from the normal-retirement-age benefit to reflect the longer payout period) don't reflect the true cost of providing the benefit, and the difference represents an increased employer cost. For small plans whose owner-employees are looking for tax savings a subsidized early-retirement program will garner bigger deductions and should be strongly considered as a planning alternative. For medium-sized and large plans some subsidy may be called for—if, for example, the employer desires to eliminate older employees—but a substantial subsidy can be prohibitively expensive.

Employers who want to offer early retirement (say for competitive reasons) but are not delighted with the prospect of losing experienced employees should consider nonsubsidized early retirement. If early retirement is not subsidized, the actuarial reduction will reflect as closely as possible the true experience of the early-retirement costs.

Deferred Retirement

A plan should always be designed to accommodate the possibility of deferred retirement—retirement after the normal retirement age. For one thing, the Federal Age Discrimination in Employment Act prohibits involuntary retirement (except for some executives and employees in high policy-making positions). For another thing, it's desirable from a business standpoint to make provisions that allow or even encourage productive employees to remain on the team. What's more, the employer must continue to make contributions in a defined-contribution plan if a deferred retirement is chosen. In a defined-benefit plan, benefits cannot stop accruing at a specified age; however, the plan can contain a maximum number of years of service for determining benefits under the plan. For example, the benefit formula could be stated as two percent of final average compensation times years of service, with service limited to 30 years.

**YOUR FINANCIAL SERVICES PRACTICE:
THE RETIREMENT-AGE RULES IN A SAMPLE
ADOPTION AGREEMENT**

Regardless of what the employer chooses with regard to early, normal, and deferred retirement, these decisions are reflected in the plan's definition section, which contains detailed descriptions of the terms *early retirement, normal retirement,* and *deferred retirement* and often spells out the actuarial reductions attributable to early retirement. In addition to containing choices regarding the plan's definition section, the adoption agreement also contains sections for choosing early, normal, and deferred retirement provisions.

The following sample illustrates how the early retirement age sections might appear in a typical adoption agreement:

Section T: Early Retirement Age (refers to Section 20 of the Plan)

(1)   Retirement Prior to Normal Retirement Age (Section S) (check one)

     ( )   will not be permitted
     ( )   will be permitted upon attaining age ___ and completing ___ years of
        ( )   service
        ( )   participation

10

Death and Disability Benefits; Top-Heavy Rules

Chapter Outline

The primary purpose of a qualified retirement plan is to provide retirement benefits to employees. The retirement plan, however, can be used to meet the insurance needs of participants by providing both death and disability coverage in the preretirement period.

INCIDENTAL RULES FOR DEATH BENEFITS

Death benefits under a retirement plan must be "incidental" because Uncle Sam is providing tax advantages to the qualified plan for retirement needs, not insurance needs. The word *incidental,* however, may be somewhat of a misnomer. The term has a special meaning that is defined through a series of revenue rulings. As a result of these rulings a fairly substantial "incidental" death benefit can be provided through the use of life insurance in a qualified plan.

The maximum death benefit that can be provided under the incidental rules is not specifically stated. Instead, a plan will be deemed to meet the incidental death-benefit requirement if it passes either of two tests—the 25 percent test or the 100-to-1 ratio test.

The rules described below apply to qualified plans and 403(b) plans, which are allowed to invest in life insurance. The rules do not apply to SEPs and SIMPLEs because these types of plans cannot have life insurance.

The 25 Percent Test

In order to determine whether life insurance is an incidental benefit provided by the plan, the cost of providing the life insurance is compared to the cost of providing all benefits. When this method is used, the total cost of the life insurance that is provided cannot exceed a specified percentage of the total cost of the benefit. You might assume that under the 25 percent test the maximum percentage of total benefits used to provide life insurance cannot exceed 25 percent, but this assumption is only half right. The 25 percent test is actually a misnomer, for it is really two tests: a 25 percent test and a 50 percent test, depending on which type of life insurance protection is involved. If term insurance or universal life is involved, the aggregate premiums paid for the policy cannot exceed 25 percent of the participant's total benefit. If a whole life policy other than universal life is used, however, the aggregate premiums paid for the whole life policy cannot exceed 50 percent of the participant's total benefit, *and* the entire value of the life contract must be converted into cash or periodic income at or before retirement. The reason for the increase from 25 to 50 percent (and the need for the conversion into cash) is that about half the premiums paid under a whole life policy represent pure insurance protection, and the other half represent the investment element of the policy.

> *Example:* Tim Rivers has a $100,000 account balance. If he uses universal life or term insurance, the aggregate premiums that can be used to pay for Tim's life insurance total a maximum of $25,000. If he has another form of whole life policy, the aggregate premiums that can be used to pay for his life insurance total a maximum of $50,000.

The 100-to-1 Ratio Test

The 100-to-1 ratio test does not look at the amount of insurance bought but concentrates on the death benefit offered. Under this safe harbor test the death benefit is limited to a maximum of 100 times the expected monthly benefit or, if greater, the reserve for the pension benefit. For example, if the expected monthly benefit is $1,500, then the total death benefit could be $150,000 or the reserve (at the date of death) if greater. The 100-to-1 ratio test was derived from the death benefit that is provided under a retirement-income contract. Retirement-income contracts are individual life products issued by insurance companies that are used to fund qualified plans (see chapter 12). As you might suspect the 100-

to-1 ratio test is best suited to a defined-benefit pension plan because the expected monthly benefit is easily determined. However, the test can be applied to any type of pension or profit-sharing plan.

Exceptions

The 25 percent test and the 100-to-1 ratio test are subject to certain exceptions. The following are the most important exceptions to these incidental-death-benefit rules:

- The incidental limitations do not apply to life insurance bought with nondeductible voluntary employee contributions.
- The incidental limitations do not apply to profit-sharing plans under certain conditions. If the profit-sharing plan permits in-service withdrawals (for example, after 2 years) and if life insurance is purchased with funds that could be withdrawn, there is no "incidental limit" on the amount of these funds that can be used to purchase life insurance. In other words, the incidental limitation applies only to funds in a profit-sharing plan that have not accumulated under the plan long enough to be distributed. If the profit-sharing plan does not permit withdrawals, however, the incidental rules will apply to all funds.
- The IRS treats universal life insurance as term insurance for purposes of the 25 percent rule, even though universal life is a form of whole life coverage that is otherwise subject to the 50 percent exception.

YOUR FINANCIAL SERVICES PRACTICE:
PROVIDING DEATH BENEFITS IN QUALIFIED PLANS

Even though the incidental rules limit the death benefits that can be provided, the financial services professional retains a good deal of discretion when designing the retirement plan's death benefit with respect to the benefit level and funding method. When designing a plan for the small employer or the professional corporation, you must keep in mind that the insurance needs of the principal individuals (business owners, key employees) will govern the death-benefit design. In the medium-sized or large organization the employees' insurance needs will be harder, if not impossible, to determine. In this situation the retirement plan's insurance benefit and other group life benefits will be decided by competition and other market factors.

When funding the plan's death benefit, you can choose either individual life insurance (as is usually the case with smaller employers) or a cash distribution made from plan assets (for example, a distribution of the account balance in a defined-contribution plan). The choice of the death-benefit funding vehicle usually dovetails with the decision about which plan funding vehicle is most appropriate. (Using qualified-plan funds to satisfy personal insurance needs will be discussed more thoroughly in chapter 12.)

- There is an exception to the 100-to-1 ratio test for split-funded plans (a split-funded plan is a plan that is funded with both individual life insurance policies and a side fund—see chapter 12). In a split-funded plan the 100-to-1 ratio can be exceeded if the life insurance policy does not provide a death benefit in excess of the 100-to-1 ratio and the amount of the death benefit is limited to the total of (1) the reserve under the policy and (2) the participant's account in the side fund. For example, under this approach the death benefit will be considered incidental for an expected monthly benefit of $1,500 if the reserve is $140,000 and the side fund is $70,000 (total $210,000), even though the 100-to-1 ratio is exceeded.

Incidental Rule for Postretirement Death Benefits

We have been looking at limitations on the amount of death benefits that can be provided if a participant dies *prior* to retirement. But there are also limitations on the amount of death benefits that can be provided *after* retirement. These rules come into play when the annuity form that is chosen provides a substantial death benefit, such as a joint and survivor annuity or a 20-year stipulated annuity. The details are somewhat complex and are discussed in depth in chapter 25. At this point simply understand that the objective of the rule is to ensure that participants cannot defer taxation of a significant portion of their benefits until after they die. For example, if a participant aged 75 elects a 100 percent survivor annuity option and the contingent beneficiary is a 25-year-old granddaughter, a larger portion of the retirement benefit will actually be paid to the granddaughter than to the participant. To prohibit this result, the rules, as they apply to this example, would limit the survivor annuity percentage that the granddaughter can receive. The incidental-death-benefit rule generally does not apply when the beneficiary is the spouse.

MANDATORY DEATH BENEFITS: QPSA AND AUTOMATIC J&S

If we think of the incidental rules as placing a ceiling on death benefits in a qualified plan, the additional death-benefit rules can be thought of as a floor under the incidental ceiling. There are two applicable rules that construct the death-benefit floor. Implementing them depends on the retirement status of a given participant. Before retirement the plan must provide a spousal benefit called a qualified preretirement survivor annuity (QPSA). After retirement the plan must protect the participant's spouse by requiring that the normal form of distribution from the retirement plan for a married participant must be a joint and survivor annuity (sometimes referred to as an automatic J&S). The legislative motive behind both these rules is to protect the spouse's right to a piece of the participant's retirement income.

The QPSA (pronounced "quip-sa") is defined differently for defined-benefit and defined-contribution plans. In both cases, however, the QPSA is required to be provided only for married participants who were married for one year before the participant's death (plans sometimes waive the one-year requirement for administrative convenience). For a defined-benefit plan the amount of the survivor annuity is basically equal to the amount that would have been paid under the qualified joint and survivor annuity (below). To determine this amount the plan administrator assumes that the participant he or she retired the day before death, or if the participant was not yet able to retire, left the company the day prior to death, survived until the plan's earliest retirement age, and then retired with an immediate joint and survivor annuity. For a defined-contribution plan the qualified preretirement survivor annuity is an annuity for the life of the surviving spouse that is at least actuarially equivalent to 50 percent of the vested account balance of the participant as of the date of death.

The QPSA need not be an employer-sponsored benefit; the employer has the choice of requiring employee contributions to fund this benefit or, conversely, reducing the normal benefit actuarially. If the second choice is the case, the employee generally has the option of electing out any time after age 35. A written confirmation of the spouse's consent to the election out is required. If the employer decides to fund the QPSA, an election out is not necessary, and the employer will save the administrative headache of accounting for employee contributions, judging the validity of spousal consent forms, and risking the potential litigation associated with a spousal consent mistake.

The qualified joint and survivor annuity (qualified J&S) must be the normal form of benefit distribution offered to a married participant at retirement. As with the QPSA, the participant can elect out of the benefit with spousal consent. The election out (which is common) must be made during a 90-day period prior to the annuity's starting date. The rationale for this short period is to prevent the employee from making a premature choice regarding what form of distribution to take from the retirement plan.

Note that the qualified preretirement survivor annuity rule only applies when a participant has a vested interest in his or her benefit prior to death.

In addition, plans of the profit-sharing type (including profit-sharing plans, stock bonus plans, ESOPs, and 401(k) plans) are not required to provide the QJSA and QPSA benefits if certain criteria are met. Most advisers encourage employers to take advantage of this exception in order to simplify plan administration. In order to qualify for the exception the plan must not allow any life annuity options, and must not accept direct transfers of plan benefits from other plans subject to the QJSA requirements. Finally, the plan must provide that if a married participant dies prior to retirement, the spouse must be entitled to receive 100 percent of the participant's plan benefit (the spouse can waive the benefit).

THE PS 58 RULE

As discussed in chapter 1, employees are generally not taxed on the benefits promised from or the contributions made to a qualified plan. Taxation occurs at the time benefits are received. The one exception is when life insurance is purchased in a plan to provide death benefits. In this case the current cost of the "pure insurance" protection is subject to taxation. The cost attributable to this pure life protection will be the lower of the actual cost as provided by the carrier or the rates supplied by the so-called PS 58 table (table 10-1).

TABLE 10-1
PS 58 Rates—One-Year Term Premiums for $1,000 of Life Insurance Protection*

Age	Premium	Age	Premium	Age	Premium
15	$1.27	37	$ 3.63	59	$ 19.08
16	1.38	38	3.87	60	20.73
17	1.48	39	4.14	61	22.53
18	1.52	40	4.42	62	24.50
19	1.56	41	4.73	63	26.63
20	1.61	42	5.07	64	28.98
21	1.67	43	5.44	65	31.51
22	1.73	44	5.85	66	34.28
23	1.79	45	6.30	67	37.31
24	1.86	46	6.78	68	40.59
25	1.93	47	7.32	69	44.17
26	2.02	48	7.89	70	48.06
27	2.11	49	8.53	71	52.29
28	2.20	50	9.22	72	56.89
29	2.31	51	9.97	73	61.89
30	2.43	52	10.79	74	67.33
31	2.57	53	11.69	75	73.23
32	2.70	54	12.67	76	79.63
33	2.86	55	13.74	77	86.57
34	3.02	56	14.91	78	94.09
35	3.21	57	16.18	79	102.23
36	3.41	58	17.56	80	111.04
				81	120.57

*These rates are used in computing the cost of pure life insurance protection that is taxable to the employee under qualified pension and profit-sharing plans. The rate at the insured's attained age is applied to the excess of the amount payable at death over the cash value of the policy at the end of the year.

If there is any good coming out of the PS 58 rule, it's that the PS 58 costs an employee pays (along with any employee aftertax contributions or employer contributions on which the employee has paid tax) are considered part of an employee's cost basis. When the employee takes retirement distributions from the plan, he or she will not be required to pay taxes on the portion of the distribution attributable to cost basis. In other words, the pure life insurance protection will not be taxed twice.

For a self-employed person with a Keogh plan, or a 5 percent owner in an S Corporation, however, the rules are applied differently. The portion of employer contribution that is allocable to the cost of pure insurance protection for the self-employed individual is treated as a nondeductible contribution. Also, at the time of payment, PS 58 costs are not recovered tax-free by the business owner.

THE IMPLICATIONS OF DEATH-BENEFIT DESIGN

There are innumerable reasons to include life insurance in an employee benefits package, including competitiveness, attraction and retention of employees, and other advantages for the business owner. By including life insurance protection in a benefit package business owners are able to (1) receive favorable group rates for themselves and their employees, (2) shift a nondeductible personal expense to the company, and (3) if necessary, gain favorable underwriting for ratable or uninsurable individuals (which potentially means life insurance protection without physical exams or medical questions).

What this boils down to is that the most important question facing the financial services professional is not whether death benefits should be provided, but rather which vehicle should provide them. Is it in the employer's best interest to provide the majority of death benefits in a group insurance plan or in a retirement plan? Which system will provide the lowest employee and employer cost for the desired benefit level?

If the tax consequences for the employee are the primary concern, as is the case with most small businesses, then the choice may be to maximize the death benefits in the group insurance plan. Reason: the applicable Sec. 79 table 1 tax rates for group plans are lower than the PS 58 costs applicable to retirement plans. This may not be true, however, when the actual costs of providing benefits in a pension plan are lower than PS 58 costs. What's more, Sec. 79 also provides a $50,000 exemption (the premiums paid for the first $50,000 of term insurance covering an employee are not taxable), which further eases the tax bite. Note, however, that the $50,000 exemption can be used with a group insurance plan that supplements a retirement plan; in other words, when it comes to the $50,000 exemption, there's no difference between group insurance plans and retirement plans as far as additional coverage over $50,000 is concerned.

If maximum retirement benefits are desired, as is the case with most closely held businesses, then a group insurance plan should be used, because the purchase of a life insurance benefit in a defined-contribution plan depletes the deductible retirement limit ($30,000). In a defined-benefit plan, however, death benefits do not inhibit the maximum retirement payout because the ultimate benefit payout ($125,000 annual pension) is not affected by incidental insurance costs.

For small organizations, however, providing the death benefit in the qualified plan may be more administratively convenient, be better serviced by the life agent, and do double duty for the retirement dollar by offering a tax-favored way of providing life insurance. In fact, the entire reason for the retirement plan may be to provide a tax-sheltered vehicle for the life insurance protection. Another reason to use life insurance in the qualified plan is that costs might be lower if turnover is high for short-service employees. Reason: the typical wait to participate in a qualified plan is longer than in a group plan.

DISABILITY BENEFITS

Designing a plan to include disability benefits is similar to designing one to include death benefits in the retirement plan. It's not a question of their inclusion in an employee benefit program but rather where these benefits belong. Most large companies that maintain separate long-term disability plans don't provide disability income benefits in their retirement program. If there is an existing disability income program, the financial services professional needs to be concerned only with the coordination of the retirement plan and the disability income plan. For example, is the retirement plan designed to provide adequate benefits after the long-term disability income benefits stop? This can be a problem if the retirement benefit is based on service and service is cut short because of disability. One way that retirement plans can be designed to deal with this problem is by stipulating that service for benefit purposes continues to accrue if disability occurs. For example, in a defined-benefit plan where the benefit at normal retirement age will be equal to 2 percent multiplied by years of service multiplied by final salary, the plan can stipulate that service will be earned during each year of disability. Another way retirement plans are able to overcome the lack-of-service problem is to immediately vest participants 100 percent in their accrued benefit or account balance if disability occurs.

Sometimes an employer has a separate disability plan in addition to a retirement plan that provides disability benefits. In this case you as the planner must coordinate your client's retirement and disability benefits so that there is no duplication of coverage.

A third possibility is for the employer to set up a retirement plan that provides all the disability benefits. If disability benefits are provided in the retirement plan, as is the case with many small plans, benefits can take several forms:

- They can be a distribution of a 100-percent-vested accrued benefit or account balance.
- They can be a distribution from a defined-benefit plan plus a plan-paid subsidy.
- They can be provided by disability insurance purchased under the plan.

No matter what form the disability benefit takes, there are two additional decisions about plan design that must be made when the retirement plan either totally or fully provides the disability benefit. First, the plan must contain a definition of *disability*. Typically the disability definition for a retirement plan is fairly restrictive. If a restrictive definition is desired, disability is said to occur when the social security disability definition is met. This makes the plan administrator's job easy—a painless verification is possible, and the social security people do all the work. If your client desires a more liberal definition of disability, you should remember to include standards for determination and verification. (*Planning Note:* One easy way to include standards for determination and verification is to purchase disability insurance and let the insurance policy definition and claims office make the determination.)

Second, consider whether or not the retirement plan's disability benefit should have age and service requirements. Reasons to include these requirements are to permit enough time for your client to properly fund the benefit and to reward only long-service employees with the benefit. What's more, if there are age and service provisions, the question of whether the disability was attributable to a preexisting condition is also sidestepped. The main reason for *not* having age and service requirements for disability is the negative impression it can create among employees.

TOP-HEAVY RULES

In chapter 1 it was implied that retirement plans were a tug-of-war. On one side of the rope are the government regulations regarding eligibility, coverage, and vesting. On the other side, pulling equally hard, are financial services professionals looking to gain tax-shelter and retirement protection for their clients who are business owners without overspending for the rank and file. The government's intervention stems from a spread-the-wealth philosophy and the desire to get the most for their money when it comes to allowing tax advantages for retirement plans.

The anchor of the government's tug-of-war team is the top-heavy rules, aimed specifically at small employers such as professional corporations and closely held businesses. The rationale for the strict scrutiny of small organizations is that employers and owners of these organizations are more prone to the temptation to shape the organization's retirement plan primarily to shelter taxes for themselves and key employees. As financial services professionals would be the first to attest, the government's suspicion is well founded. (Clients that fall into the small-plan category are almost invariably interested in tax shelter first and retirement needs second.)

The top-heavy rules are so inclusive that many financial services professionals design smaller plans according to top-heavy specifications without even bothering to take the traditional tack of designing plans according to regular pension rules and then adding contingency provisions in case the plan is or becomes top-heavy. As we shall see, under the rules for determining top-heaviness, this is a realistic approach for most small plans because they seldom can be anything *but* top-heavy.

When Is a Plan Top-Heavy?

A defined-contribution plan is top-heavy if more than 60 percent of the total amount in the accounts of all employees is allotted to key employees. Since defined-benefit plans use an accrued benefit instead of account balance, a defined-benefit plan is top-heavy if more than 60 percent of the present value of the entire amount of the plan's accrued benefits is set aside for key employees. In other words, if key employees have more than 60 percent of the retirement pie, the plan is considered top-heavy.

The top-heavy test is applied once a year (on the last day of the preceding plan year). The date the test will be performed is specified in the plan (under the definitions section) and is called the plan's determination date. Computer software is available for performing top-heavy testing, or if you prefer, a consulting or computer firm can conduct the test. What's more, there are a number of small software companies that have a telephone link to computers that perform the test under a user-fee arrangement. For a small defined-contribution plan, however, the test can be performed without assistance in a short amount of time.

The top-heavy test is detailed and replete with exceptions. For this reason an employer is fortunate to have access to such resources as consulting houses and computer software. Close scrutiny of the top-heavy rules is desirable from a planning standpoint, however, because understanding coupled with effective personnel decisions and plan design may enable the plan to escape top-heavy status.

The top-heavy test requires answers to the following questions:

- *Who is a key employee?* An individual is a key employee if any time during the current year or 4 preceding years he or she has been any of the following:

    - an officer receiving annual compensation in excess of $60,000, as indexed. (If there are 30 or fewer employees, no more than three officers are treated as key employees. If there are 31 to 500 employees, no more than 10 percent of the employees are treated as officers. And if there are more than 500 employees, no more than 50 officers are key employees.)
    - a person who owns more than 5 percent of the company (in pension parlance, a 5 percent owner). A 5 percent owner has value or voting power, capital, or profit interests in excess of 5 percent of the company.

- a person who is more than a 1 percent owner with annual compensation of more than $150,000
- one of the 10 employees owning the largest interest in the company (only employees with annual compensation in excess of $30,000 are taken into account)

To avoid top-heavy status an employer may want to keep these definitions in mind when setting up the pay scale. For example, it may design a salary range to top out at $55,000 or $29,000 instead of the $60,000 and $30,000 figures that push into the key-employee category.

- *Which employers will be treated as single employers for purposes of the top-heavy test?* Separate plans of related employers are generally aggregated for purposes of top-heavy testing. There is required aggregation of an employer's multiple plans with every plan that covers a key employee or that allows a key-employee plan to meet the applicable nondiscrimination and minimum-participation standards.

    For example, the National Paper Company maintains both a salaried-only plan, which covers some key employees, and a separate plan for hourly paid employees, none of whom is a key employee. If the salaried-only plan independently satisfies the nondiscrimination and minimum-participation rules (chapter 7), it is not aggregated and is tested independently for top-heaviness. However, if the salaried-only plan satisfies nondiscrimination and minimum-participation requirements only when considered together with the hourly plan, a required aggregation results. If the required aggregation group is top-heavy, then each plan in the group is top-heavy. If the group is not top-heavy, however, then neither plan is top-heavy.

Permissive aggregation—that is, picking and choosing whom to group together—is also possible. Planners can use permissive aggregation if the hourly plan (a nonkey-employee plan) is not needed to help the key-employee plan satisfy the nondiscrimination and minimum-participation requirements but is needed to prevent top-heaviness. In other words, if a plan covering key employees is top-heavy and permissive aggregation would avert top-heavy status, it is desirable to use these rules.

Top-Heavy Provisions

Almost all plan documents must contain top-heavy language. The plan document must specify that if the plan is or ever becomes top-heavy, certain special rules, described below, will become effective. Larger plans (covering over 100 employees) are rarely top-heavy, and top-heavy contingency language is included in the boilerplate language of the plan. However, most small plans (covering 25 or fewer employees) will be top-heavy. Therefore these plans should be designed to automatically comply with the special top-heavy provisions. In fact, many prototype plans are drafted like this.

Whether or not the plan is designed to satisfy the top-heavy requirements or contingency top-heavy provisions are included, you must ensure that the plan design (or contingency provisions) meet the following top-heavy requirements:

- special vesting rules
- minimum benefits for nonkey employees
- a special limit for situations where both a defined-benefit and a defined contribution plan are present

If these rules are met, a top-heavy plan will continue to remain qualified.

Special Top-Heavy Vesting Schedules

The top-heavy vesting schedules are similar to the schedules that were discussed earlier, only more liberal for the employee. The schedules are

1. The top-heavy version of the 5-year-cliff schedule is a 3-year/100 percent cliff schedule. (In other words, an employee must be 100 percent vested after 3 years of service.)
2. The top-heavy version of the 3-through-7 graded schedule is a 6-year graded schedule that increases the vested percentage 20 percent for each year of service after the first year. Either of these top-heavy schedules can be chosen regardless of which non-top-heavy schedule is used.

<u>6-Year Graded Schedule</u>

Years of Service	Percentage Vested
0–1	0
2	20
3	40
4	60
5	80
6	100

Employers with a top-heavy plan can choose instead to take advantage of the 2 years' required eligibility and 100 percent immediate vesting rules. Depending upon the company's turnover characteristics, this alternative may be less expensive than a 1-year-eligibility and a 3-year-cliff schedule, because contributions for an employee are not required for the extra year of delayed eligibility. When faced with this design choice, planners should take a close look at the 2-year/100 percent scenario.

Minimum Benefits and Contributions for Nonkey Employees

A top-heavy plan must provide minimum benefits or contributions for nonkey employees. For defined-benefit plans the benefit for each nonkey employee must be at least 2 percent of compensation multiplied by the number of the employee's years of service in which the plan is top-heavy up to a maximum of 10 years. In other words, a defined-benefit plan must generally fund a 20 percent benefit for nonkey employees in the years the plan is top-heavy, which could mean additional plan costs if the minimum required benefit is more than the actual plan benefit. Extra funding is typically called for if the plan is integrated with social security. Reason: a top-heavy plan cannot take into account benefits or contributions under social security to satisfy the minimum-benefit requirement. This effectively prohibits the required top-heavy minimum contribution from being eliminated or reduced by the integration of the plan with social security.

For a defined-contribution plan the minimum employer contribution must be no less than 3 percent of each nonkey employee's compensation (provided the key employees receive at least 3 percent). As with defined-benefit plans, the minimum amount cannot be eliminated or reduced through social security integration. But unlike defined-benefit plans, defined-contribution plans are less likely to incur extra plan expense because of the required top-heavy minimum contribution. Reason: defined-contribution plans generally provide a higher base amount for nonkey employees so that key employees can receive adequate benefits without discrimination.

Planning Considerations

Many—if not most—plans of small business become top-heavy within a few years of formation. This means that the top-heavy rules do have a significant impact on plan design. By far the biggest concern today are the problems that the top-heavy rules cause the small 401(k) plan. One problem is that even salary deferral only plans can become top-heavy. Remember that employee salary deferrals are treated as employer contributions and therefore count when making the top-heavy determination. If the plan becomes top-heavy the employer will be forced to make the required 3 percent contribution for non-key employees. The rules also state that the minimum can generally not be satisfied with matching contributions. The real problem comes when the plan advisor fails to notify the sponsor of this potential liability—and the business owner is surprised to find out at the end of the year that the additional 3 percent contribution must be made.

SEPs and SARSEPs are also subject to the top-heavy rules. And SARSEPs have had the same type of problems as the small 401(k) plan. Finally, Congress has come up with some solutions in the Small Jobs Protection Act of 1996. Under the new law, SIMPLEs and 401(k) plans that adopt the SIMPLE provisions will not be subject to the top-heavy rules—while traditional 401(k) plans continue to be. For this reason small businesses that are looking for a salary savings plan that has the smallest required contribution will want to explore the implications of adopting one of these alternative plan designs.

The following describe some other common issues that arise under the top-heavy rules:

- *Cross-tested plans*—If the employer establishes a plan that is intended to limit contributions for the rank-and-file employees, the top-heavy minimum generally creates a floor—or minimum—contribution that can be made.
- *Multiple plans*—If a sponsor maintains more than one plan, regulations provide that the top-heavy minimum contribution can be made to one—and not both—of the plans. Employers adopting multiple plans need to address this issue in the plan design process, to make sure that the plans don't both require minimum contributions.

11

Plan Funding and Investing—Part 1

Chapter Outline

This chapter and the next provide an overview of the issues surrounding plan funding and investing. In this chapter, three important issues are addressed. First is a review of the plan funding requirements. For defined-benefit plans, this topic is quite involved, while for other types of plans, the issue is quite straightforward. The next topic is a review of the various funding vehicles that are used in conjunction with tax-advantaged retirement plans. This discussion will also help you to become more familiar with what parties are responsible for plan investing. The third topic in this chapter addresses the legal constraints surrounding the investment of plan assets. Here we will talk about who is legally responsible for making investment decisions, what investment limitations apply, and liability for failing to meet fiduciary standards.

The following chapter focuses entirely on plan investing. There we will discuss choosing an appropriate investment policy; then we will look at various investment options. The materials first cover typical investment classes and their role in the investment mix, and then go into specialized insurance products that have been developed to meet specific needs.

PLAN FUNDING REQUIREMENTS

The financial services professional needs to be acquainted with the plan funding requirements, much as the home buyer needs to be familiar with the plumbing and heating systems of a potential purchase. In other words, a passing knowledge of some of the buzzwords and the general implications can help you avoid an unpleasant experience. And although a detailed understanding of the complex requirements and their underlying actuarial voodoo is unnecessary, you should understand enough to be able to school your client in the basics and to deal effectively with a consulting actuary.

Once a tax-advantaged retirement plan is in place, the employer must fund it in order to meet the benefit obligations promised under the plan. At one time it was possible for the employer to wait until the employee retired and monthly retirement obligations became due before providing for the employee's benefit. This pay-as-you-go system (also called a *terminal funding* approach) is no longer possible. Instead, retirement benefits must be prefunded according to the minimum funding standards that were set out in ERISA.

Under the minimum funding standards, employers are required to (1) set aside funds irrevocably (meaning that the pension money is beyond the reach of the employer or the employer's creditors), (2) place the funds with a trustee, custodian, or insurance company, and (3) fund their retirement obligations in advance. Advance funding basically means that the employer must pay the retirement liability according to specific rules

Funding Defined-Benefit Plans

This section will explore the legal requirements of defined-benefit plan funding by answering three questions: (1) What is the minimum amount of funding necessary for plan qualification? (2) What role does the plan's actuary play? (3) What is the maximum amount of funding permitted in a defined-benefit plan?

Minimum Funding Standards

Under defined-benefit plans, an organization's annual liability (normal cost) is determined by an actuarial valuation. The rules regarding actuarial valuations—which are complex to start with—become even more complicated if the plan provides benefits based on past service. (*Planning Note:* The intent of the minimum funding standards is to protect against situations where participants are left empty-handed because promised retirement benefits have not been delivered. The minimum funding standards, however, do not always effectively protect against this contingency. It is possible under current law to have a defined-benefit plan that is underfunded and unable to pay promised benefits, despite the fact that recent legislation has been enacted to tighten funding requirements.)

There are several actuarial cost methods that can be used to determine the normal cost and, if applicable, the past-service liability. These actuarial cost methods are basically a pension subspecialty handled by actuaries and are beyond the scope of this text. But we will discuss the implications that these tools of actuarial valuation, as controlled by the plan's actuary, have for your client.

The Role of the Plan Actuary

As you might imagine, the most important decision the plan actuary advises on is what cost method to use for a defined-benefit plan (how to determine the annual employer contribution for a given set of plan benefits and a given group of employees). If the wrong cost method is chosen, it will cause funding problems. Reason: the cost method can run counter to the employer's ability to fund the plan. The right cost method should provide the plan sponsor with flexibility in funding and also meet the employer's tax objectives. It ideally allows large contributions (tax write-offs) in prosperous years and minimum liability in lean years or years when there's a cash-flow crunch.

As a rule of thumb the actuary can generally recommend a cost method that will provide for relatively level costs from year to year (figure 11-1, chart 1, the projected-benefit cost method) or a method that will provide for lower liability at first but will increase until the plan reaches maturity (chart 2, the accrued-benefit cost method). If there's an attempt to fund for past service, these payments can be used either to round up the projected-benefit cost method (chart 3) or level off the accrued-benefit cost method (chart 4). If the funding for past service is not treated as enhancing the existing method, the plan is said to be with supplemental liability; if the funding for past service is treated separately, it is said to be without supplemental liability. The graphs in figure 11-1 can be compared with the projected cash-flow needs of the employer and will illustrate to the employer which system is best.

Neither the plan actuary nor the choice of an actuarial cost method bears any relationship to the ultimate cost of the plan. The ultimate cost cannot be known until the last benefit is paid and the plan is over. In other words, your client generally will never know his or her ultimate liability when adopting the plan. What the actuary does through the use of a cost method, however, is to set up a situation where there is flexibility in funding the annual liability for which your client is responsible. The actuary can help to maximize flexibility by, for example, setting up a past-service liability rather than amortizing past-service and future-service costs together.

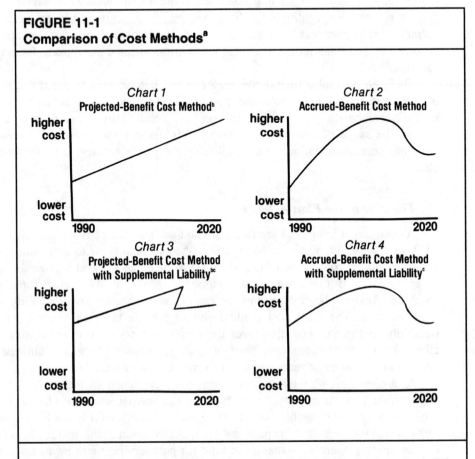

FIGURE 11-1
Comparison of Cost Methods[a]

Chart 1
Projected-Benefit Cost Method[b]

Chart 2
Accrued-Benefit Cost Method

Chart 3
Projected-Benefit Cost Method
with Supplemental Liability[bc]

Chart 4
Accrued-Benefit Cost Method
with Supplemental Liability[c]

[a] Each chart assumes an open group (one in which normal turnover occurs); if the groups are closed (just include a certain group of employees),each chart will have a sharper incline.
[b] Level funding means level as a percentage of payroll; the payroll, however, will typically increase over a given period to accommodate inflation.
[c] The drop-off for charts 3 and 4 occurs at the end of 30 years, when the past-service liability has been fully amortized. Actually the plan sponsor can choose to amortize past service in as few as 10 years (for larger write-offs; this is generally chosen by small plans looking for tax shelter) or as many as 30 years.

In addition to choosing the cost method, the actuary is responsible for making certain assumptions regarding several variables; the plan's annual costs vary depending on the assumptions used. These assumptions include the following:

- the number of employees who will be eligible to receive benefits (the higher the number of employees, the higher the annual cost)
- the final-average salary that all the employees will have, if benefits are based on final-average salary (the higher the assumption, the higher the annual cost)
- the mortality rate—the rate at which active employees and already-retired workers will die (the higher the mortality assumption, the lower the annual cost)
- the disability rate—primarily for nonretired participants (the higher the disability assumption, the higher the annual cost)
- the turnover rate, including the rate of new employee replacements (the higher the turnover assumption, the lower the annual cost)
- the retirement ages, if early retirement is an option and is subsidized (the higher the early-retirement assumption, the higher the annual cost)
- the length of the benefit period for retired employees (the longer the life expectancy, the higher the annual cost)
- the investment return—the investment income earned on the accumulated assets of the plan (the higher the investment assumption, the lower the estimated annual cost.

No matter what cost methods or assumptions the actuary chooses, he or she must satisfy the *funding standard account,* an accounting tool (required by IRS regulations) that shows whether the plan is "adequately funded." Like an income statement, the funding standard account (which is used for accounting purposes only) is annually debited with plan costs and other amounts necessary to meet the minimum funding standard. It is also credited with the employer's contribution and such other things as decreases in plan liabilities and interest gains (interest gains occur when actual interest earnings exceed expected interest earnings). The cost methods the actuary works with are basically different approaches to funding this account, with different rules for defining the permissible limits of the actual account itself. (*Planning Note:* If there is a deficiency in the funding standard account there is a 10 percent excise tax on the amount of the accumulated funding deficiency. If the funding deficiency is not corrected within the permitted time, an excise tax of 100 percent applies to the accumulated funding deficiency.)

What should be obvious by now is that the actuary has a certain leeway in setting the plan's annual cost. Note, however, that this leeway is not unlimited, because the actuary is restricted to reasonable assumptions and IRS-approved funding methods. But the bottom line is that the actuary is able to meet the cash-flow and tax needs of your client, within limits.

YOUR FINANCIAL SERVICES PRACTICE:
TEMPORARY FUNDING RELIEF

If your client's cash-flow needs become burdensome, you may wish to suggest that he or she request the IRS to waive the minimum funding standards for a particular year. The IRS may grant a waiver of the minimum funding standards and the corresponding excise tax for any year in which the employer is unable to make the necessary contributions without "substantial business hardship." Be aware, however, that the waiver will be given only if it does not harm the interests of the plan's participants. What's more, any waived contributions must be made up, with interest, in future years.

The Fully Insured Life Insurance Option

Some employers enjoy the funding flexibility available under the minimum funding standards used by defined-benefit plans. There are others, however, who would prefer fixed costs and can sleep better knowing what their liabilities are. There is relief for these employers if the plan is funded by individual insurance policies because the premiums are fixed and so is the employer liability. Under a plan that is funded by individual insurance contracts, it is the insurance company's actuary who selects the assumptions and the actuarial cost method. The premium based on that actuary's assumptions is the actual contribution due. What's more, fully insured plans (plans funded in their entirety by level-premium annuities or retirement-income contracts) are exempt from the minimum funding standards (and their corresponding administrative costs, such as actuarial fees) if (1) the insurance contract provides for level premiums from participation until retirement, (2) the benefits under the plan are equal to the benefits provided under the contract, (3) the benefits are guaranteed by a licensed insurance company, (4) premiums are paid on time, (5) there are no rights under the contract subject to a security interest, and (6) there are no policy loans.

Maximum Deductible Contributions

The minimum funding standards helped to eliminate the problem of employers who underfunded their retirement plans and eventually disappointed employees who expected to receive a retirement benefit. For some employers, however, such as small closely held corporations and professional corporations, the opposite problem exists. Small business owners generally prefer to make excessive deductible contributions to a pension fund for purposes of accelerating tax deductions and increasing the tax-shelter potential of the qualified plan. To prevent such excessive contributions, there are rules specifying the maximum deductible amount that can be made annually.

Like the minimum funding rules the determination of the maximum deductible contribution is based upon actuarial calculations. The first rule here is that the maximum allowable contribution will never be less than the required contribution under the minimum-funding rules. Then the actuary can compare this number to the contribution determined under two other calculations:

1. Determine the normal cost (the cost of the current year's liability under the plan's chosen actuarial method) plus the cost of funding one-tenth of the past-service liability (benefits based on past service).
2. Determine the unfunded cost of past and current service credits distributed at a level amount over the future service for each participant.

The maximum deductible contribution is the largest of these three calculations, but is then limited by an overriding limit referred to as the *full-funding limit*. Under this limit the maximum deduction can never exceed the lesser of (1) 150 percent of the plan's current liability (the present value of accrued benefits earned to date) less the value of plan assets or (2) 100 percent of the plan's actuarial accrued liability (the present value of all current and projected benefits).

Note that the 150 percent of the plan's current liability full-funding limit is especially troublesome. The rule was enacted to limit tax expenditures, but it inadvertently can disrupt the orderly funding of the plan. The goal of any funding method is to ensure that assets are sufficient to pay promised benefits at retirement. The 150 percent limit calculation views the plan's financial status based solely upon benefits accrued currently, and it disregards the total promised benefit. The full-funding limit has been strongly criticized by actuarial groups as being inconsistent with the policy of ensuring benefit security. Because of this limit, the maximum contribution may be significant one year and zero the next—making financial and tax planning difficult. An employer sponsoring a defined-benefit plan needs to understand the potential impact of the full-funding limit in order to avoid being surprised by the inconsistent contribution limits.

Funding Requirements for Other Types of Plans

Although the minimum funding requirements are most complex for the defined-benefit plan, it is important to note that the requirements do apply to other pension plans as well. This includes the two types of defined-contribution plans that are also pension plans—target-benefit and money-purchase pension plans. The minimum required contributions under this type of plan is the amount required under the plan's contribution formula each year. Failure to meet the required contribution would subject the plan to the 10 percent excise tax on funding deficiencies that applies to defined-benefit plans.

The minimum funding requirements do not apply to profit-sharing plans, stock bonus plans, ESOPs, SEPs, SIMPLEs, or 403(b) plans. Technically, this means that the 10 percent excise tax will not apply for failure to make contributions. However, if the plan document calls for a required annual contribution in one of these types of plans, the employer will have to make the contribution. Otherwise the plan will face disqualification since the employer failed to follow the terms of the plan.

When a plan has a specified contribution, this amount essentially constitutes the minimum and maximum allowable contributions. For discretionary profit-sharing plans, stock bonus plans, employee stock ownership plans, or SEPs the maximum contribution will be subject to the limitations discussed previously— that is, no individual can receive an annual allocation in excess of the lesser of 25 percent of compensation or $30,000 and the total employer contribution cannot exceed 15 percent of compensation of all participating employees.

FUNDING VEHICLES

A qualified plan must use a funding instrument, which must be a trust, custodial account, or group insurance contract. This section will discuss these various funding instruments and how they work, as well as the typical parties involved in the investment of plan assets. The rules are different for the other tax-advantaged retirement plans.

As discussed in chapter 6, SEPs and SIMPLEs must use individual retirement accounts and annuities, while 403(b) plans must use annuity contracts or mutual fund custodial accounts.

Trusts

Trusts are the most popular funding vehicles for qualified plans. The trust approach allows for tremendous flexibility in both investments and benefit design.

A trust used for a qualified plan is based on the same principles of trust law as trusts used for other purposes. This means that the grantor of the trust is the plan's sponsor; that the grantor transfers the *res* (the plan assets) to trustees of the trust; and that the trust makes payments as specified to the beneficiaries of the trust (the plan participants and their beneficiaries).

Like all trusts, a trust used for a qualified plan contains a trust agreement, which is set up primarily to control the receipt, investment, and disbursement of funds. A typical trust agreement spells out certain particulars:

- the irrevocability of trust assets
- the investment powers of the trustee (the investment discretion of a trustee varies from plan to plan; in some cases, the employer wants to maintain full control; in others, the trustee or investment manager has almost unchecked discretion)

- the allocation of fiduciary responsibility to a named fiduciary (who is responsible for the plan and becomes the target of legal action when required)
- the payments of benefits and plan expenses
- the rights and duties in case of plan termination

If the plan is large enough, the trustees may also keep records of employer and employee contributions, each participant's salary and service, and account and benefit information. In smaller plans this function is handled outside the trust agreement by the employer, third party plan administrator, or a consulting company.

An essential part of the trusteed plan is the plan trustees, who may be corporate (banks and trust companies) and/or individuals related to the business. The trustees carry out a variety of functions, including

- accepting and investing employer contributions
- paying benefits to plan participants
- providing periodic accounting to the employer of investments, receipts, disbursements, and other transactions involving plan assets
- maintaining administrative records, if appropriate

It's important to remember that when carrying out these duties trustees have a fiduciary relationship to plan participants. As discussed further in the next section, the fiduciaries must act in the best interest of the plan participants. Thus a business owner who is also a plan trustee cannot act in his or her own self-interest. Also the trustee must act prudently, as compared to other plan trustees, meaning that a business executive should think carefully before choosing to become plan trustee.

In large plans, sometimes the trustee acts primarily as custodian of plan assets, while the fund is invested by several investment managers. Investment managers will also be plan fiduciaries, subject to essentially the same standard of care in handling plan investments. Similarly, in smaller plans, the executives will act as trustees, while one or more corporate investment managers are responsible for investing. Regardless of the arrangement, in all cases those responsible for investing plan assets are responsible to act in accordance with the plan documents and in accordance with the funding and investment policies (discussed further in the next chapter), which are established by the employer or a committee made up of executives of the employer.

In lieu of a trust agreement, the funding vehicle can also be a custodial account with a bank (or other person as authorized by IRS regulations under Code Sec. 401(f)) as custodian. With the custodial account approach, the custodian will be the record keeper, with others actually investing plan assets.

Common Trust Funds

Generally the assets of a trust cannot be commingled or pooled with the assets of other trusts; a separate accounting and segregation of trust assets is usually required. However, an exception to this rule applies to common trust funds. Common trust funds, which are sponsored and operated by banks and trust companies, permit the pooling of funds from all participating trusts (typically many small-plan sponsors). The trust buys units of a common fund, which either increase or decrease in value depending on investment return. The common trust fund was developed because relatively small trust fund plans couldn't adequately diversify their investment portfolios on their own. In addition to eliminating the diversification problem, common trust funds also provide the potential for higher return (because of their size they can attract expert investment advice), lower brokerage fees, and liquidity of funds to meet cash requirements.

Split-Funded Plans

This term refers to a plan that uses a trust fund arrangement, but chooses to invest a portion of plan assets in insurance and annuity contracts. Insurance products can include individual insurance and annuity contracts or any of the group funding products discussed in the next chapter. This approach can be used to take advantage of the flexibility of the trust approach while also taking advantage of the guarantees of insurance products, the ability to provide significant death benefits through the plan, or simply the yields available in a group product.

Annuity Plans

A pension plan under which retirement benefits are completely provided by annuity or insurance contracts does not have to maintain a trust fund. This applies to both individual and group products. However, to avoid the trust requirement, the terms of the plan must be incorporated in the policy. This is not practical with individual policies, and therefore individual policies are generally issued under a trust fund agreement, with the trustee as owner of the policies. With a group policy, it is more common for the master contract to be the sole investment vehicle.

As you can see from the discussion of trusteed plans, split-funded plans, and annuity plans, the pension plan can be funded with really any combination of trust fund and insurance product investments. What really will distinguish the insurance product is not the type of documentation, but the strength of the investment contracts. This subject is discussed more fully in the following chapter.

LEGISLATIVE ENVIRONMENT FOR PLAN INVESTING

The legislative scheme for making sure that plan assets are invested appropriately focuses on controlling the behavior of those individuals (and business entities) most responsible for the investment of plan assets. These individuals, referred to as fiduciaries, are required to make investment decisions in accordance with certain standards and are required to avoid certain *prohibited transactions*. Below is an overview of who is considered a fiduciary, affirmative obligations, prohibited transactions, and penalties these parties may face for failing to meet appropriate standards of care.

Before beginning this discussion, it is important to note that the rules discussed in this section apply to plans that are covered by title I of ERISA. This will generally include qualified plans, SEPs and SIMPLEs, and, in some cases, 403(b) plans. As discussed in chapter 6, certain 403(b) programs that allow only for employee salary deferrals (and no other employer contributions) will not be subject to the ERISA rules discussed below.

In addition to the ERISA limitations, there are several other special investment limitations. First, plans funded with IRAs (SEPs and SIMPLEs) cannot invest in life insurance or collectibles (see chapter 6). Second, 403(b) plans have even more investment limitations, as assets can be invested only in annuity contracts, mutual funds, and life insurance. On the other hand, there are no specific prohibited investment classes for qualified plans.

Individuals Considered Fiduciaries under ERISA

Individuals who are considered fiduciaries for their role in the investment of plan assets include those persons who have discretionary authority over the disposition of plan assets and those individuals who render investment advice for a fee (or other direct or indirect compensation). Practically speaking, this will include the sponsoring company, plan trustees, investment managers (including insurance companies), and officers of the company who participate in the selection of trustees and/or investment managers.

Service providers, such as accountants, lawyers, and administrative firms, are generally not considered fiduciaries unless they have in fact control over plan assets. Even individuals selling investments to the plan will generally not be considered fiduciaries. According to DOL regulations rendering investment advice for a fee means

- exercising discretionary control over the purchase or sale of securities or
- providing investment advice regularly on the purchase and sale of assets, with such advice being the primary basis for the investment of plan assets

This definition is rather limited and excludes most individuals who sell insurance or other investment products. However, determining whether someone is a fiduciary is based on the facts and circumstances (regardless of whether the individual is specifically identified as a fiduciary), and even commissioned insurance agents have been determined to have been fiduciaries when the agent's advice has been determined to be the primary basis for the investment of plan assets.

Affirmative Fiduciary Obligations

Fiduciaries involved in the investment of plan assets are required to make decisions within the framework of four rules: the exclusive benefit requirement, the prudent person standard of care, the diversification rule, and the requirement that investment decisions conform with plan and trust documents. Below each of these rules is described in more detail.

Exclusive Benefit Rule

Fiduciaries are required to discharge their duties solely in the interest of the plan's participants and beneficiaries for the exclusive purpose of providing benefits and defraying reasonable expenses. This means that the fiduciary must act in the plan participant's interest first and foremost. However, if the investment is good for the employees, it is not necessarily illegal to have a collateral benefit for the employer. Nevertheless, investment decisions that involve any consideration other than the financial interest of plan participants can be quite tricky. The DOL, in Bulletin 94-1, has indicated that a fiduciary can consider benefits to the employees (such as job security) as long as the investment return is commensurate with alternative investments with similar risks. This opinion is considered somewhat controversial and could be changed in later opinions or by legislation. If a fiduciary sees the possibility of a conflict of loyalty between the plan participants and another party (employer), according to the DOL[1] he or she should seek the advice of a competent, independent adviser and possibly elect not to participate in the decision.

Prudence

Fiduciaries must act with the care, skill, prudence, and diligence (under prevailing circumstances) that a prudent person acting in a like capacity and familiar with such matters would use in the conduct of an enterprise of a like character and with like aims. Note that this standard compares, for example, plan trustees to other experienced plan trustees. With regard to choosing prudent investments, DOL regulations[2] refer to six factors that should be considered:

- role of the investment as part of the plan's overall portfolio
- whether the investment is reasonably designed as part of the portfolio
- risk of loss and opportunity for gain

- diversification of the portfolio
- liquidity and current return relative to the anticipated cash flow requirements of the plan
- projected return of the portfolio relative to the funding objectives of the plan

One court[3] indicated that proper fiduciary procedures included

- employing proper methods to investigate, evaluate, and structure the investment, including retaining a professional adviser if the fiduciary lacks sufficient expertise
- acting in a manner consistent with others who have a similar capacity and familiarity with such matters
- exercising independent judgment when making investment decisions

Being prudent does not mean that fiduciaries have to avoid risky investments. DOL Interpretive Bulletin 95-1 clarifies that an investment that has substantial risk is not in itself a problem as long as the expected return is commensurate with the risk and the risk is weighed against the anticipated return in the context of the plan's investment portfolio and of its funding, liquidity, and diversification needs.

Diversification of Investments

Trustees have the duty to diversify the investments of the plan to minimize the risk of large losses, unless under the plan it is clearly prudent not to do so. According to legislative history of ERISA,[4] "clearly prudent" language was intended to mean that if a fiduciary was sued for failing to diversify investments, once the plaintiff demonstrated that assets were not diversified, the defendant fiduciary would have the burden of proof to demonstrate why his or her actions were appropriate. Apparently, the diversification referred to here means both diversification among asset classes and diversification within a single asset class.

Conformance with Documents

Finally, fiduciaries are required to operate the plan in accordance with the document and instruments governing the plan. Trust instruments will spell out the types of investments that are allowed, whether any types of investments are prohibited, and who is responsible for making the decisions. Problems in this area do arise when trustees and others make investment decisions without carefully consulting relevant documents. If the plan has a funding policy, an investment policy, or both (discussed further below), these documents must be carefully followed as well.

Limitations: The Individual Account Plan Exception

Since qualified plans of the defined-contribution type allocate dollars to the separate accounts of participants, the sponsoring employer has the option either to direct the trustees to invest plan assets or to give participants some choice over the investment of individual accounts. Since SEPs and SIMPLEs are funded with individual IRAs, participants almost always have investment options. Similarly, 403(b) plans almost always give participants investment choices.

If a defined-contribution plan, SEP, SIMPLE, or 403(b) plan gives individual participants options with regard to the investment of their own plan benefits, it makes sense that the fiduciaries should not be responsible for the participant's investment decisions. ERISA Sec. 404(c) grants such fiduciary relief by providing that in the case of a participant exercising independent investment direction over his or her own account, no fiduciary will be liable for losses that arise from such participant direction.

In order to qualify for this relief, the plan must conform with strict DOL requirements. The DOL's general rule is that the plan must provide an opportunity for a participant or beneficiary to exercise control over the assets in his or her account and offer the individual an opportunity to choose from a broad range of investment alternatives.

More specifically, the rules require the following:

- *Number of investment options*—Participants must have the opportunity to choose from at least three investment alternatives, each with materially different risk and return characteristics. Also, in the aggregate, the options must offer a balanced mix appropriate for a participant and, when combined with the other investments, have the effect of minimizing risks.
- *Employer stock*—Securities of the plan sponsor can also be an investment option; however, this cannot be one of the three core options.
- *Diversification*—To meet diversification requirements, the investment options generally must be "look-through investments," such as mutual funds, pooled separate accounts, or guaranteed investment contracts.
- *Election frequency*—The opportunity to change investment elections with respect to each investment alternative must be appropriate in light of market volatility. At a minimum, the three core investment alternatives must offer the opportunity to change investment choice at least quarterly.
- *Exercise of control*—participant must be given a reasonable opportunity to give investment instructions to the fiduciary either in writing or otherwise (as long as the participant can request a written confirmation).
- *Adequate information*—The participant must also be provided with specific information regarding the investment options. The central item is a description of the investment alternatives and a general description

of the risk and return characteristics of each alternative. Participants must also be informed about procedures for making elections, any expenses involved, and whom to go to for additional information. Also note that participants must be notified that the plan is seeking to qualify for the fiduciary limitations under ERISA Sec. 404(c).

- *Information upon request*—Upon request, the participant has the right to receive additional information about each investment alternative, including copies of the prospectus, description of operating expenses (as a percentage of net assets), and other detailed financial information about each option.

Note that nothing in the regulations mandates that a plan offering individual investment options meet these requirements. If the rules are not satisfied then the fiduciary could still be liable if the participant makes an imprudent investment choice. Meeting the requirements is the best way to protect the plan fiduciaries. However, if a plan sponsor decides that meeting the requirements in the DOL regulations is impractical, yet still wants to give participants investment choices, the next best line of protection is adequate fiduciary insurance and employer indemnification. Also, in this case, employee investment education and communication can also serve to minimize risk.

If all the rules are satisfied then ERISA Sec. 404(c) indicates that the fiduciary will not be liable for a breach of duty because of the participants' exercise of control over the investment decisions. In other words, the fiduciary is not responsible for the results of the participant's asset allocation decision.

> *Example:* Emily, aged 60, decides to invest all of her 401(k) account in an aggressive growth stock mutual fund, shunning the four other, less risky alternatives. In the following year, the value of her account drops by 20 percent. Under 404(c), the fiduciary should not be liable for Emily's loss because it was her decision.

Still, 404(c) does not get the fiduciary completely off the hook. Fiduciaries are obligated to ensure that participant investment choices do not constitute prohibited transactions. Further, investment choices must conform with other fiduciary obligations—such as compliance with plan documents. Most important, fiduciaries are never granted relief from the obligation to prudently select the available options. In the example above, if the aggressive growth fund available to Emily has had inferior performance—as compared to similar aggressive growth funds—then the fiduciary may have a liability problem.

Prohibited Transactions

A large number of transactions are prohibited because they are deemed by their nature to be contrary to the interest of plan participants. Their common denominator is that they include transactions involving the plan and those parties close to the plan or employer (referred to as *parties in interest*). More specifically, these individuals are defined as any individuals in the following eight categories:

1. All plan fiduciaries, as well as plan counsel to and employees of the plan;
2. Plan service providers;
3. Sponsoring employers;
4. Employee organizations (for example, unions) whose members are covered;
5. Fifty percent owners of an employer or an employee organization described in paragraphs (3) or (4);
6. Relatives of individuals described in paragraphs (1), (2), (3), or (5);
7. Organizations (including corporations, partnerships, and trusts) that are owned by persons described in paragraphs (1), (2), (3), (4), or (5);
8. Employees, officers, directors, and 10 percent owners of the sponsoring employer or others described in paragraph (2), (3), (4), (5), (7).

There are several different categories of prohibited transactions. The first category prohibits a fiduciary from causing the plan to engage in a transaction if the fiduciary knows or should know that such transaction constitutes a direct or indirect

- sale, exchange, or leasing of any property between the plan and a party in interest;
- lending of money or other extension of credit between the plan and a party in interest;
- furnishing of goods, services, or facilities between the plan and a party in interest;
- transfer to, or use by or for the benefit of, a party in interest, of any assets of the plan; or
- acquisition, on behalf of the plan, of any employer security or employer real property in violation of ERISA Sec. 407(a).

Another category of prohibited transactions involves the investment in the sponsoring employer's stock or real property. First, a plan can only hold "qualifying employer securities," (defined as stock or marketable obligations), and "qualifying employer real property" (which is property leased from the plan to the employer). Second, a plan may not acquire any qualifying employer security or qualifying employer real property if, immediately after such acquisition, the aggregate fair market value of employer securities and employer real property held by the plan exceeds 10 percent of the fair market value of the assets of the plan. However, the 10 percent limitation does not apply to profit-sharing type plans (including profit-sharing, stock bonus, 401(k), and employee stock ownership plans), as long as the plan provides that more than 10 percent of plan assets can be invested in qualifying employer real property or qualifying employer securities.

A third category of prohibited transactions involves self-dealing. Here, the fiduciary is required to avoid using plan assets for his or her own interest or account. This prohibition includes receiving compensation from any party in connection with a transaction involving assets of the plan.

Prohibited Transaction Exemptions

As you can see, the prohibited transaction rules are extremely broad. Without exemptions, even common, everyday events—such as service providers receiving payment from the plan—would be prohibited. Because of the breadth of the prohibited transaction rules, many exceptions are provided. Exemptions come in several different forms: statutory, administrative, and individual.

Statutory Exemptions

The most commonly used statutory exemptions under ERISA include

- payment of reasonable compensation to parties in interest for services rendered necessary for the operation of the plan
- loans to parties in interest who are participants or beneficiaries of the plan if certain conditions are met. (This exception was described in chapter 9.)
- loans to employee stock ownership plans if specific conditions are met
- as provided by several statutory exemptions, relief for plans for bank employees and insurance companies that want to invest in the sponsor's investment vehicles
- certain pooled fund transactions involving banks, trust companies, and insurance companies
- distribution of assets in accordance with the terms of the plan

In addition to these exemptions, ERISA Sec. 408(c) clarifies that the prohibited transaction rules do not prohibit any fiduciary from receiving benefits as a participant from a plan, receiving reasonable compensation for services rendered to the plan (full-time employees of the plan sponsor may not be paid), receiving reimbursement for expenses incurred, or serving as fiduciary in addition to being an officer, employee, agent, or other representative of a party in interest.

Also, a plan may acquire or sell qualifying securities from any party without violating the prohibited transaction rules, as long as adequate security is paid, no commission is charged for the transaction, and the plan does not violate the 10 percent limitations.

Administrative Exemptions

ERISA Sec. 408(a) allows the Secretary of Labor to grant certain administrative exemptions from the prohibited transaction rules. These exemptions can be individual in nature, or they may be "class" exemptions, which can be relied on by the general public. Class exemptions have almost the same impact as the statutory exemptions. The DOL has granted a large number of class exemptions that can be relied upon by the employer.

Individual Exemptions

If neither a statutory nor class exemption applies, then an employer can request an individual exemption from the DOL. To grant such an individual exemption the DOL must find that the transaction

- is administratively feasible
- is in the interest of the plan and its participants and beneficiaries;
- is protective of the rights of the plan's participants and beneficiaries

Common Problems

Examples of common types of transactions that would be prohibited by the prohibited transaction rules include

- loans to the company, company owners, and relatives
- in most cases, contributions other than cash
- purchasing plan assets from the company or other party in interest
- property by the plan that is used by the business owner (such as art or other collectibles)
- property that is owned by the plan (like real estate) that is used by the company or other prohibited party

Especially in the small plan market the prohibited-transaction rules pose real problems. It may not be evident to the small business owner what's wrong with the transactions described above. There are two principal reasons for this. First, the small business owner with an entrepreneurial spirit may incorrectly look at the money in the plan as capital that should be used to build the business. As the owner often sees it, what's good for the business is good for the plan participants. Second, when a significant portion of the plan assets are for the benefit of the business owner, he or she may have a hard time distinguishing plan assets from personal assets.

Fiduciary Liability

Being a plan fiduciary is a serious matter. Remember, the fiduciaries are required to both satisfy the affirmative duties and make sure that no prohibited transactions occur. Plan fiduciaries under ERISA are personally liable to the plan to make good any losses to the plan that result from the fiduciary's breach of duty. In addition, a fiduciary is required to restore to the plan any profits realized by the fiduciary through the use of plan assets. In addition, a court can subject the fiduciary to other equitable or remedial relief as the court deems appropriate. In some egregious cases, the fiduciary can even be criminally liable.

In addition to being personally liable for his or her own breaches, a fiduciary is generally liable for the acts of cofiduciaries. A fiduciary will be liable for the breach of a cofiduciary if

- the fiduciary participates knowingly in, or knowingly undertakes to conceal, an act or omission of such other fiduciary, knowing such act or omission is a breach
- by the fiduciary's failure to comply with ERISA he or she enables the other fiduciary to commit a breach
- the fiduciary has knowledge of a breach by the cofiduciary, unless the fiduciary makes reasonable efforts under the circumstances to remedy the breach

Essentially, this means that if one fiduciary knows of a breach of duty by another fiduciary, he or she must take steps to correct that situation. In many cases this can mean suing the other fiduciary.

Other Plan Investment Limitations

Timing of Contribution of Employee Salary Deferrals

When a tax-advantaged retirement plan such as a 401(k) plan, SIMPLE, or 403(b) plan contains employee salary deferrals, the DOL has prescribed how quickly those salary deferrals must be contributed to the plan.. Under the DOL regulations, salary deferrals have to be segregated from the employer's general assets (contributed to the plan) as soon as is administratively feasible but never later than the 15th day of the month following the month of the salary deferral. For example, deferral elections for all pay periods ending in June must be contributed by July 15. This would be true regardless of whether employees were paid weekly, biweekly, or monthly.

NOTES

1. DOL Adv. Op. Lty. No. 84-09A and DOL reg. 2550.408b-2(e).

2. Reg. 29 CFR 2550.404a-1(b).
3. Lanka v. O'Higgins, 810 F.Supp. 379 (N.D.N.Y. 1992).
4. Conference Committee Report to ERISA, H.R. Rep. No. 93-1280.

12

Plan Funding and Investing—Part 2

Chapter Outline

ESTABLISHING INVESTMENT GUIDELINES

Why Establish Investment Guidelines?

Now that you are familiar with ERISA's fiduciary requirements, you can see that the rules are relatively complex and that fiduciaries have a strong incentive to meet their obligations. The first and probably most important tool for ensuring compliance will be clearly written plan investment guidelines. These are crucial for the following reasons:

- *Satisfying fiduciary obligations*—Investment guidelines help establish procedures to follow. They clarify who is responsible for what, when various tasks need to be completed, and how performance will be evaluated. They encourage a disciplined approach to fiduciary management and help to establish a paper trail.
- *First line of defense*—If the DOL or plan participants question the investment performance courts are going to be looking for a rationale for the investments chosen. The investment guidelines should be the fiduciary's most powerful shield.
- *Investing in a vacuum*—An investment decision simply cannot be made or properly evaluated in a vacuum. A treasury bill is a great investment when the main concern is protecting principal, but a terrible investment for long-term capital growth. Appropriate investment decisions have to follow clear objectives.

For all of these reasons it is extremely important to establish clear investment guidelines that tie the investment policy into the plan's objectives, clarify who is responsible for the various decisions surrounding the investment of plan assets, specify investment guidelines and goals, and establish procedures for reviewing both the investment performance and the plan's investment guidelines.

Funding Policy and Plan Objectives

Every plan is required to establish procedures for establishing and carrying out a funding policy and method consistent with the objectives of the plan and the requirements of ERISA. A funding policy addresses the level and timing of contributions necessary to fund benefit obligations throughout the life of a retirement plan.

In a defined-benefit plan, the policy should address the minimum funding requirements, provide a process for reviewing the policy periodically, and , most important, require documentation of actions taken and reasons for those actions.

The funding policy—and the investment guidelines—are driven by the plan's objectives. In a defined-benefit plan the primary objective will be to provide sufficient funds to pay both current and future benefit obligations. In addition will be the goal of minimizing long-term total required contributions. And in most cases there will be concern about the variability in annual contributions. The second and third objectives are generally at odds with one another, since minimizing costs over the long haul will require taking some risk. With risk usually comes volatility in the investment return, and thus a degree of variability in the required contributions. How important this is to a particular plan depends, in part, on how well funded the plan is—the more well-funded plan having a higher tolerance for volatility. Also the tolerance for volatility will depend upon whether the sponsoring entity is cyclical in nature.

In a defined-contribution plan, the funding policy is simpler. If the plan calls for a specified contribution the policy simply addresses the timing of contributions. With discretionary contributions in a profit-sharing plan the employer establishes a policy for determining how and when contributions will be made. Also, in a defined-contribution plan there should be less conflict with the plan's objectives. Here the employer's contribution is not tied to the plan's investment performance. The employer does not have to be concerned about the long-term cost of funding the plan or short-term variability. The only objective is providing for the retirement needs of the participants.

However, since participants will be of different ages and have different needs and risk profiles, many defined-contribution plans pass the investment decisions on to the participants. In such a plan, the objective at the trust level is some what different. Here the goal is to offer participants a number of sufficiently diverse investment vehicles—each with different risk and return characteristics—so that each participant will be able to assemble a portfolio that will meet his or her individual investment needs. Also, to assist participants in the formation of appropriate investment objectives the trustees will have to provide them with suitable education.

Investment Responsibilities

Investment guidelines should identify all the parties involved in the investment of plan assets and should address each individual's specific responsibilities. Establishing this requires first a review of the plan and trust documents. These documents offer more detail on accountability issues than most people realize. Commonly the document provides that either the employer or an investment committee is responsible for establishing and periodically reviewing the investment policy. The employer often retains the responsibility of choosing and monitoring the trustee and any investment managers. Trustees are responsible for investing plan assets in accordance with the stated investment goals and reporting to the employer or investment committee—unless some or all of this responsibility is passed on to one or more investment managers. The trustees will always account for and report on the status of plan assets. In some cases, there may also be consultants who help with selecting and monitoring investment managers.

Investment Policy

The plan's investment policy should identify the appropriate degree of risk and yield for the trust and the importance of yield in relation to safety of principal and the plan's cash flow needs. These decisions must be made in relation to the plan's objectives and the investment objectives. When trying to determine the plan's objectives, it is helpful to ask the following questions:

- Are there other resources available if investment performance is bad?
- What is the appropriate investment horizon?
- What is an acceptable level of risk?
- What is the minimum level of investment return to accomplish the goals?

These questions are relevant to the plan trustees—when they are responsible for investment decisions—as well as to plan participants in cases where they have investment control.

Investment Goals

The next step is to establish concrete performance objectives for monitoring investment performance. It is almost always more sensible to evaluate investments based on appropriate benchmarks as opposed to specific rates of return. If more than one investment manager is involved, a specific set of investment guidelines should be established for each manager, covering the following:

- Permissible categories of investments
- Asset allocation ranges among different investment classes
- Appropriate investments within categories (such as specified bond quality)
- Diversification concerns, such as maximum holding in specific investments, limits on small capitalization stocks, and limits on any particular sector
- Policies regarding proxy voting
- Limitations based on fiduciary rules, prohibited transactions, and so on

Monitoring Investment Management

Another part of the investment policy includes procedures for periodically checking performance against benchmarks. The safest course of action is to track performance on a continual basis, and meet with investment managers on a quarterly, semi-annual, or annual basis. Investment performance should be evaluated over relatively long periods although significant deviation in short-term performance can be a warning sign. Performance can be evaluated against peer groups as well as against benchmarks.

Reviewing Investment Guidelines

The final part of the investment procedures should be a plan for an annual review of the investment guidelines to insure that they are still appropriate. Again, it is important to keep accurate records of any meetings discussing and reconfirming or changing the guidelines.

INVESTMENT CONSIDERATIONS

Almost every investment option that is available to an individual investor is available to a pension plan sponsor. In fact, pension funds can be invested in such a large number of products that it's impossible to cover them all fully in this text. Instead, in the rest of this chapter, we'll concentrate on several objectives: identifying certain basic investment characteristics, clarifying the role of major asset classes in the asset mix, and finally, reviewing the makeup and merits of products that the insurance industry typically markets to pension funds.

Let's start by looking at several aspects that need to be considered before selecting investments. One factor is the investment's tax treatment. Since qualified plans and other tax-advantaged plans are tax exempt (at the trust level), investments that also have special tax advantages are generally not appropriate for the plan. This is because the investor pays a premium for the tax advantage. For example tax-free municipal bonds will have a lower investment return then comparable taxable bonds. Since the trust does not benefit from the special tax treatment, these types of investments should generally be avoided.

Another concern will be investment liquidity. This refers to the ability to convert the investment to cash in short period of time. An adequate portion of the pension assets needs to be sufficiently liquid so that benefit payments can be made without having to sell long-term investments at a bad price.

A third consideration is the investment's stability. A stable investment is one that has little fluctuation in value. Money market accounts and Treasury bills, for example, have almost no variability. As mentioned above, stability of the investments can have an impact on short-term variability of plan contributions to a defined-benefit plan. The downside of investments with little variability is that they also have low rates of return.

The variability in the value of an investment can also be called *investment risk.* Causes of investment risk are many. Here we will discuss several of the most important. First is *purchasing-power risk,* which is sometimes called *inflation risk.* With rising prices, the value of an investment asset or of the income earned thereon, or both, must increase at a rate equal to or greater than the inflation rate. Otherwise the purchasing power of the dollars invested or earned on the asset will decline. Investment assets most susceptible to this risk are fixed-dollar investments. The next type of risk is *interest-rate risk,* in which the value of an investment changes due to changes in interest rates in the market. The third major risk factor is referred to as *market risk.* Political, economic, demographic, or social events can have an impact on the market as a whole and on the specific investment, as well. A fourth type of risk, *business risk,* involves the risks associated with a particular business. Changes in consumer preference, ineffective management, law changes, or foreign competition can affect the performance of a particular business.

INVESTMENT CLASSES

Cash Equivalents

To satisfy the need to make other investment transactions and to have readily accessible money to pay benefits, plans will generally invest some of a plan's assets in instruments that are known as *cash equivalents.* Typically, cash equivalents have either no specified maturity date or one that is one year in the future or less.

A number of different investments are considered cash equivalents. The investment with the least risk of default is the U.S. Treasury bill (T-bill). These obligations of the U.S. government have maturity dates when issued of 90 or 180 days, or one year, and are backed by the full taxing authority of the government. They can be readily sold and converted to cash at a modest cost. Other federal government agencies also issue short-term marketable obligations. These will be available with a range of maturity dates, and will generally pay a slightly higher interest rate than T-bills.

Another category, bank deposits, includes savings accounts and certificates of deposit (CDs) at banks, savings and loans, and credit unions. Savings accounts face minimal risk and are subject to few restrictions on withdrawals. CDs, which are deposits for a specified period of time such as 3, 6, or 12 months, generally impose a loss of a portion of the interest earnings as a penalty for a withdrawal before maturity, although some banks have eliminated this penalty or reduced it to a minimal amount. Also, large CDs (over $100,000) can often be sold on the secondary market.

Money market instruments, including money market deposit accounts (MMDAs) and money market mutual funds (MMMFs), are other popular cash equivalents. Both MMDAs and MMMFs hold portfolios of short-term obligations of the federal government and its agencies, of state and local governments, and of businesses. The securities are, in most cases, completely liquid without penalty. Money market instruments will pay a yield slightly lower than the underlying investments (to account for management fees) but also allow greater diversification, protecting the plan from default risk.

Other investments that have the characteristics of cash equivalents include short-term obligations of state and local governments and of businesses and the long-term debt obligations of governments, businesses, and nonprofit institutions that are to mature within one year.

Bonds

Bond owners are creditors of the issuing institution, whether it is a government, business, or nonprofit organization. This status grants the investors the legal right to enforce their claims to interest income and principal repayment as contained in the agreement that specifies the terms and conditions of the debt issue. In the case of business debt instruments, debt claims have priority over any claims of its owners.

Bond issues of state and local governments (both of which are referred to as *municipals*) and of businesses typically are quality rated by Standard and Poor's Corporation (S&P) and/or Moody's Investors Service. These ratings express the likelihood that the issuer will default on the timely payment of interest or principal. Based on a financial analysis of the issuer, a letter grade is assigned to each bond issue. Bonds rated at the top of the B grade (BBB for S&P, Baa for Moody's) or higher are considered to be "investment quality." Lower ratings are assigned for bonds assessed as "speculative." The lower the quality rating, the greater the risk of default and the higher the interest rate (return) that the investor can expect to earn.

Government Bonds

Governmental debt includes securities of the federal, state, and local governments and their agencies. Some federal bonds are backed by the full faith and credit of the U.S. government. For example, all U.S. Treasury obligations have such backing. Other U.S. government bonds issued by federal agencies or organizations, such as the Tennessee Valley Authority or the U.S. Post Office, are not direct obligations of the U.S. Treasury. These bonds, known collectively as agency bonds, provide investors with a return greater than that available on U.S. Treasury bonds. A few of these agency bonds have guarantees that effectively place the full faith and credit of the U.S. Treasury behind the bonds.

Some state and local government bonds, known as *general obligations,* are backed by the taxing power of the state or local government. Others, usually issued by agencies of a state or local government, are known as *revenue bonds.* They are backed by the revenues earned from such ventures as turnpikes, airports, and sewer and water systems. Without the taxing authority behind them, these revenue bonds are viewed as riskier and pay investors a somewhat higher interest rate than do general obligation bonds.

Maturities of governmental debt instruments vary from more than one year to 30 years. Bonds with maturities of 10 years or less are often referred to as being of intermediate-term duration and have somewhat less risk than longer-term bonds. If such a risk difference does exist, intermediate-term obligations would pay a slightly lower rate than would a longer duration bond.

Corporate Bonds

Businesses are major contributors to the supply of debt securities available in the marketplace. These securities, either notes if intermediate term or bonds if long term, have various characteristics, which are detailed in the indenture. Some of the more frequently encountered characteristics include the following:

- *secured*—a promise backed by specific assets as further protection to the bondholder should the corporation default on payment of interest or principal
- *debenture*—an unsecured promise, based only on the issuer's general credit status, to pay interest and principal
- *callable*—an option exercisable at the discretion of the issuer to redeem the bond prior to its maturity date at a specified price
- *convertible*—an option exercisable by the bondholder to exchange the bond for a predetermined number of common or preferred shares

For bonds of the same quality rating, these features affect the interest rate available to the investor. If the feature provides a benefit to the bondholder, such as being secured or convertible, a lower interest rate is paid. If the feature provides a benefit to the issuer, such as the flexibility of not having specific assets pledged as collateral (debenture) or the presence of a call feature, the interest rate is higher.

Using Bonds in the Pension Environment

When plan assets are invested by the trustee, bonds are often used to ensure that the plan will have sufficient cash to pay expected benefits as they arise. For example, if a defined-benefit plan expects to pay out monthly benefits to current beneficiaries in the amount of $50,000 a month, bonds are purchased in the amount necessary to generate a stream of interest payments in such an amount. Also bonds are used simply because they provide more stable returns than equities and higher returns than the cash equivalents mentioned above.

Equity Securities

Equity investments represent an ownership position in a business. As such, they represent a higher risk for the investor than do the debt investments. Because most retirement plans have long-term investment goals, equity investments comprise a significant role in the asset mix. For example, the 1995 *Pension & Investments* survey of the 1,000 largest employee benefit funds showed that defined-benefit plans held 56.3 percent of their assets in equities, while defined-contribution plans held 51.4 percent of assets in equities.

By far the most common equity investment for pension trusts is in common stock of publicly traded corporations. Investors in common stock have the ultimate ownership rights in the corporation. They elect the board of directors that oversees the management of the firm. Each common share receives an equal portion of the dividends distributed, as well as any liquidation proceeds. If the firm is unsuccessful, losses will occur that can lead to a cessation of any dividend payments and, if losses continue, to an eradication of the common equity ownership and eventual bankruptcy.

The current income distributed as dividends to the shareholder is at the sole discretion of the board of directors. The board is under no legal obligation to make dividend payments and may instead retain the profits within the business. Only by threatening to elect or actually electing a new board can the common shareholders be in the position to force a dividend payment, regardless of the profitability of the business.

The owners of common stock also vote on major issues such as mergers, name change, sale of a major part of the business, or liquidation. Finally, common stockholders usually have a *preemptive right,* which is the right to maintain their relative voting power by purchasing shares of any new issues of common stock of the corporation.

Mutual Funds

An open-end investment company, popularly called a mutual fund, continually sells and redeems its shares at net asset value, that is, the value of the fund's assets divided by the number of outstanding shares. Mutual funds acquire a portfolio of securities in which each of the fund's shares represents a proportionate interest in the total portfolio. As sales and redemptions of the fund's shares take place, the size of the fund's total portfolio changes, increasing when additional shares are sold and decreasing when shares are redeemed.

Mutual funds can be differentiated on the basis of their portfolio objectives. These major categories include:

- *money market mutual funds*—These funds own a portfolio of short-term interest-bearing securities. As mentioned earlier, they are used by investors as an alternative to cash.
- *bond funds*—These companies own a portfolio of bonds. Subcategories include some that invest only in U.S. government issues, municipal issues, corporate issues, or low-quality (junk) bonds. Further subcategories can be short-term (up to 4 or 5 years), intermediate-term (5 to 10 years), or long-term (10 or more years in duration) bond funds.
- *common stock companies*—These companies hold a portfolio of common stocks and perhaps a small number of preferred stocks. Subcategories include those that invest primarily in conservative (defensive) stocks, growth stocks, aggressive growth stocks, or foreign stocks.

- *mixed portfolio companies*—These companies own a portfolio of bonds, stocks, and other investment instruments. Subcategories include balanced companies and income companies.

Another way to distinguish funds is to look at whether they are actively managed (securities chosen individually by management) or passively managed. A common passive strategy includes those funds referred to as *index funds*. These funds own a portfolio of that replicates a major market index such as the S&P 500. Passive strategies generally result in lower management fees.

Besides the fees charged by the management of the fund, funds have various acquisition fees. In many cases fees that would apply to individual investors are waived for the pension fund. If fees exist, they must be carefully evaluated.

Mutual funds are more and more commonly used in pension plans. With small plans, assets may be too small to be handled by an investment manager. Like the common trust fund (described in the previous chapter), mutual funds provide an easy way to achieve diversification. Mutual funds also provide liquidity and ease of entry and exit. As mutual fund return data is published and studied, it simplifies evaluation of investment performance.

When participants in defined-contribution plans are given investment choices, mutual funds (and other look-through investments such as common trust funds and insurance contracts) are becoming the primary form of investment. These types of investments allow participants to build individualized portfolios while still taking advantage of professional management and asset diversification. In addition, these look-through investments are required in order to take advantage of the fiduciary liability relief described in the previous chapter.

GROUP PENSION PRODUCTS

A full understanding of the nature of the group pension products offered today requires a knowledge of how these products evolved. Historically group pension departments of insurance companies offered a distinct contrast to plans invested directly in the types of assets discussed above under a trust agreement. For one thing, early group pension products were generally "allocated" meaning that assets were committed to provide benefits for specific employees, while trust funds were unallocated. Another distinction was that the group pension products were replete with guarantees (everything from guaranteed interest rates to annuity purchase guarantees), and trust funds offered no guarantees. While the guarantees constituted something of an advantage, they also made the early group pension products less competitive, because providing long-term guarantees required conservative actuarial projections for investment return. A third difference was that group pension contracts were inflexible in the timing of contributions and restrictive regarding the types of benefit formulas for which they were suitable. As you might expect, group pension products were less than competitive in attracting pension funds.

As time wore on, new group pension products were designed to provide the employer with more flexibility in both plan design and timing of contributions. In addition, the weighty long-term guarantees that fettered companies and kept them from offering competitive investment returns were removed and replaced with guarantees on a floor rate for investment return. What's more, companies began to segregate their pension assets from the insurance companies' general accounts, which permitted separate account investing that was tailored to diverse pension needs.

One final hurdle that insurance companies had to overcome was the commingling of contributions for the current and all prior years. In times of rising interest rates the insurance contracts appeared to be noncompetitive because they were selling a portfolio rate of interest that was weighed down by the lower rates of prior years. To counteract this, the new-money method (also known as investment-year method) was developed. Under the new-money method each deposit made by an employer is credited with the rate of interest that the funds actually earned in that year. Thus in times of rising interest rates the rates are not based on a company-based time-weighted portfolio but on a series of annual competitive rates (as a trust fund plan is).

The net result of all this change has placed group pension products on a par with trust funds. Distinctions between them remain, but that doesn't keep them from being competitive; in fact, the distinctive features of group pension products make them more advantageous under some circumstances.

Providing Full Services

Another change in the group pension area has been the evolution from a service-oriented approach (that is, providing services to help administer the plan) to a non-service-oriented approach (offering only investment). Although abandoning service has been a general trend in the insurance industry, a majority of the pension leaders continue to provide full service and support.

Offering services means several things to financial services professionals:

- The financial services professional is expected to have pension and retirement plan expertise.
- Plan services are expected. Typically helping a client with tax forms and explaining "gray areas" of the plan can call the financial services professional back to duty long after the sale is made.
- The ongoing relationship between the financial services professional and the plan sponsor is typically either uncompensated (except indirectly through contract renewal) or undercompensated.

To avoid these problems agents sometimes opt to offer contracts on a no-service basis even if the company allows for the sale of contracts on a service basis. When this occurs, however, services such as record keeping may be offered for an additional charge; in that case home-office support will minimize the agent's future involvement.

The First Generation of Group Pension Products

Many of the old group pension products, though still on the books, are no longer sold. *Group deferred-annuity contracts* were one of the first contracts designed to meet the needs of defined-benefit plans. The distinguishing characteristic of this contract is that it is funded through a series of single-premium deferred annuities—that is, the employer's annual contributions are used to purchase a deferred annuity for each participant. These products are no longer underwritten and only a few still remain on the books.

Group permanent contracts were developed to facilitate the use of cash value life insurance contracts in funding a qualified plan. Under these contracts an employer's contributions are used to purchase "retirement income" or "retirement endowment" life insurance at group rates. As the employee nears retirement the cash value of the life policy builds beyond the face amount of the insurance policy, which enables the participant at retirement to purchase an annuity.

As group permanent contracts evolved is become more common to structure the contract so the life insurance policy accumulates less cash and to use an unallocated side fund (also called a conversion fund) instead. This enables employers to have some investment flexibility regarding the timing of contributions. In other words, instead of just meeting premium payment deadlines, the employer can schedule additional payments to the conversion fund at other times.

The group underwriting and side-fund features make group permanent contracts a viable method of funding retirement plans. What's more, these contracts include guarantees on the insurance purchase rates (generally for 5 years) and annuity purchase rates (given at the outset when insurance is first issued). In spite of these features the financial services professional's contact with group permanent contracts is usually restricted to existing, in-force cases rather than new sales, because these contracts are not typically underwritten today.

The Second Generation of Group Pension Products

Three group pension products that have been in existence for some time and are still used today (although some insurance companies have discontinued underwriting them) are the group deposit-administration contract (DA), the immediate-participation-guarantee contract (IPG), and the pension-funding contract (PF). The major advantage these second-generation products had over their predecessors is that the second-generation products provide contribution flexibility and can be used with any benefit formula. (Both the group deferred-annuity contract and the group permanent contract were restricted in these areas.)

The group deposit-administration contract was the first unallocated group pension contract. The DA is funded by a series of employer contributions made throughout the year. Contributions are accounted for under two different systems—one that reflects investment guarantees that are given (the active-life fund) and one that reflects the actual investment experience. At retirement the active-life fund is debited with the amount taken out, which is enough to purchase an immediate annuity for the participant in the amount provided by the plan. The annuity purchase rates are also guaranteed in the contract. Under a DA contract, the investment experience is rated annually and dividends are paid to the contract holder if the experience fund exceeds the reserve necessary for future benefits and expenses.

The group deposit-administration contract is able to offer interest and annuity rate guarantees because it accumulates a contingency reserve, and because it has control (through dividend computations) over the rate at which actuarial gains pertaining to guaranteed items are created. Some employers object to the reserves and other insurance company controls and instead seek an immediate reflection of actual investment and mortality experience. For these employers a second (and more popular) product is available, the immediate-participation-guarantee contract. An IPG is an unallocated funding instrument that holds benefit amounts in a commingled fund. At retirement one of two things happens: (1) either the fund is charged directly with benefit payments or (2) the fund is charged with a single annuity premium. The IPG contract contains no interest guarantees, but, as the name indicates, it allows a plan sponsor to have an immediate reflection of the actual investment and mortality experience under the plan (which is the major selling point of a trust fund plan).

The IPG contract typically contains conservative guarantees of annuity rates for retired lives. They were, however, the first group pension contract that did not provide annuities as a matter of course. In other words, even though annuity rates are guaranteed, annuities are not automatically purchased at retirement.

A product that evolved from the IPG contract but spurned the use of any annuity guarantees was the pension-funding contract (PF). The only significant difference between a PF contract and an IPG contract is that under a PF contract there are no guarantees whatsoever for retirees, no annuity purchases are made, and no funds are earmarked for retired employees.

The Third Generation of Group Pension Products

The third generation of group pension products are today's big sellers. In general, these products are giving trust fund plans stiff competition and are yielding big rewards for many insurance companies. These products include

- separate-investment accounts contracts
- guaranteed-investment contracts (GICs)
- investment-guarantee contracts (IGs)

Take note that different companies tag these products with different names and/or have special variations of the generic product, so it's important to check with your own company for the product name and any variation from the generic.

Separate-Investment Accounts Contracts

The most basic of the third-generation contracts is the separate-investment accounts contract (these contracts are also offered on an individual basis—the rules discussed here apply to both the individual side of the house and the group side of the house). Under the separate-investment accounts contract the plan fund manager can either invest in one of the separate accounts offered by the insurance company or split investments among the various accounts offered. A separate-investment account is similar in concept to a mutual fund. Like a mutual fund, a separate-investment account is generally pooled (takes allocations from a variety of plan sponsors instead of from individual investors) and is always participating (that is, accounts are maintained at market value, and the actual investment experience is reflected directly in the value of the fund). A second similarity to mutual funds is that the separate-investment account has preestablished types of investments—for example, a bond or equity fund can be chosen. A third similarity to mutual funds is that each fund has a directed-investment philosophy and certain investment goals. (For example, an equity separate-investment account might have a directed philosophy of investing in dividend-producing equities.) And a fourth similarity to mutual funds is that the sales appeal of any separate-investment account is based on its competitive market history. (Planning Note: Unlike most other investment vehicles, separate-investment accounts are not generally required to be registered with the SEC. Some insurance companies do have registered accounts, however, in which case the typical prospectus is available.)

Separate-investment accounts contracts generally require a minimum deposit of $100,000 or more (less when offered by the individual pensions department). The plan sponsor can allocate these funds to one or all of the different funds available and can usually transfer funds among the accounts whenever desired. (If an account with a guaranteed interest rate is offered, however, transfer restrictions that would guard against adverse selection in plan investment may apply.) This allows the plan sponsor to play the market by changing investment strategies to meet market trends.

Separate-Investment Accounts. There are a variety of separate-investment accounts, but the basic makeup of a separate-investment accounts contract includes one or two equity accounts (a capital-growth and perhaps even a small capitalization fund), a bond account, and a short-term securities fund. In addition, some insurers offer separate-investment account funds that include balanced funds and index funds. The nature and makeup of each of these accounts varies among insurance companies. The chief selling point of any of these funds, however, is their historical performance and the pension fund sponsor's assessment of their potential.

Although separate-investment accounts are generally pooled among many pension investors, some companies also offer individual separate accounts. These individual separate accounts are generally found in the large-plan market. Companies in this category typically show an interest in segregating their assets and investing in specialized portfolios.

Unlike assets held in an insurance company's general account, assets in separate accounts are not subject to the claims of the insurance company's creditors. This makes separate investment accounts especially popular in an environment of low interest rates. In such periods, institutional investors become quite concerned about the risk of loss that could result due to the failure of the insurance company. Insulation from this risk through the use of separate accounts can be an important selling point.

However, the chief selling point of a separate-investment accounts contract is the competitiveness of the investment's rate of return.. Unlike that of most pension products, this competitive posture is generally well advertised in trade magazines, such as *Pensions and Investment Age;* therefore selling should be coordinated with the home office's advertising strategy. Another unique feature of these contracts is that there is a wealth of literature (from general philosophy reports to detailed quarterly investment reports) that can be used as a sales tool.

Guaranteed-Investment Contracts (GICs)

One of the most popular types of pension-funding products issued through group pension departments of insurance companies is guaranteed-investment contracts (GICs). As the name implies, a guaranteed-investment contract guarantees the pension plan's investment (both principal and interest). The insurance company receives plan assets at a specified date or dates, guarantees them at a stipulated rate of interest, and returns the principal and interest at a specified time or times. In fact, a GIC is analogous to a certificate of deposit for pension plans because, like a CD, it offers a predetermined rate of return. The GIC guaranteed rate is spot-rated—that is, it's based on the insurance company's ability to immediately purchase an underlying investment vehicle (for example, a zero coupon or deep discount bond).

A second similarity to a certificate of deposit is that a GIC guarantees the principal. Another similarity is that GICs permit withdrawals only on specified dates, sometimes only on the contract ending date. Some withdrawal flexibility is available, however, because GICs can be structured to pay out interest annually or to distribute the principal investment piecemeal (this is known as a strip feature). This flexibility is important for plan sponsors who must meet plan cash-flow needs, such as plan expenses and benefit payouts to retirees. What's more, although the length of a GIC is usually somewhere between 3 and 7 years (typically 5 years), investment flexibility can be achieved by the purchase of a short-term GIC for as little as one year.

When a GIC is offered as one of several investment options in a participant-directed defined-contribution plan, an exception is made to the withdrawal limitations that normally apply to a GIC. In this case there is almost never a penalty for the participant who elects to move assets within the family of available investment choices.

The withdrawal limitation for the trustee-invested plan is a real consideration for the investor. However, in exchange for leaving money with the insurance company, the pension plan is assured of guaranteed interest rates that often extend for the length of the contract. These projected investment returns provide a safety net for the pension fund manager by effectively minimizing any downside risk and by allowing plan actuaries and accountants to make accurate predictions about the GIC-invested portion of the pension portfolio. In addition, it is theoretically possible for a new type of GIC to be developed in which the investor could tie the interest-rate guarantee to a floating economic measure (for example, prime plus one percentage point). This feature would enable GICs to be sold during those hard-to-sell times when interest rates are low and expected to rise. Typically, however, the more favorable sales period for GICs is when interest rates are high and expected to fall or when interest rates are expected to remain stable.

YOUR FINANCIAL SERVICES PRACTICE: COUNSELING YOUR CLIENTS ABOUT GICs

From your client's perspective, one of the problems with the GIC is that the client is making significant investment decisions regarding both the timing of the GIC purchase and the choice of a maturity date for the GIC. For example, if your client takes a 3-year deal instead of a 5-year deal to get a higher rate when the GIC matures, he or she will get burned if interest rates drop to a point at which only lesser guarantees are available after 3 years. Obviously other scenarios could produce significant gains or losses to the plan. In order to avoid having to bet what interest rates will do, most clients try to achieve stability by making annual contributions for the same stated period. This hedging philosophy meshes nicely with the conservative approach to pension investing that many plan fund managers take.

Varieties of GICs. There are two basic types of GICs. The simpler of the two, the bullet GIC, contains a guarantee-of-interest-and-principal feature and can vary from 3 to 7 years in length.

The bullet GIC is an investment vehicle structured to take a single-sum deposit (generally $100,000 or more) for a specified period of time. Both the amount of deposit and the lock-in period are a product of the pension fund manager's investment strategy. Bullet GICs are generally marketed to defined-benefit plans because they mesh well with the timing of contributions from these plans. What puts them in sync with defined-benefit plans is that the defined-benefit contributions are generally only made quarterly. What's more, defined-benefit plans are usually large and have enough investments placed elsewhere to meet the cash-flow needs of benefit payouts, so the strip feature is not frequently used.

The inflexibility associated with making contributions to a bullet GIC led to the establishment of the other basic GIC type known as the window GIC (sometimes called a guaranteed-accumulation contract). The window GIC helps to meet the need for periodic contributions inherent in some defined-contribution plans, which credit an employee's account balance with the plan contribution when monthly or semimonthly salaries are paid. To accommodate these periodic payments a window period is established. When a window GIC is used, the interest guarantees are locked in at the contract inauguration but the timing of contributions is usually left open for up to a year. In return for this option, the guaranteed rate will be lower than the rate for a corresponding bullet GIC.

A second way the window GIC is different from the bullet GIC is that the precise contribution amount is not known. Under a window GIC the contract stipulates the timing and level of contributions, which can be stated, for example, as a specified portion of the total plan contributions. And a third way a window GIC differs from a bullet GIC is that in a window GIC the withdrawal amounts are not known. Window GICs are marketed for defined-contribution plans because under these plans the exact yearly dollar contribution is not known when the contract is signed, but only at the end of the year, after all contributions have been made. (On the other hand, a bullet GIC suits a defined-benefit plan because under these plans the precise plan contribution is actuarially determined once a year.)

Window GICs are also popular investment vehicles for defined-contribution plans in which the employer offers a fixed-income investment with a guaranteed investment rate. In these defined-contribution plans the window GIC is used for the guaranteed-investment fund, and in most cases the contract has a requirement that all of the money earmarked for the fixed-income investment fund will be paid to the window GIC.

Each basic GIC type (window or bullet) is subject to variation. For example, a forward-commitment bullet GIC allows the plan sponsor to lock in current rates for a deposit to be made on an agreed-upon future date. (*Planning Note:* A plan sponsor seeking a forward-commitment bullet GIC should realize that the guarantees will be more conservative because there is a delay in receiving the money and the insurance company may not be able to find suitable underlying investments.)

One common twist to the window GIC is to guarantee the first-year rate but leave the years 2-through-5 rate open during that first year. Pension fund managers can then lock in a rate later that year. For example, if they gamble that rates will rise and they win, they can lock in the higher rate that comes up late in the first contract year as their 2-through-5 guarantee. If they gamble that rates will rise and they don't, the insurance company can lock in the lower rate as a guarantee for years 2 through 5. Since this involves risk for the insurance company, guarantees are generally lower. A second variation of the window GIC is a provision that allows the insurance company to accept contributions up to a certain dollar amount instead of for a window period. A third variation establishes a corridor amount to be paid. If the amount actually paid is more or less than the corridor permits, the insurance company may refuse to accept the funds or additional funds may have to be paid in. In the second and third type of window GIC variation the risks to the insurance company are lower, and therefore a higher guaranteed interest rate may be offered.

Sales Appeal. The GIC market is comprised of medium-sized to large plan sponsors. One reason for this is that most insurance companies have a minimum deposit that is anywhere from $100,000 to $1 million. A second reason centers on the tendency of these plans to desire a conservative investment base for a more extensive portfolio. The major selling point of a GIC is that it provides a competitive guaranteed rate of return. A second selling point is that the risk associated with GIC investments is limited. Credit risks (the inability of the carrier to pay principal and interest at maturity) are greatly minimized when one is dealing with a company that has an established investment track record. And market risk (the possibility that rates may shift during the lock-in period) can be minimized by choosing the window GIC option of floating the guarantee for a year. The third selling point of GICs is that they fit nicely in most pension portfolios by providing a conservative investment foundation on which investments that carry more risk can be placed. A fourth selling point is that assets held in GICs can be valued at book value, while assets held in bonds, for example, have to be valued at market value. In defined-benefit plans, where variability in asset valuation can cause big fluctuations in required contributions, GICs have a clear advantage over bonds. A final selling point of GICs is their pension orientation. GICs uniquely meet the investment concern of pension managers because they maximize long-term rates of return and generate cash flow to match required benefit payments while preserving safety of principal. These are the primary concerns of any pension fund manager, and GICs meet these needs effectively.

YOUR FINANCIAL SERVICES PRACTICE: GIC SALES

The bullet GIC market is extremely sensitive to interest rates. When interest rates are high, you will be able to do a lot of bullet GIC business; when interest rates are low, however, you will have problems selling. The window GIC, on the other hand, has a fairly steady market because defined-contribution plans that have a guaranteed-interest-account option under their plan have to place their money somewhere each year, regardless of where interest rates are.

Investment-Guarantee Contracts (IGs)

A third type of no-service group pension product is the investment-guarantee contract (IG). The IG contract is similar to a GIC in many ways. Both GICs and IGs are often structured to receive predetermined contributions (based on the plan's contribution or benefit formula) and pay a guaranteed rate of interest; to receive contributions during a window period (like a window GIC); and to last 5 years typically. The major difference from a GIC, however, is that contributions are received for the 5-year period rather than for the one-year window or one-shot bullet payment. What's more, the guarantees given to the plan sponsor for years 2 through 5 are only a floor amount. Under an IG contract the funds may receive a higher interest rate than projected if the actual investment experience of an investment account exceeds the guarantees. The reason IGs can pay a rate based on actual earnings or on the guarantee, whichever is better, is because they are not spot-rated. Recall that with a GIC (which *is* spot-rated) the investment is bought up front, so the guarantee is the same as the investment experience. With an IG the insurance company makes periodic investments. The rate initially guaranteed for years 2 through 5 is then only an actuarially projected guess that the insurance company is making as to the minimum return it will be able to make on investments. A third difference between the IG and the GIC products is that the IG contract is an individually rated contract and its gain or loss to the insurance company is based on each case's own experience. Under the GIC products, however, the products are generally pooled, and the gains or losses may be absorbed by the entire pool.

Since the insurance company is taking on more risk the farther out in time it projects guarantees, the IG interest guarantees are typically on a declining scale. The guarantee for year 3 is lower than the guarantee for year 2, and these declining guarantees are attributable to the market and investment-placement risks that insurance companies take. The plan sponsor, however, is more concerned with both the initial year's guarantee and the competitive posture of the offering company. As with any participating contract, the offering company's investment history is a key selling point because the investor is hoping that the actual results will exceed the floor guarantees.

IG Variations. There are two basic types of IGs. The difference between the two (there is no generic trade name, so we'll call them "type one" and "type two") is that type one is structured to make the comparison between the guarantee and the experience account after 5 years. Under type two the interest and experience account are compared at the end of every contract year, and if the experience account has more, the plan sponsor is credited with the experience account for that year. The difference between the two types can be significant because the insurance guarantees are locked in even though they might have been unrealistically high in any one year, or investment performance could have been atypical—yet there's no 5-year average to whittle down the unusual year's performance. For this reason the guarantees are usually lower in the type two (annual look-back) IG than in the type one (5-year look-back) IG.

The difference between the two IG types also has a bearing on which market they are suited for. The 5-year look-back IG is compatible with defined-benefit plans. The annual look-back IG is best suited to defined-contribution plans, which credit (and lock in) individual accounts with an annual interest accumulation. The ability to know the exact standing of an individual's account each year is important to the defined-contribution plan's sponsor, who must prepare an annual benefit statement demonstrating the amount in the account. While a type one IG, with its look-back after 5 years, would not permit this, it's suited to a defined-benefit plan, whose actuarial assumptions can be based on the lower guaranteed rate (thus creating the need for larger tax-deductible contributions).

Sales Appeal. The major selling point of an IG contract is that it allows plan funds to receive the experience account or the guarantee, whichever is better. Thus the pension fund manager knows that downside risk is eliminated (by the guarantee) but not at the risk of locking in a static rate for an extended period. To put it another way, fund managers can sleep nights because of the guarantee, and the sky is the limit if the investment environment takes a sharp upswing turn. A second selling point is that the risks associated with IG investments are limited. As with GICs, credit risks are minimized when the offering company has a history of good performance. But for IGs, unlike GICs, the market risk of an upturn during the investment period is eliminated because the actual experience of the fund will be credited. A final selling point for IGs is their pension orientation. Like GICs, IGs uniquely meet the investment concern of pension managers because they maximize long-term rates of return and generate cash flows to match the required benefit payments while preserving safety of principal.

IGs are typically sold for both defined-benefit (5-year look-back—type one) and defined-contribution plans (annual look-back—type two). The typical IG clients are small professional corporations and small public corporations. One reason is that the minimum sale amount is generally only $50,000 a year (or $250,000 over 5 years). Another reason these clients are attracted to IGs is the market diversity that is offered in one single contract.

Using Group Pension Products in Your Financial Services Practice

Many individual life agents and other financial services professionals who have not previously worked with the group pension products are starting to include them in their stable of products. These life agents and financial services professionals have found that separate-investment account contracts, GICs, and IGs not only have a ready market but are also convenient to sell. Unlike most other pension-funding vehicles, these products do not require an intimate working knowledge of pensions. In fact, sales often depend on the rates being offered by the insurance company more than on salesmanship and/or the ability to service the retirement plan. For this reason life agents with personal contacts who are the decision makers for pension funds can step into the pension market without fearing a full-time pension-servicing commitment. But perhaps the greatest appeal to financial services professionals is that the entire process is simply done, and the payoff is quick. There is no great time lag, as with other pension products, from the time the financial services professional makes the first call to the time the commission check arrives. These are some of the reasons that financial services professionals who work in the pension field (and in other fields) find that promoting these products can be profitable. (See table 12-1 for a comparison of products.)

There are, however, some problems with selling group pension products, which are due to restrictive contract provisions. The most significant problem can occur when your client seeks to terminate the contract. A market-value adjustment is generally applied to recognize that any funds not invested in separate-investment accounts are based on fixed-income investments, which have an underlying market value; if the assets have to be liquidated, that market value becomes a significant factor. In other words, the paper gains that are offered may be lost at the termination of the contract. This can cause a strained future relationship with your client, even if the client was forewarned of the cost to get out of the contract.

In addition, group pension products have some limitations on contribution flexibility. Particularly if interest guarantees are involved, insurance companies must have requirements that will prohibit a client from seeking alternative investment opportunities that would compete with the guaranteed-interest product they are offering. Another area where there may be concerns is the limited liquidity available under the bullet GIC contract. A fourth problem area for all these guaranteed products may be the contractual restrictions imposed by the insurance company to prohibit changes in the plan's operation that might affect their risk. A final problem area is a provision in some IG contracts called the "market-value-adjustment provision." This restricts situations where the amount of money coming into a contract may be less than the amount of money going out of the contract. For example, if the total withdrawals on the guaranteed-interest account made for benefit payments and transfers to other investment media exceed the amount of contributions plus investment income, the insurance company in effect is having to liquidate some investments; and any time an insurance company liquidates investments, it may seek to protect itself with a market-value provision for this excess amount.

LIFE INSURANCE AS A FUNDING VEHICLE

As was the case with group pension products, life insurance in qualified plans has undergone an evolution of sorts. Over the years the use of life insurance in a qualified plan has shifted from emphasis on the fully insured plan to a split-funded, life-and-side-fund approach.

TABLE 12-1

Comparison of No-Service Products

Type of Contract	Amount of Contribution	Timing of Contribution	Investment Guarantees	When to Sell
Separate-Investment Accounts Contract	Typically $100,000 or more	Ongoing	None; competitive history of the offering company is important	Generally at any time; sales are easier when coordinated with home-office advertising, and/or the reporting of favorable returns
Bullet GIC	Precisely known, typically $100,000 or more	One-time, within 3 days of sale	Guaranteed at the outset for the length of the contract	When interest rates are high and expected to drop
Window GIC	Based on the plan's benefit formula, typically a percentage of annual contributions of $100,000 or more	Over a window period of up to one year	Guaranteed at the outset for the length of the contract	At all times if the client offers a guaranteed account to employees
IG Contracts	Based on the plan's benefit formula, typically $50,000 a year or $250,000 over 5 years	Over the length of the contract	Guaranteed at the beginning of each contract year and the outset of the contract	When interest rates are low and expected to rise, or if the market is unstable and the client wants to keep options open.

A major drawback to fully funded plans was their inflexibility with regard to the timing of employer contributions (premium deadlines). What's worse, fully funded plans were far too concerned with the insurance element and didn't provide a competitive investment return. (The noncompetitive investment return stemmed from the fact that the long-term nature of the guarantees required conservatism.)

In time fully insured plans were replaced with a split-funded approach, which combined an ordinary life contract with a side fund. The ordinary life contract generates the lowest scale of cash values, so a significant amount of funding can be provided through the side fund. This approach offers the best of both worlds—the preretirement death-benefit coverage of a fully funded plan and the investment discretion and contributions-timing discretion that's built into the side fund.

YOUR FINANCIAL SERVICES PRACTICE:
RETIREMENT-INCOME CONTRACTS

One product that is frequently used, whether the plan is fully insured or a side fund is used, is a retirement-income contract. Retirement-income contracts are a form of life insurance policy specifically designed to provide a high enough cash value at retirement age to ensure a monthly income equal to $10 per $1,000 of the policy's face value (which satisfies the incidental-death-benefit rules). In other words, if the plan is fully insured, retirement-income contracts will provide enough cash value for the plan-promised retirement benefit without running afoul of the rule that death benefits must be incidental in a retirement plan.

Insured Plans

Plans using life insurance are structured to include the following features:

- One or more separate contracts are issued on the life of each employee. (These policies are referred to as allocated funding instruments because each individual policy is intended to provide benefits to one specific

- A trust agreement is executed between the employer and the trustee. (Recall that a pension fund must either be a trust or a life insurance contract; because only a single individual is covered under each policy, life insurance policies are not considered life insurance contracts, so a trust is mandated.)

- The trustee applies for the insurance, pays the premiums when due, is custodian of the individual contracts, and—even though the insured individual applies for the contract—has legal ownership of the insurance contract. Because a trustee is involved, the term *pension trust* is commonly used to describe pension plans funded with individual life policies.

- The insurability of individuals is seldom a serious problem under a life-insurance-funded plan because (1) evidence of insurability is sometimes waived, (2) substandard rates can be used, and (3) graded or graduated death benefits can be used. What's more, like group term life insurance plans, some individual policy plans establish nonmedical amounts using a formula based on the amount of volume under the particular plan.

- The plan's disability benefit can be provided either through a waiver-of-premium clause or a rider or by fully vesting the cash value.

- If a defined-benefit formula is used, the plan's benefit formula is typically designed to prevent increases in retirement benefits as a result of increases in compensation during the 5-year period just before retirement. This is because otherwise it would be too difficult to predict earnings to fund the exact benefit, and there is no time to fund the additional amounts that are needed for the higher benefits.

- If an employee leaves before retirement, disability, or death, his or her vested interest can be taken care of in several ways: (1) the contract can be transferred to the participant; (2) a paid-up policy in the amount that's currently funded can be transferred; (3) the trustee can borrow the unvested portion and assign the contract; or (4) the policies can be cashed in for their surrender value.

What makes the individual life/separate-account method unique is the nature of the products involved. Some individual life policies allow a competitive investment return that is market sensitive. The separate-accounts side fund allows investment discretion, a desirable feature for today's sophisticated investor. The combination of these two products embodies the best of what a partially insured plan has to offer. But before this approach is taken, the financial services professional should first assess the desirability of using life insurance to fund the retirement plan.

Why Life Insurance?

If you consider retirement plans in the abstract—solely as retirement vehicles—using life insurance to fund the plan doesn't make much sense. After all, even if investment earnings on the life insurance policy are competitive with other investments, there's still the pure life cost to consider. What's more, the use of life insurance may lead to PS 58 costs that are currently taxed to the participant. But retirement plans do not exist in a vacuum; they are a piece of the entire financial plan of the individual, whether it be the 25,000-person megacorporation or the 3-person doctor's office. And as part of their financial plan these people need life insurance protection.

In the large corporation life insurance is seldom used to fund retirement plans (except for nonqualified plans). A group life plan is all that's necessary to keep these organizations competitive in the employee benefit field, and financial planning considerations for the individual come second to those of the company. But for the small professional corporation or closely held business owner the use of life insurance to fund a qualified plan may be the best method to pay for life insurance—and therefore to fit in two pieces of the financial planning puzzle with one move. Using life insurance in the qualified plan satisfies the need for life insurance protection for the owner and gives a tax deduction to the business. Recall that the business owner cannot deduct life insurance as a business expense on the corporate tax sheet. But with the imposition of a retirement plan the corporation gets a tax deduction, and the business owner is insured at a substantial savings (the only nondeductible amounts being those amounts of pure insurance protection subject to PS 58 costs).

There are of course other reasons to use individual life insurance policies to fund a qualified plan. These include

- maximizing the preretirement death benefit
- dealing with a single individual or coordinated group in doing financial planning
- minimizing paperwork, administrative hassles, and the extra expenses resulting when death benefits are provided both inside and outside the plan
- not having to meet the requirements of the minimum funding standard rules if the plan is fully insured (discussed in chapter 11)

Naturally the life insurance need must exist before funding a qualified plan with life insurance becomes a prudent maneuver. If life insurance needs have been treated adequately elsewhere in the financial plan, then the client needn't carry it in the retirement plan.

ANNUITIES AS A FUNDING VEHICLE

Annuities are traditionally thought of as a common method of distributing retirement funds to retirees. However, they can play another role when it comes to funding the retirement plan. Like the use of life insurance, the use of annuities to fund retirement plans has undergone an evolution of sorts. The original retirement annuity products offered a noncompetitive investment return and lacked contribution flexibility—two drawbacks that led to their downfall. Under these contracts the objective was to fund the retirement benefit by funding an annuity that built sufficient cash values at retirement to pay out benefits.

Annuity contracts used to fund retirement plans are typically deferred annuities, with the plan sponsor agreeing to fund (over the employee's career) an annuity that will begin spinning out payments at retirement. These annuities can be either fixed (where the monthly return is predetermined and guaranteed) or variable (where the underlying annuity investments, such as stocks, bonds, and money markets, let the annuities' return float with market conditions). The variable annuity tends to be the more popular of the two because it gives the plan sponsor more investment discretion—within limits. This is particularly important when the plan sponsor is a small business owner who wants some investment control over his or her own retirement. It is in this small closely held business/professional-corporation market that most plan-funding annuities are sold.

Annuities are sometimes used to fund plans in situations where life insurance is not available because of underwriting considerations. Although life insurance underwriting requirements are not typically stringent in the retirement arena, there are times when a prospect is uninsurable and the "guaranteed issue" or graded death benefit amount is not sufficient. In these cases annuities are suitable substitutes for life insurance in filling the funding need. A second reason annuities are used to fund plans is the guaranteed payout rates they sometimes offer. If this is the case, the same annuity that is used for funding purposes is also used for payout purposes.

A new approach to funding retirement plans with annuities is to use modified guaranteed annuities. These allow high interest rates that are guaranteed only if the contract is kept up until maturity. If the contract is cashed in before maturity, interest rates are adjusted to current market values.

13

Plan Installation and Administration

Chapter Outline

Once the plan has been selected and designed according to employer specifications and the funding approach has been decided upon, the tasks of plan installation and plan administration begin. The role of the financial services professional in these processes varies from case to case. Some clients desire that you provide ongoing consulting, while others allow you to take a more passive posture. Most financial services professionals will want to choose the latter role and delegate the responsibilities associated with plan installation and administration to a third-party administrator. This will enable you to use your time more efficiently, freeing you up for sales and design consulting. There are, however, occasions that call for client hand-holding and troubleshooting on your part. For these times you need a general understanding of the installation and administration processes, and the documents that are an integral part of these processes. The objective of this chapter is to provide you with this understanding through an overview of plan installation and plan administration. If a more detailed review of the plan installation and administration process is needed, the loose-leaf services described in chapter 2 should be consulted. These services provide a wealth of information about filing requirements, as well as supplying copies of current forms and instructions.

SETTING UP A CORPORATE PLAN

The first step in the plan installation process is for the employer to legally adopt the plan. This can be done through a resolution of the corporate board of directors, which can either adopt a particular plan document or simply adopt the major provisions of the plan. The corporate resolution should be adopted before the end of the tax year if the employer wants the plan to be effective in that year. If the company's securities are offered in the open market, the plan is also generally submitted for stockholder approval (although it's not legally necessary). Notice of the establishment of the plan and details about the plan should be presented to stockholders in a proxy statement.

At the same time that the plan is approved, the corporate board of directors should also approve the trust instrument (if any) that will be used. Recall that a trust provides for the irrevocable deposit of plan assets. In other words, once assets such as individual life insurance policies or cash are transferred to the trust, the employer or the employer's creditors cannot recapture these assets. (The employer may, however, recapture assets that exceed promised benefits at the termination of the plan.) Under some state laws a nominal contribution to the trust may be necessary in order to establish its existence.

If a group pension contract is used instead of a trust, the board will review a specimen contract. If the board wishes to adopt the contract, it will authorize the submission of a letter of application with premium. Note that the group pension contract must be submitted for approval to the state insurance department in the state where the corporation is domiciled. The state insurance department reviews the contract to see if the insurer has sufficient reserves to pay benefits and if the contract meets other state specifications. For this reason, group pension contracts are issued conditional upon state insurance department approval and are subject to any modifications that the state insurance department requires. Fortunately, however, most state insurance departments tend to rubber-stamp approval of these contracts in a timely fashion because model contracts have been preapproved well before the time of the individual submission. (*Planning Note:* New York and Pennsylvania take a more restrictive and time-consuming approach to the approval of group pension contracts. Allow extra time if you are dealing with these insurance departments.)

Another step that must be completed before the end of the first tax year is notifying the participants of the new plan. This can be an oral explanation at an employee meeting or a written letter that is either mailed or posted at work—for example, "It is our pleasure to announce the ABC Company is adopting a qualified 401(k) plan. The details of the plan are as follows. . . ." Alternatively, the summary plan description (see below) can be used to satisfy this requirement.

For a plan funded with employer contributions, the employer typically adopts the plan at the end of the tax year in which it wants to receive a tax-deductible contribution. The reason is that the employer may not know until the end of the year whether it has funds available to contribute to a plan. In this case, the plan is made effective retroactive to the first day of the year, and a tax-deductible contribution can be made for the whole year. For example, if the employer is on a calendar tax year, the plan may be adopted on December 31, effective as of the previous January 1. However, if the plan is a contributory plan (a 401(k) plan or 403(b) plan), it should be adopted prior to the beginning of the first year of the plan's operation. This is necessary to allow time to enroll participants in the program. For such a plan application is best accomplished through one or more enrollment meetings.

If the plan is contributory or if salary reductions are required under a 403(b) plan or a 401(k) plan, an additional step must be taken. When this is the case, the employees are asked to attend an enrollment meeting. The enrollment of an adequate number of employees in the plan is crucial for purposes of meeting the nondiscrimination rules and passing the actual deferral percentage test (401(k) plans only). Employers usually request the financial services professional to attend the enrollment meeting and use his or her selling skills to persuade the rank-and-file employees to make the necessary contributions or salary reductions.

The enrollment meeting starts out with the financial services professional describing the plan and spelling out the benefits and trade-offs of plan participation for the employees. The meeting typically contains a question-and-answer period during which the employees get to voice their concerns and receive clarification on important issues. (*Planning Note:* Many financial services professionals present a slide show or movie that addresses the most typical questions. This often heads off the common problem of having one or two employees cause trouble by harping on the negative aspects of the plan.) The meeting typically concludes with the completion and signing of enrollment forms and salary reduction agreements or authorization to withhold mandatory contributions from an employee's pay.

The enrollment meeting (or if an enrollment meeting is not required, a separate meeting) can be used to secure the information to apply for individual life insurance contracts if they are being used wholly or in part to fund the plan. In addition, medical examinations can also be conducted at this time, if required by underwriting.

Regardless of whether a trust or group pension contract is used, the entire first year's contribution should be made by the time for filing the employer's tax return for the year in which the plan is adopted. (For a corporate employer using a calendar year, the date for filing the tax return for a given year is generally March 15 of the following year, but this can be extended to September 15.) As long as this requirement is met and the plan is in final form, the employer will be able to deduct contributions if the plan qualifies. (*Planning Note:* The plan should be adopted subject to the right to be rescinded if it does not qualify, and the trust or group pension contract should allow contributions to be returned if the plan does not qualify.)

In order to determine whether the plan qualifies, the employer should file an application for an advance-determination letter with the IRS. The employer is not required to receive IRS approval, but instead can wait for an IRS audit to determine whether the plan is qualified. However, this is not recommended because of the risk of disqualification (which means a retroactive loss of the tax deduction). The forms and documents used to file for an advance-determination letter include the following:

- IRS Form 5300 (Application for Determination for Employee Benefit Plan) or IRS Form 5307 (Short Form Application for Determination for Employee Benefit Plan—this form is used for master or prototype plans)
- IRS Form 8717 (User Fee for Employee Plan Determination Request)
- IRS Form 5302 (Employee Census)
- IRS Form 2848 (Power of Attorney and Declaration of Representative)
- copies of the plan and the trust or group pension contract
- specimen copies of any individual life insurance or annuity contract involved
- specimen copies of the formal announcement and detailed description made available to employees (notice to interested parties—see below)

Make sure the determination letter is applied for before the tax return filing date (plus extensions). If the request for an advance-determination letter is submitted before the tax return is due, the IRS will extend the time limit for amending the plan. A retroactive amendment will then be possible, enabling the employer to receive a deduction for the current year. If the filing deadline is missed, it is highly unlikely that the IRS will allow the plan to be amended retroactively or that a deduction will be allowed for the initial contribution. Retroactive amendment is common if the IRS objects to some provisions of the proposed plan. (*Planning Note:* A determination letter is typically issued within 6 months after the application is filed. Although the IRS has a maximum of 270 days to make a ruling, no determination letter will be received before 60 days so as to give interested parties a chance to comment.)

Immediately preceding the filing of the request for an advance-determination letter the employer should issue the notice to interested parties of the intent to install a qualified plan. The IRS will not issue an advance-determination letter unless interested parties have been notified that an application for one has been filed. The notice to interested parties goes to all employees eligible to be in the plan and to ineligible employees if they work at the same location as the eligible employees (except nonparticipating union employees). If the notice is posted or given in person it must be given no less than 7 days or more than 21 days before the request for a determination letter is filed. If the employees are notified by mail, the postmark can't be less than 10 days or more than 24 days before the application for the determination letter is filed. The notice should indicate that qualification is being sought and that the employees have the right to submit comments on the plan to the IRS and the Department of Labor. The notice should also contain

- a brief description of the class of interested parties

- the name of the plan and the plan administrator and the employer identification number
- a description of eligible employees (for example, salaried only)
- the procedures that an employee may use for commenting to the IRS and DOL
- other specified information (consult one of the loose-leaf services described in chapter 2)

The final and most important step in the employee communications process is the issuing of the summary plan description (SPD). A summary plan description is an easy-to-read booklet that explains the plan to the participants. The SPD may be prepared by the financial services professional, the insurer, or the employer. In any case employers are required to give summary plan descriptions to participants within 120 days after the plan is adopted by the board of directors. Within this time the SPD should also be filed with the Department of Labor. (*Planning Note:* In addition to being used with retirement plans, summary plan descriptions are also required for most welfare benefit plans. For this reason it may be wise to suggest that your client combine all the summary plan descriptions [and other information] in an employee handbook.)

A summary plan description bridges the gap between the legalese of the pension plan and the understanding of the average participant by effectively communicating how a plan works, what benefits are available, and how to get these benefits. The SPD must strike a balance between clarity and depth. To this end, the Department of Labor suggests the frequent use of examples, the elimination of technical jargon and long complex sentences, the inclusion of a table of contents, and the use of clear cross-references. Other good ideas include the following:

- cross-referencing only to materials already discussed, not to materials that have yet to be discussed
- using short paragraphs (three or four sentences)
- using short sentences (20 words or less) and short, familiar words with few syllables

A summary plan description must be fair and evenhanded. It can't be used to persuade employees to join the plan, but must merely explain the plan. The regulations specifically state that a summary plan description can't downplay the negative consequences of involvement—for example, it can't gloss over plan terms that may cause a participant to lose benefits or fail to qualify for them. Any limitations, exceptions, reductions, or other restrictions on plan benefits must be duly noted. It's not clear, however, whether the positive plan consequences can be overplayed. This is certainly desirable in a 401(k) plan, 403(b) plan, or a contributory plan because the employer may want to entice employees to participate in order to meet the actual deferral percentage test, 401(m) test, or the 410(b) nondiscrimination tests, respectively. It may also be desirable if the employer wants to get a little more mileage out of his or her benefit dollar. In either case, however, it's probably limited to the extent that it can't be misleading. In other words, there seems to be some leeway, but one thing is clear: "overselling the plan" is not acceptable. (*Planning Note:* Your client's summary plan description should contain a disclaimer stating that if there is a conflict between the plan and the summary plan description, the plan provisions will be determinative. Despite these disclaimers, however, courts are increasingly ruling that the summary plan description's provisions are binding on the employer. For this reason, encourage your staff and/or your clients to take a hard look at the accuracy of their summary plan descriptions.)

The summary plan description was born with ERISA and is governed by final regulations that appeared in 1976. These regulations dictate what kind of language to use, what kind of information to have, and which group of people must get the information. The regulations also require that every 5 years participants whose plans have been modified must receive an updated summary plan description, and every 10 years—regardless of whether the plan has been modified—a new summary plan description must be issued. Here's a list of items that the SPD must contain:

- a provision identifying the plan—for example, "This is the ABC Company profit-sharing plan"
- the names and addresses of people responsible for the plan
- the employer identification number
- the plan administrator's name, address, and telephone number
- the name and address of the person designated for service of legal process
- the name, title, and business address of each trustee
- if the plan is collectively bargained, a statement to that effect
- an explanation of the plan's eligibility requirements for participation and benefits and normal retirement age
- an explanation of any joint and survivor benefits
- an explanation of any terms that could result in a participant's losing benefits
- a PBGC insurance provision, if applicable
- a description and explanation of the plan provisions for determining years of service for eligibility to participate, vesting, breaks of service, and benefit accrual
- a list of the sources of plan contributions
- the name of the funding agency
- the plan year's ending date
- procedures for presenting claims for benefits under the plan and remedies for benefits denied under the plan
- a statement of ERISA rights (this statement is standard text promulgated by the Department of Labor)

Table 13-1 below summarizes all the steps required to establish a qualified retirement plan.

TABLE 13-1 **Summary of Steps in Setting Up a Corporate Plan**	
Steps	Timetable
1. Secure a corporate resolution adopting the plan.[1]	Before the end of the tax year.
2. Secure a corporate resolution approving the trust document or group pension contract.[2]	Before the end of the tax year.
3. Notify participants of the plan's adoption and its major terms.	Before the end of the tax year.
4. Conduct an enrollment meeting if necessary.	For 401(k) and 403(b) plans, shortly after plan adoption.
5. Give notice of the filing for advance determination to interested parties.	Before the date for filing the employer's tax return.
6. File for an advance-determination letter.	Before the date for filing the employer's tax return.
7. Make the first year's contribution.	Before the date for filing the employer's tax return.
8. Communicate the plan to employees (which can be done through the SPD).	Typically, shortly after the notice to interested parties has been sent.
9. Supply a summary plan description to employees and file it with the DOL.	Within 120 days after the plan is adopted.
[1] If not in final form when adopted by the board of directors, finalize the plan before filing for an advance-determination letter. [2] If not in final form when adopted by the board of directors, finalize the trust before the end of the year of adoption.	

ADMINISTRATION OF A CORPORATE PLAN

Every qualified plan has a plan administrator who is responsible for the administration of the plan. Typically the plan administrator is the employer (in larger plans, the employer's director of human resources) or an individual or committee designated by the employer. The plan administrator receives help from a variety of sources. If the plan has a trust, the trustee may assist the plan administrator with administrative matters, but more frequently the trustee restricts his or her activities to investing the plan's assets. With insured plans the insurer will generally provide a great number of administrative services, from computer support to producing manuals, which guide the plan administrator through the administrative process. In addition to the trustee or insurance company the plan administrator can also look to a variety of third-party administrators (TPA) who perform everything from turnkey services to only one specific service, such as administering the actual deferral percentage test. As a financial services professional you will sometimes be asked to suggest or secure a TPA. (A list of third-party administrators can be found in chapter 2.)

One of the principal duties of the plan administrator is compliance with the reporting and disclosure requirements of ERISA. All qualified plans are subject to these reporting and disclosure requirements (except some church and state plans). The most important reporting and disclosure requirement is filing the annual return/report with the IRS. (*Planning Note:* Financial services professionals are sometimes asked to advise plan administrators on how to comply with the reporting and disclosure requirements and may be called on to help in the filing of forms.)

There are several types of forms, depending on the nature of the employer and the number of employees. These forms are generally referred to as the 5500 family of forms and include detailed financial and accounting information, as well as actuarial information for a defined-benefit plan. These forms must be filed annually. The 5500 family of forms are required to be filed by the last day of the seventh month after the plan year ends. An extension of time up to 2 1/2 months may be granted if Form 5558 is filed. Here's a list and explanation of the most commonly used members of the 5500 family of forms (see table 13-2):

- Form 5500 (Annual Return/Report of an Employee Benefit Plan [with 100 or more participants]). This form is filed if the employer has 100 or more participants at the beginning of the plan year.
- Form 5500 C/R (Return/Report of Employee Benefit Plan [with fewer than 100 participants]). This form is filed if your client has fewer than 100 participants. Your clients need only fill out the first two pages of the 5500 C/R form 2 out of every 3 years. This serves as a registration of the plan without requiring extensive paperwork. In the initial year and every third year thereafter, your clients are required to fill out the longer version of the form (page one and pages three through six). This represents a more thorough filing.
- Form 5500EZ (Annual Return/Report of One-Participant Pension Benefit Plan). This form is used if the plan is a "one-participant" plan. A plan is considered to be a one-participant plan if it covers (a) your client or your client and spouse, and the business is wholly owned by your client or your client and spouse, or (b) only partners in a business partnership, or the partners and their spouses.
- Schedule A of Form 5500 (Insurance Information). This form is filed if any benefits are provided by an insurance company. Two exceptions

TABLE 13-2
Summary of IRS Filing Requirements

Form 5500.

Summary of Filing Requirements for Employers and Plan Administrators (File forms ONLY with IRS)

Type of plan	What to file	When to file
Most pension plans with only one participant or one participant and that participant's spouse	Form 5500EZ	File all required forms and schedules for each plan by the last day of the 7th month after the plan year ends.
Pension plan with fewer than 100 participants	Form 5500-C/R	
Pension plan with 100 or more participants	Form 5500	
Annuity under Code section 403(b)(1) or trust under Code section 408(c)	Form 5500 or Form 5500-C/R	
Custodial account under Code section 403(b)(7)	Form 5500 or Form 5500-C/R	
Welfare benefit plan with 100 or more participants	Form 5500	
Welfare benefit plan with fewer than 100 participants (see exceptions on page 3 of these instructions)	Form 5500-C/R	
Pension or welfare plan with 100 or more participants (see instructions for item 26)	Financial statements, schedules, and accountant's opinion	
Pension or welfare plan with benefits provided by an insurance company	Schedule A (Form 5500)	
Pension plan that requires actuarial information	Schedule B (Form 5500)	
Pension or welfare plan with 100 or more participants	Schedule C (Form 5500)	
Pension plan with ESOP benefits	Schedule E (Form 5500)	
Fringe benefit plan under Code section 6039D	Schedule F (Form 5500)	
Financial Schedules for item 27	Schedule G (Form 5500)	
Pension plan filing a registration statement identifying separated participants with deferred vested benefits from a pension plan	Schedule SSA (Form 5500)	

exist. First, Schedule A need not be filed if a form 5500EZ is used. Second, certain master trusts submitted by insurance companies make a Schedule A unnecessary. When this is the case, however, a Department of Labor filing may be required.

- Schedule B of Form 5500 (Actuarial Information). This form is used for most defined-benefit plans.
- Schedule E of Form 5500 (ESOP Annual Information). This form is used if the plan is an ESOP.
- Schedule P of Form 5500 (Annual Return of Fiduciary of Employee Benefit Trust). This form starts the statute of limitations running on fiduciary responsibilities.
- Schedule SSA of Form 5500 (Annual Registration—Statement Identifying Separated Participants with Deferred Vested Benefits). This form is filed if a covered participant separates from service and the participant is entitled to a deferred vested benefit.

In addition to filing the 5500 family of forms with the IRS, plan administrators must also satisfy the reporting requirements prescribed by the Department of Labor, most notably the requirements pertaining to the summary plan description. What's more, administrators of defined-benefit plans must also supply the Pension Benefit Guaranty Corporation with annual premiums and filings (Form PBGC-1). Form PBGC-1 is due no later than 7 months after the close of the plan year (July 31 for a calendar-year plan).

Plan administrators are required not only to file forms with appropriate federal agencies, but also to keep plan participants informed. Two of the most important ways of doing this are through the summary plan description (for an existing plan, the SPD must be furnished to an employee within 90 days of becoming a participant) and employee meetings. Other paperwork is also required, however; this includes supplying plan participants with a summary annual report each year. This document is a summary of the information on the annual report—5500 form(s)—and is provided to each participant in the plan every year.

In addition to a summary annual report, plan participants must also be supplied with a summary of material modification. A summary of material modification informs the employees about changes in the plan. For example, if the vesting schedule was changed from 10-year-cliff vesting to 5-year-cliff vesting, the participants should be supplied with notification of the change within 210 days after the close of the plan year in which the material modification occurred. A material modification does not include every plan change but only the major changes shown in table 13-3.

Furnishing plan participants with a personal benefit statement is another important aspect of plan administration. Upon written request each plan participant or beneficiary is entitled to receive a statement of the individual's own accrued benefit or account balance under the qualified plan. This statement need not be furnished more than once in any 12-month period but must be furnished upon a participant's termination of employment. Many plan administrators, however, feel it appropriate to provide a personal benefit statement every year to each participant and beneficiary even if there is no formal request for one. This is good practice because it makes employees more aware of their benefits and enables the employer to meet the organizational objectives of retaining and motivating employees.

TABLE 13-3 List of Material Modifications
name and address of sponsor/employer name and address of plan administrator structure of plan name of plan type of plan agent for service of process persons performing functions for the plan sources and method of determining contributions method of asset accumulation procedure for presenting claims eligibility requirements vesting provisions features of portability or reciprocity length of service to determine participation, vesting, benefit accrual break-in-service rules requirements for pension benefits basis for computing retirement benefits circumstances causing loss of pension benefits joint and survivor annuity rules disposition of employee's contributions requirements for welfare benefits circumstances causing loss of welfare benefits fiduciaries' names and addresses

Another aspect of plan administration is counseling participants about plan choices—especially the retirement options available to them (for example, 90 days prior to the time that the retirement annuity begins married participants must be notified of their right to waive the joint and survivor option in favor of another annuity form). In addition, annuity options must be explained and other retirement preparations must be finalized. This may take the form of private counseling or it may be written material provided to the plan administrator through a plan administrator's manual. A plan administrator's manual is usually supplied by the insurance company to the plan administrator to help with administrative matters and contains handouts with simplified explanations that can be distributed to participants.

Yet another duty of plan administration is issuing certain tax forms to participants (copies of these forms are also sent to the IRS):

- 1099R forms (filed with the IRS and sent to any participant or participant's beneficiary who receives a lump-sum or periodic distribution)
- withholding forms (withholding taxes on benefit payments—whether in a lump sum or periodic payments. This must be done unless the participant elects to have no tax withholding taken out.)

Another facet of plan administration involves amending plan documents. This has become an increasingly larger part of the plan administrator's duties because retirement plans have undergone frequent and sweeping legislative changes that have mandated plan amendment. In general, when a plan is amended some of the same procedures that are followed in the initial qualification process (such as submitting a Form 5300) are repeated. In addition, the new law itself and subsequent IRS rulings and procedures typically contain procedures and timetables for amending plans. One final note: if four or more substantive changes are made to a plan in a given year the plan must be "restated." A restated plan filing subjects the entire plan to close scrutiny. Conversely, an amended filing subjects only the amendments to close scrutiny. (See table 13-4.)

TABLE 13-4
Summary of Plan-Administration Responsibilities

Filing annual return or report (5500 family of forms)
Filing summary plan descriptions with DOL
Filing annual premiums with PBGC (Form PBGC-1)
Holding employee meetings
Supplying participants with summary annual report
Supplying participants (and DOL) with summary of material
  modification
Furnishing personal benefit statements
Counseling participants on options
Issuing appropriate tax forms
Amending and restating the plan when necessary

SETTING UP AND ADMINISTERING A KEOGH PLAN

The rules for setting up and administering a Keogh plan are roughly the same as the rules for a corporate plan. For example, even in a one-person sole proprietorship a summary plan description is required and a formal adoption of the plan must take place. However, some differences do exist, such as the following:

- A Keogh plan must be established by December 31 in order for a deduction to be taken for the year. Plan contributions, however, can be made up until the tax return deadline plus extensions.

- A business owner can shift from one master plan to a different one without incurring any penalties. (*Planning Note:* If your client is currently under another organization's master Keogh plan, the possibility for a "painless" switch exists.)
- A letter or some other document should be used by a sole proprietorship or partnership to formally adopt the plan. This is the corollary to the corporate resolution that adopts the plan.

(*Planning Note:* The role of the financial services professional takes on greater significance when the client establishes a Keogh plan because such clients typically do not have an administrative arm to carry out the multiple functions associated with plan installation and administration.)

SOFTWARE PACKAGES USED FOR PLAN INSTALLATION AND ADMINISTRATION

A variety of software packages are available from insurance company home offices and pension vendors that aid in the process of plan installation and administration. Software packages are widely available in the following areas:

- actual deferral percentage test calculation (monitors whether 401(k) plans meet the ADP test)
- actuarial valuations (a must for firms with defined-benefit plans)
- claims processing (typically used in conjunction with welfare benefit plans)
- document preparation (both plan and summary plan description)
- employee benefit statement preparation (typically used in conjunction with welfare benefit plans)
- nondiscrimination testing (monitors whether plans meet 410(b) and 401(a)26 tests)
- top-heavy analysis (monitors top-heavy status of plan)
- 5500 forms preparation (very popular method for simplifying government filings)
- pension check processing (processes benefit payments)
- loan processing (useful for processing loans and tracking plan loan repayments)

14

Plan Termination

Chapter Outline

Business owners contemplating the establishment of a retirement plan need to know that qualified plans must be permanent, rather than temporary, programs. The IRS seeks assurances that the plan is intended to meet the retirement needs of present and future employees rather than as a tax shelter for key employees. This does not mean, however, that the business owner must be saddled with a plan indefinitely. If business conditions change substantially, the plan can still be terminated, as long as the plan has been drafted to reserve the employer's right to terminate it.

The term *plan termination* used herein means the complete dissolution of the plan: participants receive no additional plan benefits, contributions cease (after meeting remaining obligations), plan assets are liquidated, and benefits are distributed. The employer considering termination of a plan may not be fully aware of the consequences and administrative burdens of such a decision. This reading explores the procedures and ramifications of plan termination and reviews less drastic alternatives.

TO TERMINATE OR NOT TO TERMINATE

Why Plan Termination?

The employer may wish to terminate a plan for any number of business reasons. The following are common ones:

- The employer is no longer in a financial position to make further plan contributions.
- The plan benefits are not meaningful amounts, and participants are limited in their ability to make deductible IRA contributions.
- To lower plan costs and ease administrative complexity, the employer may want to switch plan designs (for example, switching from a defined-benefit to a defined-contribution approach).
- The company may want to switch to an employee stock ownership plan (ESOP) to purchase the stock of a retiring owner.
- The employer wants to accommodate a substantial change in business operations, such as the sale or merger of the business.

Alternatives to Plan Termination

Plan termination is much more than simply ceasing additional employer contributions. It also means notifying proper governmental agencies, liquidating assets, and distributing funds to participants—all of which generate a great deal of paperwork and administrative expense. Before deciding to terminate a plan, the employer should consider other alternatives.

Ceasing Further Benefit Accruals

A defined-benefit or defined-contribution plan can be amended to cease further benefit accruals—as long as benefits already earned are not reduced. With defined-contribution plans, this strategy can be used to cease employer contributions. This approach may make sense to the employer who expects to resume making contributions later or who is concerned about participants squandering retirement benefits if they receive them now. Ceasing accruals in a defined-benefit plan does not always result in a complete cessation of contributions, depending upon the funding status of the plan. Ceasing accruals will, however, limit the plan sponsor's future funding obligations.

Regardless of the type of plan involved, one issue that must always be considered is whether additional benefit accruals must be awarded for the current year. Under ERISA, benefit accruals cannot cease until 15 days after plan participants have been notified of the amendment. Therefore the effective date of the amendment ceasing accruals must be a minimum of 15 days after notice is given. Once the effective date is established, a determination is made whether participants are entitled to another year of benefit accrual. The rule is that *they are entitled to an accrual if they meet all service eligibility requirements prior to the effective date of the amendment.*

> *Example:* Alpha Corp. maintains a money-purchase pension plan with a calendar plan year. The plan is amended to cease accruals effective September 1 (and participants are given notice of the amendment by the preceding August 15). If the plan awards a benefit accrual to participants completing 1,000 hours of service, full-time employees will have met the 1,000-hour requirement by September 1 and will be entitled to an accrual for the current plan year.

An amendment ceasing accruals for current participants usually should include a provision prohibiting other employees from becoming new plan participants. Since new participants will not be eligible for any benefits, adding them simply compounds the administrative burden. Under the law, a plan that is not currently providing benefit accruals does not have to satisfy any minimum coverage requirements, so prohibiting new members does not cause any coverage problems.

Effect on Defined-Benefit Plans. Ceasing further benefit accruals in a defined-benefit plan does not change the plan's essential nature—the plan is still required to pay promised benefits as they become due, employees continue to vest under the same vesting schedule,1 and the employer is still required to meet the minimum funding obligations. If assets are not sufficient to meet the projected payouts, the actuary may determine that additional contributions are still necessary. Plans subject to the PBGC insurance program must continue paying insurance premiums. The rising costs of these premiums over the last few years could weigh in favor of terminating the plan versus discontinuing further benefit accruals.

Effect on Defined-Contribution Plans. In a money-purchase plan, or any other plan with required contributions, the only additional contributions necessary when accruals cease are those to fund the prior or current year's obligation.

Whether the same vesting provisions can continue to apply or whether full vesting occurs depends upon the type of plan involved. Any defined-contribution plan that is a pension plan (money-purchase and target-benefit plans) should be able to continue using the same vesting schedule. On the other hand, in profit-sharing plans, participants become fully vested when employer contributions are completely discontinued. (See below for more complete discussion.)

Amending the Plan into Another Type

In some circumstances, the employer has the choice to amend the plan into another type of plan, rather than terminating the plan and starting up a new one. This is a tricky area and legal consultation should be sought out. However, some general guidelines can be provided. A defined-contribution plan of one type usually may be amended into another type of defined-contribution plan; for example, a money-purchase plan can be amended into a profit-sharing plan. The amendment must be carefully drafted to ensure that subtle differences between the types of plans are addressed.

Likewise, a defined-benefit plan of one type may be amended into another type of defined-benefit plan. In the large plan market, this sometimes happens when a traditional defined-benefit plan is amended into a cash-balance-type plan. One type of amendment is clearly prohibited: defined-benefit plans cannot be amended into defined-contribution plans, and defined-contribution plans cannot be amended into defined-benefit plans.

Limitations on Plan Termination

Several issues may discourage or prohibit the plan sponsor from terminating the plan. These issues are addressed below.

Temporary Tax Shelters

As a general rule, retirement plans may not be set up as a subterfuge to tax-shelter funds for the benefit of key employees. If they have been, plan termination can result in retroactive disqualification. For plans terminated within a few years after establishment, the IRS presumes that the employer did not intend for the plan to be permanent. To rebut this assumption, the employer must provide a reason of "business necessity beyond the employer's control." Acceptable reasons for an early termination appear to be change in ownership by merger, the liquidation or dissolution of the business, a change in ownership by sale or transfer, adverse business conditions, a significant change in the pension law, or a change in the company's retirement plan strategy, resulting in the adoption of a replacement plan. Practically speaking, the permanency issue is not a concern when the plan has been maintained for at least 10 years.

Insufficient Plan Assets

In defined-contribution plans, plan benefits are based upon the individual accounts, which represent all the assets held by the plan. This means that additional employer contributions are generally not required when a plan is terminated. However, for any plan that requires specified employer contributions, promised contributions that have not been made at the time of termination must still be made.

Defined-benefit plans, on the other hand, are a totally different story. In defined-benefit plans, assets never equal the present value of promised benefits. The plan will either have more than enough or not enough assets to pay promised benefits. When assets are insufficient to pay benefits, plans subject to the PBGC insurance program may not be able to be terminated at all. The PBGC has a financial interest at this point, and strict rules (described below) apply. If the plan cannot be terminated, the employer generally will want to amend the plan to cease all further benefit accruals in order to limit its future liability. If a plan with insufficient assets is not subject to the PBGC program, the plan may be terminated, and strict rules regarding how plan assets are allocated to the participants apply. The rules that apply to plans with excess assets are discussed more fully below.

Plan Problems

Plan termination is a time when the IRS scrutinizes the operation of the plan. The sponsor of a plan should correct any compliance problems prior to considering plan termination. The IRS currently maintains a voluntary compliance program, which allows sponsors willing to correct compliance problems to do so with a minimum of penalties.

TERMINATING A DEFINED-CONTRIBUTION PLAN

Compared with the termination of a defined-benefit plan covered by the PBGC insurance program, termination of a defined-contribution plan is relatively easy. However, each of the following steps will still need to be taken.

- A corporate resolution terminating the plan must be adopted, and the plan and trust must be amended to terminate further accruals. As discussed above, the issue of whether participants have accrued a benefit for the current year has to be carefully considered.
- The plan termination date must be scheduled at least 15 days after participants are notified. Since the termination effectively ceases benefit accruals, the ERISA rule requiring that participants be notified 15 days before the amendment becomes effective applies.
- The employer must make any remaining required contributions for the previous year or for this year's benefit accruals.
- Sometimes when the laws regarding qualified plans change, plan sponsors are allowed an extended period in which to incorporate amendments reflecting the new law. If this is the case at the time of a plan termination, conforming amendments should be added to the plan.
- Plan assets must be liquidated in preparation for distribution. Note that assets can be distributed in kind as long as the highly compensated employees are not given special treatment.
- Benefit distribution paperwork (described below) must be prepared.

- In the year that benefits are distributed, when the annual IRS Form 5500 is filed, it is marked as the "final form."

Submitting the Plan to the IRS

At the time of plan termination, the sponsor of a qualified plan can voluntarily request an IRS approval letter. If granted, the IRS letter states that the plan termination does not adversely affect the qualified status of the plan. Although the submission is voluntary, in recent history the IRS has audited a large number of plans that terminate without requesting such a determination letter.

The determination letter gives the sponsor and plan participants the assurance that distributed benefits will be eligible for the special tax treatment afforded to qualified plans. Unfortunately, the IRS determination letter is not a guarantee that the plan will not be audited later. However, the auditing process should go more smoothly if the determination letter had been requested. For these reasons, it is generally a good idea for the plan sponsor to request the IRS determination letter.

To request a determination letter, the plan sponsor must complete and submit Form 5310. Also, all plan participants and beneficiaries must be given notice of the submission. Besides announcing the submission, the notice should inform participants that they are allowed to send comments to the IRS or Department of Labor (DOL). Strict rules apply to who must receive the notice as well as how and when it is to be distributed.

TERMINATING A DEFINED-BENEFIT PLAN

An extremely complex termination procedure applies for defined-benefit plans covered under the PBGC insurance program. For plans that are not covered, the procedures are similar to those described above.

Plans Covered under the PBGC Insurance Program

Overview

The Pension Benefit Guaranty Corporation (PBGC) is a federal agency that insures participants against the loss of benefits arising from complete or partial termination of a defined-benefit plan. When this agency was discussed in chapter 2 of the textbook, we mentioned that the PBGC

- covers all qualified defined-benefit plans (except for plans of professional-service employers with 25 or fewer active participants)
- collects compulsory premiums
- guarantees benefits (up to a maximum) in case of employer default; the maximum monthly guaranteed benefit for 1996 was $2,642.

- oversees plan terminations initiated by the employer
- initiates terminations if a plan is financially strained
- taps up to 30 percent of the net worth of employers whose plans have terminated and left the PBGC liable for payments

Here we will explore the PBGC's practices and requirements for plan terminations initiated voluntarily by the employer. But note that the PBGC also has the right to terminate a plan in financial difficulty (as discussed further at the end of the chapter).

Voluntary Plan Termination

When an employer wishes to terminate a defined-benefit plan covered under the PBGC program, the employer faces three issues:

- Can the plan be voluntarily terminated?
- When can the plan be terminated?
- How can the plan be terminated?

The Single Employer Pension Plan Amendments Act (SEPPAA) addresses and provides answers to each of these questions. SEPPAA introduced a major change to the plan termination process. Now a plan can be terminated only if it meets specific conditions; if not, the plan must continue until the conditions are satisfied. Technically speaking, a termination is allowed only if the plan satisfies conditions for a standard or a distress termination.

Standard Termination. The employer can initiate a standard termination only if the plan has sufficient assets to pay all plan benefits. If the plan does not currently have sufficient assets, the plan may still qualify for a standard termination if the employer agrees to make up the difference with a single payment, or if a 50 percent owner of the company agrees to waive benefits due under the plan.

Distress Termination. If the plan does not have sufficient assets to pay promised benefits, the plan may qualify—in extreme circumstances—for a distress termination. To qualify, the employer must fall within one of the following categories:

- It faces liquidation in bankruptcy or insolvency proceedings.
- It faces reorganization in bankruptcy or insolvency proceedings.
- It can demonstrate to the PBGC that it will be unable to pay its debts when due and will be unable to continue the business.
- It can prove that the cost of providing coverage has become unreasonably burdensome as a result of a decline in the workforce.

Setting the Termination Date. Assuming an employer is able to terminate the plan under SEPPAA, the next consideration is the termination date. This date has great importance because it establishes the limits on the employer's liability. The date is contingent upon notification of participants of the upcoming termination. The actual termination date must be from 60 to 90 days after the notification.

Steps in a Plan Termination. Once the date is established, in order to keep the termination date, all of the following PBGC-required procedures must be completed in a timely manner:

- issuing a notice of intent to terminate to participants and beneficiaries at least 60 days and no more than 90 days before the proposed termination date
- filing a notice of the termination on Form 500 (including an actuaries certificate that assets are sufficient to pay promised benefits) with the PBGC on or before the 120th day after the proposed termination date
- distributing assets to satisfy plan obligations within 240 days after the PBGC filing

In addition to the requirements established by the PBGC, the plan also must take each of the steps required for terminating a defined-contribution plan. To summarize, these include:

- adopting a corporate resolution to terminate the plan and amending the plan and trust to terminate further accruals
- making any remaining required contributions
- adopting plan amendments to conform with law changes
- deciding whether to voluntarily request IRS approval on Form 5310 and notifying participants
- liquidating plan assets in preparation for distribution
- preparing benefit distribution paperwork (described below)
- filing the final 5500 annual return/report

Plans Not Covered under the PBGC Insurance Program

When a plan is not subject to PBGC regulation, it need not conform to the PBGC's rigid termination procedures. Because of this, a non-PBGC plan can be terminated even if it does not have sufficient assets to pay all plan benefits. When this is the case, the law prescribes a specific method for dividing the plan assets among the participants. In many cases, to avoid bad feelings (and potential lawsuits), the owners will decide to have all of the deficiency taken from their own benefits.

The administrative burden is not as great with the non-PBGC plan, since the PBGC filing requirements do not have to be satisfied. However, the sponsor does have to take all of the steps required for terminating a defined-contribution plan, as described above.

Reversion of Excess Plan Assets

As stated earlier, a defined-benefit plan may, at any point in time, have more assets than necessary to pay benefits promised under the plan. This generally occurs when plan assets outperform the actuaries assumptions. Before the mid-1980s, an employer could terminate a plan and receive an asset reversion from an overfunded terminated defined-benefit plan without penalty (although the amount was and still is treated as taxable income to the employer).

However, beginning in the mid-1980's, the law began to make the practice of terminating plans to recover surplus assets less desirable by adding penalty taxes to the amount of excess assets returned to the employer. Congress took its strongest action to date in promoting these goals when it passed the Revenue Reconciliation Act of 1990. The Act (new Code Subsection 4980) created a 50 percent excise tax on all reversions except when the employer shares the reversion with employees, in which case the excise tax is only 20 percent.

To qualify for the 20 percent tax rate, the employer must either (1) establish a qualified replacement plan to which it transfers assets equal to the excess of 25 percent of the reversion, or (2) provide pro rata increases in benefits of qualified participants in connection with the plan termination equal to at least 20 percent of the reversion.

Note that in order to revert plan assets to the employer, the plan must specifically state that excess assets will revert at the time of plan termination. Under a recent law change, a plan that does not have such a provision may not be amended to do so at the time of the termination.

When a plan has excess assets, the employer is not under any obligation to revert the excess. The assets may be, and often are, allocated among plan participants. The law provides some discretion in the allocation method, and the actuary should provide several alternatives. In the small-plan setting, the actuary generally looks for a method that allocates the lion's share of the excess to the business owner. This can work quite well, unless the owner's benefit is already approaching the maximum benefit limitations. If the owner can get a significant piece of the excess, the reallocation method has clear tax advantages—benefits can be rolled into an IRA and tax deferral can continue. On the other hand, if the owner's share of the excess is limited, he or she may prefer the reversion approach.

DISTRIBUTIONS FROM A TERMINATING PLAN

In one significant way, the process of distributing plan benefits at the time of plan termination is different than in other situations. If the plan is to pay single-sum benefits, then the paperwork involved is the same as for normal benefit payouts. On the other hand, if participants are to receive deferred annuity payments at retirement, the plan purchases deferred annuities and much of the normal distribution paperwork will be completed at the time the annuity begins.

The form of benefit payout at plan termination depends solely upon the terms of the plan. If the plan does not offer a lump-sum option, the employer purchases a single-premium annuity contract (SPAC) from an insurance company, and all benefit payouts are made through that contract. If the plan does offer a lump-sum option, participants must be given a choice to receive a single sum or the deferred annuity. At the employer's election, a single-sum option can be added at the time of termination; however, such an option may not be removed. When a plan has a lump-sum option, in most cases, participants elect this option.

The employer considering the addition of a lump-sum option in a defined-benefit plan should do so carefully. Under the law, single-sum benefits are calculated using the lower of the plan's specified interest rate or a rate specified by the PBGC. When interest rates in the market are low, the PBGC rate can also be quite low. Therefore, providing benefits in the form of a lump sum can prove to be more expensive than purchasing a deferred annuity in many cases.

Single-Premium Annuity Contracts

Employers wishing to purchase paid-up annuities to satisfy the distribution obligation from a terminating plan purchase a single-premium annuity contract. SPACs are issued through group pension departments of insurance companies and sold to plans that are terminating. In return for the single premium, the insurance company assumes the transferred plan liabilities and issues annuity certificates that ensure participants receive their benefits.

At the time that participants retire, they choose a distribution option from among the various ones available. The law requires that the SPAC distribution options match the original plan distribution options. At the time of payout, the insurer provides election forms, qualified joint and survivor notices, and so on.

SPACs are typically difficult for an insurer to price (that is, to determine how much money is required from the employer to pay the benefit obligations under the plan). The insurer must first assess the liabilities under the plan, a process complicated by discrepancies in terminology from plan to plan and the presence of any atypical design features. The second step, finding the present value of future obligations, can be even trickier. At this stage, the insurer must apply assumptions regarding interest return, mortality, early retirement (which is particularly important if the early-retirement benefit is subsidized), and other variables. A third difficult aspect of pricing a SPAC lies with the one-time expense charge. Theoretically the employer could be making benefit payments 50 years or more in the future. Determining expenses for that length of time can be almost impossible. All these pricing difficulties affect the insurance company because (1) the single premium required can vary significantly from company to company, and (2) a SPAC that is priced too high will not be competitive and a SPAC that is priced too low will lose money.

With the recent failure of several insurance companies, note that the DOL is quite concerned about the choice of carriers when a SPAC is purchased. The employer and other plan fiduciaries may be held personally liable if the insurer cannot pay up—if it is determined that the fiduciaries did not use reasonable care when choosing the carrier. On a practical level, this means that the fiduciaries should:

- obtain several SPAC quotes
- document how and why the particular choice was made
- review the company's insurance ratings using a number of rating services
- be especially careful when they choose a lower quote, if that insurer is also rated lower than the competition
- consider hiring independent consultants to further analyze the financial condition of the company

Remember that fiduciaries are not liable simply if the insurer fails—only if they behaved in an imprudent manner.

YOUR FINANCIAL SERVICES PRACTICE:
SELLING SPACs

The SPAC is a relatively convenient product for the financial services professional to sell. The market is easily identifiable (terminating plans), the sale depends solely on the single premium being requested, and commissions are received promptly. The sale of a SPAC is a one-step process that does not call for an ongoing commitment to the client. The most difficult part of the sale is making sure the home office receives the proper documents for underwriting purposes and that the single-premium quote is competitive with other quotes. Also, the agent needs to carefully consider the fiduciary issues mentioned above.

Distribution Paperwork

If the plan does not allow lump-sum payments and a SPAC is being purchased, participants do not make a distribution election at the time of the termination. The actual benefit election is made later at retirement. However, if participants have the option to receive a lump sum, then the paperwork is similar to any other plan distribution. The following summarizes the various items that must be given to and completed by participants:

- benefit election form

- notice and election forms for applicable qualified joint and survivor annuity rules
- notice and election forms for the right to have benefits transferred directly to an IRA or other qualified plan
- IRS Form 1099R for lump-sum distributions

TERMINATIONS BY OPERATION OF LAW

In the preceding part of this reading, we discussed plan terminations initiated by the employer. Here we discuss a quite different topic, plan terminations that occur due to the operation of law. This may occur in three separate situations:

- a partial termination of any qualified plan, resulting from a sudden reduction in the number of plan participants or a reduction in plan benefits
- the termination of a profit-sharing plan as a result of a complete discontinuance of contributions
- the involuntary termination of a defined-benefit plan by the PBGC

Partial Terminations

As mentioned previously, when a plan is terminated, the Tax Code requires that plan benefits become fully vested. This rule also applies to those participants affected by a partial plan termination. Unfortunately, this term is not defined in the Code. Under the regulations, the decision whether a partial termination exists is based on a review of all the facts and circumstances. The factors in this determination are

- whether the number of plan participants has been substantially reduced, *and*
- whether plan amendments have adversely affected the rights of employees to vest in benefits under the plan

When there is a reduction in the number of participants, there is no specified number or percentage drop that triggers a partial termination. Each case is decided by the facts and circumstances. However, any time plan participation drops by more than 20 percent, corporate counsel should look into the issue. Drop-offs in participation may occur due to layoff, an amendment excluding previously eligible participants, or (in rare occurrences) voluntary termination of employment. Under the various cases and rulings, a partial termination is certainly more likely if the reduction is within the control of the employer; however, the IRS has indicated that a partial termination may exist even when participants terminated employment voluntarily. The result of a determination that a partial termination exits is that all participants eliminated from the plan become fully vested.

Reduction in the number of participants is the most likely scenario in which the partial termination issue will arise; still, whenever the plan's vesting provisions are amended, the second rule must be considered. Amendments adversely affecting participants' rights to vest can result in a partial termination. This provision seems unnecessary, since other provisions in the Code prohibit the reduction of vested benefits already accrued and allow participants with 3 years of service to select an old vesting provision over a new, less favorable one.

The regulations identify a third type of partial termination. Under this special rule, a defined-benefit plan is deemed to be partially terminated if the reduction (or cessation) of benefit accruals results in—or increases the possibility of—a reversion to the employer. This means that the determination depends entirely on the plan's funding status at the time of the amendment. In other words, an amended plan that is not fully funded does not result in a partial termination, whereas a plan with excess assets at the time of the amendment would create a partially terminated plan. When a partial termination exists under this special rule, all participants become fully vested in their benefits as of the time of the amendment.

Profit-Sharing Plans

The same Code section governing partial terminations states that in profit-sharing type plans (which includes 401(k) plans and ESOPs), participants become fully vested at the time of a complete "discontinuance of contributions."

Again, the determination is based on a facts-and-circumstances test. In making the determination, the IRS considers whether contributions have been recurring and substantial, and whether there is any reasonable probability that the lack of contributions will continue indefinitely. This vague standard makes it difficult for the sponsor to determine whether the rule applies in a particular case. As a practical matter, the issue should be reviewed if no substantial contributions are made to a plan for 2 years or more.

The IRS—especially at the time a plan terminates—will definitely review the complete discontinuance issue. In many situations, plans are terminated well after the date that contributions have ceased. In this scenario, the IRS is likely to determine that benefits became fully vested at the time contributions stopped, not when the plan was actually terminated. Such a determination can cause major headaches when forfeited benefits have already been reallocated to other participants.

Involuntary Terminations of Defined-Benefit Plans

In the case of a defined-benefit plan covered by the PBGC insurance program, the PBGC has the right to involuntarily terminate a plan in very limited circumstances. The reason that it does so is to protect itself from mounting liabilities under a plan that shows no promise of meeting its obligations. The PBGC can institute termination proceedings if it determines that the interests of the plan participants would be better served by the termination, and if any one of the following occurs:

- Minimum funding standards have not been satisfied.
- Benefits cannot be paid when they are due.
- A substantial lump-sum payment has been made to a substantial owner who is a plan participant.
- The long-run liability of the company to the PBGC is expected to increase unreasonably.

NOTE

1. Participants may have to become fully vested in accordance with the rule discussed in the section on partial plan terminations. Under this rule, full and immediate vesting is only an issue if the plan has excess assets at the time the amendment is adopted.

15

Nonqualified Retirement Plans: An Overview

Chapter Outline

Up to this point the emphasis has been on the use of a tax-sheltered qualified plan to meet the needs of the small business and the small-business owner. However, a second lucrative market is open to financial services professionals who are servicing the retirement needs of the business and the business owner. This market is the nonqualified plan market, which includes nonqualified deferred-compensation plans and executive-bonus plans. These plans help the business owner and selected employees save for retirement without being subject to the requirements that apply to qualified plans. As a trade-off for allowing the employer complete discretion in plan design and in choosing which employees will be covered by the plan, the employer loses the central advantage of a qualified plan—that is, the ability to make a before-tax contribution on the employee's behalf that is simultaneously deductible to the business. Instead, the employer is entitled to an immediate deduction only if the employee is currently taxed, or conversely, the employee may defer tax only if the employer's deduction is deferred.

One housekeeping detail needs to be discussed before we start to explore the nonqualified market. Nonqualified deferred-compensation plans are sometimes referred to as salary continuation plans, deferred-compensation plans, and nonqualified plans. These aliases, however, can be misleading because they all have other meanings too. For example, the term *salary continuation plan* is sometimes used to refer to sick days and disability benefits. Likewise, *deferred compensation* sometimes refers to qualified pension and profit-sharing plans. The term *nonqualified plans* can refer to a myriad of plans that fail to meet various qualification standards. Since we are going to discuss only nonqualified deferred-compensation plans in chapters 15 and 16, we'll call them nonqualified plans for short. In the marketplace, however, it is wise to make sure everybody is on the same wavelength and isn't tripped up by the confusing nomenclature.

**YOUR FINANCIAL SERVICES PRACTICE:
THE ALLURE OF THE NONQUALIFIED MARKET**

Several factors prompt financial services professionals to become involved in the nonqualified market. Some get involved because nonqualified deferred-compensation and executive-bonus plans help them to provide comprehensive services to their clients. A combination of life insurance, individual annuities, qualified plans, and nonqualified plans allows the financial services professional to provide a comprehensive umbrella of retirement coverage. Others prefer the nonqualified market because it means contact with an upscale clientele, and this in turn provides networking opportunities. A third reason to be involved in the nonqualified market is to be able to sell insurance and annuity products to the nonqualified plan. As we shall see in chapter 16, insurance and annuity products are a popular employer choice for funding nonqualified plans.

PROBLEM SOLVING WITH NONQUALIFIED PLANS

The nonqualified market is a very important part of a financial services practice in the retirement field because it allows financial services professionals to successfully deal with client situations that are otherwise unsolvable, such as these:

- *The client desires an alternative to the qualified plan because he or she is fed up with legislative changes.* Frequent legislative changes to qualified plans (see chapter 2) have cost employers a small fortune in plan-amendment fees, while at the same time giving them less of what they want out of the plan. When they weigh the tax advantages offered by a qualified plan against the discretion, discrimination, and cost effectiveness possible under a nonqualified plan, some employers may feel the scales have tipped toward the nonqualified plan.

- *The client needs to bring executive retirement benefits up to desired levels by adding a second tier of benefits on top of the qualified plan.* Despite the tax advantages offered by a qualified plan, a client may desire to limit the income-replacement ratio under the qualified plan because of the cost of covering employees on a nondiscriminatory basis. When this is the case, a nonqualified plan should be set up to provide executives with the proper level of retirement funding.

- *The client desires to circumvent the nondiscrimination requirements of a qualified plan.* If your client wishes to have absolute discretion regarding which employees should be covered under the plan, a nonqualified plan should be used because it allows your client to reward selected employees on a discriminatory basis.

- *The client desires to exceed the maximum benefit and contribution limitations of a qualified plan.* If your client is looking to maximize retirement benefits for executives beyond the 25-percent-of-salary-or-$30,000 defined-contribution limit or the $125,000 defined-benefit limit a nonqualified plan should be considered.

- *The client desires to reduce the reporting and disclosure workload required by a qualified plan.* Companies that are tired of meeting the reporting and disclosure requirements associated with qualified plans will find substantial relief because most nonqualified plans have only nominal reporting and disclosure requirements. What's more, fewer formalities are required to establish a nonqualified plan than a qualified plan.

- *The client wants to provide a stand-alone benefit that allows highly compensated employees to defer current income as a means of supplementing retirement income.* When used in this manner a nonqualified plan is usually part of a package of perks offered to key executives. This deferred-compensation arrangement differs from one utilizing a supplemental nonqualified plan, because under this arrangement the client's aim is not to provide additional retirement compensation, but rather to permit an executive to defer salary until retirement.

- *The client is an owner of a closely held business who is looking to temporarily save taxes.* In a closely held business corporate dollars are interchangeable with personal dollars. Therefore when the corporate tax rate is lower than the individual tax rate it behooves the business owner to shelter retirement funds in the business by setting up a deferred-compensation program for tax purposes. For example, if Dr. Shombert has the option of taking an extra $10,000 as income or leaving the money in the corporation, and if Dr. Shombert's marginal rate is 39.6 percent and the corporate rate is 15 percent, Dr. Shombert will save

$2,460 in taxes by using a nonqualified plan—$1,500 owed on corporate income as opposed to $3,960 in taxes owed on personal income.

- *The client is the owner of a closely held business that is just starting up.* Closely held businesses that are just starting up often lack the cash to pay owner-employees their full salaries. A nonqualified plan allows these employees to contractually arrange for their salaries to be paid at a later date without having the IRS raise questions about the reasonableness of the compensation at that time.

- *The client wants to meet the organization objectives of attracting executives, retaining executives, and providing for a graceful transition in company leadership.* Although qualified plans can achieve similar objectives, nonqualified plans are more effective in managing what financial services professionals call the three Rs—recruiting, retaining, and retiring. That's because nonqualified plans are not encumbered with qualification rules and can be designed to achieve company objectives by providing for the forfeiture of benefits unless certain requirements are met. For example, a nonqualified-plan provision stating that an employee must provide consulting services after retirement or else lose nonqualified benefits enables the organization to be weaned from its current leaders smoothly. Such a provision is not permitted in a qualified plan.

DETERMINING THE COMPANY'S NEEDS

Once your client has indicated that one or more of the above situations is applicable, your next step is to focus the client on the important issues involved in selecting and designing a nonqualified plan. In addition, you need to discern the organization's needs and objectives. The device used to accomplish these steps is a nonqualified plan fact finder. The following fact finder will

- provide a working framework for soliciting the client's goals
- serve as a due-diligence checklist, which will ensure that important discussions haven't been omitted
- operate as a training tool for those who have little or no experience with nonqualified plans
- educate the client about the various needs, objectives, and considerations that are relevant to plan selection and design

Use this nonqualified supplement in conjunction with the qualified plan fact finder from chapter 3.

NONQUALIFIED PLAN FACT FINDER

Client Name: _____

Step 1: Identify concerns.

Listed below are some typical concerns that organizations have when instituting a nonqualified plan. Grade each of these concerns by scoring 1 for very valuable, 2 for valuable, 3 for moderately valuable, and 4 for least valuable.

1.   Avoid the nondiscrimination requirements of a qualified
     plan.   [1][2][3][4]

2.   Allow executives to defer current income for their
     own tax-shelter purposes.   [1][2][3][4]

3.   Exceed the 415 maximum benefit and contribution limits
     of a qualified plan.   [1][2][3][4]

4.   Supplement qualified-plan benefits that are not stretched
     to the maximum limits.   [1][2][3][4]

5.   Recruit talented executives from outside the company.   [1][2][3][4]

6.   Retain executives by inducing them to stay with the company.   [1][2][3][4]

7.   Induce executives to take early retirement.   [1][2][3][4]

8.   Induce executives to provide consulting services
     after retirement.   [1][2][3][4]

9.   Keep executives from competing with the company.   [1][2][3][4]

10. Adjust executive retirement benefits to include not only
     the compensation considered under the qualified plan but
     all compensation.   [1][2][3][4]

Step 2: List in order the primary reasons for establishing a nonqualified plan.

1.

2.

3.

CHOOSING THE BEST NONQUALIFIED RETIREMENT PLAN

Once you have a full understanding of the client's objectives, you can choose the proper nonqualified plan. There are many varieties of nonqualified plans, but we will focus on deferred-compensation plans and executive-bonus plans because of their importance to the financial services practice of the CLU and ChFC. There are, however, several other popular plans:

- *Incentive stock options* allow executives to acquire stock at a bargain without incurring a taxable interest when the stock is acquired.
- *Phantom stock plans* are plans in which deferred-compensation units are created and assigned a value equal to the company's stock. These deferred-compensation units are awarded to selected executives, who have a paper account balance (no actual stock is transferred to the executive), which may be enhanced by capital increases in the company's stocks and by declared dividends.
- *Restricted stock plans* provide an executive with employer stock that is forfeited if the executive's performance is subpar or if the executive leaves employment before a stipulated amount of time.
- *Golden handshakes* are additional benefits that are intended to induce early retirement.
- *Golden parachutes* are substantial payments made to executives who are terminated upon change of ownership or corporate control.
- *Incentive pay* refers to bonuses given for accomplishing short-term goals that can be used by the executive for retirement purposes.

YOUR FINANCIAL SERVICES PRACTICE:
THE NONQUALIFIED VERSUS THE QUALIFIED MARKET

When contrasted with the complexity involved in choosing a qualified plan, choosing a nonqualified plan seems relatively simple. In the qualified situation the client tends to have multiple objectives that conflict with the qualification rules. In a nonqualified situation the client tends to have fewer objectives, which can be provided for fully and effectively because the nonqualified plan can be tailored in an unfettered fashion. In fact, the most crucial decision involved with nonqualified plans is not which plan to choose, but whether to choose a nonqualified plan or some other form of executive- compensation technique, such as salary increases or executive perquisites.

NONQUALIFIED DEFERRED-COMPENSATION AND SALARY CONTINUATION PLANS

There are four different types of nonqualified deferred-compensation plans: top-hat plans, excess-benefit plans, supplemental executive-retirement plans, and 457 plans. Each plan type reflects a different employer objective.

Top-Hat Plans

If the employer's objective is to provide a method for executives to defer current income (in essence, to allow a nonqualified 401(k) look-alike arrangement), a so-called top-hat plan can be used. Top-hat plans are perhaps more accurately described by their alias, nonqualified salary-reduction plans, because under a top-hat plan selected executives forgo receipt of currently earned compensation (such as a portion of salary, a bonus, or commissions) and defer this income until retirement.

Top-hat plans can be set up to provide executives with additional compensation without limitations on the amount of the funds that can be contributed and without regard to which employees the plan excludes. Under ERISA a top-hat plan is defined as a plan that is typically unfunded (plan funding is discussed later) and is maintained by an employer primarily for the purpose of providing deferred compensation for "a select group of management or highly compensated employees." The exact definition of "a select group of management or highly compensated employees" is not spelled out, however; instead, a facts-and-circumstances approach determines whether a top-hat plan covering only these employees is bona fide. Two polar situations can provide some guidance. In Department of Labor advisory opinion 85-37A the DOL ruled that a certain plan was not a top-hat plan (and therefore was subject to the Title I requirements of ERISA) because the group of covered employees was too broad. This plan covered 50 of 75 employees, including a departmental foreman, factory superintendents, and officers. The average compensation of those covered was $21,000. At the other extreme is the decision in *Belka v. Rowe* (571 F. Supp. 1249). In this case a bona fide top-hat plan was said to exist because less than 5 percent of the work force was covered by the plan and the average salary (in 1980) was nearly $55,000. In *Belka* all employees covered by the plan either were salesmen or held management positions. The court ruled that the plan met the "select group of management or highly compensated employees" requirement—although the salesmen were not managers and some managers were not highly compensated—because the plan had been established for *either* management or highly compensated employees.

A top-hat plan can either be initiated at the individual option of an executive during contract negotiations or be offered as a package of perks to selected managers or highly compensated employees. In either circumstance, however, the agreement of deferral should be entered into prior to the date that the services are actually performed to avoid unwanted tax consequences.

Candidates for a top-hat plan include

- employers who are looking to provide a low-cost benefit for highly compensated and management employees (the only employer cost is the cost of the deferral of the tax deduction)
- small closely held businesses whose owners' individual tax rate is higher than the corporate tax rate

- organizations that wish to set conditions on a certain amount of executives' salaries to induce desired results (discussed later)

Excess-Benefit Plans

If the employer's objective is to provide a benefit (or contribution) that exceeds the 415 limits, then an excess-benefit plan should be used. ERISA defines an excess-benefit plan as a plan maintained by an employer solely for the purpose of providing benefits for certain employees in excess of the limitations on contributions and benefits imposed by Sec. 415 of the Internal Revenue Code, without regard to whether the plan is funded. In other words, an excess-benefit plan picks up where the maximum-contribution and benefit limits for a qualified plan leave off.

Excess-benefit plans are considered a type of employer-provided salary continuation plan (as opposed to an employee-elected deferred-compensation plan). In other words, under a salary continuation plan the executive does not forgo receipt of currently earned income but instead receives an additional retirement benefit (or contribution).

Excess-benefit plans are dovetailed with an underlying qualified plan and provide the benefit or contribution that is blocked out by the Sec. 415 limits.

> *Example:* The Celtic Company offers a qualified defined-benefit plan with a benefit formula that provides for 90 percent of final average salary. Owners Locke and Jefferson earn $160,000 each and are effectively prevented by the $125,000 Sec. 415 limit from receiving their full 90 percent benefit ($144,000). The Celtic Company can, however, set up an excess-benefit plan that complements the qualified plan benefit and brings Locke and Jefferson's total benefits up to the desired 90 percent level.

Candidates for an excess-benefit plan include

- employers who have plans that are fully "maxed out" (at the maximum 415 level)
- employers looking to provide adequate retirement income for highly paid executives

Supplemental Executive-Retirement Plans

A supplemental executive-retirement plan (SERP) satisfies the employer objective of complementing an existing qualified plan that is not already stretched to the maximum limits, by bringing executive-retirement benefits (or contributions) up to desired levels. SERPs have some of the characteristics of both top-hat plans and excess-benefit plans. Like a top-hat plan, a SERP is typically unfunded and is maintained by an employer primarily for the purpose of providing deferred compensation for a select group of management or highly compensated employees. And like the excess-benefit plan, the SERP is a form of salary continuation plan (that is, it provides a deferred benefit, as opposed to the deferral of a reduced salary).

SERPs operate much the same as excess-benefit plans, being dovetailed with the underlying qualified defined-contribution or defined-benefit plan. The major difference, however, is that SERPs complement qualified plan limitations that are below the 415 limits.

Regular and Offset SERPs

SERPs can complement the underlying qualified plan in one of two ways. They can be designed to provide the "missing piece" of retirement benefit (or contribution) that the employer wants the executive to have. For example, if the employer is looking to provide a replacement of 60 percent of an executive's final average salary and the underlying qualified plan only provides for a 40 percent replacement, the SERP can be designed to provide a benefit equal to 20 percent of the final average salary. In cases where the exact benefit (or contribution) is unknown, however, such as when an integrated unit-benefit formula is used, SERPs can be designed a second way: to provide for the total benefit or contribution desired (for example, all 60 percent) taking into account, or offsetting, the benefits provided by the qualified plan. This type of SERP is called an offset SERP (not to be confused with a social security offset plan).

Special Uses for SERPs

When a company is less concerned with providing supplemental executive-retirement benefits than it is with accomplishing a particular objective, a SERP can be used to accommodate the company's special needs. For example, one unique use of an offset SERP is to reduce an executive's benefit by the amount he or she receives under the retirement plans of *other* employers. This type of offset SERP is used if the employer's primary objective for establishing the SERP is to attract desired executives from other companies. By providing an offset SERP that subtracts out benefits received from other employers, your client can maintain a cost-effective benefit package while at the same time allaying recruited executives' fears of losing a substantial pension benefit if they transfer out of their current plan.

Candidates for SERPs

Candidates for SERPs include employers who want to

- cut back benefits under their qualified plan because of increased costs

- provide a higher income replacement ratio for executives than they can afford (or want) to provide for all employees
- defeat the $160,000 cap on compensation that can be considered in determining benefits

457 Plans

Sec. 457 of the Internal Revenue Code provides rules governing all nonqualified plans of government units, governmental agencies, and non-church-controlled tax-exempt organizations. A nonqualified plan that is sponsored by one of these organizations is referred to as a 457 plan, and it is the only type of nonqualified plan permitted for these organizations. A 457 plan is similar to a 401(k) plan and a top-hat plan in that salary can either be taken as cash or deferred. Under the rules governing 457 plans the maximum amount that can be deferred in any year can't exceed $7,500 (as indexed) or one-third of the participant's compensation, whichever is less. For employees reaching retirement there is a "catch-up provision" that extends the amount contributed under a complicated set of rules. In addition, the following rules apply:

- Elections to defer compensation must be made before the compensation is earned.
- Special distribution restrictions apply.
- The employer may discriminately choose any or all employees for coverage.

Since the employer in a Sec. 457 plan does not pay federal income taxes, deductibility is not an issue.

DESIGN CONSIDERATIONS

To the extent that they are subject to ERISA (discussed later), all top-hat, excess-benefit, and supplemental executive-retirement plans must conform to the applicable ERISA rules. Since these plans are usually designed to *avoid* being subject to ERISA, however, top-hat and excess-benefit plans and SERPs can be designed in a wide variety of ways. Plan design is an interesting and challenging assignment because the financial services professional is not inhibited by legislative and regulatory constraints. Let's look at the most common design features used in these plans.

Forfeiture Provisions

A forfeiture provision in a nonqualified plan sets forth certain conditions under which an employee forfeits the benefits he or she would normally get under the plan. For business and tax reasons, forfeiture provisions are an essential part of an excess-benefit plan and a SERP. From a business standpoint the employer's objective in installing the plan can be satisfied by choosing the proper forfeiture provision. The tax implications which we'll discuss in chapter 16 are also beneficial. Top-hat plans do not typically contain forfeiture provisions because they represent an employee election to reduce salary. The analogy can be made to the fact that salary reductions under a 401(k) plan or 403(b) plan are always 100 percent vested and not subject to forfeiture. But forfeiture provisions are very common in excess-benefit plans and SERPs because they help to achieve a multitude of employer objectives. Let's look at some client problems and see how forfeiture provisions can help solve them.

Client Problem: Successful Transition of Company Leadership. Some businesses are dependent on the special contributions of a few key executives (executives who have specialized knowledge, unique talents, or personal contacts that are important to the business). The retirement of these executives may prove devastating to the profit-making ability of the organization. To prevent a drop in revenue and to ensure a smooth transition, a nonqualified deferred-compensation plan can contain a provision that requires the executive to provide consulting services after retirement or else forfeit any benefit under the plan.

A consulting provision can be an effective tool for solving your client's problem. Care should be taken, however, not to create additional problems for the executive. If the consulting provision is poorly designed, the "retired" executive may be construed as still being employed by the employer. If an employer-employee relationship exists, the executive will forgo receiving social security benefits that would have been payable (this is not a factor if the rendering of consulting services amounts to performing substantial services as a self-employed individual), and the executive will lose the right to the special 5- or 10-year-averaging tax treatment on distributions from the qualified plan (a condition of which is that an employee must be separated from service). To avoid these problems the consulting provision

- should not contain any formal schedule of duties or assignments for the former executive
- should not allow the former employer to exercise the direction and control that under common-law rules establishes an employer- employee relationship (for example, the employer must not supervise the former executive in the performance of advisory services)
- should not establish a work schedule that requires the employer to give permission for the former executive to be absent from work

If these requirements are met, the business can accomplish its goals without adversely affecting the tax and social security picture of the executive.

Client Problem: Retention of Executives. If your client is concerned about inducing an executive to stay on board instead of leaving prematurely, a so-called golden-handcuffs provision should be incorporated into the plan. A golden-handcuffs provision discourages executives from leaving the employment of your client by specifying that substantial benefits will be forfeited if service is voluntarily terminated prior to normal retirement age. There are any number of ways to design this provision. The employer who is not concerned about recruiting executives will probably prefer a provision requiring the executive to forfeit *all* rights under the plan if he or she terminates employment prior to normal retirement age. If executive recruiting is a strong concern, the forfeiture of benefits can be designed to include liberal vesting requirements. For example, the plan may provide *no* vesting to an employee who works less than 5 years, 50 percent vesting to an employee who terminates between 5 and 10 years, and 100 percent vesting to an employee who terminates after 10 or more years. If executive recruiting is a concern but not a priority, a more conservative vesting schedule can be used (for example, 50 percent vesting after 10 years, 75 percent vesting after 15 years, and 100 percent vesting after 20 years).

Client Problem: Competition from Former Employees. A major problem for employers in service industries (such as doctors and lawyers) is an associate who leaves the business and goes to work for a competitor or uses his or her pension money to open up a competing business. In order to deter this behavior your clients should put a covenant-not-to-compete provision in their nonqualified plans. A covenant-not-to-compete provision calls for the forfeiture of nonqualified benefits if the employee enters into competition with the employer by opening a competing business. In order to be considered valid under state law, the covenant-not-to-compete provision must be carefully drafted or else state courts will hold the provision void because it violates public-policy employment goals. The provision should be reasonable in terms of the geographical area and the time period it covers. For example, a covenant that says a former employee can't compete in the Northeast for 10 years after the employee leaves employment is probably a violation of public policy and not valid. If the employee is restricted from working for 2 years in the same county, however, the provision is probably valid. The acts and circumstances—particularly the type of industry involved—will be determinative. (*Planning Note:* The rules for noncompetition clauses vary from state to state. To make sure that the most restrictive schedule possible is used without risking judicial nullification, your client should consult an attorney.)

Designing a Nonqualified Plan for Executives

Up to this point the assumption has been that your client is a business entity. However, your financial services practice may also include solving retirement problems for executives who are negotiating a nonqualified arrangement with their employer. If this is the case keep the following points in mind:

- A supplemental executive-retirement plan can be set up to protect selected executives against involuntary termination if the company changes hands, by structuring the SERP to pay out or increase benefits under this contingency (a so-called takeover trigger—the executive's alternative if a golden parachute does not exist.)
- Nonqualified plans can be designed to protect your client against involuntary termination because of declining earnings or change in control of the business by providing immediate vesting in nonqualified benefits if either of these contingencies occurs. This provision is called an insolvency trigger. If the plan with an insolvency trigger is properly structured, the executive will be taxed only when the triggering event occurs. At the time your client will willingly trade off the tax consequences of immediate taxation for the security of receiving his or her benefits. The challenge, however, is to design the nonqualified plan so that the existence of an insolvency trigger does not trigger immediate taxation. If a rabbi trust is used (discussed in chapter 16), this probably cannot be done. If the plan is completely unfunded, however, the insolvency trigger can be incorporated into the plan.
- Nonqualified plans can be designed to allow withdrawals prior to termination in cases of financial hardship. When this is desired the plan should spell out the exact circumstances that constitute a hardship, or it should provide for an independent third party to make the determination. By doing this your client can avoid adverse tax consequences.
- Your client should ask for a binding-arbitration clause in case of a dispute. This will help to save litigation costs.

Other Features in Plan Design

Besides forfeiture provisions there are several other important design features to be considered in nonqualified plans. In fact, if a plan is not required to meet ERISA standards, the only real constraints on plan design are the market forces at work and the designer's imagination. In general, however, the design features of a nonqualified plan are similar to those of a qualified plan except that they are not inhibited by IRS restrictions. Here's an overview of some standard design features.

Benefit or Contribution Structure

Nonqualified plans can be designed as either defined-benefit or defined-contribution plans. Top-hat plans are usually designed as defined-contribution plans because they allow executives to *contribute* a deferred amount of salary each year. Salary continuation nonqualified plans (excess-benefit plans and SERPs) can also be set up as defined-contribution plans but are more frequently set up as defined-benefit plans. When excess-benefit plans or SERPs are set up as defined-benefit plans, the benefit formula should jibe with the employer's objectives. This may mean supplementing the employer's qualified plan or avoiding duplication in benefits by the coordination of all benefits received under the employer's qualified and other benefit plans, retirement benefits earned with other employers, and social security benefits. Meeting employer objectives may also mean indexing benefits, weighing benefits for length of service (such as in a unit-benefit formula), or both.

Eligibility

Participation in nonqualified plans is typically restricted to company executives. An excess-benefit plan can include rank-and-file employees, but the benefits of the rank-and-file employees never even approach, let alone exceed, the qualification limits. A top-hat plan or a SERP, however, *must* by definition be maintained "primarily" for a select group of management or highly compensated employees. In fact, care must be taken to restrict participation so that the plan is considered to be a top-hat plan or SERP for ERISA purposes.

In a top-hat plan or a SERP the executive's title or position typically dictates inclusion in or exclusion from the plan (for example, all executives above the level of first vice president might be included). A second way to determine eligibility is by salary. When salary determines eligibility, the chosen dollar amount should be indexed; by taking this precaution the employer doesn't risk substantial cost increases caused by the inclusion of executives who are not at the top level but whose salaries have inflated over time. A third common way to determine eligibility is to appoint a compensation committee. When this is done, the employer, who heads the committee, retains absolute control over plan membership.

Disability Provisions

Nonqualified plans frequently contain disability provisions. The employer can stipulate whether disability will be treated like any other termination of employment or whether special disability provisions (such as full vesting or benefits or a special benefit computation) will apply. In addition, the employer must choose whether service will continue to accrue if a disability occurs—in which case the plan should contain a definition of disability.

Regardless of how the employer decides to treat disability under the nonqualified plan, the planner should be careful to coordinate benefits between the nonqualified plan and other employer plans. This will prevent costly duplication of benefits.

Retirement Age

Another key plan design to be considered is retirement age. In general, the normal retirement age of the nonqualified plan is the age at which benefits become payable without any forfeiture. The employer's personnel objectives determine whether a "young" retirement age (50–62) or an "old" retirement age (65–70) is chosen. If the employer wants to control salary costs by keeping a young work force, then a young retirement age should be chosen (typically, this is coordinated with a young normal retirement age in the qualified plan). If the executives involved have knowledge or experience that is crucial to the company, however, a later retirement age should be selected.

Death Benefits

Nonqualified plans can provide death benefits, which can cover the preretirement period, the postretirement period, or both. The death benefit chosen depends in part on what type of life insurance is used to fund the plan (if any) and what type of annuity is used for distribution from the plan. The choice of a death benefit should therefore be closely coordinated with the life insurance product used in the plan.

EXECUTIVE-BONUS LIFE INSURANCE PLANS

An alternative that can be used in combination with, or in lieu of, the previously discussed deferred-compensation plans is an executive-bonus life insurance plan (also known as a Sec. 162 plan). Like a deferred-compensation plan, an executive-bonus life insurance plan can be provided on a discriminatory basis to help business owners and select executives save for retirement. The executive-bonus life insurance plan, however, does not provide for the deferral of income. Under an executive-bonus life insurance plan the corporation pays a bonus to the executive for the purpose of purchasing cash-value life insurance. The executive is the policyowner, the insured, and the person who designates the beneficiary. The corporation's only connection (albeit a major one) is to fund premium payments and in a few cases to secure the application for insurance. Bonuses can be paid out by the corporation in either of two ways. The corporation can pay the premiums directly to the insurer or pay the bonus to the executive, who in turn pays the policy premiums. In either case the corporation deducts the contribution from corporate taxes at the time it is made (this is in direct contrast to most deferred-compensation plans—see chapter 16) and includes the amount of the payment in the executive's W-2 (taxable) income.

Since payments made under executive-bonus life insurance plans are W-2 income, bonuses are subject to federal, state, and local withholding requirements and to social security taxes (unless the wage base has already been exceeded).

Implementation of Sec. 162 Plans

Executive-bonus plans are fairly easily implemented. First, as with all forms of nonqualified compensation, a corporate resolution authorizing the business expenditure should be obtained. Second, those in charge should select the executives to be included in the plan and the amount of benefits they will receive. Third, they should notify the Department of Labor that the plan is in effect (see chapter 16). Fourth, either the executive or the corporation should secure the application for insurance. And finally, the executive should apply for the policy as the owner and designate the policy's beneficiary.

Double-Bonus Plans

Concern over the receipt of additional taxable income from executive-bonus life insurance plans has caused many employers to provide a second bonus to alleviate any tax that the business owner or executive may pay. (These plans are typically called double-bonus plans.) There will be a tax on the second bonus, so the work sheet below helps calculate the total amount needed for both bonuses.

YOUR FINANCIAL SERVICES PRACTICE:
NONRETIREMENT APPLICATIONS FOR EXECUTIVE-BONUS PLANS

Besides being a retirement planning tool, executive-bonus life insurance plans can be used in several other ways to serve your clients. Some planners use them in lieu of superimposed group term life insurance (life insurance over the tax-sheltered $50,000 limit). This usage has grown in popularity recently owing to COBRA changes that increase employer costs by inflicting benefit contribution requirements on group plans. Another use of Sec. 162 plans is to help the executive to purchase an insurance policy to fund a cross-purchase buy-sell agreement. Without these agreements partners may not have the assets to continue the business when one of them retires or dies. A third use of executive-bonus life insurance plans is to provide the executive's estate with a source of liquid funds to pay estate taxes. Restrictions on the amount of insurance that may be used under group term life plans and qualified retirement plans make the liquidity issue an important executive concern.

TABLE 15-1
Double-Bonus Work Sheet

Step 1: State the target premiums (the amount of the first bonus).	_____
Step 2: Specify the applicable tax rate (including federal state, local, and all other applicable taxes).	_____
Step 3: Subtract the step 2 amount from 1.00.	_____
Step 4: Divide the step 1 amount by the step 3 amount to find the amount of both bonuses.	_____

Example: JANCO wants to provide executive Kathy Beamer with a $10,000 nontaxable bonus to pay the premium under her cash-value life policy. JANCO will have to provide Kathy with $16,666.67, determined as follows:

Step 1: State the target premiums. $10,000.00
Step 2: Specify the applicable tax rate.   .40
Step 3: Subtract the step 2 amount from 1.00.   .60
Step 4: Divide the step 1 amount by the step 3
              amount to find the amount of both
              bonuses. $16,666.67

Note that the 40 percent tax rate used in the example includes a 31 percent federal tax rate, a 4 percent state tax rate, and city taxes of 5 percent. In lieu of the work sheet the following formula can be used:

$$\frac{\text{Amount of first bonus}}{1 \ - \ tax \ rate} = \text{Amount of both bonuses}$$

16

Nonqualified Retirement Plans: Issues and Answers

Chapter Outline

Chapter 15 served as an introduction to the nonqualified market by surveying nonqualified plan use, choice, and design. In order to fully understand the nonqualified market, however, we also need to review many of the issues involved in the implementation of nonqualified plans. The questions that must be addressed include the following:

- Is it more advantageous for a cost-conscious client to use a qualified or a nonqualified plan?
- What tax considerations underlie the use, design, and funding of a nonqualified plan?
- Should a plan be funded, unfunded, or informally funded?
- Should a rabbi trust be used, and if so, how can it be designed in a state-of-the-art manner?
- Should a secular trust or a surety bond be used to secure payments under a nonqualified plan?
- What are the ERISA implications of using nonqualified plans?
- How are nonqualified plans installed and administered?
- Should life insurance products be used to pay for nonqualified plan benefits?

It is only after understanding these issues that we can accurately serve our clients' needs.

NONQUALIFIED VERSUS QUALIFIED

As we have seen, qualified pension and profit-sharing plans are retirement plans that meet standards set out in the Employee Retirement Income Security Act (ERISA) and Internal Revenue Code. The major requirements for qualification have been identified and discussed in earlier chapters. As a payback for adhering to these burdensome rules, plan contributions are immediately deductible by the employer, earnings on plan funds are tax deferred, and when qualified plan funds are distributed to employees several tax-saving strategies such as forward averaging and rollovers may be available. The case study in chapter 2 illustrates the vast economic gain available through this tax-saving "interest-free loan."

In contrast a nonqualified plan cannot simultaneously give the employer the benefit of an immediate tax deduction and give the employee the benefit of a tax deferral. Most nonqualified plans are structured to defer the taxation of retirement benefits for executives. Unlike qualified plans, however, nonqualified deferred-compensation plans postpone the employer's deduction until the benefit has been paid to the executive and has been included in his or her income. In addition, earnings on money put aside to fund the plan will be taxed in the year it is earned unless a tax shelter such as life insurance is used. Finally, distributions from nonqualified plans cannot be forward averaged to reduce the effective tax rate or rolled over to delay taxation (see table 16–1).

Despite the dismal tax comparison, nonqualified plans are favored over qualified plans in many cases for a variety of reasons, including

- design flexibility (chapter 15)
- lower administrative costs
- cost-saving discriminatory coverage

This last reason is perhaps the chief motivation for an employer to install a nonqualified plan. Business owners claim they can save significant sums of money by excluding rank-and-file employees from the plan. In the minds of many employers the tax savings garnered under a qualified plan are overshadowed by the ability to avoid paying benefit costs for the majority of their employees. A short case study helps to illustrate this point (see also table 16-1).

TABLE 16-1 **Qualified and Nonqualified Plans Compared**		
Characteristic	Qualified Plan	Nonqualified Plan
Tax deferred to employee	Yes—always	Yes (unless considered funded)
Tax consequences to employer	Immediate deduction	Deduction deferred (unless considered funded)
Earnings accumulate tax free	Yes—always	No (unless tax shelter used)
Special tax treatment at retirement for employee	Yes (rollovers and forward averaging)	No
Ability to lower costs by only covering selected employees	No (must meet nondiscrimination rules)	Yes—always
Plan administration requirements	Burdensome and expensive	Minimal and inexpensive
Reporting and disclosure requirements	Burdensome and expensive	Minimal and inexpensive
Ability to attract, retain, and motivate employees	Effective	More effective

CASE STUDY: THE SMALLCO COMPANY

Smallco is a company of 10 people and is owned by two sisters. The sisters earn a salary of $100,000 each; the payroll for the additional employees is $240,000 (average salary, $30,000). If Smallco were to install a profit-sharing plan that provides a benefit of 15 percent of salary to all employees, the qualified plan would cost $66,000 plus administrative expenses ($66,000 equals 15 percent of the total payroll, $440,000). If Smallco were to provide a 15 percent nonqualified plan for the two owners and no benefits for the other employees, however, then the cost to the plan would be reduced to $30,000 plus the cost of deferring the deduction.

Determining the Cost of Deferring the Deduction

Smallco pays corporate taxes at the 34 percent rate. The deferral of the deduction would thus immediately cost Smallco 34 cents on every dollar put into the plan. Since $30,000 is being contributed, Smallco would thus "lose" $10,200 in tax savings (34 percent tax rate multiplied by the $30,000 contribution). In addition, Smallco loses the amount it could have gained by investing the $10,200. This of course will be offset by the amount that will be deducted when the benefits are paid. There is no way to accurately predict the employer's cost for deferring the deduction because of the interest and time assumptions that must be used (not to mention potential shifts in tax rates). But even assuming that it costs Smallco $1.40 (a conservatively high figure) to provide $1 in benefits, the total plan cost in real dollars will only be $42,000. This amount is $24,000 less than the qualified plan would cost. In addition, Smallco's administrative costs will be significantly lower. To put it another way, even though it will cost Smallco more than a dollar to provide a dollar's worth of benefits, the additional cost is more than offset by increased benefit costs brought about by providing benefits for rank-and-file employees.

YOUR FINANCIAL SERVICES PRACTICE:
EFFECTIVE COMPENSATION PLANNING

Clients often mistakenly believe that implementing a qualified plan will increase costs because the benefits are an additional compensation—sort of a windfall—for rank-and-file employees. This commonly held opinion is correct only if benefits are an increase to the overall compensation package. If benefits are a piece of what is already being paid to an employee, however, employer costs are not increased. In other words, the employer should focus on how employees are paid, not how much he or she pays them. Effective compensation planning dictates that employers give employees (and themselves) the opportunity to save for retirement with the tax advantages that are only available through a qualified plan. Unfortunately, for many employers it's the perception that counts, not the reality.

One way to satisfy stubborn prospects is to *gradually* shift current compensation to deferred compensation. This can be accomplished by lowering future salary increases by a small percentage, which will be used to fund a deferred-compensation plan.

TAX CONSIDERATIONS

A client who desires a nonqualified plan must be made aware of the tax implications of having such a plan.

It goes without saying that salary is taxable to an employee in the year it is paid to the employee. But what happens when the salary is deferred to a later tax year?

Constructive Receipt

Under IRS regulations an amount becomes currently taxable to an executive even before it is actually received if it has been "constructively received." Constructive receipt will be deemed to occur in a nonqualified plan if the deferred compensation is credited to an executive's account, set apart for the executive, or made available to the executive so that he or she may draw upon it anytime or could draw on it if notice of intention to draw had been given. In other words, if the executive had the choice of taking compensation but refused to take possession, the IRS will treat that person as having taxable income. There is, however, no constructive receipt if either of the following conditions is met:

- The deferred compensation is subject to substantial limitations or restrictions.
- The election to defer compensation is a mere promise to pay, not represented by notes or secured in any way (that is, if it is an unsecured promise to pay).

Consequently, an executive in a top-hat plan, for example, will be deemed to be in constructive receipt of income because he or she is in effect postponing income in order to avoid current taxation—*unless* the nonqualified plan meets either one of the two criteria outlined above. Since the major advantage to an executive of a nonqualified plan is the deferral of taxes, it is essential that the plan be designed to meet one of the two specified criteria.

Substantial Limitation or Restriction

Whether or not constructive receipt applies is a facts-and-circumstances decision. Substantial limitations have been held to exist if the executive must wait until the passage of a given period of time to receive the money (under a golden-handcuffs provision, for example). In addition, the employer can avoid constructive receipt by setting up the plan to require the occurrence of an event that is beyond the executive's control. (Recall the forfeiture provisions discussed in chapter 15).

Unsecured Promise to Pay

What constitutes an unsecured promise to pay will be covered in detail when unfunded plans, informally funded plans, and rabbi trusts are discussed later. The question of *when* the unsecured promise to pay should be made is another matter, however. The executive is better off entering into the agreement to defer compensation before services are rendered. If the executive waits to make an election later, the plan can only avoid constructive receipt if there is a "substantial risk of forfeiture." A substantial risk of forfeiture is a significant limitation or duty that will require a meaningful effort on the part of the executive to fulfill, and there must be a definite possibility that the event that will cause the forfeiture could occur. In other words, the executive will have a much higher hurdle to jump to avoid IRS claims of constructive receipt if he or she procrastinates in making the election.

When Does It End?

One final point concerning constructive receipt needs to be made. The problem of constructive receipt can last beyond the asset buildup period. In other words, plan provisions also have to ensure that the executive isn't taxed on more than he or she receives in the distribution period. For example, an executive can't elect to accelerate the balance of payments due under the plan after retirement. An executive can, however, elect the time and manner of payment under the nonqualified plan without triggering constructive receipt if the election is made before the deferred amount has been earned.

Economic Benefit

Under the economic-benefit doctrine an economic or financial benefit conferred on an executive as compensation should be included in the person's income to the extent that the benefit has an ascertainable fair market value. In other words, if a compensation arrangement provides a current economic benefit to an executive, that person must report the value of the benefit even if he or she has no current right to receive the benefit. The economic-benefit doctrine is different from the constructive-receipt doctrine because the tax issue is *not* whether the taxpayer can control the timing of the actual receipt of the income (as it is in constructive receipt); the issue is whether or not there has been an irrevocable transfer of funds made on the executive's behalf that provides an economic benefit to the executive. The economic-benefit doctrine is a higher hurdle for taxpayers to jump than the constructive-receipt doctrine because it requires the executive to be taxed when funds are irrevocably paid out on the executive's behalf to a fund in which the executive has vested rights—regardless of whether there are substantial limitations or restrictions on the deferred income. For purposes of the economic-benefit doctrine a fund is created when property is irrevocably placed with a third party. *The economic-benefit doctrine does not apply, however, when the property involved is subject to the rights of the employer's creditors, because theoretically no property has been transferred and the obligation remains an unsecured promise to pay.*

Section 83

Under Sec. 83 of the Internal Revenue Code the executive is not taxed until his or her rights in the property become transferable or are no longer subject to a substantial risk of forfeiture (discussed above). A substantial risk of forfeiture is deemed to occur if the plan contains forfeiture provisions, that is, if the rights to deferred compensation are conditional on the performance—or nonperformance—of substantial services. Whether or not the forfeiture provisions accomplish this is a facts-and-circumstances determination. *One final note: "property" that is transferred and is subject to the creditors of the corporation is not really property for tax purposes, because the transferred interest cannot be valued and the obligation remains an unsecured promise to pay.*

Let's look at some examples.

Example 1: Employer Able sets up a separate account that will be used to pay off nonqualified benefits. Able retains ownership over the assets in the fund and can direct the fund's assets to business use if necessary. Under this scenario the executives avoid taxation because they cannot control the timing of the actual receipt of the income, and the employer has not made an irrevocable transfer of funds on the executives' behalf. The executives in this example, however, may not feel secure that they will receive their benefit because they have only an unsecured promise to receive benefits.

Example 2: To provide the executives with more security employer Able transfers the funds to a trust. The assets placed in the trust cannot revert back to the employer and are not subject to attack by the employer's creditors if the company files for bankruptcy. Under this scenario the executives are certain that they will receive their nonqualified benefit—but they are also subject to immediate tax on the transferred assets. Reason: the transferred assets are no longer an unsecured promise to pay and are not subject to a substantial risk of forfeiture; therefore the executives have constructively received and derived an economic benefit from the assets—even though they have not actually received the assets.

PLAN FUNDING

Nonqualified plans can be funded, unfunded, or informally funded. As you have probably concluded by now, plan funding for tax purposes and "storing assets" to pay future nonqualified promises are two different things from a tax standpoint. Let's take a closer look.

Funded Plans

A nonqualified deferred-compensation plan is considered funded for tax purposes when, in order to meet its promise of providing benefits under the plan, the company contributes specific assets to an escrow or trustee account in which the executive has a current beneficial interest. In other words, to pay benefits the company sets aside funds that are beyond the reach of the general creditors of the corporation. In addition, a nonqualified plan will be considered funded if the executive's obligation is backed by a letter of credit from the employer or by a surety bond obtained by the employer. If a nonqualified deferred-compensation plan is considered funded, the executive will be subject to immediate taxation under the rules of constructive receipt (unless substantial limitations apply), economic benefit and Sec. 83; and ERISA rules concerning participation, funding, vesting, fiduciary enforcement, and reporting and disclosure will apply (discussed later). Since this defeats the purpose of the plan, most plans are designed to be unfunded for tax purposes.

Unfunded Plans

A nonqualified deferred-compensation plan is considered unfunded for tax purposes if there is no reserve set aside to pay the promised benefit under the plan. Rev. Rul. 60-31 states that a mere promise to pay that is not represented by notes or secured in any way is not regarded as a receipt of income. Therefore an unfunded, unsecured promise by an employer to pay compensation at some future date will not constitute current taxable income to an executive.

Informally Funded Plans

Unfunded plans that do not make contingencies for storing funds to pay nonqualified promises pose a major problem for the executive because benefit payments hinge on the fiscal health of the employer at the time benefits become payable. What's more, many executives wonder if their own status will be different by the time they collect. Management change, business buyouts (through hostile takeover or otherwise), or a demotion due to performance problems or "office politics" may put the employee in an untenable position when he or she approaches the time to collect benefits. The executive is relying mainly on the corporation's unsecured (albeit contractual) promise to pay. Thus executives are caught in the horns of a dilemma. On one hand if the plan is funded executives will be taxed immediately. On the other hand executives don't want to risk their retirement on an unsecured promise to pay. Because executives want the best of both worlds—as much security as possible without triggering immediate taxation—many plans are informally funded. A plan is informally funded when a reserve is set up to pay the nonqualified benefit, but the assets of the reserve are retained as assets of the corporation, subject to attack by creditors of the corporation. In other words, as long as the executive does not have a current beneficial interest, the plan is considered unfunded for tax purposes. When a plan is informally funded, it is important to consider the other side of the equation—the employer's deduction.

Income Tax Effects on the Employer

Under the cash method of accounting a taxpayer is not entitled to a deduction until benefits have been paid to executives. Some employers are subject to the accrual method of accounting, however. Under the accrual method of accounting a taxpayer is entitled to a deduction in the year during which all events have occurred that gave rise to the liability and the amount of such liability can be determined with reasonable accuracy. However, the timing of deductions for the payment of nonqualified deferred compensation comes under special IRS regulations. Unlike the usual tax accounting rules applicable to other deductions, Reg. 1.404(b)-1T allows a deduction for nonqualified deferred compensation only in the year in which the payment is includible in the employee's gross income. Although unfunded deferred-compensation arrangements would often qualify as deductible expenses under the usual accrual requirements, Reg. 1.404(b)-1T will take precedence and delay the deduction for the employer until the income is taxable to the employee.

RABBI TRUSTS

The tax and funding implications of nonqualified plans boil down to one simple question: How can executives secure their interests in a nonqualified plan without triggering plan funding for tax purposes? The answer is a rabbi trust.

The so-called rabbi trust is a trust established and funded by the employer that is subject to the claims of the employer's creditors (thus escaping current taxation for the executive), but the funds in the trust cannot be used by or revert back to the employer. It was invented in 1981 by a rabbi who came up with a better idea for funding his deferred-compensation plan. Under the plan his congregation set aside deferred-compensation funds in an irrevocable trust to be paid out to the rabbi at retirement. The major difference between this trust and other trusts set up at that time was that the funds remained subject to the congregation's general creditors and could be paid to them if the congregation defaulted on any of its obligations. The rabbi obtained a private-letter ruling in which the IRS agreed with him that since the money remained subject to the congregation's creditors, even though he was vested he had not really received it and should only be taxed when the benefits were actually paid to him. The IRS reasoned that since the payments were subject to the congregation's general creditors, they were subject to a substantial risk of forfeiture and therefore did not fall under the rules of Sec. 83. In addition, the IRS ruled that they were an unsecured promise to pay and thus did not constitute constructive receipt or economic benefit. The new planning tool was quickly dubbed a rabbi trust.

Since the time that the rabbi trust was first implemented, its limits have been more clearly defined. For many years a sponsor wanting the IRS to rule on the validity of the rabbi trust agreement had to request a private letter ruling. In Rev. Proc. 92-64 the IRS made the use of the rabbi trust more secure by providing a model trust agreement. In order to have IRS approval of a deferred compensation agreement today, the sponsor in almost all cases must use the IRS's model rabbi trust form.

The model trust generally conforms with IRS guidelines already well known from prior IRS private letter rulings. Optional paragraphs are provided to allow some degree of customization. The model contains some relatively favorable provisions. For example, it allows the use of "springing" irrevocablility. That is a provision under which, if there is a change of ownership of the employer, the trust becomes irrevocable. Similarly, at the change in control the employer can be required to make an irrevocable contribution of all remaining deferred compensation. Also, the model permits the rabbi trust to own employer stock. However, the model does not allow "insolvency triggers" that hasten payments to executives when the employer's net worth falls below a certain point. (The IRS fears that accelerating benefit payments when the employer's financial position deteriorates may result in all benefits being paid before any creditors have a chance to attach the assets of the trust.) Other requirements either contained in the model trust or in prior rulings include the following:

- The assets in a rabbi trust must be available to all general creditors of the company if the company files for bankruptcy or becomes insolvent.
- The participants must not have greater rights than unsecured creditors.
- The plan must provide clear rules describing when benefits will be paid.
- The company must notify the trustee of any bankruptcy or financial hardship that the company is undergoing. When a bankruptcy or financial hardship occurs, the trustee should suspend payment to the trust beneficiary and hold assets for the employer's general creditors.

Unique Uses for Rabbi Trusts

The rabbi trust has evolved into a planning tool that has many uses. As stated above, a rabbi trust can have a springing irrevocability provision, protecting an executive's rights in the case of a management takeover. This permits the executives to be secure while at the same time allowing the company to have the current use of assets that might be transferred to the trust. Another way to protect the participants in the event of a hostile takeover is to give the trustee control over the investment of plan assets upon the change in control. This prevents the "bad guys" from making investments in illiquid employer-leased real estate or an employer-related venture. The ability to require employer contributions to the trust upon a change in control can provide another layer of protection for the covered executives. Such a provision opens the door for the use of a new generation of "as-needed" rabbi trusts.

The IRS has also confirmed that a single rabbi trust can be used to fund the assets of multiple deferred-compensation plans sponsored either by a single employer or by an employer and its subsidiaries.

Participants can elect the form of distribution from the rabbi trust when contributions to the trust are made without triggering constructive receipt. In addition, a change in the form of business organization by the employee's company (from a partnership to an S corporation, for example) will not adversely affect the rabbi trust.

Finally, executives can take a hardship withdrawal from a rabbi trust without triggering constructive receipt. The withdrawal is limited to an amount reasonably needed to meet the emergency. What's more, the emergency must be unforeseeable, that is, pose a severe financial hardship to the participant or result from a loss of property due to casualty or other similar extraordinary and unforeseeable circumstances beyond the control of the participant.

A Final Word on Rabbi Trusts

Although rabbi trusts accomplish the dual objective of deferring taxation and providing a measure of retirement security to executives, they have one important disadvantage: rabbi trusts provide no benefit security for executives should the employer go bankrupt. In other words, the executive must stand in line with other creditors if the employer files for bankruptcy. Rabbi trusts, therefore, are very effective in providing retirement security if the employer is unwilling to pay promised benefits, but they do not provide security if the employer is unable to pay benefits.

SECULAR TRUSTS

In situations where the employer's ability to pay promised benefits comes into question some professionals have been recommending a so-called secular trust in lieu of a rabbi trust. Like a rabbi trust, a secular trust calls for an irrevocable contribution on the employer's part to finance promises under a nonqualified plan. Unlike a rabbi trust, however, funds held in a secular trust cannot be reached by the employer's creditors. This means that executives can expect to receive promised benefits even if the employer goes bankrupt. It also means, however, that employer contributions to a secular trust are taxable.

Unfortunately, several recent IRS private-letter rulings have questioned the continued viability of secular trusts. In these rulings the IRS indicated that in some circumstances trust earnings would be subject to double taxation, once when earned at the trust level and again when actually paid out to the employee. This change would certainly discourage the use of the secular trust; however, these rulings are unclear and presently the fate of secular trusts is in doubt. If you decide that a secular trust is appropriate, you should seek professional guidance.

How Secular Trusts Work

Secular trusts work like rabbi trusts—up to a point. That is, the trust agreement is adopted and funded by the employer, and payments are made to an independent trustee. They are unlike rabbi trusts, however, because to compensate for the additional tax burden on the executive, the trust typically makes annual distributions to the executive, equals the amount of the executive's current tax liability.

Secular Trusts: The Employer's Perspective

From the employer's standpoint the secular trust has several advantages over a rabbi trust. The greatest advantage to the employer is that funds placed in a secular trust are deductible in the year transferred. This makes it less expensive to provide the nonqualified benefit because the deduction is not deferred. In addition, earnings on plan funds are taxable to the executive, not the employer. In a small closely held business whose corporate rates are higher than individual rates, accelerating the deduction to the employer and shifting earnings to the individual can be worth more in tax savings than postponing the income of the business owner.

Secular Trusts: The Executive's Perspective

The big advantage of secular trusts for executives is the security they derive from such an arrangement. If executives are so inclined, then forgoing deferral to secure nonqualified promises is a good idea. From the executives' standpoint, however, the question needs to be asked: Why not take the payments as current compensation? Aside from the fact that the employer may not be willing to give the employees ready access to their retirement funds, there is no good reason for them to abrogate control over the money while being taxed currently on it. Since executives typically have a significant amount of say over their nonqualified benefit, secular trusts are not widely used. In other words, executives who are concerned about security typically demand their "deferred compensation" currently.

YOUR FINANCIAL SERVICES PRACTICE:
SURETY BONDS

For the executive who feels uncomfortable with the possibility of benefits going unpaid from a rabbi trust because of an employer bankruptcy but wants to avoid the use of a secular trust because of the tax consequences, an alternative may be available. For these executives you should look into the use of a surety bond. A surety bond provides for a bonding company to pay promised benefits if the employer defaults on the promise to pay nonqualified benefits—thus providing the executive with an indirect means of securing the employer's unsecured promise.

In order to prevent the purchase of a surety bond from triggering a constructive-receipt, economic-benefit, or Sec. 83 problem, certain precautions must be taken. The executive must bear the cost of the surety bond, and the employer should not have an involvement with the bonding company. If these precautions are taken, the executive can have the security of continued protection for nonqualified retirement payments.

The downside is that surety bonds for nonqualified plans can be expensive and difficult to obtain. Premiums are typically 1 to 3 percent of the annual amount deferred, plus earnings. In addition, very few companies provide this coverage. Finally, renewal of the bond can be difficult if the employer experiences an economic downturn. Surety bonds are issued for from 3 to 5 years and may not be renewed if bankruptcy is on the horizon. Ironically, this is when they are most needed!

TABLE 16-2
Comparison of Funding Approaches

Type of Plan	Funds Set Aside Prior to Retirement	Secured against Unwillingness to Pay	Secured against Employer Insolvency	Delayed Taxation for Executives
Unfunded pay-as-you-go plan	No	No	No	Yes
Rabbi trust	Yes	Yes	No	Yes
Secular trust	Yes	Yes	Yes	No

ERISA CONSIDERATIONS

In addition to understanding the tax implications for funding nonqualified plans, your clients need to understand the ERISA implications as well.

As mentioned earlier, nonqualified plans may be subject to certain ERISA provisions that your clients generally wish to avoid. These provisions deal with reporting and disclosure (chapter 13), participation (chapter 7), vesting (chapter 9), funding (chapter 11), fiduciary (chapter 2), and ERISA enforcement (employee access to federal courts to claim ERISA rights). In general an excess-benefit plan that is unfunded will not be subject to any of these requirements. If it's funded, the excess-benefit plan will be subject to limited reporting and disclosure requirements and ERISA enforcement provisions only but not the participation, vesting, funding, and fiduciary standards. Unfunded top-hat plans and SERPs are treated the same for ERISA purposes. If these plans are unfunded, only the reporting and disclosure, fiduciary, and ERISA enforcement provisions will be applicable but not the ERISA participation, vesting, and funding requirements. If these plans are funded, however, all the above-mentioned ERISA requirements apply.

TABLE 16-3
Summary of ERISA Application to Nonqualified Plans

ERISA Requirement	Unfunded Plans			Funded Plans		
	Excess-Benefit	Top-Hat	SERP[a]	Excess-Benefit	Top-Hat	SERP
Reporting and disclosure	NA	App*	App	Limited[b]	App	App
Participation	NA	NA	NA	NA	App	App
Vesting	NA	NA	NA	NA	App	App
Funding	NA	NA	NA	NA	App	App
Fiduciary	NA	App	App	NA	App	App
ERISA enforcement	NA	App	App	App	App	App

[a] This refers only to a SERP that constitutes an unfunded plan maintained by an employer primarily to provide deferred compensation for a select group of management or highly compensated employees.
[b] Limited reporting and disclosure requirements include only furnishing participants with summary plan descriptions or annual reports and termination reports about individual benefits, as well as furnishing the Department of Labor with the name and address of the employer, the employer's identification number, and a declaration that the employer maintains the plan primarily to provide deferred compensation to a select group of management or highly paid employees, plus a statement identifying the number of such plans and the employees in each.
* Abbreviation for applicable

"FUNDING" NONQUALIFIED PLANS WITH LIFE INSURANCE

Corporate-owned life insurance (COLI) is a popular way for most publicly held and almost all closely held businesses to set up a reserve against future obligations under a nonqualified plan. No single type of contract is best. Most employers, however, prefer policies with premium and investment flexibility and low mortality and expense costs. In addition, since the policy values are generally used to finance retirement benefits, permanent rather than term coverage is indicated.

Advantages of COLI

The use of COLI is attractive for many reasons:

- The tax-free inside buildup that occurs in a life insurance policy is important to a nonqualified plan because, unlike those of a qualified plan, earnings on nonqualified-plan assets are not tax deferred.

- Life insurance proceeds received by the company can protect the company against the premature death of an executive. This works two ways. If the executive is not fully vested in his or her promised benefit at death, or if no death benefit is provided at all, the excess death benefit received by the company can be used to cushion the company against anticipated losses owing to the executive's death. If the executive is fully vested in a substantial death benefit and dies shortly after entering the plan, the life insurance policy will be able to pay the promised benefit in full, whereas the other reserves would have been inadequate.

- Life insurance proceeds received by the company upon the death of the executive are tax free.

- Policies can be borrowed against to help pay the cost of future premiums. Knowing that if cash flow is a problem the funding of his or her benefit won't suffer should give the executive an added sense of security. An added benefit of a leveraged insurance contract is that the employer is allowed to deduct any interest paid on policy loans that total $50,000 or less. (*Planning Note:* The $50,000 ceiling on policy loans was added by TRA '86. Prior to that time leveraged life insurance products had been a highly desirable way to fund nonqualified plans, but the trend now seems to be away from leveraged policies and toward variable life insurance.)

- Life insurance funding provides the employer with flexibility. The employer may either use the cash values of the policy to pay nonqualified benefits or use other assets and keep the policy in force until death. If the latter course is taken, the employer can often receive more from the insurance company as death proceeds than it pays out under the plan.

- Life insurance policies can be used to provide a supplemental disability benefit. The waiver-of-premium clause in a life policy will enable the executive to get the full nonqualified benefit even if he or she becomes disabled.

- If life insurance purchased on the life of the executive is owned by the company, premiums are paid by the company, and the company is the sole beneficiary, then constructive-receipt, economic-benefit, and Sec. 83 problems are avoided.

- If the nonqualified plan requires the plan to pay a life income to the executive, by electing a life-income option the employer can pass on to the insurance company the risk that the executive will live beyond his or her normal life expectancy.

Disadvantages of COLI

Two major disadvantages of using life insurance to fund a nonqualified plan concern the limitation on a corporate deduction for interest paid on policy loans (previously discussed) and the alternative minimum tax on corporate assets. The alternative minimum tax offers some impediment to the use of life insurance to fund a nonqualified plan because the life insurance that is payable to the corporation, although not subject to regular taxes, may be subject to the alternative minimum tax (AMT). If so, employer costs are increased. Employers should be advised that they may need to purchase additional insurance so that they can pay any AMT as well as their obligations under the plan. Although the AMT will usually be about 15 percent of the death benefit (and in many cases far less), some experts suggest that the employer obtain slightly over 15 percent more life insurance than the amount needed to fund the plan. In any case the employer's tax adviser should be consulted to determine whether the alternative minimum tax will apply.

THE INSTALLATION AND ADMINISTRATION OF NONQUALIFIED PLANS

The final issue we will consider in this chapter is the installation and administration of your client's nonqualified plan. In order to install a nonqualified plan the employer should adopt a corporate resolution authorizing the purchase of life insurance to indemnify the business for the expenses it is likely to incur. A second restriction should authorize the production of either a contract or plan document that will spell out both the corporation's and executives' benefits and obligations. In addition, a rabbi trust document or a secular trust document should be created. Finally, a one-page ERISA notice should be completed and sent to the Department of Labor. This notice is a letter informing the DOL that a nonqualified plan exists and that certain named employees are covered by the plan.

17

Individual Retirement Arrangements—Part 1

Chapter Outline

Individual retirement arrangements have been called the little guy's tax shelter and Congress's greatest gift to working Americans. Although tax reform blew some of the wind out of their "sales," these arrangements remain an important product for financial services professionals and their clients. Individual retirement arrangements go a long way toward providing retirement security for a majority of Americans, and the financial services professional can help clients achieve this goal by explaining the IRA rules, encouraging saving for retirement, and marketing IRA investments.

Individual retirement arrangements are similar to qualified plans in many ways. Both are tax-favored savings plans that encourage the accumulation of savings for retirement because they allow contributions to be made with pretax dollars (if the taxpayer is eligible) and earnings to be tax deferred until retirement. These special tax advantages represent a real bargain for taxpayers because, although funds will be taxed when distributed, the ability to deduct contributions and consequently to lower taxable income, plus the ability to defer taxation on earnings, is like receiving an interest-free loan from Uncle Sam. This taxation on earnings, is like receiving an interest-free loan from Uncle Sam. This windfall for taxpayers comes at the government's expense. The federal government and most state and local governments postpone collecting taxes on accumulated interest and/or contributions in order to encourage people to plan for their retirement. By postponing the receipt of tax revenue, the government actually loses revenue because under the time-value-of-money concept, money must be discounted over time. For example, a dollar collected today would be worth only 23 cents if collected 30 years from now, assuming the government could have invested the money at 5 percent. Because of this significant loss of revenue, stringent rules are in place to ensure that the goal of encouraging retirement savings is achieved and the revenue loss is minimized.

TYPES OF INDIVIDUAL RETIREMENT ARRANGEMENTS

There are three types of individual retirement arrangements, distinguished by their underlying investment vehicles as follows:

- individual retirement accounts
- individual retirement annuities
- individual retirement bonds

Individual Retirement Accounts (IRAs)

Individual retirement accounts are the most popular type of individual retirement arrangement. An IRA, like all individual retirement arrangements, is a savings program for individuals to which yearly tax-deductible contributions can be made. The IRA document itself is a written trust or a custodial account whose trustee or custodian must be a bank, a federally insured credit union, a savings and loan association, or a person or organization that receives IRS permission to act as the trustee or custodian (for example, an insurance company). No one will receive IRS permission to be the trustee of his or her own IRA, because the IRS mandates arm's-length dealing between the beneficiary of the IRA trust and those in charge of enforcing IRA rules.

IRAs and all individual retirement arrangements are subject to certain limitations. First, contributions to an IRA cannot exceed $2,000 a year or 100 percent of compensation, whichever is smaller. (There are two exceptions to this rule: a spousal IRA can be set up, and rollover contributions of any amount can be placed in an IRA. Both exceptions are discussed later.) Second, IRA contributions cannot be made during or after the year a taxpayer reaches age 70 1/2. Third, IRA funds may not be commingled with the taxpayer's other assets; the fund can contain only IRA contributions and rollover contributions. Fourth, IRA funds may *not* be used to buy a life insurance policy. Fifth, funds contributed to an IRA cannot be invested in collectibles. Sixth, no loans may be taken from these savings programs.

Individual Retirement Annuities (IRA Annuities)

An IRA annuity is an annuity contract typically issued by insurance companies. IRA annuities are similar to IRAs except that the following additional rules apply because of their annuity investment feature:

- The IRA annuity is nontransferable. In other words, unlike the proceeds from other annuities, the IRA annuity proceeds must be received by either the taxpayer or a beneficiary. Individuals cannot set up an IRA annuity and pledge the annuity to another party or put the annuity up as a security for a loan. For example, if loans were made under an automatic premium-loan provision, the plan would be disqualified.
- IRA annuities may not have fixed annual premiums. It is allowable, however, to charge an annual fee for each premium or to have a level annual premium for a supplementary benefit, such as a waiver of premium in case of disability.

Individual Retirement Bonds

Individual retirement bonds are a third form of individual retirement arrangement. These bonds were issued by the federal government prior to May 1, 1982, but subsequently taken off the market because they could not effectively compete with private investments. Individual retirement bonds have these features: (1) interest is paid when the bonds are cashed in; (2) no interest is paid after the taxpayer reaches 70 1/2 (obviously the bonds should be cashed in before this age), and, if the taxpayer dies, interest payments stop 5 years after the taxpayer's death or on the date he or she would have reached 70 1/2, whichever is earlier (again, the bonds should be cashed in before this age); (3) the bonds are nontransferable; and (4) the bonds cannot be sold, discounted, or used as collateral or security. Even though these bonds are no longer available for sale, you may find a client who needs advice on how and when to cash them in.

THE GROUND RULES

Individual retirement arrangements have certain ground rules regarding eligibility, contribution and deduction limits, and distributions. Generally these rules ensure that the federal government is promoting retirement savings, not merely providing a tax shelter. These rules also ensure against the loss of excess federal revenue by limiting the amount of contributions, prescribing the dates by which distributions must occur, and limiting participation to those who are considered middle class or below or who are not considered active participants in a pension program.

Who's Eligible

Any person under age 70 1/2 who gets compensation (either salary or self-employment earned income) can make a contribution to an IRA. For some the contribution will not be deductible, but the interest earnings will be tax deferred. For others the contribution (as well as any interest earnings) will be tax deferred through an income tax deduction. The contribution will be deductible if neither the taxpayer nor the taxpayer's spouse is an active participant in an employer-maintained retirement plan. If the participant and/or the spouse is an active participant then the contribution is deductible only if his or her adjusted gross income falls below prescribed limits (designed to approximate a middle-class income).

Active Participant

The first issue that arises under the eligibility question is specifying who an active participant is in an employer-maintained plan. The employer-maintained plan basically takes into account every type of qualified plan: defined-benefit pension plans, money-purchase plans, target-benefit plans, profit-sharing plans, stock plans. It also includes 403(b) tax-sheltered annuity plans, SEPs, and SIMPLEs. Federal, state, or local government plans are also taken into account. Not included, however, are nonqualified retirement arrangements. An employee who is covered only by a nonqualified plan won't be considered an active participant and can therefore make deductible IRA contributions.

Simply being associated with an employer-sponsored plan does not affect the taxpayer's ability to make deductible IRA contributions. Deductibility of IRA contributions is only jeopardized if the taxpayer is an active participant in the employer-sponsored plan. *Active participant* has a special meaning that depends on the type of plan involved.

Defined-Benefit Plans. Generally a person is an active participant in a defined-benefit plan unless excluded under the eligibility provision of the plan for the entire year. And this is true even if he or she elects not to participate in the plan. For example, ABC Company has a plan that requires employees to contribute in order to participate. Since Kim does not feel she can afford to make contributions, she doesn't participate. But she is still considered an active participant for IRA purposes, even though she isn't active in the plan.

Nevertheless, there are situations in a defined-benefit plan when a client won't be considered an active participant as follows:

- if your client is not covered under the plan's eligibility provisions (for example, employees who are not currently eligible or who will never be eligible for plan participation)
- if the defined-benefit plan is frozen—meaning that no additional benefits are accruing currently for any participant

Defined-Contribution Plans. In general, a person is an active participant in any type of defined-contribution plan if the plan specifies that employer contributions must be allocated to the individual's account. This category also includes SEPs, 403(b) plans, and SIMPLEs. In a profit-sharing or stock plan where employer contributions are discretionary, the participant must actually receive some contribution (even if the contribution amounts to a reallocated forfeiture) for active-participant status to be triggered. Furthermore, mandatory contributions, voluntary contributions, and contributions made pursuant to a salary reduction SEP, 403(b) plan, SIMPLE, or 401(k) arrangement will also trigger active-participant status.

A special rule applies when contributions are completely discretionary under the plan (like a profit-sharing plan) and contributions are not made until after the end of the plan year (ending with or within the employee's tax year in question). In this case, to recognize that a plan participant may not know whether he or she is an "active participant" by the time the IRA contribution deadline arrives, the employer's contribution is attributable to the following year.

> *Example:* Sally first becomes eligible for XYZ Corporation's profit-sharing plan for the plan year ending December 31, 1996. The company is on a calendar fiscal year and does not decide to make a contribution for the 1996 plan year until June 1, 1997. Sally is not considered an active participant in the plan for the 1996 plan year. However, due to the 1996 contribution, she is an active participant for the 1997 plan year.

When the plan year of the employer's plan (regardless of whether the plan is a defined-benefit or defined-contribution plan) is not the calendar year, an individual's active participant status is dependent upon whether he or she is an active participant for the plan year ending with or within the particular calendar year in question.

> *Example:* Susan first becomes eligible for the ABC money-purchase pension plan for the plan year June 1, 1995 to May 30, 1996. Susan is an active participant for 1996 (but not 1995) because the plan year ended "with or within" calendar year 1996.

Finally, note that in determining active participant status, participation for any part of the plan year counts as participation for the whole plan year, and that whether or not the participant is vested in his or her benefit has no bearing on the determination.

Income Level

The second issue that arises under the eligibility question is whether the taxpayer can make deductible contributions under the income-level rules. In general, people who are not active participants can deduct contributions to an IRA no matter what they earn. For an active participant, however, fully deductible contributions are allowed only if the taxpayer has adjusted gross income below a specified level. If the adjusted gross income exceeds the specified limit but falls below a maximum level, the $2,000 IRA limit is proportionately reduced by a formula (table 17-1).

TABLE 17-1
Limits for Deductible IRA Contributions

Filing Status	Full IRA Deduction	Reduced IRA Deduction	No IRA Deduction
Individual or head of household	$25,000 or less	$25,000.01– $34,999.99	$35,000 or more
Married filing jointly	$40,000 or less	$40,000.01– $49,999.99	$50,000 or more
Married filing separately	Not available	$0.01–$9,999.99	$10,000 or more

The level for unreduced contributions depends upon the taxpayer's filing status. Married couples filing a joint return will get a full IRA deduction if their adjusted gross income is $40,000 or less. Marrieds filing separately cannot get a full IRA deduction. Individual taxpayers and the taxpayers filing as head of household will get a full IRA deduction if their adjusted gross income is $25,000 or less.

The maximum level for deductible contributions is $49,999.99 for marrieds filing jointly; $9,999.99 for marrieds filing separately; and $34,999.99 for those using head-of-household or individual filing status. In other words, if an active participant's adjusted gross income exceeds these levels, no part of an IRA contribution can be deducted.

For taxpayers whose adjusted gross income falls between the no-deduction level and the full-deduction level, their reduced deduction can be computed by using the following formula:

$$\text{Deductible amount} = \$2,000 - \frac{\text{adjusted gross income} - \text{filing status floor}}{5}$$

Example 1: Bob and Rita Dufus (a married couple filing jointly) are both working and have a combined adjusted gross income of $46,000. Bob and Rita can each make the full IRA contribution of $2,000 (total $4,000). The formula shows that each can deduct $800 (total $1,600):

$$\text{Bob and Rita's deductible amount} = \$2,000 - \frac{\$46,000 - \$40,000}{5}$$

Bob and Rita's deductible amount = $800 each

Therefore of the $4,000 contributed to an IRA, $2,400 will be on an after-tax basis.

Example 2: Anne Le Flamme (filing as a single taxpayer) has an adjusted gross income of $30,000. She too can make a $2,000 contribution, but only $1,000 will be deductible:

$$\text{Anne's deductible amount} = \$2,000 - \frac{\$30,000 - \$25,000}{5}$$

Anne's deductible amount = $1,000

Anne might, however, choose to limit her contribution to the $1,000 deductible permitted and seek tax shelter elsewhere for the other $1,000 she has targeted for retirement savings.

Three important rules apply to taxpayers who fall into the reduced IRA category. First, the IRS allows the adjusted limitation to be rounded up to the next $10 increment. For example, if the formula for Kay shows her eligible to make a deductible contribution of $758.43, her deductible contribution is rounded up to $760. The second rule that applies to the reduction formula is that there is a $200 floor. In other words, even if Ed's deductible IRA contribution works out to $57, Ed is still entitled to make a $200 deductible contribution. If Ed's deductible amount is zero, however, no deductible contribution is allowed, not even the $200 floor amount. The third rule that applies is that in order to be able to receive distributions tax free, a taxpayer can designate contributions as nondeductible even when they are actually deductible. This is useful only if the taxpayer has little or no taxable income or if the taxpayer anticipates large tax increases in the future.

(Planning Note: Be sure to watch your client's adjusted gross income carefully, because a one-cent difference can mean the loss of a $200 deduction. For example, Faye and Roger Maloney (married and filing jointly) have $50,000 in adjusted gross income, which means no deductible IRA. If Faye and Roger could reduce the amount of adjusted gross income by one cent, to $49,999.99, they would be entitled to a $200 deductible IRA contribution.)

Contribution Limits

The limit for annual contributions to an IRA or an IRA annuity is the lesser of $2,000 or 100 percent of compensation. Taxpayers need not contribute the full $2,000 or the full deductible amount. In other words, taxpayers are always free to contribute as little as they want or make no contribution at all for any year. It's important to remember that a contribution cannot exceed a person's *compensation.* Compensation is earnings from wages, salaries, tips, professional fees, bonuses, and any other amount a taxpayer receives for providing personal services. In addition, alimony and separate-maintenance payments are also considered compensation for IRA and IRA annuity purposes. Compensation does not include earnings and profits from property, such as rental interest and dividend income, or amounts received as a pension or annuity. As a general rule, if it is income the taxpayer worked for in a given year, the contribution can be made; if it is derived from investments or retirement income, it is not eligible.

Self-employeds who have a net loss from self-employment can make IRA or IRA annuity contributions if they had salary or wage income, and they don't have to reduce the amount of salary income by the net loss. If there are both salary or wage income and net income from self-employment, the two amounts are combined to determine the amount that can be contributed.

> *Example 1:* In his first year in business, Donald, a self-employed creator of computer software, has a net loss of $17,000, largely because of start-up costs. However, he did receive $4,000 from part-time teaching at the university. Donald may contribute up to $2,000 to an IRA because his salary will not be reduced by his self-employment loss.

> *Example 2:* Patty, an aspiring self-employed artist and part-time day-care worker, received only $1,000 in income from her day-care job, but her net self-employment income from paintings she sold was $3,000. Patty may contribute up to $2,000 for an IRA because the combination of salary income and self-employment income exceeded $2,000.

Timing of Contributions

Contributions to an IRA can be made at any time. The year for which a contribution can be deducted, however, depends on when the contribution is made. If the contribution is made between April 16 and December 31, it is deductible only for the year in which it is made. If the contribution is made between January 1 and April 15 (the tax-return due date not including extensions), it may be deductible either for the year in which it is made or the preceding year (assuming, of course, that contributions haven't already been made for that year). What this means is that a contribution to an IRA can be made after the tax year is over up until the tax-filing deadline for the preceding year (April 15). If the taxpayer desires, $4,000 can be contributed at one time. For example, on January 15 a $4,000 contribution can be made with $2,000 applying to the prior year and $2,000 applying to the current year.

Spousal IRAs and IRA Annuities

The rules for spousal IRAs and IRA annuities were changed under the Small Business Jobs Protection Act of 1996 so that now a couple in which one person earns at least $4,000 (and the other does *not* have employment earnings) will be on the same footing as when both work. Under the new rules, an individual can contribute up to $2,000 to a spousal IRA as long as the working party earns at least $4,000. Other conditions include the following:

- The taxpayer is married at the end of the year.
- The spouse earns less than the taxpayer.
- A joint tax return is filed for the tax year for which the contribution is made.

Spousal IRAs or IRA annuities can be set up even if the taxpayer does not contribute to his or her own account, or contributions can be made for both spouses, or the taxpayer can make contributions just to the taxpayer's IRA or IRA annuity even though a spousal IRA or IRA annuity already exists. But no more than $2,000 can be placed in either IRA for any year.

Spousal IRAs are subject to the same deductibility rules that apply to nonspousal IRAs—active participants are barred from deducting a spousal IRA unless they fall under the prescribed income ranges that were discussed earlier. In other words, nonactive participants may deduct spousal IRAs; active participants whose adjusted gross income is $40,000 or less can take a full spousal IRA deduction of $2,000; and active participants whose adjusted gross income is $40,000.01 – $49,999.99 can take a reduced spousal deduction. Like the nonspousal IRA, the spousal IRA requires a mathematical formula to determine the appropriate deductible amount:

$$\text{Deductible amount of spousal IRA} = \$2,000 - \frac{\text{adjusted gross income} - \$40,000}{5}$$

Example: Joe and Jane Morgan would like to contribute to a spousal IRA in addition to their regular IRA. Joe and Jane have an adjusted gross income of $46,000 that enables them to make an $800 deductible contribution to Joe's IRA. Jane does not have any income because she stays home with the children. Joe and Jane want to maximize their deductible contribution by setting up a spousal IRA for Jane.

$$\text{Deductible amount for spousal IRA} = \$2,000 - \frac{\$46,000 - \$40,000}{5}$$

$$\text{Deductible amount for spousal IRA} = \$800$$

Note that the total deductible limit will be $1,600 ($800 for Joe's IRA and $800 for Jane's spousal IRA).

Excess Contributions

An excess contribution is any amount contributed to an individual retirement arrangement that exceeds the $2,000 limit. One common way of falling into the excess contribution trap is to make a rollover that does not meet the prescribed rules. An improper rollover and other excess contributions will result in an excise tax of 6 percent on the excess. If the excess amount (plus interest) is withdrawn by the tax deadline in the year the excess contribution is made, however, the taxpayer does not have to pay the penalty. The taxpayer does have to include the excess amount in his or her gross income for that year and may have to pay a 10 percent premature distribution penalty on the interest. But there is no premature distribution penalty on the principal amount.

ROLLOVER CONTRIBUTIONS

To facilitate portability of pensions and transferability when a taxpayer changes jobs, distributions from a qualified plan (except life insurance distributions) or from an individual retirement arrangement can be made on a tax-free basis if the distribution is reinvested within 60 days in an individual retirement arrangement. This transaction is known as a *rollover*—the tax-free transfer from one retirement program to another.

There are several types of rollovers involving individual retirement arrangements:

- *Rollovers from one individual retirement arrangement to another individual retirement arrangement.* Taxpayers can withdraw all or part of the balance in an IRA or IRA annuity and reinvest it within 60 days in another IRA or IRA annuity. The reasons for doing this include changing trusts or custodial accounts (because of dissatisfaction with investment performance or service) or temporarily boosting cash flow.

  Rollovers, however, are permitted only once a year. One way around the one-year rule is to make a trustee-to-trustee transfer—a transfer of IRA or IRA annuity funds from one trustee directly to another trustee. A trustee-to-trustee transfer does not constitute a rollover, because the money is never distributed.

- *Rollover from a qualified plan to an IRA or IRA annuity.* Under the rules applicable today, most distributions made from a qualified plan, tax-sheltered annuity, or a Keogh plan can be rolled over into a new or existing IRA or IRA annuity. The only exception is for distributions that are a part of a series of periodic payments over the life expectancy of the participant or over a period of 10 years or more. When a participant wishes to make a rollover from a qualified plan or 403(b) plan, he or she should elect what is referred to as a *direct transfer* from the plan to the IRA. When the participant makes this election, the distributing plan is not required to withhold any portion of the distribution for income taxes.

If, instead, the participant received the distribution directly and then rolled the benefit over, the distributing plan would have to withhold 20 percent of the distribution. Electing the direct rollover is relatively easy to accomplish, since the law now requires that qualified and 403(b) plans give participants the option to make the direct transfer to an IRA.

- *Conduit rollovers.* Amounts received from an employer's qualified plan may later be moved to another qualified plan by using a conduit IRA or IRA annuity. A conduit IRA or IRA annuity "stores" plan assets for transfer to another plan. The following rules apply to conduit IRAs and IRA annuities:

  - The conduit IRA or IRA annuity may consist *only* of the assets transferred from a qualified plan (and any earnings). In other words, plan assets cannot be transferred into an existing IRA and later rerolled over. Taxpayers may have both a conduit IRA and other IRAs or IRA annuities.
  - If the original distribution to the IRA was made before 1993, the funds in the IRA had to be attributable to a rollover of a qualified total distribution as that term was defined in the Internal Revenue Code as of the time of the rollover. Amounts contributed to the IRA after that date are not subject to any restrictions.

In addition to the conduit IRA or IRA annuity rollover, the qualified-plan-to-IRA-annuity rollover, and the individual-retirement-arrangement-to-individual-retirement-arrangement rollover, funds from a divorce or similar proceeding may be rolled over to an individual retirement arrangement under the following conditions:

- They are assets of the former spouse's qualified plan.
- They are made pursuant to a qualified domestic-relations order (a judgment issued under a state law that allows a participant's plan assets to be used for marital property rights, child support, or alimony payments).
- They are received within one calendar year.

In addition, the taxpayer need not roll over the entire amount distributed but may roll over only part of it if desired.

Why Roll Over?

Two reasons to roll assets over into an IRA or IRA annuity are to avoid taxation of plan distributions and to continue to accrue tax-deferred interest. In this manner taxation can be delayed until distributions must begin. A third reason to roll over plan distributions is to gain control of the investment direction of retirement funds. Frequently an alternative to taking a distribution is to let the pension amount sit with a former employer who typically will have investment control over the funds. The IRA rollover enables the taxpayer to take distributions and direct the investment of the funds.

One reason to use a conduit IRA or IRA annuity is to avoid the harsh distribution rules governing IRAs, if the distribution rules of the new plan are more lenient. For example, if Samantha's new plan allows early retirement at age 55 and Samantha is planning to retire then, her funds should be rerolled over into the new plan instead of rolled into an IRA. The reason is that if the funds remain in the IRA, Samantha is barred from receiving them without penalty until she is 59 1/2; however, if the funds are rerolled over, the plan will distribute them without penalty at age 55.

YOUR FINANCIAL SERVICES PRACTICE:
YOUR IRA AS A SWING LOAN

Often people need cash for a short period of time; for example to cover the closing costs of a new home before selling the old one—or to buy a new car to replace a clunker when the clunker inconveniently dies a month before the big commission check is due.

The IRS ruled in Letter Ruling 9010007 that the rollover provisions apply regardless of the use made of the funds distributed from the IRA, as long as the 60-day deadline is met. Therefore the IRA can be used as a source of short-term, interest-free funds. However, if the IRA owner doesn't have a foreseeable source of funds to replace the IRA distribution used as a short-term loan, he or she should be prepared to pay the tax resulting from failing to meet the 60-day limit. In addition to federal income tax, a 10 percent early distribution penalty may be payable on a "failed" rollover unless the distribution was made after age 59 1/2, death, or disability. Finally, clients should be made aware that the IRS ruling only applies to the taxpayer who made the ruling request. Cautious taxpayers may feel uncomfortable without more authoritative rulings.

DISTRIBUTIONS

Taxpayers can make withdrawals of all or part of their individual retirement arrangements anytime they want. Once a withdrawal is made, however, the amount withdrawn becomes part of the taxpayer's income for tax purposes. The taxpayer also loses the special advantage of tax-deferred interest accumulation. This deterrent encourages some to leave their account untouched; they prefer never to take distributions and to leave the funds as a legacy. On the other hand, others don't care that distributions are taxed and desire to withdraw their funds almost as quickly as they contribute them. Since the government trades off revenue in order to encourage retirement savings through the use of individual retirement arrangements, it has established some rules to make sure that IRAs, IRA annuities, and retirement bonds are used for retirement purposes only.

Premature Distributions

The first rule, called the *premature distribution rule,* is aimed at those who want to withdraw funds before retirement. This rule puts a 10 percent excise tax on distributions that occur prior to age 59 1/2 (unless distributions are made in the form of a life annuity or its equivalent), death, or disability. Taxpayers wishing to withdraw funds prior to these events not only have to include funds in gross income, they also have to pay the 10 percent penalty. Unfortunately this rule discourages IRA or IRA annuity participation by the young and deters substantial contributions by the not-so-young. There is no reason for this, because the government penalty does not do what it purports to, namely, stop IRA and IRA annuity contributions from being used as capital-accumulation vehicles. There is a point at which it pays a taxpayer to make IRA or IRA annuity contributions even when a premature withdrawal is the taxpayer's intention. The break-even or get-ahead date depends on the tax bracket of the employee when contributions are made, the interest earned under the IRA or IRA annuity, the tax bracket of the person when distributions are withdrawn, and the ratio of nondeductible contributions to the total IRA balance at the time of withdrawal.

A few caveats about using IRAs for capital-accumulation purposes:

- There is always the possibility that the federal government will increase the penalty or, even worse, restrict distributions altogether until retirement.
- If the taxpayer's tax bracket is higher at the time of withdrawal, the break-even point will be longer. (The converse is also true: a lower tax bracket at distribution time will mean a shorter break-even point.)
- It is possible the IRA distribution will put the taxpayer into a higher tax bracket. One way to avoid this is to split distributions over 2 years. For example, the taxpayer could take half of what is needed in December and the second half in January.
- The projected time for withdrawing the funds may not be the most advantageous time to liquidate the taxpayer's account. For example, the underlying stocks may be at a low point.
- The taxpayer may need these funds for retirement, and any premature distribution could undermine a potential retirement date or standard of living during retirement.

Excess Accumulations

The second rule regulating distributions, called the tax on excess accumulations, is more successful in accomplishing the government's goals. This rule is targeted at those who would keep funds in their IRAs or IRA annuities indefinitely. Under the excess-accumulation rule, taxpayers must begin receiving distributions by April 1 of the calendar year following the year they reach age 70 1/2. If the proper amount is not withdrawn, a 50 percent excise tax is placed on the amount that should have been distributed. The government goal of encouraging the IRA or IRA annuity funds to be used for retirement is sure to be met under the excess-accumulation rule. In addition, the government is sure to recoup taxes on retirement savings during the taxpayer's expected lifetime. Since these rules apply to qualified plans as well as IRAs and IRA annuities, they will be discussed in greater detail in chapter 25.

Distributions on Account of Death

Distributions from an individual retirement arrangement because of the owner's death are subject to special rules and tax treatment depending on whether the distributions have already started. If the owner dies after distributions have begun, the remainder of the funds must be distributed at least as rapidly as they were before the owner's death (unless the taxpayer is receiving distributions under the excess-accumulation rules). In other words, if the beneficiary will be taxed on payments and wants to delay receiving them, the prior payment schedule should be followed. If the beneficiary desires to receive all funds immediately, however, this is also allowed. If the owner dies before distributions have begun (and the excess-accumulation rule is not applicable), distributions depend on whether there is no beneficiary, a nonspouse beneficiary, or a spouse beneficiary. If there is no beneficiary, the funds must be distributed within 5 years. If there is a nonspouse beneficiary, the funds can be distributed over the life of the beneficiary but must start one year after the taxpayer's death. If the spouse is the beneficiary, he or she can delay taking distributions until the date the deceased would have been 70 1/2. The beneficiary can, of course, take distributions immediately if so desired.

18

Individual Retirement Arrangements—Part 2

Chapter Outline

In addition to the legal and tax implications concerning IRAs, there are also several financial applications. Let's take a closer look.

TYPES OF INVESTMENTS

Individual retirement accounts can be invested in a multitude of vehicles running the gamut from mutual funds to limited partnerships, from investments with minimal risk and modest returns to speculative investments with promises of greater return. IRAs are typically invested in certificates of deposit, money market funds, mutual funds, limited partnerships, income bond funds, corporate bond funds, and common stocks and other equities. Self-directed IRAs (IRAs in which the taxpayer is able to shift investments between general investment vehicles offered by the trustee) are also popular because they allow the investor to have investment flexibility and to anticipate or react to interest-rate directions and market trends.

Choosing the best investment for an individual retirement arrangement is similar to choosing any other investment: lifestyle, other financial resources, and the client's degree of risk aversion must be considered. There is, however, one hitch with an IRA or IRA annuity investment: The *R* stands for *retirement*. The retirement goals of a client must be considered to make the proper IRA or IRA annuity investment. In rendering IRA or IRA annuity advice the job of a financial services professional is to get the client to come up with a retirement strategy first and an investment strategy second.

Investment Restrictions

Investment of IRAs is generally open to all the investment vehicles available outside IRAs. There are, however, a few exceptions:

- investment in life insurance
- investment in collectibles
- prohibited transactions

Life Insurance

Investment in life insurance is not allowed for an IRA even though defined-benefit and defined-contribution retirement plans allow an "incidental" amount of life insurance. IRAs, however, are not subject to the same rules (or underlying logic) and are considered to be strictly for retirement purposes. Therefore no incidental insurance is available. But there is an interesting method for linking the sale of life insurance with an IRA.

YOUR FINANCIAL SERVICES PRACTICE:
LIFE INSURANCE AND IRAs

Dividend-paying cash value life insurance (for example, whole life) can be used to fund an IRA indirectly. The client should use an existing policy or purchase a life policy capable of generating $2,000 worth of dividends after a sufficient time has passed to allow cash buildup. The $2,000 can then be distributed as a "tax-free" dividend if it's used to fund an IRA or IRA annuity. The taxpayer gives up contributions to a life policy for several years but gains the face value (plus any reinvested dividends) as insurance coverage, a perpetually tax-free-funded IRA or IRA annuity, and a possible IRA or IRA annuity tax deduction.

Collectibles

If an IRA or IRA annuity is invested in collectibles, the amount invested in collectibles is considered a distribution in the year invested. This means that the tax advantages of IRAs or IRA annuities have been eliminated, and if the investment is made prior to age 59 1/2, a 10 percent excise tax will be applicable unless the payment is made in the form of a life annuity or its equivalent. Collectibles include works of art, Oriental rugs, antiques, gold, rare coins, stamps, rare wines, and certain other tangible property.

There is one exception to the prohibition on investments in collectibles. Any gold or silver coin issued by the United States can be bought with IRA funds. However, gold and silver coins of other countries are still prohibited as an IRA purchase.

Prohibited Transactions

A prohibited transaction for purposes of an individual retirement arrangement is any improper use of the account or annuity. Prohibited transactions for an IRA or IRA annuity include borrowing money from the account or annuity, selling property to the account, and using the account or annuity as security for a loan. If a nonexempt prohibited transaction occurs, the IRA will be "disqualified" and the taxpayer must include the fair market value of part or all of the IRA or IRA annuity assets in his or her gross income for tax purposes in the year in which the prohibited transaction occurs. There also will be a 10 percent premature distribution penalty (if prior to age 59 1/2). In effect, prohibited transactions are treated as distributions from the plan.

Although there is no general restriction on investing in tax-sheltered vehicles such as municipal bonds, they are an imprudent investment for IRA purposes because the tax shelter is not necessary. Since an IRA provides for tax deferral already, the overkill of investing in a tax-free bond won't make it worthwhile for an investor to take the lower yield that municipal bonds offer.

Individual Retirement Annuities (IRA Annuities)

The primary reason for choosing one IRA funding vehicle over another is the investor's desired return balanced against the amount of risk the investor is willing to accept. There are, however, secondary reasons that make IRA annuities worth considering when the return/risk factors are comparable with other investments: the waiver-of-premium coverage in case of disability and the lifelong payments that are afforded by a life annuity. The waiver-of-premium coverage provides an investor with valuable protection should disability occur. This is especially important for those relying on individual-retirement-arrangement funds as a major source of retirement income. In fact, for some people the waiver of premium in case of disability may be the only assurance of retirement income (aside from social security). The lifetime payments offered by an annuity are a second reason for choosing an IRA annuity. As with any annuity, the investor is betting he or she will outlive the mortality table. If the investor does, the excess payments represent mortality gain, which can be thought of as an additional return on investment. The IRA annuity also quells a common fear of retired persons—running out of funds and becoming dependent on others. Ideally investors would like to live off the interest provided by their personal savings and IRA, but this is not possible for many. Life annuities provide a structured way to use up both principal and interest without the danger of funds running out.

IRAs AND THE FINANCIAL SERVICES PROFESSIONAL

For the financial services professional, understanding IRAs requires more than just knowing the various rules, restraints, and tax implications associated with IRAs. The financial services professional must also analyze whether a current client's interests are best served by making IRA contributions and must identify potential clients who need IRA assistance. Many financial services professionals must even ask themselves whether selling IRAs is appropriate for them.

Should Your Client Make an IRA Contribution?

There are any number of valid reasons why people don't make IRA contributions:

- IRA contributions are unaffordable because of present income level or current cash flow.
- Large expenses, such as a child's college education, are close at hand, and the money would have to be withdrawn before the break-even point.
- Tax rates for the client are very low (for example, for someone in graduate school), and it's reasonable to assume he or she will be in a much higher bracket at retirement time.
- Savings can't be tied up because of insecure prospects for future income (for example, for someone involved in a speculative employment situation).

If, however, your client's excuse for not contributing is having a lack of knowledge about IRAs or lack of interest in them, being too young, or having an adequate retirement plan, then careful reconsideration is warranted. For example, does your client who is "too young" know that by making just nine $2,000 contributions from age 18 to age 26—and no contributions thereafter—an IRA at age 65 will be larger than an IRA funded with a $2,000 contribution each year from age 27 to age 65 (table 18-1)? Does your client whose retirement plan is "adequate" consider that postretirement inflation at a modest increase of 4 percent per year means that a $1.00 loaf of bread at age 65 will cost $2.19 at age 85?

One of the most important considerations in deciding whether to put money into an IRA is whether your client can deduct the initial contribution. Taxpayers who can make contributions on a before-tax basis have a huge advantage over those whose only benefit is the interest accumulation on a tax-sheltered basis. Those whose only advantage is tax-deferred interest accumulation must look carefully at net aftertax investment return and the desirability of keeping the contributions tied up until the break-even point.

Regardless of whether pretax contributions can be made, it is important to know if the "risk" of tying up income justifies the return of the IRA tax advantage(s). Generally it's a justified risk if the client is committed to saving for retirement, but it won't be justified if the client is likely to raid the IRA before the appropriate time. Undisciplined IRA withdrawals represent ineffective money management, and planners who feel withdrawals are too great a temptation for their clients may want to avoid the IRA in the first place. On the other hand, some planners think of the lock-in of retirement funds as a hidden advantage of IRA savings because the client is coerced into leaving savings for retirement and won't be tempted to withdraw funds under marginal circumstances. In either case, knowing your client's financial habits and forecasting his or her willpower is the deciding factor.

The IRA Market—Potential Clients

Just about every taxpayer is a candidate for an IRA. In fact, because of their broad-based appeal and general attractiveness to the public, IRAs make a great door opener. What's more, mass marketing of IRAs is possible—and this opens the way to an increased client base. Once in the door you can easily explain IRAs, which will lead naturally into a discussion of the overall retirement and financial plan.

For financial services professionals who work primarily with employers, employer-sponsored IRAs are possible. The usual IRA rules apply, and there is none of the qualified retirement plan hassles, such as reporting requirements and nondiscriminating coverage. In fact, there is no requirement that employer-sponsored IRAs be available to all employees, so it's possible to provide them just for key employees and owner-employees. Contributions to an employer-sponsored IRA may be made as additional compensation or as a salary reduction, and in the latter case payroll deduction is a good way to simplify administration.

If you decide to advise your employer-client to have employer-sponsored IRAs, your client must consider the following factors:

- Amounts contributed are taxable to the employee; if an employee earns under the compensation limits for his or her particular tax bracket, the employee may deduct the contribution.
- Social security and unemployment taxes are applicable, since the contribution represents extra compensation. If the employer believes that the employee will be entitled to an IRA deduction, however, no federal income tax withholding is required.

Whether you're involved with IRAs in the individual market or through the employee benefit market, it's important to be aware that selling IRAs has its drawbacks. First, IRA commissions are generally not generous. (They are typically lower than on most insurance products.) Second, because of the wide variety of investments and the fluctuating returns offered, clients tend to shift investment vehicles, which translates into administrative and financial headaches. Many planners believe, however, that despite these headaches IRAs can represent an ideal supplemental sale and that involvement with the IRA products leads to financial success for themselves and their clients.

TABLE 18-1
IRA Funding Plans[1]

Plan One			Plan Two		
Age start		18	Age start		27
Age end		26	Age end		65
Amount per year		$2,000	Amount per year		$2,000
Rate of return		10%	Rate of return		10%
Value at age 65		$1,229,194	Value at age 65		$883,145
Total amount contributed		$18,000	Total amount contributed		$78,000

Age	Amount	Value	Age	Amount	Value
18	$2,000	$ 2,240	18	0	0
19	2,000	4,749	19	0	0
20	2,000	7,559	20	0	0
21	2,000	10,706	21	0	0
22	2,000	11,990	22	0	0
23	2,000	13,429	23	0	0
24	2,000	15,041	24	0	0
25	2,000	16,846	25	0	0
26	2,000	18,867	26	0	0
27	0	21,131	27	$2,000	$ 2,200
28	0	23,667	28	2,000	4,620
29	0	26,507	29	2,000	7,282
30	0	29,688	30	2,000	10,210
.	.	.	.	.	.
.	.	.	.	.	.
.	.	.	.	.	.
60	0	763,233	60	2,000	540,049
61	0	839,556	61	2,000	596,254
62	0	923,512	62	2,000	658,079
63	0	1,015,863	63	2,000	726,087
64	0	1,117,449	64	2,000	800,896
65	0	1,229,194	65	2,000	883,185

[1] This comparison is hypothetical; no guarantees are implied for specific investments. The interest rate is assumed to remain unchanged for the entire period.

Book Two

19

Introduction to Individual Retirement Planning

Chapter Outline

All too often clients are only vaguely aware of problems associated with the retirement years. Other clients recognize that retirement problems exist but feel there is no way to cope with the magnitude of the financial requirements. Instead they choose to concentrate on today and let tomorrow take care of itself. Many clients used to feel the same about life insurance until efforts by the insurance industry and its agents brought about the general acceptance that life insurance is a basic piece of a client's financial plan. This change has been fostered by agents educating their clients about the problems that exist when a major source of income is lost because of death and about how life insurance products can help. A similar effort by agents is now required to educate an aging population about the need to plan for retirement and to provide the financial planning tools that can be used to replace lost income in the retirement years. If the track record of the insurance industry is any indication, retirement planning will soon be included in every individual's financial plan.

WHY PLAN FOR RETIREMENT?

Because a larger percentage of the population will live until retirement and will live longer during retirement than previous generations, it is more essential than ever that today's population plan for retirement. Retirement planners need to help their clients understand the following:

- the magnitude of the financial requirements facing them during retirement
- the impact of inflation on retirement
- the effect that financial well-being has on the quality of life
- the importance of planning to achieve financial self-sufficiency

In addition, clients who are complacent about saving for retirement should be made aware of the financial problems that force retirees to worry about the adequacy of their retirement income or that make them financially dependent on others. Have your clients consider the following:

- Retirees are often forced to reduce or eliminate their consumption of some "nonessential items" so that they can afford the increasing costs of items necessary for the maintenance of life. These nonessential items (such as home maintenance), however, are themselves critical to a person's self-dignity and future financial welfare.
- Studies indicate that 75 percent of elderly families cannot afford luxury items because the routine costs of living absorb all of their income.
- Even in the most generous employer-sponsored retirement plans the employer typically only replaces about one-half of a person's salary.
- The combination of an employer-sponsored plan and social security will not provide adequate funds for maintaining the preretirement standard of living during retirement.
- Clients should be sensitive to the long-term viability of social security as it exists today. They should consider the economic trouble the Medicare system is experiencing today and the bailouts of the social security system in the early 1980s. If these problems can occur when only one out of eight Americans is retired, what will happen in the year 2027 when one out of five Americans will be retired?
- Many clients will have to deal with deteriorating health during retirement. Poor health not only creates the problem of increased medical bills, but also means increases in the purchase of services that clients were once able to do for themselves (for example, home maintenance).
- Rising inflation during retirement forces many retirees to either work part-time at low wages to replace lost purchasing power or liquidate the family home or other financial or personal assets to pay bills.

- If inflation goes up 4 percent per year, an item that costs $1 at age 65 will cost $2.19 at age 85.

ROADBLOCKS TO RETIREMENT SAVING

The question remains, Why don't more Americans plan for retirement? After all, the so-called golden years are part of the American dream. The answer lies in the many distractions that hinder retirement savings.

Perhaps the biggest roadblock to retirement planning is the tendency of many working people to use their full aftertax income to support their current standard of living. These people will not have any private savings to supplement social security and pension funds. Many of them also may have experienced adversities like unemployment that pushed them into debt. In other cases a lifestyle that incurs debt may stem from a spendthrift attitude or from the desire to emulate or improve upon their parents' standard of living. Whatever the reason for their lack of retirement savings, clients must follow a budget that allows them to live within their means and that also provides for retirement savings. (*Planning Note:* Make your clients aware that a 90/10 spending ratio is generally desired. Under a 90/10 spending ratio 90 percent of your clients' earnings is directed toward their current standard of living, and at least 10 percent is directed toward other long-term financial objectives, such as their children's education and their own retirement. For example, a family with a gross annual income of $60,000 should allocate no more than $54,000 (including taxes) of its total income to standard-ofliving and lifestyle items, leaving at least $6,000 for long-term objectives. Furthermore, as income rises, the percentage spent on the current standard of living should decline, eventually approaching an 80/20 split.)

A second impediment to retirement saving is unexpected expenses, including uninsured medical bills; repairs to a home, auto, or major appliance; and periods of unemployment. (*Planning Note:* The client should set up an emergency fund to handle these inevitable problems. Approximately 3 to 6 months' income is usually set aside for this objective. If a client's salary is stable and other income such as dividends is part of the individual's income flow, then a 3 to 4 months' income level in the emergency fund can be sufficient. However, if the main source of income is commissions that fluctuate between pay periods, 6 months' income held for emergencies is more appropriate.)

Inadequate insurance coverage is a third impediment to retirement saving. Regardless of whether it is life, disability, health, home, or auto, many individuals continue to remain uninsured or underinsured. Because the client cannot always recover economically from such losses, one important element of retirement planning is protection against catastrophic financial loss that would make future saving impossible. (*Planning Note:* Agents should conduct a thorough review of their clients' insurance needs to make sure they are adequately covered. Two often overlooked areas are disability insurance and liability insurance for the professional. Make sure your client is adequately protected in both areas.)

YOUR FINANCIAL SERVICES PRACTICE:
UNDERSTANDING QDROs

There are two ways in which a settlement of pension rights can be made under a Qualified Domestic Relations Order (QDRO):

- an immediate cash settlement (which is often made from non-pension sources)
- a settlement under which payments to the nonparticipant spouse are deferred until payments are due to the participant spouse

In both cases valuation is fundamental. Before the parties can agree on how to divide the pension, its value must be determined. If the plan is a defined-contribution plan, valuation is relatively easy; the participant has an individual account and the plan sponsor must provide its value to the participant at least annually. However, if participation in the plan has extended over a period longer than the marriage, this amount must be reduced by a "coverture fraction" that is based on the relation between the length of the marriage and the duration of the plan coverage. This can be a simple mathematical ratio, or it can reflect rates of contribution and interest over time.

If the plan is a defined-benefit plan, the parties will probably need an actuary's assistance in determining the present dollar value of pension benefits. For a participant in a defined-benefit plan, the benefit at any time before retirement is expressed as an amount of expected pension at retirement age that the participant has accrued up to that point. For example, if the participant is aged 45, the plan might express his accrued benefit as "$10,000 per month beginning at age 65." In order to determine current worth, at age 45, an actuarial calculation must be made. In this calculation, the interest rate and mortality assumptions are critical. The assumptions don't necessarily have to be the same as those used by the plan for funding purposes. There is no federal standard for actuarial assumptions in this area, although PBGC interest rates for valuing plans on termination are sometimes used as guidelines. The total amount determined must also be multiplied by a coverture fraction, as for the defined-contribution plan where the participant was not married to the current (imminently departing) spouse during the entire time of his or her plan coverage.

Many open and controversial issues exist in these determinations. For example, should the valuation take taxes into account? What about inflation? Or possible future increases in the participant's salary? These are issues of state law that may vary and may not have been considered or decided by the state's courts. The use of an expert actuary is advisable, particularly in disputed cases, so that the actuarial assumptions and other valuation assumptions can be supported in court proceedings if necessary.

A fourth roadblock to saving for retirement occurs in the case of a divorced client. Divorce often leaves one or both parties with little or no accumulation of pension benefits or other private sources of retirement income. They only have a short time to accumulate any retirement income and are not able to earn significant pension or social security benefits. If the marriage lasted 10 years or longer, divorced persons are eligible for social security based on their former spouse's earnings record. In addition, a spouse may be entitled to a portion of the former spouse's retirement benefits if the divorce decree includes a qualified domestic relations order (QDRO). QDROs are judgments, decrees, or orders issued by state courts that allow a participant's plan assets to be used for marital property rights, child support, or alimony payments to a former spouse or dependent.

Another common retirement planning problem is the lack of a retirement plan at the place of employment. Some workers have never had the opportunity to participate in a qualified pension plan because their employer(s) did not provide such benefits.

Workers who have frequently changed employers also face the problem of arriving at retirement with little or no pension. Statistics show that employees today are unlikely to remain with one employer for their working life and will typically hold seven full-time jobs during their career. Generally these people will not accumulate vested pension benefits because they never stayed with an employer long enough to become vested. Even if they did become vested, they may have received a distribution of their accumulated pension fund upon leaving the job and probably spent this money rather than investing it or rolling it over for retirement. (*Planning Note:* Advise clients who change jobs to roll over vested benefits into an IRA or into their new qualified plan to preserve the tax-deferred growth on their retirement funds. Advise clients who have recently changed jobs that if they have not met the participation requirements of their new employer's plan, then annual tax-deductible contributions can be made to an IRA in those years, regardless of salary.)

Loss of assets held jointly with children or others who experience debt problems is another reason people have insufficient retirement assets. Some parents have had disastrous experiences when they have put investment assets or property in joint names with children. Problems occur because debts of their children can subject the retirees' assets to creditor's claims, forfeiture in bankruptcy, or foreclosure. Such events could happen for reasons such as an auto accident, unemployment, or the joint owner's disability.

A final impediment to acquiring adequate retirement savings is the tendency to direct retirement funds for other purposes. The down payment on a primary residence and/or vacation home and the education of children can consume any long-term savings that people have managed to accumulate. Since these objectives have a greater urgency for completion than retirement, they supplant retirement as a saving priority. Although these objectives are worthy, it is important to remind clients that savings must be carved out for retirement purposes in addition to other long-term objectives.

Whatever distractions face your clients, it is important to educate them about the need to plan and save for retirement. Clients must realize that saving is possible only for a limited time period during their life, but consumption occurs throughout their lives and can drastically increase at any time because of illness or inflation. This imbalance makes it essential for clients to save sufficient assets during the working years in order to ensure attainment of retirement goals. You cannot force clients to make lifestyle choices that will provide an adequate source of retirement funds. You can, however, make clients aware of the large sums needed for retirement and point out that a spendthrift lifestyle (one which uses the full aftertax income to support the current standard of living) hurts retirees in two ways. First, it minimizes their ability to accumulate savings that will produce an adequate income stream to complement their employer pension and social security. Second, retirees become accustomed to an unnaturally high standard of living. By living below their means before retirement, clients will establish a lifestyle that is more easily maintained in the retirement years. You can motivate clients to undertake a savings plan by first helping them to identify the retirement objectives for which they should be striving.

RETIREMENT OBJECTIVES

Clients' objectives will vary significantly depending on many factors, including health, age, marital status, number and ages of children, differences in the ages of the husband and wife, and personal preferences. Table 19-1 contains a ranking of some typical retirement objectives. (The ranking identifies how a surveyed group of CLUs, ChFCs, and members of the Registry of Financial Planning Practitioners feel their clients would generally rate their retirement objectives.)

TABLE 19-1
Ranking of Retirement Objectives in Order of Priority
Retirement Objectives
1. Maintaining preretirement standard of living 2. Maintaining economic self-sufficiency 3. Minimizing taxes 4. Retiring early 5. Adapting to noneconomic aspects of retirement 6. Passing on wealth to others 7. Improving lifestyle in retirement 8. Caring for dependents

Maintaining Preretirement Standard of Living

Maintaining their preretirement standard of living despite the loss of income from employment can mean a variety of things to clients. For some clients it may mean being able to stay where they are (in the same home or the same area) without a dramatic loss of purchasing power. Other clients may be willing to move to a less costly area in order to maintain their purchasing power. Clients who are active in leisure activities such as golf or clients who hold memberships in such groups as the local Rotary club will want to continue (if not expand) these activities. It is important to remind clients that a continued subscription to the local orchestra's performances or continued winter trips to Florida can be as important a planning objective as providing food and shelter. (*Planning Note:* The client's priorities often differ from the planner's. Thus planners should be careful not to impose their own values on the client.)

Maintaining Economic Self-Sufficiency

An objective that goes hand in hand with maintaining one's preretirement standard of living is the desire to remain self-sufficient throughout retirement. Many clients fear becoming dependent on children, charity, or the government. Financial independence takes on even more importance when one considers that many other constraints may be imposed on their independence such as their ability to work or be mobile.

Minimizing Taxes

An important objective common to all clients is their desire to be taxwise regarding their retirement funds. Paying the least amount of taxes on their retirement distribution(s) (chapter 26), investing for the best aftertax yield (chapter 24), and maximizing tax-shelter opportunities with their retirement capital (chapter 24) are special priorities that your clients will have. One reason clients strive for tax savings is a propensity to play the tax-game by concentrating on tax consequences as opposed to economic consequences. While this motivation *may* serve your clients in the proper manner, their primary concern should be aftertax income, not paying less taxes, and a risky venture that promises tax deductions may not be as profitable as some taxed investments.

Retiring Early

A characteristic of modern times is that many people want to "get out of the rat race" as soon as possible. According to a study done by Charles D. Spencer & Associates, most workers choose to retire prior to age 65 (see table 19-2). This data shows that early retirement is a common client priority. If a client seeks an early retirement, it is even more important to start retirement planning at a young age and to accurately estimate or even overestimate the retirement need. These extra precautions are necessary because the lengthened retirement period is subject to compounded increases in inflation. Furthermore the shortened preretirement period is subject to increased drain on current cash in order to fund the extended retirement period and pre-age 65 costs for medical protection.

TABLE 19-2
1994 Retirement Experience*

Timing of Retirement	Number	Percent of Total
Retirement prior to age 65	14,001	74.78%
Retirement at age 65	2,004	10.70
Retirement after age 65	2,229	11.91
Disability retirement, all ages	488	2.61
Total	18,722	100.00

*Based on a survey by Charles D. Spencer & Associates of the 1994 retirement experience of 144 private sector corporations. From Spencer Research Reports, June 9, 1994.

Adapting to Noneconomic Aspects of Retirement

In addition to the relevant economic objectives your clients will have to meet, they will also have noneconomic objectives, such as

- using leisure time more effectively
- adapting to a nonworking environment
- coping with deteriorating health
- adapting to a fixed income
- relocating after retirement
- finding the best residence for the retirement years

These and other noneconomic factors also have important economic implications. For example, relocating after retirement can affect the overall pool of retirement assets because the sale of the home may provide surplus assets.

Passing on Wealth to Others

For some clients the wherewithal for an adequate retirement income is not the problem. Instead the problem is how to plan their estate without subjecting the "family money" to inheritance or gift taxes. These clients present the financial services professional with an entirely different set of planning problems. In essence, the need is not to secure enough money to finance retirement but rather to shelter as much as possible from taxes as money passes from generation to generation.

Improving Lifestyle in Retirement

Clients with the objective of improving their lifestyle in the retirement years are willing to make extra sacrifices prior to retirement in order to enjoy some luxuries, such as travel, during retirement. Another set of planning problems is created if the person's objective is to plan for a more costly lifestyle during retirement. These individuals will need extra resources in order to fulfill their dreams.

Caring for Dependents

Another retirement objective for some people is to have the ability to support a dependent. This typically occurs when a dependent needs frequent physical or medical care. Special and distinct planning considerations are required depending on whether the dependent is a child, sibling, or parent. In addition to the normal living expenses during the dependent's life expectancy, the planner must also consider whether there will be medical bills, additional living expenses, and any other financial drains on the client's retirement income.

**YOUR FINANCIAL SERVICES PRACTICE:
IMAGE-BUILDING MATERIALS**

Asking clients to complete a questionnaire concerning their retirement goals will help them think about their retirement objectives as well as acquire valuable information. The questionnaire should include a list of common client goals with room for the clients to explain exactly how these goals relate to them. Both the financial and nonfinancial aspects of retirement planning should be included. For clients near retirement a retirement information sheet should be provided as a companion to the survey. The information sheet should contain (1) local phone numbers, such as the social security office, the senior citizens office, and the American Association of Retired Persons; (2) information about local stores that give discounts to the retired; and (3) a listing of benefits for the retired provided by the local government, such as bus fare discounts.

Other Objectives

In addition to the general retirement objectives, your client may have one or more of the following specific retirement objectives:

- *providing for secure investments*—investing assets to minimize potential losses and make the client feel secure about his or her investments
- *coping with health care costs*—purchasing a medicare supplement may be required to cover health care costs not covered under the medicare program

- *continuing the family business*—special planning is needed for clients who would like to see their business successfully continue after their retirement
- *obtaining reasonable value for the sale of a closely held business*—maximizing the amount received upon the sale of a business if clients wish to discontinue operations after retirement
- *staying as healthy as possible*—ensuring adequate funding for health clubs and other leisure activities

THE RETIREMENT PLANNER

Holistic Retirement Planning

Retirement planning is a multidimensional field that requires the planner to be schooled in the nuances of many financial planning specialties as well as other areas. Unfortunately many so-called planners approach retirement planning from only one point of view (for example, investments). The perspective offered by specializing, however, is inadequate for dealing with the diversified needs of the would-be retiree. A client is better served by a team of planners who have specialized backgrounds that are complementary or by a single planner who is experienced in a variety of important retirement topics.

Whether the retirement team or the multitalented individual is the vehicle, the holistic approach to retirement planning is the only means by which a client's needs can be fully and adequately met. Under the holistic approach to retirement planning, the planner is required to communicate with clients concerning the following topics:

- employer-provided retirement plans
- social security
- income tax issues
- insurance coverage
- investments
- long-term care options
- retirement communities
- relocation possibilities
- wellness
- nutrition
- lifestyle choices

Your Retirement Planning Practice

A 1987 survey conducted by The American College found that over 80 percent of the participants, including CLUs, ChFCs, and members of the Registry of Financial Planning Practitioners, anticipated increasing the time they spend providing retirement planning for clients. In the same survey, over 70 percent of the respondents indicated that they expected to increase the number of clients for whom they provide retirement-planning advice. These statistics are indicative of a trend among financial services professionals to include or expand retirement planning in their financial services practice. The reason for this trend is that many planners feel that retirement planning is a better way to serve existing clients and is an integral part of comprehensive financial planning. Planners also feel that having a reputation as a retirement planner makes them more appealing to new clients.

Retirement planning requires planners to undertake several responsibilities that may not have been a part of their traditional financial practice. These aspects of a retirement planning practice include the following:

- *incorporating retirement planning as a segment of comprehensive financial planning.* This means using financial planning techniques such as fact finding, budgeting, income-flow regulating, and rendering investment advice.

- *dealing with other professionals who advise the client.* These professionals include the client's lawyer, accountant, banker, investment adviser, and—if the planner is not the client's sole insurance agent— other insurance agents. By communicating with this group planners gain many advantages, including a better understanding of the client's needs, a team approach for motivating the client to save for retirement, and referral sources for future business.

- *dealing with relatively young clients.* One common mistake is to start retirement planning only after a client has satisfied his or her other long-term responsibilities such as buying a home or educating a child. Retirement planning is best, however, if clients start saving for retirement at a relatively young age. For this reason an insurance agent who has the advantage of seeing clients before other professionals can frequently become their primary retirement planner. (*Planning Note:* When approaching a younger client about retirement, planners often refer to retirement planning as "financial independence planning.")

- *monitoring and updating the client's plan.* The client's plan needs continued service because of changes in family circumstances (such as job changes, births, deaths, divorces, and the acquisition of inheritances) and because of changes in the tax and economic environment.

- *conducting seminars for employers.* Many planners are asking employers for time to speak to employees during working hours. The employer sees this as an opportunity to provide a low-cost employee benefit, and the employees appreciate a retirement-planning seminar offered by the employer. Planners who are also designing the employer's qualified or nonqualified plan can point out to the employer that work-sponsored retirement-planning seminars help the plan accomplish its main objective—a successful retirement for employees.

In addition to undertaking these obligations, retirement planners must also familiarize themselves with the various resources available in the retirement-planning field. Organizations such as the American Society of CLU & ChFC, the International Association of Financial Planners, and the International Society of Retirement Planners offer a forum that provides newsletters, conferences, and a chance for interaction with other planners. In addition, planners should make their clients aware of the American Association of Retired Persons (AARP), an organization that provides information on services for the elderly and is a valuable resource for retirement information. Planners may also want to have their library include the following sources:

- *Comprehensive financial planning software* such as that offered by Softbridge, Inc. This software often contains retirement-planning data sheets.
- *Retirement Planning*, Vicker (demonstrates how to start a lifetime money-management program, talks about planning for retirement, investing, and provides an overview of the many retirement-planning considerations)
- *Modern Maturity*, AARP (the widely read retirement magazine published by AARP)
- *Home Health Care Services Quarterly*, Reif and Trager (covers all aspects of nutrition for the elderly)
- *Journal of Housing for the Elderly*, Pastalan (talks about the home equity resource and retiring to public housing)
- *Retirement Communities*, Hunt (discusses retirement communities in the United States)
- *The Encyclopedia of Aging*, Maddox (provides a comprehensive look at aging)
- *Long-Term Care*, Hughes (discusses the providers of and delivery systems for long-term care)
- *Guide to Social Security*, Detlefs and Meyers (complete booklet that answers a variety of social security questions)
- *Comfort Zones*, Chapman (a workbook used at most employee retirement-planning seminars that helps the preretiree better understand the future)

20

Planning for the Client's Needs

Chapter Outline

There are many factors that affect a client's ability to achieve his or her retirement goals. Despite careful planning, events occur that are beyond the client's control (for example, a merger or plant closing that forces the client into early retirement). Furthermore, as people mature their goals and situations also change. In addition, the fact that each client is unique and requires planning that accommodates his or her individual needs provides a challenge that will test the best of planners. This chapter explores this challenge and provides strategies that deal with the many obstacles to effective retirement planning.

THE NATURE OF CLIENTS AND THE ROLE OF THE PLANNER

It is often said by financial services professionals that the only thing that clients have in common is that they are different. As a planner you must become familiar with each client's attitude and conduct retirement planning consistent with the unique situations that make up the client's profile. Understanding these factors starts with an overview of the following:

- attitudes toward retirement
- health issues
- perception of life expectancy
- attitudes toward saving for retirement
- client investment savvy
- stability of the marriage

(*Planning Note:* For retirement-planning purposes the "client" constitutes *both* the husband and wife. Many planners mistakenly meet with only one spouse and later find out that the retirement plan must be revamped to accommodate the other spouse's input. For this reason when dealing with married individuals, planners should make every effort to understand the feelings of both the husband and wife and the influence each exerts over important planning decisions.)

Attitudes toward Retirement

Planners should take into account their clients' attitudes toward retirement when developing a retirement plan. In general, clients who have many activities that they have been unable to pursue because of the demands of the workplace usually look forward to retiring as soon as it is economically feasible. Retirement is not a panacea for all workers, however. Persons who have no outside interests or hobbies to pursue after they leave the workforce often find retirement boring and unfulfilling. For these individuals retirement takes the regimen out of life by eliminating the scheduled workday.

Clients may defer retirement as long as desired because recent amendments to the Age Discrimination in Employment Act (ADEA) prohibit involuntary retirement at any age (subject to a few exceptions, such as the exception for certain highly paid executives). On the other hand, there has been a recent trend among employers to offer employees lump-sum incentive payments to take early retirement. These so-called golden handshakes coupled with the possibility to take early retirement under qualified plans have enticed many to leave employment early.

From a financial standpoint the longer retirement is deferred, the better it is for the client. Continued employment generally means an opportunity to continue the accumulation of assets for retirement and the continuation of full medical benefits. In addition, some less obvious benefits of continued employment exist. These benefits include

- inflation protection, assuming your client's salary keeps pace with inflation
- continuation of employment-related activities, such as memberships in athletic clubs and other organizations
- travel on behalf of the employer, which makes it less costly to travel with the spouse because the client need only pay the spouse's costs

- continued interaction with colleagues in the workplace
- a bolstered sense of self-esteem for clients who base their sense of self-worth on employment production

Health Issues

In addition to your client's attitude toward retirement, you must also account for your client's health when planning for retirement. Persons in extremely poor health may not be able to continue employment after early retirement regardless of their desire to continue working. In contrast, persons in good health may decide to remain in the workforce until normal retirement age or to defer retirement beyond normal retirement age. Be wary, however, because health issues are not restricted to the client alone but may also encompass family members. For example, a spouse in extremely poor health may need extra care and attention that could be provided by the employed spouse. This can serve as an impetus to retire early. In addition, a permanently disabled child who requires expensive care may make the worker feel that employment must be continued as long as possible regardless of his or her own health.

When developing a client's retirement plan, it may be impossible to say with certainty whether a given health condition will prompt the client to retire early or to remain longer in the workforce. It is important, however, to recognize that the client's retirement plan may have to be adapted to changes in the health of the client or of his or her family.

Perception of Life Expectancy

As we shall see later, one of the most important assumptions a planner will make when liquidating retirement assets is the life expectancy of the client. Therefore the planner must be familiar with the client's perception of his or her life expectancy and, if married, his or her spouse's life expectancy. This perception is often generated by the ages at which parents and grandparents have died. If family life expectancy reaches into the 80s and beyond, the client is often concerned about the adequacy of accumulated funds for the enjoyment of a relatively long retirement. Conversely, in families where most relatives die before the end of their 60s, working family members frequently seek early retirement in order to enjoy some of their accumulated retirement benefits. Persons whose ancestors have widely varied life expectancies may not have any strong personal perception about their own life expectancy. In any case, the planner should also keep in mind the projected life expectancies used by insurance companies for annuity purposes (appendix 3). These life expectancies provide guidelines for choosing life-expectancy assumptions. Note that many planners typically add 5 to 10 years to a life expectancy because the effect of using a projected life expectancy and consequently underestimating the actual life span can be disastrous.

Attitudes toward Saving for Retirement

Most retirement planning comes down to a question of now or later. Is the individual willing to allocate funds toward retirement now and reduce current standard of living so that an adequate standard of living will be possible during retirement? Conversely, is there an unwillingness to reduce the current living standard and allocate funds toward retirement that will result in a forced reduction in the standard of living at the onset of retirement? Most clients easily consume their disposable income during years of employment. Human wants seem to be insatiable as spending up to and beyond an individual's means is typical. Furthermore, people would like to increase whatever standard-of-living level they currently enjoy. However, by cutting back on the standard of living (or forsaking increases) during the employment years, individuals can accumulate assets and sources of income that will help fund retirement needs. Compound interest and the ability to secure higher yields on long-term investments allow clients to accumulate sizable funds over long periods of time with relatively small periodic contributions.

Example: Jane Jones (aged 30, 28 percent tax bracket) can accumulate $400,000 by the time she reaches age 65 by investing $251 a month between the ages of 30 and 65 (assuming a 9 percent taxable yield). If, however, Jane waited until age 55, she would be required to invest $2,378 a month (at 9 percent taxable yield) to acquire the same $400,000.

**YOUR FINANCIAL SERVICES PRACTICE:
CASH VALUE LIFE INSURANCE AND ANNUITIES**

Two products that can be used to accomplish the goal of periodic saving over a long accumulation period are cash value life insurance and deferred annuities.

Cash value life insurance holds the following retirement planning advantages:

- Forced savings occur in a painless way. If the premiums are paid in a direct deposit manner, the client never has a chance to spend the money.
- Cash-value buildup is tax deferred until withdrawn at retirement.
- Interest rates used with some products are market sensitive and yield earnings that may outdistance inflation.
- Death benefits are offered which can be used for a surviving spouse's retirement.

If there is no need for additional life insurance protection, deferred-annuity contracts are well suited for accumulation and provide many of the advantages offered by cash value life insurance, including forced savings, tax deferral, and market-sensitive yields, without the expenses associated with the life insurance element. Flexible premium annuities are also available for those who are unable to make level premium payments.

Investment Savvy of the Client

A 1985 survey of American households by *Money* magazine concludes, "Americans are . . . remarkably ill-informed about the nuts and bolts of personal finance." Only 50 percent of those surveyed understand bank certificates of deposit or IRAs. If these are accurate percentages for such relatively simple products, consider for a moment what the percentages might be for more complex investments such as common stocks, options, real estate syndications, or futures.

It is essential for the planner to ascertain the degree of the client's investment expertise for two reasons. First, to recommend investment vehicles that go beyond the understanding of the client would be unproductive. If the client lacks understanding, the planner should explain the investment characteristics of the vehicles being suggested. Second, for every investment alternative that is suggested investment risks must be thoroughly explained to prevent unpleasant surprises for the client and potential legal liability for the planner. In addition to educating clients about the risk characteristics of various investment media, the planner must assess the propensity of both the client and spouse to accept risk. In general, many Americans want to avoid undue risk when it affects their financial affairs. Consequently most clients will tend to opt for investment media that produce relatively low returns. A second consequence of your client's risk propensity is that any recommended investments must be consistent with the client's risk profile; otherwise, the recommendation will either not be accepted or, if acquired, will not be retained.

Stability of the Marriage

When assembling a retirement plan, it is essential that you become aware of the status of the client's marriage. If a divorce or separation is a possibility, separate retirement planning for each spouse (although funded out of the family income) may be prudent. Even if the marriage seems sound, the high divorce rate and the increasing frequency of both spouses being employed dictate that the planner raise the issue of separate planning with both parties. Regardless of the status of the marriage, however, the client must make the decision and the planner should not force a client into an awkward situation.

Not only are the consequences of divorce important for the planner to consider, but it is also important to consider the consequences of remarriage on the retirement plan. This is particularly important when there are children from the prior marriage(s). Until the children are self-supporting, child support and education payments may constrain the noncustodial parent's ability to adequately plan for retirement. In addition, a client might want to provide for offspring from several marriages after his or her death. When this is the case, target amounts for retirement income purposes are established that do not include liquidation of principal during retirement.

STRATEGIES FOR THE CLIENT'S SITUATION

One of the most challenging aspects to retirement planning is dealing with the many issues confronting clients. These issues include a variety of personal decisions that are made by your client (such as the desire to relocate after retirement) or that are a result of the client's specific circumstances (such as the ownership of a business). In either case any retirement plan must effectively accommodate the client's personal decisions or account for the client's special circumstances.

Planning for a Business Owner

Retirement planning for clients who have an ownership interest in a business is strongly influenced by the nature of the business, the decision-making power of the client, and the long-term stability of the business. These factors determine whether the client has the influence to maximize contributions or benefits under the qualified plan, whether (or to what extent) saving outside the business is necessary, and whether the client will be able to use his or her ownership-interest as a retirement asset. For example, if the client has the ability to maximize benefits under a business's qualified plan, then little, if any, additional retirement saving will be necessary. Furthermore, funds saved in a qualified plan are not subject to the reach of the business's general creditors in case of bankruptcy. On the other hand, a business owner may be forced to forgo making contributions to a qualified plan or to tap personal retirement funds to keep the business from failing, and the business may go bankrupt in spite of these efforts.

When planning for the business owner the planner's primary obligation is to set up a qualified plan for the business and to monitor the plan to make sure it meets the retirement planning needs of the business owner. Reason: Provided saving for retirement is economically feasible, the tax advantages available under a qualified plan make this plan the most effective method of saving for retirement. In the event that the business owner has maximized contributions or benefits under a qualified plan or it is prohibitively expensive to maximize benefits because of the nondiscrimination requirements for qualified plans, an alternate plan can be set up to save funds for the owners on a nonqualified basis, or the client can use personal income from the business for retirement savings.

In addition to becoming involved with the client's qualified plan, nonqualified plan, and individual retirement savings from company compensation, the planner must also

- *monitor the performance of the business*—retirement planning must account for the fact that a failing business will put constraints on savings and a successful business will require special tax planning
- *account for the business owner's ability to receive payment for business interests sold at retirement*—this can involve setting up a buy-sell

agreement that includes methods for valuing the business whenever needed

- *plan for the continued employment of the former business owner as a consultant to the business*—especially if the business remains in the family

Planning for the Client Whose Plan Is Terminated

When your client is not the business owner, he or she may still be a participant in a company pension plan. Your client may be counting on this plan to provide a significant portion of his or her retirement benefit and will be quite upset if the plan is terminated. You should be aware of the protection that the law provides your client in such a case. The law provides that if a plan is terminated (or partially terminated), participants under the plan are endowed with certain rights. One of the most important rights is that the participant becomes 100 percent vested in the account balance (defined-contribution plans) or accrued benefit (defined-benefit plans). One hundred percent vesting occurs whether the participant was zero percent vested or 80 percent vested on the day before the termination. A second right that your clients have is to be informed by the employer about the terminations. Employer communications include

- a notice of the termination
- a notice that the IRS's approval of the termination is being sought
- modifications of the summary plan description, describing coincident changes to the terms of the plan
- the issuance of election forms that explain distribution options, describe the tax consequences of each option, and request participant elections

For participants in a defined-benefit plan the consequences of plan termination trigger PBGC protection. If the employer is unable to make benefit payments, the PBGC will guarantee the payment of certain benefits known as basic benefits (special benefits and benefits that become vested due to the plan termination are generally not covered). The PBGC insurance only covers up to a maximum benefit level. The maximum insured benefit equals the lesser of

- $2,642 (as indexed in 1996) a month, adjusted upward each year to reflect changes in the social security wage base, or
- 100 percent of average monthly wages during the participant's 5 highest-paid consecutive years

Since not all benefits are guaranteed by the PBGC, participants may not get all their benefits. Also some defined-benefit plans are not covered under the PBGC insurance program, and these plans may terminate with insufficient assets to pay benefits. In either case, the insufficient assets are distributed to participants in a required priority. From high to low priority, the order is

- employee voluntary contributions
- employee mandatory contributions
- annuity payments begun at least 6 years before the termination of the plan
- all other guaranteed benefits
- all other vested benefits
- all other benefits under the plan

If the plan owns life insurance policies, it may, and generally will, allow participants the right to purchase the policies. If the participant elects to receive the policy, he or she will be taxed on the cash value of the policy less any basis (PS 58 costs) and will assume premium payments thereafter. To minimize taxation, the trustee can take out the full loan value of the policy and have the stripped policy distributed out of the plan. If the trustee takes out the loan, the loan proceeds will then be distributed to the participant as part of the cash portion of his or her distribution.

Coordinating Retirement Planning with Estate Planning

For some clients retirement planning plays a secondary role to estate planning. In many respects the goals of retirement and estate planning seem incongruous. Retirement planning involves the accumulation of funds primarily for consumption during the client's (and/or spouse's) retirement. The primary goal of retirement planning is to maintain the preretirement lifestyle. This generally requires the expenditure of a significant percentage of the client's accumulated wealth, particularly if the client lives well past the chosen retirement age.

The primary goal of estate planning, on the other hand, is to accumulate assets during the client's lifetime for the appropriate distribution to selected heirs at a client's death. Generally speaking, clients wish to pass as much wealth to their heirs as circumstances permit. Methods employed to reach this goal include the conservation of wealth during retirement and minimization of the federal and state tax costs of transferring wealth.

The first of these methods requires little explanation. The less wealth consumed by a client during retirement, the greater the distributable estate will be at his or her death. The ability to conserve wealth during retirement is a client-specific question. That is, the amount of wealth consumed necessarily depends upon the client's target retirement lifestyle, continued health, and actual lifespan.

The minimization of estate taxes depends on the answer to the "who," "what," and "how" questions. The "who" question determines the level of transfer tax based on the target of the client's distribution. The net amount of assets passing to heirs depends upon their relationship to your client. Assets passed to the surviving spouse will be free of transfer taxes under typical circumstances due to a federally permitted 100 percent marital deduction. A new generation-skipping transfer tax, however, may cause a double federal tax burden for gifts or bequests to grandchildren. Furthermore, state transfer taxes are often higher if assets are distributed outside of the client's lineal heirs.

The "what" question refers to the difference in taxes resulting from various types of transferred wealth. Under some circumstances property is transferred to the surviving spouse free of federal estate tax. In other circumstances, however, transfers to a spouse will not qualify for the estate tax marital deduction. For this reason a large part of the estate-retirement planning dichotomy is the determination by the client of which assets to consume during retirement and which to leave to his or her heirs. (*Planning Note:* Because there are estate tax implications concerning consumption of certain assets during retirement, planners should consult with their clients' estate planner to determine which assets should be used during retirement and which assets should be left intact.)

Finally, the "how" decision determines the manner in which property passes to the heirs. Some transfer mechanisms create greater tax liability than others. For example, direct probate transfers cause full imposition of estate and/or inheritance tax (ignoring marital deduction and unified credit). On the other hand, properly designed irrevocable life-insurance-trust transfers will result in substantial wealth passing to the beneficiaries at zero tax costs. Of course, the client may have to reduce current consumption and lose some degree of control to gain these transfer planning advantages.

Planning for a Homeowner

Retirement planning for a homeowner requires special consideration regardless of whether the homeowner intends to continue ownership after retirement or relocate to a new residence.

Continuing to Live in the Preretirement Residence

If your client decides to stay in the preretirement residence, you must account for the stream of mortgage payments, if any, and the cost of home maintenance and repair when determining the postretirement standard of living. From an emotional standpoint continued ownership may be desirable considering that the very act of retirement is sufficiently stressful without experiencing other important lifestyle changes at the same time. From an economic standpoint, however, it may be desirable for the client to take some equity out of the home to be used for retirement purposes. Even a mortgage-free house can be costing your client income. Reason: The equity that can be pulled from a home can be annuitized or used as capital to produce an income stream for retirement.

If your client would like to take some equity out of his or her house but is reluctant to leave the home, alternatives are available that can achieve the desired results without bringing the negative consequences. One option is to engage in a transaction known as a reverse annuity mortgage (RAM). Under one type of reverse annuity mortgage the client sells a remainder interest in the home but retains the right to occupy the house until death. The purchaser of the remainder interest acquires the right to take possession of the property after the homeowner's death (or the death of the homeowner and the spouse). The consideration for acquiring the remainder interest in the house is that the purchaser agrees to make periodic payments to the seller during the seller's life.

Under another type of reverse annuity mortgage the annuity payments plus interest are held as a series of loans against the value of the home. In this case the amount paid out in an income stream plus interest will be recovered by the lender from eventual sale proceeds after the death of the retiree.

The reverse annuity mortgage is a relatively new concept, and only a few financial institutions are currently active in this market. Therefore this option may not be available in all parts of the country or to all those homeowners in areas where the service is available. A second potential impediment to the use of a reverse annuity mortgage is that the homeowner may not have enough home-equity to make a reverse annuity mortgage feasible. This is especially true for clients who have just recently taken out a second mortgage on their home. A third problem with a reverse annuity mortgage is that the financial institution making the purchase has a vested interest in preserving the value of the property. This typically means that the client must go through the unpleasant tasks of (1) acquiring permission to make renovations, (2) maintaining the property according to contractual specifications, and (3) allowing periodic inspections of the property by the purchaser. (*Planning Note:* Reverse annuity mortgages have not yet become popular because of the feeling clients have about giving up their home. Furthermore the feelings of clients' children may preclude this course of action. Make sure the family has settled the matter before proceeding with the transaction.)

A second option available to the client who wants to remain in his or her home but needs to capitalize on its value is to rent space to occupants. A tenant may prove to be not only a valuable financial resource but also a companion for the retiree. Conversely, minor alterations of the property could be made so that the retiree and the tenant have full privacy. (*Planning Note:* Have your clients check with their local zoning boards before renting out space. In some communities taking in tenants may not be permitted, or the town may impose restrictions on the property. In addition, have the client check his or her homeowner's policy to see if additional coverage is necessary.)

Another means of unlocking the equity tied up in your client's home while allowing the client to remain in the residence is a sale-leaseback arrangement. Under a sale-leaseback your client sells the house to an investor and rents the property from the investor for the rest of his or her life (or if married, both lives). The sale-leaseback agreement can specify future rents or can provide for an agreement about how changes in the rental rate will be determined (for example, a periodic market value appraisal by a neutral third party).

The most desirable type of a sale-leaseback involves younger family members buying the home for investment purposes. The family relationship between the buyer and seller often makes the arrangement run more smoothly. Regardless of who the buyer is, however, the new owner will be able to deduct mortgage interest, depreciation, and other expenses, and must include the rents as income.

Relocation to a Retirement Residence

If your client decides to sell his or her home and relocate to a smaller, less expensive residence, the money made available from the transactions should be counted as a retirement asset. For example, if your client can sell the house for $200,000 after taxes and relocate to a new residence costing $100,000, the extra $100,000 can be used to produce an extra $10,000 a year in income (assuming a 10 percent interest rate). As discussed, this can be very desirable from a financial perspective because retirees can capitalize on what for many is their single most important financial asset—their home. In addition, this can be very desirable from a tax standpoint because the IRS allows a one-time exclusion of up to $125,000 on the taxation of gain from the sale of a home. The $125,000 exclusion is subject to the following restrictions:

- The individual taking the exclusion must be age 55 or older.
- If the individual is married and files a separate return, the exclusion is cut to $62,500.
- The exclusion only applies if the property has been owned and used by the client as a principal residence for 3 years of the 5-year period ending on the date of the sale or exchange (the years need not be consecutive).
- The client must make an election to exclude the gain from gross income.
- The exclusion can be made only once during the client's lifetime.

Another technique for using the home as a means of providing retirement income is for the retiree to enter into a split-interest purchase of property. To do this, the residence of the retiree is sold and part of the proceeds are used to purchase the retiree's interest in a different residence. However, the retiree does not have full ownership of all interests in the new residence because the property interest is separated into two distinct parts—a life estate and a remainder interest. The retiree retains a life estate and is entitled to the exclusive use and benefit from the property from the date of purchase to the date of the retiree's death. (*Planning Note:* The life estate can be a joint and survivor form whereby the spouse of the retiree would also have a life estate.) The second party to the transaction purchases the remainder interest and will receive full ownership of the property at the death of the retiree (and death of the spouse if a joint life estate were established).

A split-interest purchase of property can provide retirement income for your client in several ways. First, even if the second home is of equal market value to the one sold, the retiree is only purchasing a life estate and so the full amount of the proceeds from the sale would not be needed. In this case some of the equity in the home is available for investment in income-producing assets while the retiree has a comparable residence for retirement. Secondly, if a lesser value home is purchased, then a larger portion of the proceeds are available for investment purposes.

In addition to advising a client who is relocating about the one-time exclusion of gain from the sale of a home or a split-interest purchase of property, you must also give advice on several alternative decisions. One such decision is about the relocation itself. Typical relocation patterns today include moves to less expensive housing in the same town as well as moves to the preferable climates of southeastern or southwestern United States.

Many planners advise caution when relocating to an unfamiliar geographic area. It might be advantageous for retirees to retain ownership of their previous home by renting it out while they temporarily rent in the new geographic area. By retaining their family home retirees have a house to return to if the relocation proves to be unsatisfactory. Problems with relocations occur because retirees miss the close proximity to friends and family or because retirees move to a location where they frequently vacationed prior to retirement and find postretirement year-round living undesirable.

Whether relocating across town or across country, the client will have to decide on the type of housing facility that best suits his or her needs. In general, smaller one floor units in a home or an apartment are preferred. A smaller unit minimizes the cleaning drudgery, maintenance burdens, and heating and cooling expenses.

Some retirees choose not to move into either single family homes or apartments, but instead move into life-care retirement communities. These communities often provide some level of housekeeping and meal preparation in addition to facilities for activities, including crafts, tennis, golf, and swimming. Some of these retirement communities can be quite expensive, however, and frequently require a substantial nonrefundable fee for admission as well as an ongoing monthly fee. Paying a nonrefundable fee makes the decision almost irreversible for your client. For this reason, you should recommend that the client spend time conversing with current residents of the community and try to experience living in the community before making a financial commitment. Communities that promise lifetime care, especially those without ongoing fees, should be scrutinized by the planner. The communities' funding calculations should be based on sophisticated actuarial evaluations. An absence of proper management and financing could lead to inadequate funding and subsequent financial failure of the community. Some retirement communities failed financially from inadequate pricing and inadequate subscriptions.

Planning for Postretirement Employment

Some retirees continue working beyond retirement on a part-time basis as either a consultant to their former employer or in another capacity. Retirees who work as consultants to their former employer benefit by continuing to interact with coworkers and friends and maintaining the sense of purpose and self-worth they received from employment. Employers who hire former employees as consultants gain the advantage of being able to capitalize on the former employees' expertise, skills, and business connections.

A potential problem with providing consulting services to a former employer (or working after retirement in any capacity) is that retirees can lose social security benefits if earnings exceed specified limits. In general, for the 62- to 65-year-old retiree social security benefits will be reduced $1 for every $2 in earnings in excess of prescribed limits. For retirees aged 65 to 69 the social security reduction will be $1 for every $3 in earnings. For clients under age 65 the earnings limit is $8,640 (this 1997 figure is increased annually to reflect inflation). So if your 63-year-old client earns $10,000, his or her social security benefits will be reduced $680 annually. (To calculate the reduction, subtract the earnings limit ($8,640) from the actual amount earned ($10,000) and divide by 2.) For clients aged 65 to 69 the earnings limit is $13,500 in 1997. Note that under a new law, the earnings limit for this age group will be increased gradually until it reaches $30,000 in 2002. If a 66-year-old client earns $15,000 in 1997, his or her social security benefits will be reduced $500 annually ($15,000 actual salary minus $13,500 earnings limit, divided by 3). There is good news for clients aged 70 or older, however, because there is no reduction to social security regardless of the amount earned.

21

Determining Postretirement Monetary Needs: Preliminary Concerns

Chapter Outline

One major question that almost every individual encounters when planning for retirement is whether sufficient income and assets exist to provide for the retirement years. There is no exact method that calculates how much is enough. However, the planner can take several steps to create a workable retirement plan. This chapter and chapters 22 and 23 will explore these steps by

- addressing four crucial elements of postretirement monetary need (chapter 21)
- exploring the various sources of retirement income (chapter 22)
- providing a method for computing and for funding the client's retirement need (chapter 23)

In this chapter we will look at four of the five major components of the postretirement monetary need: the expected standard of living during retirement, the estimate of the first year's retirement needs, the expected starting date for retirement, and the expected inflation rate before and after retirement. Chapter 22 will address the fifth major factor in determining the postretirement monetary need—the client's sources of retirement income.

EXPECTED STANDARD OF LIVING DURING RETIREMENT

The standard of living enjoyed during the years just prior to retirement largely influences the client's expectations for his or her postretirement standard of living. For this reason the planner encounters different situations depending on how close the client is to his or her retirement date. With this in mind, let's examine the differences that exist between clients of various age groups.

Late-Career Clients

For almost all clients the years immediately prior to retirement represent their peak earning years and their highest standard of living. Clients who are near the end of their careers are concerned about maintaining their current standard of living. As a group these clients are the most interested in retirement planning and are the most willing to make some adjustments to their preretirement lifestyle to compensate for inadequate retirement savings. Reason: Their close proximity to retirement makes planning for retirement one of their highest priorities.

Mid-Career Clients

The client who is in the middle of his or her career has a different perspective on his or her postretirement standard of living. Employment has permitted this client to establish a comfortable standard of living, but the client envisions still further increases in income and in lifestyle. For these clients the desired standard of living during retirement will be based on their expectations of success in their career and the attendant increases in their standard of living. In other words, these clients will prefer to enjoy an unknown and yet to be realized standard of living during their retirement years. This expectation provides planners with a special challenge. Although sufficient time remains to develop and implement accumulation plans to provide for the client's retirement years, the actual retirement standard of living is speculative at best. For this reason planners must first make the best estimate possible based on the client's educational background, job experiences, personal ambitions, and career plan. The estimated retirement standard of living can be computed by applying a growth factor to the client's current salary (for example, 1 1/2 times an expected inflation rate of 4 percent) and approximating the client's final-average salary. A second method would be to estimate the current annual expenses that are owed by a person in the position the client aspires to by the end of his or her career and inflate this amount. Regardless of which method is used, it is important for planners to monitor the careers of their younger clients and make corresponding adjustments to the retirement plan to reflect the difference between their actual growth rate and their estimated growth rate. If this is done as the client gets closer to retirement, the estimated standard of living becomes more accurate.

Early-Career Clients

These clients typically have too little experience to estimate what their retirement needs will be and probably have not thought too much about the standard of living they will expect at that time. Most likely, if any such thought has been entertained, these clients anticipate a standard of living approximately equal to or slightly greater than their parents' current standard. For this reason, estimating a retirement standard of living at this stage is too tentative. The planner should instead concentrate efforts on encouraging their clients to use IRAs, to make voluntary nondeductible contributions to the employer plan, or to acquire long-term savings vehicles such as deferred annuities.

Note also that early-career clients as well as mid-career clients are less likely than a late-career client to adjust their current lifestyle for retirement planning purposes. Younger clients are more likely to be distracted by other priorities and will tend to ignore the future because current problems take precedence. In this situation the retirement planner must try to make saving for retirement a priority in spite of these distractions.

ESTIMATING THE FIRST YEAR'S INCOME

In addition to understanding the standard of living the client expects during retirement, planners must also be prepared to estimate the income stream that a client will need during retirement. One of the essential parts of this process is estimating the income that a client will need in the first year of retirement. Let's examine the two generally accepted methods for determining this, the replacement-ratio method and the expense method.

The Replacement-Ratio Method

One way to estimate how much a client will need in the first year of retirement is to apply the replacement-ratio method. The replacement-ratio method assumes that the standard of living enjoyed during the years just prior to retirement will be the determinant of the standard of living needed in the first year of retirement. Under the replacement-ratio method the planner can estimate the amount needed in the first year of retirement regardless of the client's age by using a replacement ratio that is geared to continue the same standard of living (for late-career clients) or the estimated standard of living (for mid-career clients). In general, a 70 to 90 percent replacement ratio is used. In other words, the amount of income needed to be financially independent in the first year of retirement without drastically altering the client's standard of living varies between 70 and 90 percent of the average gross annual income of the average of the last 3 years of employment. For example, if a client with an income in the years prior to retirement of $95,000, $100,000, and $105,000 respectively has an 80 percent target rate, then the client should target a replacement ratio of about $80,000 (80 percent of the $100,000 average). Support for this range rests upon the elimination of some employment-related taxes and some expected changes in spending patterns that reduce the retiree's need for income (such as expenditures that will either decrease or disappear in the retirement years).

Factors That Influence the Amount of Income Needed during Retirement

Reductions in Taxation

In many circumstances, retirees can count on a lower percentage of their income going to pay taxes in the retirement years. Some taxes are reduced or eliminated, and in other cases retirees may enjoy special favorable tax treatment. Let's take a closer look at the potential reductions in taxation that are granted to retirees.

Social Security Taxes. FICA contributions (old-age, survivors, disability, and hospital insurance) are levied solely on income from employment. Distributions from pensions, IRAs, retirement annuities, and other similar devices are not considered income subject to FICA or SECA taxes. Hence, for the retiree who stops working entirely, social security taxes are no longer an expenditure. Tables 21-1 and 21-2 indicate the amount of social security taxes that must be paid in 1997. These amounts will increase each year to reflect increases in the wage base for the old age, survivors, and disability portion of social security (in 1997, 6.2 percent of $65,400). The hospital insurance portion of social security is not subject to a wage cap, and the tax in 1997 is 1.45 percent of all covered wages.

Increased Standard Deduction. For a married taxpayer aged 65 or over, an additional $800 (in 1996) is added to the standard deduction. If the taxpayer's spouse is also 65 or older, an additional $800 increase in the standard deduction can be taken ($800 for each spouse, or $1,600 total). For any taxpayer over age 65 who is not married and does not file as a surviving spouse, $1,000 is added to the standard deduction.

TABLE 21-1
FICA Taxes That Must be Paid by Both
Employers and Employees

Salary	1995[1] FICA Tax	1996[2] FICA Tax	1997[3] FICA Tax
$ 25,000	$1,912.50	$1,912.50	$1,912.50
50,000	3,825.00	3,825.00	3,825.00
75,000	4,881.90	4,974.90	5,142.30
100,000	5,244.40	5,337.40	5,504.80
125,000	5,606.90	5,699.90	5,867.30
150,000	5,969.40	6,202.40	6,229.80

[1]6.2% x salary up to $61,200 (OASDI) + 1.45% x salary
(Medicare)
[2]6.2% x salary up to $62,700 (OASDI) + 1.45% x salary
(Medicare)
[3]6.2% x salary up to $65,400 (OASDI) + 1.45% x salary
(Medicare)

TABLE 21-2
SECA Tax Paid by Self-Employeds

Net SE Earnings	1995[1] SECA Tax	1996[2] SECA Tax	1997[3] SECA Tax
$ 25,000	$3,825.00	$3,825.00	$ 3,825.00
50,000	7,650.00	7,650.00	7,650.00
75,000	9,763.80	9,949.90	10,284.60
100,000	10,488.80	10,674.80	11,009.60
125,000	11,213.80	11,399.80	11,734.60
150,000	11,938.80	12,404.80	12,459.60

[1]12.4% x salary up to $61,200 (OASDI) + 2.9% x salary
(Medicare)
[2]12.4% x salary up to $62,700 (OASDI) + 2.9% x salary
(Medicare)
[3]12.4% x salary up to $65,400 (OASDI) + 2.9% x salary
(Medicare)

Social Security Benefits Exclusion. Until 1984, all social security benefits were received free of federal income taxation. Since then, however, the rules have changed several times, so that now many individuals are required pay tax on a large portion of their benefits. Until 1994, the maximum amount of social security benefits subject to tax was 50 percent. However, beginning in 1994, the maximum percentage increased to 85 percent for certain taxpayers.

The portion of the OASDI benefit that is subject to tax is based on what is referred to as the individual's *provisional income.* Provisional income is the sum of the following:

- the taxpayer's adjusted gross income
- the taxpayer's tax-exempt interest for the year
- half of the social security benefits for the year

If the provisional income is less than what is referred to as the *base amount*—$25,000 for a single taxpayer and $32,000 or less for a married taxpayer filing jointly—social security benefits are not taxable. If the provisional income is between the base amount and $34,000 ($44,000 for a married taxpayer filing jointly), up to 50 percent of the social security benefit will be includible in taxable income. If the provisional amount exceeds $34,000 ($44,000 for a married taxpayer filing jointly), up to 85 percent of the social security benefit will be includible in taxable income. To summarize, the table below identifies the various cutoff points.

TABLE 21-3 Portion of OASDI Benefits Subject to Federal Income Tax		
Taxpayer Filing Status	Provisional Income Threshold	Amount of Benefits Subject to Federal Income Tax
Single	under $25,000	0 percent
Single	$25,000-$33,999	up to 50 percent
Single	$34,000 or more	up to 85 percent
Married filing jointly	under $32,000	0 percent
Married filing jointly	$32,000-$43,999	up to 50 percent
Married filing jointly	$44,000 or more	up to 85 percent
Married filing separately (and living in the same household)	$0	up to 85 percent

The general description of how much is included and the various cutoffs is often sufficient for planning purposes. However, the planner may have occasion to actually calculate the specific amount of benefits includible as taxable income. The following explanation and example can be used to make this determination.

Step 1: Calculate provisional income.

Step 2: Determine appropriate thresholds, based on the individual's tax filing status.

Step 3: The amount of social security benefits included as taxable income is the smallest number obtained from performing the following three calculations:

(a) 50 percent of any provisional income that exceeds the base threshold plus 35 percent of any amount in excess of the second threshold

(b) 85 percent of the benefits

(c) 50 percent of the benefits, plus 85 percent of any amount in excess of the second threshold

Example: Peggy and Larry Novernstern are married and file jointly. They have an adjusted gross income of $40,000 (not considering social security benefits) plus $5,000 of tax-free bond interest, and are entitled to a $15,000 social security benefit.

Step 1: Provisional income equals:

preliminary adjusted gross income	$40,000
tax-free bond interest	5,000
50 percent of social security benefits	7,500
provisional income	$52,500

Step 2: Determine income in excess of the applicable thresholds.
Excess over base threshold:
($52,500 – $32,000) $20,500
Excess over second threshold:
($52,500 – $44,000) $8,500

Step 3: Amount includible in taxable income is the lowest of the following three amounts:

(a) 50 percent of excess over base threshold plus 35 percent of excess over second threshold
(.5 x $20,500 + .35 x 8,500)   = $13,225
(b) 85 percent of $15,000   = **$12,750**
(c) 50 percent of $15,000 +
85 percent of 8,500   = $14,725

In this case the $12,750 (85 percent of the benefit) is included as adjusted gross income.

State and Local Income Taxation. In some states social security benefits are fully exempt from state income taxation; in others some taxation of these benefits might occur if the state's income tax is assessed on the taxpayer's taxable income as reported for federal income tax purposes. In addition, some states grant extra income tax relief for the elderly by providing increased personal exemptions, credits, sliding scale rebates of property or other taxes (the amount or percent of which might be dependent on income), or additional tax breaks.

Deductible Medical Expenses. For taxpayers that itemize deductions it might be easier to exceed the 7.5 percent threshold for deductibility of qualifying medical expenses owing to the reduced retirement income level and often increased medical expenses.

Reduced Living Expenses

In addition to the possible reductions in taxation, retired individuals can experience reduced living expenses that permit them to maintain their same standard of living on a lower income. Let's take a closer look at some of the reduced living expenses.

Work-Related Expenses. The costs of proper clothing for work, commuting, and meals purchased during work hours are eliminated when a person retires. In addition, other expenses, such as membership dues in some professional or social clubs, may be reduced because of retired status or may be eliminated if no longer necessary.

Home Ownership Expenses. By the time of retirement, many homeowners have "burnt the mortgage" and no longer have this debt reduction expenditure. (*Planning Note:* It may be worthwhile for a client to pay off the mortgage at or near the date of retirement. This mortgage redemption not only eliminates the debt repayment expenditure but also reduces income from interest or dividends on assets used to pay the mortgage, thereby reducing income for federal and state tax purposes. For taxpayers of modest means, the income reduction might place them just below the threshold for taxation of social security benefits. Also, most of the monthly mortgage payments typically are applied to principal reduction, thus interest deductibility would be a minor tax benefit. Furthermore the interest being paid could exceed the rate of earnings on invested funds, thereby producing a real saving for the retiree.)

Absence of Dependent Children. The expense of supporting dependent children is usually completed by the time a client enters retirement. Be cautious, however, because retirees, especially those who married later in life, occasionally have children who are not self-supporting and will require continued financial support during some of the clients' retirement years.

Senior Citizen Discounts. Special reductions in price are given to senior citizens. Some reductions, such as certain AARP discounts, are available at age 50. Many businesses, however, require proof of age 65 (usually by having a medicare card) to qualify for discounts on prescriptions, clothing, and restaurant meals. Discounts typically range from 5 to 15 percent of an item's cost.

No Longer Saving for Retirement. For many retirees retirement is not a time to continue to save for retirement. Payments to contributory pension plans, lack of eligibility for IRA or Keogh plan contributions, or just the psychological fact of being retired help to weaken retirees' motivation to save for the future. Note that a retired worker's income can fall by the amount being saved with no concurrent reduction in standard of living. Therefore a retired worker who has been saving 20 percent of income needs only to maintain an "inflation protected" 80 percent (before tax) of income to enjoy the same purchasing power.

Fewer Automobiles. Retirees often consciously decide to reduce their automobile expenditures either by owning fewer automobiles or by purchasing a replacement less frequently. In either case the dollar cost for automobile insurance and the cash flow for financing automobiles tend to decline during the retirement years.

ILLUSTRATION 21-1
Justification of a 70 to 90 Percent Replacement Ratio

Joe Jones, aged 64, has a fixed salary of $100,000 and would like to maintain his current purchasing power when he retires next year. If Joe has no increased retirement-related expenses, Joe can do this by having a retirement income of 70 percent of his final salary as illustrated below. If Joe has increased retirement-related expenses, a somewhat higher figure should be used. (Note that postretirement inflation will be accounted for later.)

Working salary			$100,000
less retirement savings		18,000.00	
less FICA taxes	(TABLE 21-1)	5,504.80	
less reduction in federal taxes	(extra $1,000 deduction for being 65)	280.00	
	(no tax on portion of social security received)	1,138.40	
less annual commuting expenses to work		450.00	
less mortgage expenses	(mortgage expires on retirement date)	4,626.80	
Reductions subtotal			30,000
Total purchasing power needed at 65			$ 70,000
Percentage of final salary needed			70%

Increased Living Expenses

Some retirement planners are rather uncomfortable with recommending a planned reduction in income in the first year of retirement. These planners believe that certain factors suggest that during the first year of retirement at least as much if not more income will be required to maintain the preretirement standard of living. Let's take a closer look at these factors.

Medical Expenses. Without question medical expenses will increase over time for virtually all clients. The mere act of aging and the associated health problems generate additional demands for medical services. Even if advancing age does not create an increase in an individual's demands for medical services, inflation in these costs will. Furthermore, increases in inflation are not evenly distributed in the various medical care disciplines, and those services that will potentially affect retirees have been hit hardest. For example, the cost of hospital rooms rose 719 percent; professional medical services rose 406 percent; and prescription drugs rose 196 percent over the past 20 years. This does not consider the prices for some of the newer, more costly wonder drugs. Although retirees are often covered by medicare and other health insurance, the trend in these coverages has been toward cost containment—defined by the government and the insurance companies as that of shifting more of the medical cost to the insured by means of larger deductibles and coinsurance payments. These higher medical expenses would be in addition to the increased premiums for the insurance.

**YOUR FINANCIAL SERVICES PRACTICE:
WARNING YOUR CLIENTS ABOUT THE RISKS**

Whether or not your clients accept a 70 to 90 percent replacement ratio or feel something more is necessary, it should be stressed that there is no definitive answer to absolutely determine if the postretirement income should be less than, equal to, or greater than that of the preretirement years.

Estimating financial needs during the first year of retirement is like trying to hit a moving target when you are blindfolded: Your aim is obscured by many unknown variables and the target is hard to draw a bead on. For example, the planner and client must establish what standard of living is desired during retirement, when retirement will begin, what inflation assumptions should be made before and after retirement, and what interest can be earned on invested funds. In addition, for clients who are forced by economic necessity to liquidate their retirement nest egg, the client and planner must estimate the life expectancy over which liquidations will occur. Many of these variables can dramatically change overnight and without warning, for example:

- The client may be planning on retiring at age 65 when health considerations or perhaps a plant shutdown forces retirement at age 62.
- A younger client may be planning on a relatively moderate retirement lifestyle, but business success mandates that a more lucrative retirement lifestyle be planned.

Travel, Vacations, and Other Lifestyle Changes. Many clients expect to devote considerably more time to travel and vacations upon retirement than they did during their working years. Increased leisure time, once a scarce commodity, now provides the opportunity to travel. Unfortunately vacationing can be an expensive activity. Indeed, an increase in vacation activities represents a rise in the standard of living and will require additional income.

Dependents. As previously stated, parents usually need less income during the first year of retirement because they no longer financially support their children, who typically become self-supporting prior to parental retirement. However, many retirees still have dependents to support. Many parents have children with mental or physical problems who will require long-term custodial and financial care throughout the retirement years. Other retirees, because medical care, surgical techniques, and drugs are helping to prolong life, may have to provide for their aged parents who no longer possess the wherewithal to do so themselves.

THE EXPENSE METHOD

A second way planners can estimate their client's retirement needs is by using the expense-method approach. The expense method of retirement planning focuses on the projected expenses that the retiree will have in the first year of retirement. As with the replacement ratio method it is much easier to define the potential expenses for those clients who are at or near retirement. For example, if the 64-year-old near-retiree expects to have $3,000 in monthly bills ($36,000 annually), then the retirement income for that retiree should maintain $36,000 worth of purchasing power in today's dollars. If, however, a younger client is involved, more speculative estimates of retirement expenses must be made (and periodically revised).

A list of expenses that should be considered includes expenses that may be unique to the particular client as well as other more general expenses.

Some expenses that tend to increase for retirees include the following:

- utilities and telephone
- medical/dental/drugs/health insurance
- house upkeep/repairs/maintenance/property insurance
- recreation/entertainment/travel/dining
- contributions/gifts

Conversely, some expenses tend to decrease for the retiree. These include the following:

ILLUSTRATION 21-2
Understanding the Expense Method

Your clients, Bob and Betty Smith, both aged 64, would like to maintain their current purchasing power when they retire next year. They can do this by having an annual income of $40,860 as illustrated below. Note that the figures are estimates of their expenses during retirement (some are higher than their current expenses and some are lower than their current expenses). Also note that postretirement inflation will be accounted for later.

Estimated Retirement Living Expenses and Required Capital (in Current Dollars)

	Per Month x 12 =	Per Year
1. Food	500	6,000
2. Housing:		
a. Rent/mortgage payment	400	4,800
b. Insurance (if separate payment)	25	300
c. Property taxes (if separate payment)	150	1,800
d. Utilities	180	2,160
e. Maintenance (if owned)	100	1,200
3. Clothing and Personal Care:		
a. Wife	75	900
b. Husband	75	900
4. Medical Expenses:		
a. Doctor (HMO)	75	900
b. Dentist	20	240
c. Medicines	75	900
5. Transportation:		
a. Car payments	130	1,560
b. Gas	50	600
c. Insurance	50	600
d. Car maintenance (tires and repairs)	30	360
6. Miscellaneous Expenses:		
a. Entertainment	150	1,800
b. Travel	200	2,400
c. Hobbies	50	600
d. Other	100	1,200
e. Club fees and dues	20	240
7. Insurance	100	1,200
8. Gifts and contributions	50	600
9. State, local, and federal taxes (if any)	800	9,600
10. Total expenses (current dollars)	3,405	40,860

- mortgage payments
- food
- clothing
- income taxes
- property taxes
- transportation costs (car maintenance/insurance/other)
- debt repayment (charge accounts, personal loans)
- child support/alimony
- household furnishings

EXPECTED STARTING DATE FOR RETIREMENT

Estimating the target date for the start of retirement is another crucial element in determining postretirement monetary needs. The advent of social security in the 1930s created an image that Americans would retire when social security benefits began. Until recently most pension planning tended to support this perception by specifying retirement to occur at age 65. Thus workers and planners almost invariably planned, economically and psychologically, for retirement to begin at age 65.

This assumption may not be wise, however, when you consider the following factors:

- The retirement date for full social security benefits will be gradually increased to age 67 between 2003 and 2027.
- According to one study nearly five out of six individuals retire early.
- Health issues will affect the choice of a retirement date.
- An increasing number of individuals are forced to retire early in cases where jobs are being eliminated.
- The average retirement age of American workers is age 62.

Planners must therefore rely on their best judgment and account for the client's specific circumstances when estimating a retirement date. (*Planning Note:* If you err on the conservative side and plan for a retirement date that occurs prior to your client's actual retirement date, you will overestimate the retirement need, and consequently the client will have more funds than necessary. Conversely, a planned retirement date that occurs after the actual retirement starting date will tend to underestimate the retirement income need and leave the client with less funds than necessary.)

Planners who feel that retirement prior to age 65 is likely to occur should keep in mind its impact on their clients' pension benefits. In a defined-contribution plan the account balance will be lower than if the client continued working until normal retirement. In a defined-benefit plan early retirement benefits are usually actuarially reduced to account for the longer payout period. Therefore it is not unusual for a plan that provides a 50 percent replacement ratio of final-average salary at normal retirement age to provide a 40 percent replacement ratio at the plan's early retirement age (less, if the early retirement benefit is not subsidized by the employer). Note also that the final-average salary at an early retirement age will be less than if the client remained employed until normal retirement age. This plus the actuarial reduction tends to severely restrict the amount of pension income you can count on for a client who retires early compared to a client who retires at normal retirement age.

The planner must also account for the retirement dates for the two-wage-earner family. In two-wage-earner families the spouses will often choose to coordinate their retirement dates. If the spouses are close in age, they typically desire to retire in the same year. If a wide age disparity exists, clients typically stagger retirement dates. Keep these trends in mind when planning for the two-wage-earner family.

A final consideration when determining a target retirement date is the burdensome fixed long-term liabilities of the client. In some cases the client has very little discretion over the retirement date until these liabilities have been paid. For example, the client may have large debts from medical expenses and/or educational expenses.

EXPECTED INFLATION BEFORE AND DURING RETIREMENT

A final element that greatly affects the postretirement monetary need is the amount of expected inflation before and after retirement. Forecasting inflation is not an easy task. Lacking a crystal ball, a proxy for the expected inflation rate is needed. Since retirement income planning can encompass a long time span, one school of thought is to recommend taking a long-term view of inflation. For example, for the period from December 1951 to December 1986 inclusive, the average compound increase in prices was 4.3 percent, and proponents of the long-term view would perhaps use 4.5 percent as a reasonable measure for expected inflation.

A second school of thought suggests that the structure of the economy and prices have changed too drastically to use long-term figures. This group would argue that the figures from the last 5 or 10 years are a more appropriate measure of inflation. For the 5 years ending December 1986, the compound inflation rate was 3.3 percent; for the 10 years ending December 1986, the rate was 6.6 percent.

Rather than accept any one of these inflation rates, or any other historical rate, the planner must be aware of the forces that were operating during those periods and the forces that are likely to operate in the future. For the most recent 5-year period, oil has declined and farm prices have been relatively stable. Thus these two major components of consumer spending did not contribute to the inflation rate, and hence the 3.3 percent figure might not be sustainable for a long period of time. The 10-year rate of 6.6 percent, however, included sizable oil increases, rising farm prices, and rising interest rates; and it might have actually overstated the long-term inflation rate. Furthermore, the long-term rate of 4.3 percent from December 1951 to December 1986 included the 1950s and 1960s when inflation was not the factor that it is today and when the structure of the economy was substantially goods producing as opposed to today's service producing.

Since there is no method of determining the inflation rate based on historical data, you must use your best judgment as to future economic prospects and your clients' risk-aversion tendencies. A risk-averse client will probably want a more conservative figure projected, whereas a risk taker may feel comfortable with an optimistically low-inflation assumption. For someone in the middle, a 4 percent assumption could prove to be a viable rate to use during both the accumulation period and the retirement period. However, both you and your client must recognize that if actual inflation begins to exceed the expected rate, revisions in the planning must be made. (*Planning Note:* If you err on the conservative side and assume a higher inflation rate than the actual inflation rate, you will overestimate the retirement need and consequently the client will have more funds than necessary. Conversely, an estimate that assumes a lower inflation rate than the actual inflation rate will underestimate the retirement need and leave the client with less funds than necessary.)

ILLUSTRATING THE EFFECT OF INCREASES IN INFLATION AND STANDARD OF LIVING

In general, the higher the inflation rate and standard-of-living increases that a client experiences, the greater the amount of retirement income that will be needed. The compound interest formula can be used to make the necessary projection for the purpose of illustrating this. This formula is

$$FV = PV(1 + r)^n$$

where FV = the target dollar expenditures at retirement
PV = the dollar expenditures for the current standard of living
r = a rate of growth in the dollar expenditures for the standard of living
n = the number of years from time of planning until target retirement date

The rate of growth, or r, can stand for either (1) the rate of increase in the level of the standard of living, (2) the rate of inflation that requires more dollars being spent to maintain the current standard of living, or (3) a combination of both. For example, if no inflation is expected, but the client anticipates a 20 percent increase in his or her standard of living between now and retirement 10 years hence, the result is an average annual 1.84 percent compound increase in the standard of living and r equals .0184 in the formula. If no growth in the standard of living is anticipated before retirement, but inflation is expected to average 4 percent annually over the 10 years to retirement, then r equals .04 in the above formula.

When the standard of living is expected to rise during the planning period and inflation is expected to continue, then r, the growth rate, can be *approximated* by adding the rates of growth in both the standard of living and inflation to estimate the needed income at or during retirement. For example, if the standard of living is expected to rise at 1.84 percent annually and inflation at 4 percent annually, then the combined result is a needed 5.84 percent increase in income. In this case r equals 5.84. (For technical accuracy these rates should be multiplied together (1.0184 x 1.04 = 1.059) rather than added, but because of the many necessary assumptions about the future the inaccuracy from approximating is acceptable.)

Applying the Formula

Earlier in this chapter, we introduced three disparate clients: the late-career client, the mid-career client, and the early-career client. At this point, the concepts developed in this chapter can be applied to illustrate the effect that inflation and standard-of-living assumptions have on his or her needed retirement income.

For the purpose of simplicity, the following assumptions will apply to each client:

- target retirement at age 65
- inflation of 4 percent each year until retirement
- a retirement standard of living equal to 90 percent of the preretirement standard of living

The Late-Career Client

This client, Ed Ferguson, aged 60, currently is spending $50,000 per year to maintain his standard of living. Ed does not anticipate any increase in his standard of living between now and retirement. To begin planning for Ed's retirement, the starting point requires an estimation of his needed retirement income at and during retirement. Using the compound interest formula Ed's estimated retirement income need at age 65 would be

$$FV = \$50,000 \, (1.04)^5$$
$$FV = \$60,832$$

This is the amount Ed would be spending on standard of living before retirement. Since it is assumed that the retirement standard of living will be 10 percent less than the preretirement standard, the following adjustment determines the amount Ed needs for his first year's retirement income:

1st year   Retirement Income = 90% of preretirement standard of living
                                                          expenditures
              Retirement Income = .90 ($60,832)
              Retirement Income = $54,749

Since inflation will continue after retirement, Ed will need income in his second year of retirement.

$$FV = 54,749 (1.04)^1$$
$$FV = \$56,939$$

By the same process Ed's retirement income could be calculated for each and every year. Table 21-4 shows the retirement income needed in 5-year increments until age 80 and in 10-year increments until age 100.

Note that there will be a change in retirement needs for Ed if the inflation or standard-of-living assumptions are altered. In general, the higher the inflation and standard-of-living assumptions the greater the amount of income that is needed and vice versa. For example, if a 2 percent inflation rate is assumed and an 80 percent of final salary replacement ratio is used, Ed will need only $44,163 at age 65 (that is $10,586 less income needed at age 65 than is shown in table 21-3). If, however, a 6 percent inflation rate is assumed and a 100 percent of final salary replacement ratio is desired, Ed will need $12,162 more than shown in table 21-4 at age 65, or $66,911.

TABLE 21-4 Retirement Income for Ed Ferguson	
Ed's Age	Income
65	$ 54,749
70	66,610
75	81,042
80	98,600
90	145,951
100	216,044

The Mid-Career Client

Susan Hughes, aged 43, currently is spending $40,000 to maintain her standard of living. But Susan feels that her future is bright and she expects expenditures for standard of living will grow by 2 percent over inflation each year from now until retirement. She, like Ed in the preceding example, will want to use a 90 percent replacement ratio to maintain her preretirement standard of living. Based on this information, Susan's preretirement standard-of-living expenditures will be

$$FV = \$40,000 \ (1.06)^{22}$$
$$FV = \$144,141$$

Her first year's retirement income will be

1st year's Retirement Income $= .90 \ (\$144,141)$
1st year's Retirement Income $= \$129,727$

Table 21-5 shows the estimated retirement income for Susan until age 100 using the formula $FV = \$129,727 \ (1.04)^n$.

TABLE 21-5 Retirement Income for Susan Hughes	
Susan's Age	Income
65	$129,727
70	157,833
75	192,028
80	233,632
90	345,832
100	511,916

As with Ed, Susan's retirement income needs will vary with the inflation and replacement ratio assumptions used. In addition, if Susan expects more than a 2 percent per year growth to occur in her living standard, her retirement income need will increase. For example, if Susan expects a 4 percent per year growth to occur, she will need $195,715 at age 65 (that is $65,988 more than the amount needed at 2 percent). Note also that if Susan has a 4 percent growth per year but inflation drops to an average of 2 percent a year, then the numbers in table 21-5 will still be correct.

The Early-Career Client

John Jones, aged 25, currently spends $15,000 to maintain his standard of living. He is less optimistic about the future than Susan is and expects his standard-of-living expenditures to increase about 1.25 percent annually until retirement. He expects the standard of living during retirement to be equal to 90 percent of his last year of employment. Thus John would have anticipated standard-of-living expenditures during his last year of employment as follows:

$$FV = \$15,000 \ (1.0525)^{40}$$
$$FV = \$116,138$$

His first year's retirement income will be

1st year's Retirement Income = .90 ($116,138)
1st year's Retirement Income = $104,524

Table 21-6 shows John's retirement income needs to age 100 using a 4 percent rate of inflation.

TABLE 21-6 Retirement Income for John Jones	
John's Age	Income
65	$104,524
70	127,170
75	154,722
80	188,241
90	278,644
100	412,462

Summing Up

As can be observed from the three estimates, if the assumptions used to develop the estimated retirement income needed to maintain a particular standard of living are valid, each client will require, if he or she lives to age 100, an amount of income beyond expectations.

Suppose, however, inflation was ignored. If the inflation assumptions during employment and retirement could be zero, then table 21-7 shows the resulting retirement income needs.

TABLE 21-7 Retirement Projections without Inflation	
Client	Income
Ed	$45,000 (.90 x $50,000)
Susan	$55,655 [.90 x $40,000 $(1.02)^{22}$]
John	$22,188 [.90 x $15,000 $(1.0125)^{40}$]

There is quite a difference. Think how much easier the potential for meaningful retirement income planning could be for both the client and the planner if the rate of inflation were zero. Unfortunately, like death and taxes, long-term inflation is a fact of life and the prudent planner must assume it will continue and plan accordingly.

22

Determining Postretirement Monetary Needs: Sources of Postretirement Income

Chapter Outline

In addition to analyzing the expected standard of living during retirement, the expected starting date for retirement, and the expected inflation rate before and after retirement, planners must also account for the resources that the client has available for retirement. These resources are compared to the client's expected retirement needs to determine the short fall—the amount of additional savings needed. These resources typically include benefits payable under social security and medicare, pension benefits from employer-provided plans, and private savings that the employee has accumulated for retirement purposes. These three sources have come to be known as the three-legged stool of retirement security. This chapter analyzes these resources with an emphasis on the facets that are important for the retirement planner to know.

SOCIAL SECURITY

When people use the term *social security*, they are actually referring to the old-age, survivors, disability, and health insurance (OASDHI) program of the federal government. For retirement planning purposes planners should be familiar with the entire social security system, particularly the old-age insurance programs and health insurance programs. Let's take a closer look at these two programs.

Old-Age Insurance under Social Security

Eligibility

Your client is eligible for retirement benefits under the old-age provisions of social security if he or she is covered by social security (groups that are not covered are discussed later) and has "credit" for a stipulated amount of work. Credit for social security purposes is based on *quarters of coverage.* For 1997 a worker receives credit for one quarter of coverage for each $670 in annual earnings on which social security taxes are paid. However, credit for no more than four quarters of coverage may be earned in any one calendar year. Consequently a worker paying social security taxes on as little as $2,680 (that is, $670 x 4) during the year will receive credit for the maximum four quarters. Furthermore, the amount of earnings necessary for a quarter of coverage is adjusted annually according to changes in the national level of wages. Also note that prior to 1978 a worker could receive credit for only one quarter of coverage in any given calendar quarter. In the past, it was necessary to earn wages throughout the year to receive the maximum number of credits. Now a worker with the appropriate level of wages can receive credit for the maximum number of quarters even if all wages are earned within one calendar quarter.

Fully Insured Status

A person is fully insured for purposes of receiving social security retirement benefits if he or she has 40 quarters of coverage. Once a person acquires this much credit, he or she is fully insured for life even if covered employment under social security ceases.

Retirement Benefits

A worker who is fully insured is eligible to receive monthly retirement benefits as early as age 62. Electing to receive benefits prior to age 65, however, results in a permanently reduced benefit. In addition, the following dependents of persons receiving retirement benefits are also eligible for monthly benefits based on the retiree's own account:

- *a spouse aged 62 or older*—Benefits are permanently reduced if this benefit is elected prior to the spouse's reaching age 65. This benefit is also available to a divorced spouse under certain circumstances if the marriage lasted at least 10 years.

- *a spouse of any age if the spouse is caring for at least one child of the retired worker*—The children must be (1) under age 16 or (2) disabled and entitled to a child's benefit as described below. This benefit is commonly referred to as a mother's or father's benefit.
- *dependent, unmarried children under 18*—This child's benefit will continue until age 19 as long as a child is a full-time student in elementary or secondary school. In addition, disabled children of any age are eligible for benefits as long as they were disabled before reaching age 22.

It is important to note that retirement benefits are not automatically paid upon eligibility. Instead workers must apply for retirement benefits, as well as all other social security benefits.

Benefit Amounts

Old-age insurance benefits are based on a worker's primary insurance amount (PIA). The PIA, in turn, is a function of the worker's average indexed monthly earnings (AIME) on which social security taxes have been paid. For retirement planning purposes the planner need not know how to calculate the AIME and PIA. Instead, the best method to estimate a client's expected social security benefits would be to request the employee's data from the social security administration. To obtain this information your client must mail in either Form SSA-7050-F3 or Form SSA-7004-PC-0P1 (appendix 4). The social security office will provide data relating to your client's earnings history and estimated primary insurance amount. (*Planning Note:* One of the social security forms referred to above should be submitted to the social security office every 3 years to verify that social security is keeping an accurate record of your client's earnings history.)

Table 22-1 can be used to estimate social security benefits for those clients who are retiring at age 65.

Cost-of-living Adjustments. Old-age insurance benefits are increased automatically each January as long as there has been an increase in the Consumer Price Index (CPI) for the one-year period ending in the third quarter of the prior year. The increase is the same as the increase in the CPI since the last cost-of-living adjustment, rounded to the nearest 0.1 percent.

There is one exception to this adjustment. In any year that the combined reserves of the social security trust funds drop below certain levels, the cost-of-living adjustment will be limited to the lesser of the increase in the CPI or the increase in national wages used to adjust the wage base for social security taxes. When benefit increases have been based on wage levels, future cost-of-living increases can be larger than changes in the CPI to compensate for the lower benefit increases in those years when the CPI was not used. However, this extra cost-of-living increase can be made only in years when the reserve is equal to at least 32 percent of expected benefits.

Benefits Taken Early. If a worker elects to receive retirement benefits prior to age 65, benefits are permanently reduced by 5/9 of one percent for every month that the early retirement precedes age 65. For example, for a worker who retires at age 62, the monthly benefit will be only 80 percent of that worker's PIA. A spouse who elects retirement benefits prior to age 65 will have benefits reduced by 25/36 of one percent per month; a widow or widower will have benefits reduced by 19/40 of one percent per month. In the latter case benefits at age 60 will be 71 1/2 percent of the worker's PIA. If the widow or widower elects benefits between the ages of 50 and 60 because of disability, there is no further reduction.

Delayed Retirement. Workers who delay applying for retirement benefits until after age 65 are eligible for an increased benefit. For persons born from 1917–1924, the increase is 3 percent for each year of delay up to age 70. For persons born from 1925–1926, the increase is 3 1/2 percent per year. To encourage delayed retirement, the percentage will gradually increase to 8 by 2009.

Social Security Coverage

Although most workers in the United States are covered under the social security program, some clients may belong to a group that is not covered. Let's examine these groups and what, if any, alternatives they offer to social security coverage.

One of the largest groups of employees not covered by social security are most civilian employees of the federal government who were employed by the government *prior to 1984* (those hired after 1984 and others who elected social security coverage are covered by social security). Most of those hired before 1984 are typically covered under the Civil Service Retirement System, which is similar to the social security system. Information regarding the Civil Service Retirement System's benefits can be obtained from the Advanced Sales Reference Service (a loose-leaf service used in the insurance industry) and from a book entitled *Federal Insurance Benefits*, both are published by National Underwriter (Cincinnati, Ohio).

A second group generally not covered by social security is the railroad workers. Railroad workers are covered under a benefit system similar to social security known as the Railroad Retirement Act. Information on the Railroad Retirement Act can be obtained from the sources cited above and in write-ups found in tax loose-leaf services such as Commerce Clearing House and Prentice Hall.

TABLE 22-1
Sample Social Security Benefits—As of 1996

Your Age in 1996	Who Receives Benefits	Monthly Benefits At Age 65				
		Your Present Annual Earnings				
		$15,000	$24,000	$36,000	$48,000	$62,700 & Up
65	You	$622	$845	$1,100	$1,179	$1,248
	Spouse	311	422	550	589	624
64	You	637	865	1,128	1,213	1,289
	Spouse	318	432	564	606	644
63	You	626	850	1,110	1,197	1,277
	Spouse	313	425	555	598	638
62	You	626	850	1,111	1,203	1,287
	Spouse	313	425	555	601	643
61	You	627	851	1,114	1,210	1,299
	Spouse	313	425	557	605	649
55*	You	604	821	1,077	1,193	1,308
	Spouse	298	406	532	598	646
50*	You	594	809	1,057	1,186	1,323
	Spouse	291	397	519	582	650
45*	You	598	815	1,061	1,197	1,356
	Spouse	293	400	521	587	666
40*	You	587	802	1,040	1,174	1,338
	Spouse	286	391	507	572	652
35*	You	562	768	994	1,122	1,281
	Spouse	270	369	477	539	616
30*	You	566	774	997	1,127	1,287
	Spouse	272	372	479	542	618

Source: *1996 Guide to Social Security and Medicare*, 1996, William M. Mercer, Inc.
*These amounts are reduced for retirement at age 65 because the Normal Retirement Age (NRA) is higher for these persons.

Employees of some state and local governments and subdivisions of state and local governments make up a third group that is not covered by social security. These employees are covered under a state or local pension system. Information about a particular state or local system can be obtained from the human resources department of the applicable governmental agency. Note, however, that most state and local governments and their subdivisions have entered into voluntary agreements with the Social Security Administration resulting in social security coverage for employees.

Other groups not covered by social security include ministers who elect out of coverage because of religious principles or conscience and some American citizens who work abroad for foreign affiliates of U.S. employers.

Medicare

In addition to understanding the amount of retirement benefits provided by social security and the people who are covered by social security, retirement planners need to understand the medicare system.

Eligibility for Medicare

Part A, the hospital portion of medicare, is available at no monthly cost to any person aged 65 or older as long as the person is entitled to monthly retirement benefits under social security or the railroad retirement program. In addition, civilian employees of the federal government aged 65 or older are also eligible. Workers do not have to be actually receiving retirement benefits, but they must be fully insured for purposes of retirement benefits. In addition, dependents aged 65 or older of fully insured workers aged 62 or older are also eligible for medicare.

Most persons who are 65 or over and do not meet the previously discussed eligibility requirements may voluntarily enroll in medicare. However, they must pay a monthly premium. In addition, these persons must also enroll in part B.

Any person eligible for part A of medicare is also eligible for part B. However, a monthly premium must be paid for part B. This monthly premium, $43.80 in 1997, is adjusted annually and represents only about 25 percent of the cost of the benefits provided. The remaining cost of the program is financed from the federal government's general revenues.

Persons receiving social security or railroad retirement benefits are automatically enrolled in medicare if they are eligible. If they do not want part B, they must elect out in writing. Other persons eligible for medicare must apply for part B benefits. Anyone who elects out of part B or who does not enroll when initially eligible may later apply for benefits during the general enrollment period between January 1 and March 31 of each year. However, the monthly premium will be increased by 10 percent for each 12-month period during which the person was eligible but failed to enroll.

Medicare: Part A Benefits

Part A of medicare provides benefits for expenses incurred in hospitals (for stays up to 90 days in each benefit period), skilled nursing facilities (if a physician certifies that skilled nursing or therapeutic care is needed for a condition that was treated in a hospital within the last 30 days), and hospices (for terminally ill persons who have a life expectancy of 6 months or less). In addition, home health care benefits are covered. In fact, part A of medicare will pay the full cost for an unlimited number of home visits by a home health agency. In order for benefits to be paid, the facility or agency providing benefits must participate in the medicare program. Virtually all hospitals are participants, as are most other facilities or agencies that meet the requirements of medicare.

Medicare: Part B Benefits

Part B, the supplementary medical insurance portion of medicare, provides benefits for the following medical expenses not covered under part A:

- physicians' and surgeons' fees that result from house calls, office visits, or services provided in a hospital or other institution (under certain circumstances benefits are also provided for the services of chiropractors, podiatrists, and optometrists)
- diagnostic tests in a hospital or in a physician's office
- physical therapy in a physician's office, or as an outpatient of a hospital, skilled nursing facility, or an approved clinic, agency, or public-health agency
- drugs and biologicals that cannot be self-administered
- radiation therapy
- medical supplies, such as surgical dressings, splints, and casts
- rental of medical equipment, such as oxygen tents, hospital beds, and wheelchairs
- prosthetic devices, such as artificial heart valves or lenses after a cataract operation
- ambulance service if a patient's condition does not permit the use of other methods of transportation
- pneumococcal vaccine and its administration
- mammograms

With some exceptions part B pays 80 percent of the approved charges for covered medical expenses after the satisfaction of a $100 annual deductible.

Exclusions. Although the preceding list may appear to be comprehensive, numerous medical products and services are not covered by part B. Some of these products and services that represent significant expenses for the elderly include the following:

- drugs and biologicals that can be self-administered
- routine physical, eye, and hearing examinations
- routine foot care
- immunizations, except pneumococcal vaccinations or immunization required because of an injury or immediate risk of infection
- cosmetic surgery unless it is needed because of an accidental injury or to improve the function of a malformed part of the body
- dental care unless it involves jaw or facial bone surgery or the setting of fractures
- custodial care
- eyeglasses, hearing aids, and orthopedic shoes

In addition, benefits are not provided to persons who are eligible for workers' compensation or treated in government hospitals. Benefits are provided only for services received in the United States, except for physicians' services and ambulance services rendered for a hospitalization that are covered in Mexico or Canada under part A.

FINDING OUT ABOUT PENSION BENEFITS

Information concerning the benefits available from the employer's pension plan is typically provided to plan participants on an annual basis. A client participating in an employer-sponsored plan usually receives a statement containing the following information:

- vesting percentage (all participants are 100 percent vested at retirement)
- dollar amount of pension benefit from plan at normal retirement age in current (uninflated) dollars (defined-benefit plans)
- current account balance (defined-contribution plans)
- estimated social security benefit
- benefit to spouse from pension plan should the employee die prior to normal retirement age
- value of contributions made by the plan participant and other payments that are considered part of the participant's basis

If your client's employer does not provide an annual benefit statement, the planner should have the client request a statement. Under the Employee Retirement Income Security Act (ERISA) most employers (the federal government and some other employers are exempted) are required to provide benefit statements on request (no more than one per year, however).

Another way to analyze your client's pension benefits is to examine your client's summary plan description (SPD). ERISA requires that most employers (the federal government and some other employers are exempted) provide a description of the plan to employees. The SPD will contain a wealth of information about your client's options under the plan, including information about

- early retirement
- normal retirement age
- benefit accruals after normal retirement (defined-benefit plans)
- contributions after normal retirement (defined-contribution plans)
- annuity options available at retirement
- lump-sum payouts (if allowed)
- claims procedures for denial of benefits

In addition to the summary plan description and the annual benefit statements, the employer will supply *1099R Forms*. These forms are filed with the IRS and sent to any participant or participant's beneficiary who receives a lump-sum or periodic distribution. They will indicate the amount of the distribution and whether any portion of the distribution will not be subject to tax.

The following checklist should be used to help you in your fact-finding process.

WORKSHEET 22-1
Employer-Provided Documents Used for Retirement Planning
Name of Plan Administrator_____
Phone Number_____
1. Summary Plan Description   [ ]
2. Annual Benefit Statements   [ ]
3. 1099R Form   [ ]

WILL EMPLOYER PENSIONS AND SOCIAL SECURITY PROVIDE ENOUGH RETIREMENT INCOME?

Clients having retirement expectations need to plan so their expectations can be fulfilled. In many ways it is similar to taking a trip. Just knowing that you want to go somewhere is not enough to get you there. You have to make plans depending on the availability of funds at the time the trip will be made. The situation is the same in retirement—what can be done in retirement depends on the funds the retiree has accumulated. Unfortunately some clients do not approach you about planning for retirement until it is too late to accumulate sufficient retirement assets. These clients probably assumed that the combination of pension benefits and social security would be adequate for retirement needs. In most cases, however, social security and pension benefits will not provide enough retirement income to enable a retiree to continue his or her preretirement standard of living. Consider the following:

- Most defined-benefit plans are geared toward providing a replacement ratio between only 40 and 60 percent of final-average salary. This amount generally will only be paid if the employee has 25 or more years of service with the employer (for employees whose service is less, the replacement ratio is reduced accordingly). Furthermore the defined-benefit pension is often reduced for payments to social security, and under typical circumstances the actual replacement ratio can drop to between 20 and 30 percent of final average salary for a rank-and-file employee.
- Defined-contribution plans are not protected against preretirement inflation. Defined-contribution plans can only provide benefits based on the average earnings of your client, which are less than the earnings in your client's final years. This means that half the contributions to your client's account were made based on salaries that were lower than the average salary your client earned during his or her participation in the plan. These contributions based on lower "uninflated salaries" tend to limit the replacement ratio in a defined-contribution plan. What's more, poor investment performance of the defined-contribution account or lack of contributions for employees who joined a defined-contribution plan later in their careers also tends to limit the amounts that are available under these plans.
- Most profit-sharing plans allow employers to skip annual contributions and allow employees to make in-service withdrawals.
- Assuming the employer's plan has a loan provision, any loaned amount may reduce the pool of plan assets available at retirement if the loan was taken out within 5 years of retirement, since the outstanding balance will not be distributed to the participant.
- Employers may terminate their qualified plans leaving employees to continue working without any future benefits or contributions.
- Social security is geared toward providing benefits for the lower paid. For example, a person with a $10,000 salary prior to retirement will receive approximately a 50 percent income replacement ratio from social security whereas a person with a $100,000 salary will only receive a 10 percent income-replacement ratio.
- Most nonqualified plans provide for abundant retirement savings for an employee. Retirement planners must be wary of certain traps

awaiting their clients. First, lump-sum distributions from a nonqualified plan will be subject to significantly more taxes than similar distributions from a qualified plan, because qualified plan distributions are eligible for favorable 5- or 10-year averaging and nonqualified distributions are not. Second, retirement funds are more secure in a qualified plan than in a nonqualified plan. Promised benefits from a nonqualified plan are subject to loss for a variety of reasons.

  – *The nonqualified plan may contain a forfeiture provision.* For example, the plan may provide that benefits are forfeited if the employee terminates employment prior to age 65.
  – *The nonqualified plan will typically not pay benefits if the employer goes bankrupt.* Nonqualified plan funds are typically held as corporate assets, which are subject to the claims of corporate creditors.
  – *Benefits payable under a nonqualified plan may be defaulted by an employer who has not prefunded the plan and who lacks current resources to pay.*

Case Study

(The following case study illustrates the fact that the combination of just pensions and social security will not provide an adequate retirement benefit.)

Gene Splicer went to work as a biologist for DNA Corporation in 1964 for a $10,000 salary. Gene's salary has increased at an annual rate of 7 percent over his 32 years with DNA and in 1996, Gene, aged 65, earned $81,443. During his tenure with DNA a 7-percent-of-salary contribution was made annually on Gene's behalf into a money-purchase plan which earned 7 percent interest. The amount of money in Gene's plan in 1996 was $182,450. Gene has approached you about retirement and has disclosed that he has always believed that his pension and social security would be enough to sustain him through retirement. Thus he has virtually no personal savings (the personal savings he had managed to accumulate were recently spent on his children's education). Gene would like answers to the following questions:

  • How much per month will the $182,450 money-purchase plan provide if an annuity is purchased that provides for equal payments to Gene's spouse should he die first?
  • How much social security will Gene and his (nonworking) spouse receive?
  • Will these amounts be enough to sustain Gene's current standard of living through retirement?

For Gene and his wife (both aged 65) the $182,450 account balance in his money-purchase plan will provide a $1,976 a month benefit in the form of a 100 percent joint and survivor benefit. Gene and his wife can also expect to receive an additional $1,752 a month from social security (a combined $21,024 annual benefit according to table 22-1). The combination of the $1,976 pension benefit and $1,752 social security benefit will give Gene a gross monthly salary of $3,728. Gene's current gross monthly salary is $6,787, which is about twice the amount he will receive in retirement! Gene's replacement ratio will be an inadequate percentage of his final average salary. Gene will have to suffer drastic cutbacks in his standard of living during the retirement years.

**YOUR FINANCIAL SERVICES PRACTICE:
PLANNING FOR CLIENTS WHO HAVE PROCRASTINATED**

The client who starts planning for retirement within a few years of the retirement date is precluded from pursuing options that could have been available with a minimal amount of planning and preparation. These clients have lost the ability to set aside savings on a systematic basis and to let compound interest work for them. This does not mean, however, that planning cannot be conducted for these clients. Important decisions must be made about distributions from qualified plans, liquidation of personal assets, and investment of any private savings. In addition, developing a retirement plan for the client who has procrastinated includes determining what funds are available for retirement and creating strategies even if the funds are inadequate.

One such strategy calls for the planner to suggest that the client postpone retirement. The combined effect of both lengthening the accumulation period and shortening the retirement period is financially desirable. If delaying retirement from his or her current job is not feasible, the client can achieve similar results by working for another employer after forced retirement. A second strategy is to recommend that the client move to an area with a lower cost of living. This move will enable the client to stretch his or her retirement dollars. By freeing up some of the equity in the home the client can make available assets for investment purposes. In addition to recommending these strategies, it is an essential part of the planner's job to help the client change his or her expectations about retirement. By forcing the client to look realistically at the lifestyle he or she will be able to afford, you can save your client from overspending during the early retirement years and thus from becoming financially destitute in the later retirement years.

PRIVATE SAVINGS

Clients commonly have savings for retirement even before they seek help in retirement planning. These savings must be considered for planning purposes. Typically these savings will be inadequate to fully fund the retirement need and additional saving will be required. Finally, the pattern of saving used by the client provides the planner with good ideas about potential investments that the client may be comfortable with for retirement-accumulation purposes. (*Planning Note:* One saving technique that should be suggested to clients is to have any income earned on investments immediately reinvested in the accumulation vehicle, such as dividend reinvestments. These convenient reinvestments promote long-term saving because the client never has the chance to spend the money.)

Clients will typically have retirement savings in one or more of the following vehicles:

- *IRAs*—IRAs can contain both private savings and amounts rolled over from a former employer's qualified plan. In addition, IRAs can contain funds that will be subject to taxation at distribution and funds that will not be taxed because they were originally contributed on an after-tax basis. (*Planning Note:* If the client intends to make both deductible and nondeductible contributions, separate IRAs should be established for each type of contribution to simplify record keeping.)

- *Retirement Annuity Plans*—Your client is likely to have a personally owned deferred-annuity contract issued by a life insurance company and designed to accept contributions over a period of years. Upon the individual's retirement the accumulated sum can be either converted to an annuity or withdrawn in a lump sum.

- *Personally Owned Life Insurance*—Upon reaching retirement an individual often finds that the amount of cash value life insurance carried on his or her life is more than adequate for the future needs of providing protection for survivors or for estate liquidity purposes. Thus the policy surrender value for one or more policies can be taken either in the form of an annuity or as a lump sum used for investment in alternative income-producing investment vehicles.

- *Financial Assets*—Many clients have accumulated a portfolio of stocks, bonds, mutual funds, master limited partnership units, unit trust shares, real estate investment trust shares, ownership interests in nontraded limited partnerships, CDs, or other investment assets.

- *Tangible Assets*—Some individuals have acquired considerable tangible investment assets. These can take the form of investment real estate, precious metals or gemstones, art, or other collectibles. (*Planning Note:* Most tangible assets require an annual cash outlay for their protection. This outlay could be for insurance, storage costs, or other expenses associated with their ownership. Unless the client's income level exceeds the amount needed for maintaining the retirement standard of living, these negative cash-flow investments become candidates for resale when the client nears retirement. This transaction will not only eliminate the cash drain but more importantly convert the investment into an income-producing form.)

23

Determining Postretirement Monetary Needs: Case Study

Chapter Outline

In this chapter we turn our attention from the various pieces of the retirement-planning puzzle (the expected standard of living, the expected retirement date, the expected inflation rate, and the sources of retirement income) to a method for actually solving the puzzle of putting together a retirement plan. Putting together a retirement plan for a client is basically a three-step process. In the first step the planner conducts fact finding to become familiar with the client's feelings, goals, and factual circumstances. In the second step the planner must calculate the amount of the client's retirement need. This process is complicated by the mathematical equations that are involved, because planners must account for the time value of money and inflation (in other words, a dollar today is not the same as a dollar tomorrow). The third and final step in putting together a retirement plan is to establish a savings schedule and investment portfolio for the client so that he or she can fund the amount of the needed savings.

Since the best way to understand these steps is to examine how they apply in a particular situation, this chapter presents a case study that examines the retirement needs of Joe and Betty Brown.

FACT FINDING

Your client, Joe Brown, has revealed the following information:

- Joe is married and his wife, Betty, is a homemaker.
- Both Joe and Betty are currently 55 years old.
- Joe expects to retire at age 65.
- Joe earns $54,000 a year.
- Joe is in the 28 percent tax bracket.
- Joe's company has a defined-benefit pension plan. If Joe continues employment until age 65, he can expect to receive a $20,000-a-year pension. (That figure is in today's dollars; his actual pension at retirement will be larger.) Joe's pension will be payable in the form of a 50 percent joint and survivor annuity (see chapter 25). Joe's pension will *not* be offset by social security payments.
- Joe owns $150,000 in common stock, which pays $6,000 per year in dividends. Joe has reinvested all aftertax income from the portfolio every year except one, when he and Betty spent the money on a trip to Europe.
- Joe owns some non-income-producing assets, such as a home (current market value $250,000) and personal effects (worth about $100,000). The mortgage on the home will be paid off in 2 years.
- Both Joe and Betty have a fairly sophisticated understanding of investments.
- Joe and Betty have been married for 30 years, and the marriage is very stable.
- Both Joe and Betty are in good health.
- Both Joe and Betty feel they have average, or better than average, life expectancies.

FINANCING THE DESIRED RETIREMENT LIFESTYLE

Several steps must be taken to determine the finances necessary for providing Joe and Betty with a continuation of their current lifestyle throughout retirement. These steps are

(1) adding up the current sources of retirement income
(2) finding the amount of income needed to achieve the desired retirement lifestyle
(3) estimating the retirement-income status (RIS)

(4) determining which resources need inflation protection

(5) calculating the target amount

Step 1: Adding Up the Existing Sources of Retirement Income

Joe indicates that he will have the following sources of income:

- *Social Security*—The Social Security Administration has informed Joe that he will receive $1,407 monthly ($938 for Joe and $469 for Betty) in social security benefits (current dollars) at age 65. This translates into a $16,884 annual income in current dollars.
- *Pension*—Joe's pension is $20,000 a year in current dollars.
- *Private Savings*—Joe does not intend to liquidate his $150,000 equity portfolio. Joe will, however, use the $6,000 in dividends for living expenses during retirement. Since Joe has no desire to either take the equity out of his home or sell any personal effects, these assets will not be used to produce a stream of income for retirement.

Step 2: Finding the Amount of Income Needed to Achieve the Desired Retirement Lifestyle

To find the amount of income needed to achieve the desired retirement lifestyle, you can either apply the desired replacement ratio to your client's salary or use the expense method approach.

Ratio Method

If the client expects an increase in his or her standard of living, a growth factor must be incorporated to determine Joe's final salary. Joe, however, would like his retirement income to provide a standard of living comparable to his existing standard of living and does not need to apply a growth factor to his current lifestyle. Since he will no longer be saving for retirement, paying social security taxes, or incurring work-related expenses, Joe estimates that 80 percent of his preretirement income from employment will be sufficient. In other words, in today's dollars Joe wants to have $43,200 (80 percent of his current salary of $54,000) when he retires. In tomorrow's dollars Joe is looking to have this amount keep pace with inflation. (For example, if inflation rose 4 percent per year for 10 years, Joe would need $63,947 to have his current purchasing power during the first year of his retirement.)

Example: Suppose instead that Joe had anticipated that his standard of living would increase 2 percent per year until retirement. (In other words, his salary would increase 2 percent more than inflation, and Joe would use the commensurate increase in real income to improve his lifestyle.) If this is the case, a growth factor of 2 percent should be applied to Joe's current $54,000 salary using the future value formula discussed in chapter 21:

$$FV = PV(1 + r)^n$$

where n = number of years before target retirement date
r = inflation rate

In this case, however, instead of inflation the r would stand for the desired growth rate that the client expects (2 percent). Under these circumstances the salary considered would be

$$V = \$54,000 (1 + r)^n$$

$$= \$54,000 (1 + 1.02)^{10}$$

$$= \$65,826$$

Since Joe only needs 80 percent of this salary in current dollars, Joe would want $52,660 in today's dollars when he retires in order to maintain his anticipated purchasing power. In tomorrow's dollars Joe would want this amount to keep pace with inflation.

Since Joe had not anticipated any real growth or inflation factor, we can use the $43,200 target achieved by applying an 80 percent replacement ratio to his current salary when estimating Joe's retirement income status.

Expense Method

If Joe were to use the expense method to determine the amount of income he would need during retirement, he and Betty would sit down with the planner to estimate their expenses in their first year of retirement. Let's assume that Joe will have annual expenses of $43,200 (the same as the ratio method). Note, however, that the expense and ratio method will seldom provide the same number.

Step 3: Estimating the Retirement-Income Status (RIS)

To determine the amount of additional savings he will need to accumulate, Joe must subtract his annual target for retirement income from his estimated amount of annual retirement income (table 23-1).

The retirement-income status (RIS) can be either a positive or negative number. A positive RIS indicates a surplus since current sources exceed the target amount. A negative RIS indicates a deficit and suggests the need for additional savings. When the RIS is negative, it will be labeled RID (retirement-income deficit) and used with a positive sign to avoid dealing with negative numbers.

TABLE 23-1 Calculation of Annual Retirement-Income Status (in today's dollars)		
Estimated annual retirement income		
Social security	$16,884	
Pension	20,000	
Private savings (dividends)	6,000	42,884
Annual target retirement income		$43,200
Annual retirement-income status (RIS)		$ − 316

In current dollars Joe appears to be in the enviable position of having nearly adequate retirement income to meet his desired retirement standard of living (a RID of only $316). However, this may be misleading because these values ignore the effects of inflation before and after retirement.

Step 4: Determining Which Resources Need Inflation Protection

Up to this point we have determined that Joe will have a $316 gap between what his social security, pension, and private savings will provide and what his desired annual income during retirement will be. At this point, we have a partial picture of the retirement need for Joe and Betty. To calculate the true retirement need, however, we must provide inflation protection, both before and after retirement, for all Joe's retirement resources. In chapter 21 when the effect of inflation was explored, it was determined that a 4 percent rate of inflation could be used as an estimate. Using that estimate let's take a closer look at each of the retirement resources.

Social Security

To a certain extent social security is inflation protected because it is geared toward increases in the consumer price index (CPI). This assumes, however, that the law will remain unchanged and that the CPI accurately reflects inflation as it affects Joe. For Joe's purposes we can assume that the law will not change and that the indexation of social security is a reasonable reflection of inflation increases.

Pension

We can assume that Joe's pension is inflation protected until retirement because it is a defined-benefit plan based on final-average salary. We cannot, however, assume any inflation protection after retirement. For this reason, in addition to funding the retirement-income deficit (RID), Joe will need to fund an amount that can be used to bolster his non-inflation-proof pension benefits (that is, to keep pension purchasing power constant). This amount is called the decline in purchasing power (DIPP).

Dividends

Dividend income from a stock portfolio is generally considered to be inflation protected if the principal is left intact. For Joe's purposes we can assume his dividend income will be inflation protected both in the preretirement and postretirement periods. The fact that Joe is not liquidating his principal provides a hedge against inflation, because he can annuitize the principal if he needs additional retirement income.

Retirement-Income Deficit (RID)

Joe must account for the effect of preretirement and postretirement inflation on the purchasing power of the income from the monies that he will accumulate to fund the RID. For example, when a 4 percent rate of inflation is added to the RID ($316 in today's dollars), the RID grows to $468 by the time Joe reaches age 65.

Table 23-2 summarizes the impact of inflation on Joe's resources.

TABLE 23-2 Inflation's Impact on Joe's Resources	
Source of Income	Inflation Protected
Social security benefits	Yes
Pension	Not after retirement
Dividends	Yes
Retirement-income deficit	No

Step 5: Calculating the Target Amount

The next step is to examine how much Joe will need to accumulate to fund the RID and the pension DIPP. This sum is the target amount of funds that Joe needs in addition to his current stock portfolio to achieve his desired standard of living during retirement. To accomplish this the planner must first make many assumptions about the future. In addition to estimating inflation at, for example, 4 percent, assumptions must be made about the amount of investment return that Joe will earn on accumulated funds and about the method that Joe will use to liquidate his saved funds.

Investment Return

As a general rule, a higher rate of return means a greater variability of the return and hence a greater risk. Thus, if your client seeks a higher return on invested monies, there will be a commensurate increase in the likelihood that the targeted amount of retirement funds will not be accumulated. A general guideline for this risk-return tradeoff is that the more important the financial objective is to the client, the less the risk that should be assumed. Some planners believe that accumulating funds for retirement is the most important reason for investing and would consequently recommend investment vehicles that have relatively low risk. Even if you do not adhere to this philosophy, you must recognize that since Joe's retirement date is only 10 years away, he will have little opportunity to make up any investment losses that might occur during this relatively short period. For this reason a conservative investment strategy should probably be chosen.

An additional consideration is whether Joe can use a tax-deferred investment vehicle, such as an IRA, or can make a nondeductible voluntary contribution to his pension plan during the accumulation period. If so, earnings on monies set aside would accumulate free of current income taxation. With such a vehicle 8 percent could be earned on relatively low-risk investments. If currently taxable investments of the same risk characteristic were employed, then the return (r) times one minus the client's marginal tax rate (t), or $r(1 - t)$, would be earned after tax. In other words, since Joe is in the 28 percent marginal tax bracket, he would have an aftertax yield of 5.76 percent on an investment that yields 8 percent interest before tax [$.08(1 - .28)$].

Liquidation of Funds

Several paths can be followed when using the funds accumulated to meet Joe's retirement-income deficit and to meet the decline in purchasing power of Joe's pension. One such option is to not liquidate the assets at all. Under this option Joe will need to accumulate a fund that would earn sufficient income each year without reducing the accumulated capital. A second alternative would involve accumulating a fund that could be systematically liquidated over a specified number of years. At the end of the specified time the capital would be depleted. (*Planning Note:* The longer the liquidation period that is assumed for depleting assets, the greater the amount of funds that will be needed for the retirement target.)

**YOUR FINANCIAL SERVICES PRACTICE:
PROTECTING CLIENTS FROM OUTLIVING INCOME**

A planner should exercise caution when liquidating a client's assets over a specified period of time. Many planners mistakenly rely on the figures given in mortality tables to determine the liquidation period. The problem with this approach is that one-half of the population lives beyond the tabular life expectancy. For this reason many planners underestimate the client's life expectancy when determining the liquidation period. Even when extending the liquidation period beyond the tabular life expectancies, planners can encounter trouble. Statistics show that 20 percent of the people who reach age 65 will live to age 95.

One way for a planner to be cautious is by recommending that a client purchase a life annuity with his or her accumulated savings. A life annuity permits clients to continue to receive payments until they die, regardless of how long they live. In those cases when clients live beyond the life expectancy on which the annuity was based, the client experiences what is known as mortality gain. The insurance company does not necessarily lose money when it pays mortality gain, however, because theoretically an equal number of people die before the life expectancy on which the annuity was calculated and experience mortality loss.

The Mathematics

Once the planner has made assumptions about the investment return and the liquidation period, these assumptions as well as the client's retirement-income deficit (RID) and decline in purchasing power (DIPP) are applied in mathematical equations to calculate the client's target accumulation. To simplify the process let's do two separate calculations, one for the RID fund and one for the DIPP.

Amount Needed to Fund the Retirement-Income-Deficit (RID) Fund. Let's assume that Joe wants to have the inflation-protected income stream last for only a specified period, such as 25 years from the date of his retirement, at which point the fund would be exhausted. In this situation you need to calculate the stream of payments that Joe would like to receive from an inflation-protected retirement-income deficit and discount the payments to the value at retirement age assuming the principal will be paid out along with the interest. The appropriate equation for doing this is as follows:

EQUATION 23-1
Funds Needed at the Client's Retirement Date for Total
RID—Liquidating Principal*

$$
\begin{array}{c}
\text{Funds needed} \\
\text{(RID funds)}
\end{array}
=
\begin{array}{c}
\text{Retirement} \\
\text{date RID}
\end{array}
\times (1 + \text{int}) \times
\left[
\frac{1 - \left(\dfrac{1 + \text{inf}}{1 + \text{int}}\right)^n}{\text{int} - \text{inf}}
\right]
$$

where n = liquidation period expressed in years
     int = interest rate
     inf = inflation rate

---

*This equation calculates the funds needed to provide an income stream that is inflation protected and will continue forever (no liquidation of principal). The payments will increase each year by the rate of inflation.

Assuming that inflation stays constant at 4 percent, that Joe retires at age 65 (recall that Joe's retirement-income deficit had risen from $316 to $468 at age 65), that Joe expects to liquidate the fund over 25 years, and that Joe earns an aggressive 8 percent interest after tax, Joe will need $7,717 at retirement according to the following calculation:

$$
\begin{array}{c}
\text{Funds needed} \\
\text{(RID fund)}
\end{array}
= \$468 \times (1 + .08) \times
\left[
\frac{1 - \left(\dfrac{1.04}{1.08}\right)^{25}}{.08 - .04}
\right]
$$

$$= \$7,717$$

If Joe's desired liquidation period was 35 years with the same inflation and interest rates, he will find, using equation 23-1, that $9,264 would be the sum needed at retirement.

If Joe desires to have income growing but not have the principal reduced, however, he must use a different equation. This equation calculates the stream of payments that Joe would like to receive from an inflation-protected retirementincome deficit fund and discounts the payments to the value at retirement age assuming the principal will not be liquidated and only interest will be paid out. The appropriate formula to use is as follows:

EQUATION 23-2
Funds Needed at the Client's Retirement Date for Total
RID—Not Liquidating Principal*

$$\text{Funds needed} \atop \text{(RID fund)} = \text{RID} + \frac{\text{RID (1 + inf)}}{\text{int} - \text{inf}}$$

where int = interest rate
inf = inflation rate

---

*This equation calculates the funds needed to provide an income stream that is inflation protected and will continue forever (no liquidation of principal). The payments will increase each year by the rate of inflation.

With the same interest and inflation assumptions, this equation becomes

$$\text{Funds needed} \atop \text{(RID fund)} = \$468 + \frac{\$468 \ (1.04)}{.08 - .04}$$

$$= \$12,636$$

Table 23-3 summarizes Joe's situation for determining the retirement-income-deficit fund.

TABLE 23-3
Retirement-Income-Deficit Fund

Liquidation Method	Sum Needed at Age 65
25-year liquidation	$ 7,717
35-year liquidation	$ 9,264
Income only	$12,636

Amount Needed to Fund the Decline in Purchasing Power (DIPP). In addition to funding the retirement-income deficit, Joe needs to set aside additional funds to maintain the purchasing power of his pension. In this case, you need to first calculate the present value of the stream of payments that Joe should be receiving from an inflation-proof pension and then determine the present value of a stream of level payments for the same period. The difference between these present values represents the supplemental funds Joe needs to make his pension benefits inflation proof. The appropriate equation for solving this problem is as follows:

EQUATION 23-3
Funds Needed at the Client's Retirement Date for Total DIPP—
Liquidating Principal*

$$\text{DIPP} = \begin{array}{c}\text{income} \\ \text{needing} \\ \text{inflation} \\ \text{protection}\end{array} \times (1 + \text{int}) \times \left[\frac{1 - \left(\dfrac{1 + \text{inf}}{1 + \text{int}}\right)^n}{\text{int} - \text{inf}}\right] -$$

$$\begin{array}{c}\text{income} \\ \text{needing} \\ \text{inflation} \\ \text{protection}\end{array} \times (1 + \text{int}) \times \left[\frac{1 - \left(\dfrac{1}{1 + \text{int}}\right)^n}{\text{int}}\right]$$

where n = liquidation period expressed in years
    int = interest rate
    inf = inflation rate

*This equation calculates the funds needed to provide an inflation-protected
supplement to a level or fixed-income stream for a given number of years. This
provides increasing payments to supplement the fixed-payment stream.

The income to be protected in this case is only the pension income.

Note that it is projected that Joe's pension at age 65 will have grown from
$20,000 (at age 55) to $29,605, assuming a 4 percent inflation rate. Therefore
Joe will need $146,877 at retirement determined as follows:

$$\text{DIPP} = \$29,605\,(1.08)\left[\frac{1 - \left(\dfrac{1.04}{1.08}\right)^{25}}{.08 - .04}\right] - \$29,605\,(1.08)\left[\frac{1 - \left(\dfrac{1}{1.08}\right)^{25}}{.08}\right]$$

$$= \$29,605\,(1.08)\,(15.26850409) - \$29,605\,(1.08)\,(10.67477619)$$

$$= \$488,186 - \$341,309$$

$$= \$146,877$$

Using the same formula for 35-year liquidation, the amount needed will be
$258,364. If Joe desires, however, to have income growing but not have the
principal reduced, he must use a different equation that will not liquidate the
principal. The following equation should be used:

EQUATION 23-4
Funds Needed at the Client's Retirement Date for Total
DIPP—Not Liquidating Principal*

$$
\text{DIPP} = \begin{matrix} \text{income} \\ \text{needing} \\ \text{inflation} \\ \text{protection} \end{matrix} \times 1 + \left(\frac{1 + \text{inf}}{\text{int} - \text{inf}} \right) -
$$

$$
\begin{matrix} \text{income} \\ \text{needing} \\ \text{inflation} \\ \text{protection} \end{matrix} \times (1 + \text{int}) \left(\frac{1}{\text{int}} \right)
$$

where int = interest rate
inf = inflation rate

---

*This equation calculates the funds needed to provide an inflation-protected
supplement to a level or fixed-income stream for an unlimited number of years.
This provides increasing payments to supplement the fixed-payment stream.

Using the same interest and inflation rate assumptions Joe would need

$$
\text{DIPP} = \$29,605 \times 1 + \left(\frac{1.04}{.04} \right) - \$29,605 \times 1.08 \times \frac{1}{.08}
$$

$$
= \$29,605 \times 27 - \$29,605 \times 13.5
$$

$$
= \$399,667
$$

Table 23-4 summarizes Joe's situation for determining the decline in the purchasing power fund.

TABLE 23-4
Decline in Purchasing Power Fund

Liquidation Method	Sum Needed at Age 65
25-year liquidation	$146,877
35-year liquidation	$213,363
Income only	$399,667

Adding Up the Total Funds Needed. To determine exactly how much he will
need at retirement Joe must add together the amount necessary to fund the RID

and the amount necessary to fund the DIPP. Note that Joe could choose different liquidation methods for the retirement-income-deficit fund and the decline in the purchasing-power fund. For example, he could use a 25-year liquidation for the RID fund and a 35-year liquidation for the DIPP. This method would be most appropriate if he wanted to hedge on his and Betty's life expectancy. Assuming Joe chooses the same liquidation for both, which is the more common choice, table 23-5 indicates the target amount that Joe will need to accumulate in addition to other retirement resources.

TABLE 23-5 **Target Accumulation**			
Liquidation Method	Retirement- Income- Deficit Fund	+ Decline in Purchasing- Power Fund	= Total Target Fund
25-year	$ 7,717	$146,877	$154,594
35-year	9,264	$213,363	$222,627
Income only	$12,636	$399,667	$412,303

YOUR FINANCIAL SERVICES PRACTICE:
CALCULATING YOUR CLIENT'S TARGET

When calculating your client's target you should keep in mind the following:

- The decline in purchasing power (DIPP) is not just for pensions. The DIPP calculation also applies to any other sources of income that will not be adjusted for inflation after retirement. For example, a cash value life insurance policy that will be converted to level annuity payments at retirement to use as a retirement resource is not inflation protected after retirement and will be added to the pension income to get the income needing inflation protection in equations 23-3 and 23-4.
- Equations 23-1 and 23-2 are applicable to the retirement-income deficit and calculate an annuity due (payments start immediately). Equations 23-3 and 23-4 are applicable to the decline in purchasing power and calculate an immediate annuity that delays the start of payments for one period (in this case one year).

IMPLEMENTING A SAVINGS SCHEDULE TO FUND THE TARGET AMOUNT

Once a target has been calculated, the planner's focus turns toward using this data to set up a savings schedule. Joe could use a variety of techniques to fund his retirement target, including making a lump-sum payment from gain realized on the sale of his home and/or the liquidation of his stock portfolio. (If the portfolio is liquidated, a new target must be calculated because the old target included dividends from the portfolio as a source of retirement income.) Besides making a lump-sum payment, Joe could fund the payments in the remaining years until retirement. The two most popular methods of doing this are (1) funding the payments on a level basis until retirement or (2) using a stepped-up annual funding method that increases payments annually to coordinate payments with increasing income.

Level Annual Funding

If Joe wanted to use level annual funding until retirement at age 65, equation 23-5 should be used. Equation 23-5 essentially calculates the amount of annual payments (based on the fact that the payments made are earning compound interest) so that a level amount is saved annually.

EQUATION 23-5
Level Annual Funding*

$$\text{Annual funding} = \frac{\text{Target amount (from table 23-5)}}{\left[\dfrac{(1 + int)^n - 1}{int}\right] \times (1 + int)}$$

where int = interest rate
n = number of years in accumulation period

---

*This equation provides a way to calculate the level investment (savings) payment necessary to accumulate the target amount over a given number of years (n) if those funds earn interest at the assumed interest rate throughout the n-year accumulation period. (If the funds are producing taxable income, the interest rate should be an aftertax rate.) Any target amount can be used, and it should represent the dollar amount desired at the end of the n-year period.

For example, if Joe wanted to have a 25-year liquidation (target amount $154,594), he would need to make $9,881 payments at the beginning of each year until retirement, determined as follows:

$$\text{Annual funding} = \frac{\$154,594}{\left[\dfrac{(1 + .08)^{10} - 1}{.08}\right] \times (1 + .08)}$$

$$= \$9,881$$

Using this same formula the level annual amount needed to fund for a 35-year liquidation target ($222,627) would be $14,229 and to fund the income-only

Using this same formula the level annual amount needed to fund for a 35-year liquidation target ($222,627) would be $14,229 and to fund the income-only target ($412,303) would be $26,353. Table 23-6 summarizes the level annual payments needed.

TABLE 23-6 Level Annual Funding	
Liquidation Method	Level Annual Payment
25-year liquidation	$ 9,881
35-year liquidation	$14,229
Income only	$26,353

Stepped-Up Annual Funding

If Joe wanted to use stepped-up annual funding, equation 23-6 should be used. Equation 23-6 calculates an increasing scale of payments that Joe would need to fund the target amount.

Equation 23-6 only gives you the first year's annual payment. To determine payments in the subsequent years of the accumulation, multiply the prior year's payment by one plus the inflation rate.

For example, if Joe wants to use a stepped-up annual funding method to coordinate savings increases with increases in salary and have a 25-year liquidation (target amount $154,594), he would need to make a first payment of $8,437, determined as follows:

$$\text{Annual funding} = \frac{\$154,594 \times (.08 - .04)}{1 - \left[\frac{1.04^{10}}{1.08}\right] \times (1.08)^{11}}$$

$$= \$8,437$$

Joe's second-year payment would be $8,774.48 ($8,437 x 1.04), and his third-year payment would be $9,125.46 ($8,774 x 1.04). Table 23-7 shows all ten of Joe's payments.

EQUATION 23-6
Stepped-Up Annual Funding*

$$\text{First - year funding } = \frac{\text{Target amount x (int } - \text{ inf)}}{\left[1 - \left(\frac{1 + \text{inf}}{1 + \text{int}} \right)^n \right] \times \left[(1 + \text{int})^{(n + 1)} \right]}$$

where int = interest rate
inf = inflation rate
n = number of years in accumulation period

---

*This equation calculates the level of first-year investment (saving) contribution to an accumulation fund that will accumulate a target amount by the end of a given period of years (n) if the fund earns the assumed interest rate throughout the n-year period and the contributions to the fund increase at the assumed inflation rate. Note that what we call inflation rate is really the growth rate of the funding contribution each year. It could be any rate the client is capable of contributing to the accumulation fund.

TABLE 23-7
25-Year Liquidation Target/Stepped-Up Payments

Age	Year	Payment
55	1	$ 8,437
56	2	8,775
57	3	9,125
58	4	9,490
59	5	9,870
60	6	10,265
61	7	10,675
62	8	11,103
63	9	11,547
64	10	12,008

For the 35-year target ($222,627) an initial payment of $12,149 is required. Table 23-8 illustrates payments under this system.

TABLE 23-8
35-Year Liquidation Target/Stepped-Up Payments

Age	Year	Payment
55	1	$12,149
56	2	12,635
57	3	13,140
58	4	13,666
59	5	14,213
60	6	14,781
61	7	15,372
62	8	15,987
63	9	16,627
64	10	17,291

For the income-only target ($412,303) an initial payment of $22,500 is necessary. Table 23-9 illustrates the payments under this system.

TABLE 23-9
Retirement-Income-Only Target/Stepped-Up Payments

Age	Year	Payment
55	1	$22,500
56	2	23,400
57	3	24,336
58	4	25,309
59	5	26,322
60	6	27,375
61	7	28,470
62	8	29,608
63	9	30,793
64	10	32,025

SOURCES OF FUNDING

Joe will probably decide to use savings from his current income to meet whatever payment schedule he chooses. If Joe can manage to save 22.5 percent of his salary (note that this becomes increasingly feasible after mortgage payments cease), he can meet the 35-year stepped-up annual funding schedule (table 23-8). This strategy is illustrated in table 23-10.

TABLE 23-10
Joe's Savings Strategy

Age	Salary	22.5 Percent Savings	35-year Liquidation (from table 23-8)
55	$54,000	$12,150	$12,149
56	56,160	12,636	12,635
57	58,406	13,141	13,140
58	60,743	13,667	13,666
59	63,172	14,214	14,213
60	65,699	14,782	14,781
61	68,327	15,374	15,372
62	71,060	15,989	15,987
63	73,903	16,628	16,627
64	76,859	17,293	17,291

In addition to a 22.5 percent savings from Joe's current salary, Betty could become employed in an effort to earn additional savings. (Note that if this is the case, a recalculation might be necessary to account for an increased social security benefit as a retirement resource.)   Another option is for Joe to delay retirement until beyond 65, thereby increasing the amount of time to save and decreasing the target amount.

Regardless of which method Joe and Betty choose, they will be faced with making additional investments of the funds being used to provide for the targeted amount. Planners should give advice concerning these investments and should make investment-return assumptions that are consistent with expected investment results. Investments will be covered in depth in the next chapter.

24

Investing for Retirement

Chapter Outline

RISK-RETURN CONSIDERATIONS

In order to properly advise clients about investing for their retirement, planners must first understand the relationship between risk and return. In general, the higher the potential risk of any investment the higher must be the potential return in the long run. Conversely, the lower the risk of an investment means the lower the return in the long run. Risk includes the variation in the amount of the annual income as well as the potential for gain or loss of all or some of the assets' value. From this perspective, investing for retirement can be seen as a trade-off between what is acceptable to the client and what is appropriate for the client. For example, despite the fact that high-risk investment vehicles might enhance the client's ability to accumulate the needed funds for retirement, if the client is unwilling to accept that degree of risk, then the high-risk, high-return investment will not be a viable alternative for retirement accumulation purposes. Thus a willingness to accept or not accept a high degree of investment risk can have a large effect on the amount of assets that a client will need to accumulate to fund his or her retirement income target. In addition, that choice will affect the annual saving required to accumulate that fund.

Example: Recall that we used an 8 percent after-tax investment assumption, a 4 percent inflation rate, and a 25-year liquidation period for Joe Brown when figuring his retirement target was $154,594. If we change only the after-tax interest rate for the 10-year accumulation period to a 5 percent after-tax return, Joe will need to accumulate $233,747, which is an additional $79,153 to reach the same retirement standard-of-living objective.

A second consideration is not what level of risk a client can withstand, but what level of risk is appropriate for retirement planning purposes. For example, as a client nears his or her retirement date, the amount of risk that can be taken must be reduced as a means of preserving the funds needed for retirement. This shift to lower-risk, lower-return investments will reduce the total amount of funds accumulated for retirement. To offset this reduced return, additional annual saving will be needed during all, or at least the last few years of the accumulation period.

Example: If Joe Brown reduced his after-tax return from 8 percent to 5 percent after he attained age 60 and had been contributing $14,940 per year to achieve his objective, Joe would need to save an additional $4,525 during each of the remaining 5 years to meet his objective.

LIFE-CYCLE CONSIDERATIONS

In addition to accommodating the client's risk profile, retirement planners also need to be aware of the unique characteristics of retirement investing at each stage of a client's life cycle. When planning for a client's retirement the following three time periods are important:

- the long-term accumulation period
- the portfolio-restructuring period
- the preservation and retirement-income period

LONG-TERM ACCUMULATION PERIOD

The long-term accumulation period starts when the client first begins to accumulate funds for retirement purposes and continues until the client is within 5 to 15 years of retirement. During the long-term accumulation period the planner must

- recognize the client's preference for risk and choose investment vehicles that correspond to the client's "zone of acceptance"
- monitor the portfolio's performance
- revise the portfolio to correspond with changes in the client's personal finances, the client's attitude toward risk, and the economy

- account for inflation's influence on the client's need for retirement funds

Regardless of an individual's willingness to bear investment risk, the long-term accumulation period is the time when a client can take on the highest tolerable risks to strive for the largest possible accumulation of assets. A greater risk can be taken during this period because clients still have many years of employment remaining and are in a position to alter their saving habits should investment losses occur.

Thus the client who can be categorized as a risk-taker would build a high-risk, high-return portfolio that would include some high-risk investments such as stocks of newly formed publicly traded businesses, master limited partnership units, or other investments near the peak of the risk-return triangle shown in figure 24-1. The risk-blender would prefer a medium-risk, medium-return portfolio that would hold some investments such as common stocks, mutual funds, and other vehicles from the middle of the risk-return triangle. The risk-avoider, on the other hand, has a preference for a low-risk, low-return portfolio and would want investments largely selected from the bottom portions of the risk-return triangle.

An appropriate portfolio for the long-term accumulation period includes a mix of investments that are both consistent with the client's attitude toward risk and appropriate for meeting the client's long-term objectives. These objectives may not be met, for example, if a risk-avoider chooses an extremely conservative portfolio. Reason: In addition to the investment risk, retirement investing faces the risk that long-term inflation will reduce the buying power of the monies placed into the investment vehicle. (This is the purchasing power risk.) Therefore, during the long-term accumulation period, even the risk-avoider should consider some investments that will have as two of their characteristics a higher return and a potential for appreciation. Such investments provide a means of offsetting some of the purchasing power risk even though risk of capital loss is increased. Without some investment returns that will counterbalance the effects of inflation, the task of accumulating sufficient retirement funds becomes even more formidable.

However, there is not one best portfolio for any one client-risk profile that will achieve these objectives. Figure 24-2 shows three widely different portfolios that offer similar degrees of risk and approximately the same opportunity for long-term gain for each of the three different client-risk attitudes. (Other portfolio configurations could also be developed.) For example, the risk-avoider could construct a portfolio consisting of 80 percent very low-risk, very low-return investments and 20 percent very high-risk, very high-return investments. And although this particular portfolio would have results similar to the two other portfolios for this risk preference, the presence of 20 percent of the investable monies in a high-risk, high-return investment might be inappropriate for some clients within this profile. Therefore a portfolio configuration that is consistent with risk and return objectives for the general risk category might be unacceptable for a client within that profile.

(*Planning Note:*   The retirement planner must exercise caution when recommending investment vehicles during the long-term accumulation period. The portfolio must fall within the client's "zone of acceptance." Otherwise, the client may reject the full set of recommendations and either do nothing, which would be detrimental to the client, or, worse yet from the planner's standpoint, look for someone else to do his or her retirement planning.)

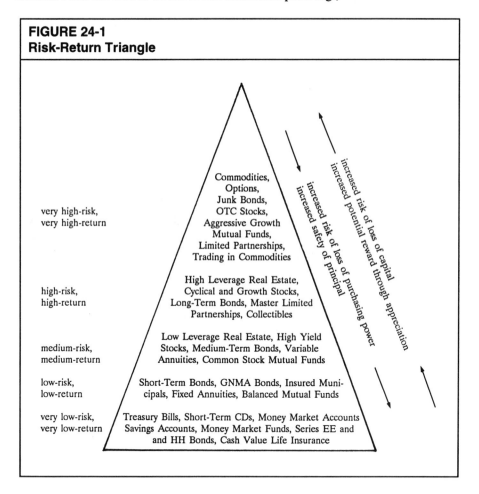

FIGURE 24-1
Risk-Return Triangle

Other Investment-Related Issues

In addition to the client's risk profile, there are other elements of the portfolio building and long-term accumulation phase that apply to virtually all clients. The first of these elements is that investors are planning for a long-term objective. Portfolio design should not be swayed by short-term impulsive changes in conventional wisdom as to what is the right investment for the moment. Unless fundamental, long-term changes are occurring that will affect the investment portfolio path chosen by the client, long-term goals are more likely to be achieved by using a buy-and-hold strategy that includes periodic monitoring and selective repositioning. (*Planning Note:* Dollar-cost averaging (DCA), an approach in which a fixed-dollar amount is invested in a security in each period, is consistent with a buy-and-hold strategy. Clients who use this

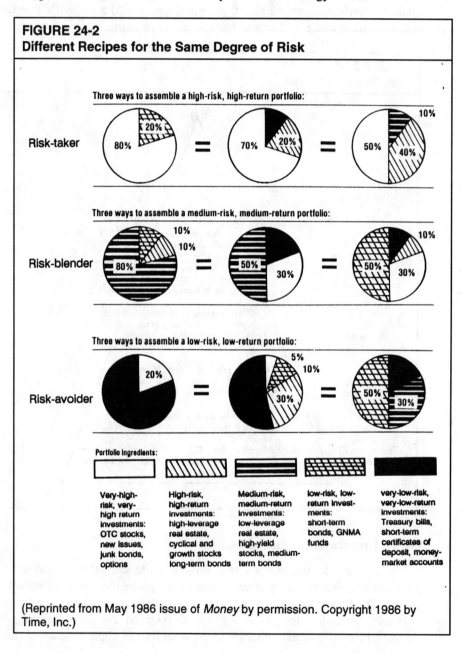

FIGURE 24-2
Different Recipes for the Same Degree of Risk

(Reprinted from May 1986 issue of *Money* by permission. Copyright 1986 by Time, Inc.)

approach will purchase more units of a security when its price is low and fewer units of the security when its price is high. Over a long period of time the investor ends up with a lower average cost for the security than was the average acquisition price for each transaction. For example, reinvestment of quarterly dividends within a common stock mutual fund would be one form of DCA. Periodic contributions of additional funds to purchase a deferred variable annuity would be another illustration of DCA.)

A second common issue, alluded to in the last planning note, that aids effective retirement investment planning is the process of consistently setting aside investment funds. Unless the client is willing to invest funds on a regular basis as part of his or her routine money management, the financial goals for retirement will not be achieved.

The fact that each client's financial affairs will undergo change is another common element. Therefore an annual review of the client's situation should be an integral part of the retirement planning process. This review is important for the following reasons:

- As the standard of living grows, the need for additional saving to fund the increased standard of living also increases.
- Planners may want to suggest that as real income grows the current standard of living should grow at a somewhat reduced pace. Assume real after-tax income increases by 10 percent. If the client limits any increases in lifestyle expenditures to 5 percent of the increase in income, then there will be a sizable increase, proportionately, in funds available for retirement accumulation purposes. For example, if a client has income of $100,000 and allocates $80,000 for lifestyle and $20,000 for retirement purposes, a 10 percent increase in real income will provide an additional $10,000. If the increase in lifestyle expenditures can be kept to $4,000 (or 40 percent of the $10,000 increase), then $6,000 is available for retirement. This $6,000 represents a whopping 30 percent increase in annual retirement funding! In addition, the $4,000 increase in lifestyle expenditures raises the current standard of living by 5 percent.
- Planners must consider downward revisions of funding goals because of job-related reversals or other economic reversals.

A fourth factor is that a client's risk propensity changes over time. This can occur for many reasons such as having a poor experience with previous investments. For example, the sharp stock market decline in October 1987 may have been so devastating psychologically to a client that investments in common stocks (or common-stock-based mutual funds or variable annuities), previously within that client's zone of acceptance, may no longer be an acceptable investment choice. Should this occur, the client needs to (1) reevaluate the expected return from the accumulated funds, (2) restructure the portfolio of accumulated funds, (3) change the allocation of new funds regularly being invested, and (4) alter the amount of annual funding to achieve the retirement target.

The widespread opportunity for clients to participate in an employer-sponsored defined-contribution retirement plan is a fifth common element. Many such plans give investment discretion to the employee. When the client has this opportunity, the investment vehicle(s) chosen should be considered a part of the aggregate portfolio mix for the purpose of assessing the match of the portfolio with the clients risk profile. (*Planning Note:* Employer-sponsored plans often permit additional voluntary contributions (typically on an after-tax basis) that can be made through payroll deductions. This option can provide both the forced element of retirement saving that some individuals need as well as the opportunity to purchase securities with little, if any, transaction costs to the plan participant. More importantly, however, all earnings on qualified plan assets are tax deferred.)

A sixth factor for many clients is the direct ownership of common stocks. Many corporations encourage stockholders to increase their ownership interest in the corporation by offering two attractive methods. One method is for corporations to permit stockholders to make contributions, generally not more frequent than quarterly and within minimum and maximum dollar amounts, to purchase additional shares through this stockholder plan. Another method is the automatic reinvestment of dividends into additional shares of the corporation's stock. In addition to the ease of purchasing additional shares, the attractiveness of these two methods is that the transaction costs are subsidized since the corporation either pays that cost or acquires shares in the market in large volume so that the corporation obtains a negotiated and reduced brokerage commission that can be passed on to the shareholders in the form of lower transaction costs.

When this technique is used, the corporation's stock should be evaluated with respect to its risk-return characteristics and be within the acceptable criteria for the overall retirement portfolio. Clients should be advised against relying so heavily on acquiring these stocks that they do not have a diversified portfolio.

PORTFOLIO RESTRUCTURING PERIOD

The time when major restructuring of a retirement portfolio occurs will vary depending on the client. The restructuring typically begins somewhere between 5 and 15 years prior to the planned retirement date. Therefore, if the client's target retirement age is 65, this phase could begin as early as age 50, but is often delayed until the middle or late 50s or until the early 60s.

As a client approaches retirement, he or she becomes less growth orientated and begins to be more concerned about having enough income from the portfolio for retirement income needs. This change in emphasis occurs for several reasons. First, as the client realizes that since only a few years remain until retirement, he or she has less time in which to recover losses should the higher-risk investments suffer reverses. Therefore the client is now less willing to bear risk within the portfolio and less willing to invest additional funds in or even retain some or all of the currently owned higher-risk investments. Consequently annual retirement funding during these years is directed into investment media near the bottom of the risk-return triangle in figure 24-1. Even if the client retains the currently owned, higher-risk investments acquired in the accumulation period, the risk profile of the total portfolio declines.

A second factor influencing the structure of the client's portfolio is the perceived need for an increased level of income during the retirement years. Assets whose main attraction was that of long-term appreciation during the accumulation period lose their appeal as clients become increasingly concerned about having sufficient current income to maintain the desired standard of living during retirement. This increased focus on income combined with the downward risk profile of the portfolio has the effect of generating more current annual income but less total return each year from the portfolio. As a consequence, until retirement actually takes place, the reinvestment of the portfolio's annual income stream becomes an ever-increasing segment of total portfolio management.

This process of redirecting the portfolio composition continues as the client ages, leading to a portfolio mix at or around retirement that contains significantly less risk than the one held at the beginning of this period. Accompanying this risk reduction is the portfolio's production of a much larger current income stream. The planner and the client must both keep in mind that a higher current income stream does not necessarily equal a higher annual return. The form of the return will change. Investments that produce high current income streams may realize little or no appreciation. The *total* return from the portfolio will most likely decrease over time. If the return does decrease during this period, the client may not, in the absence of increased annual funding, have accumulated the desired amount of assets at retirement. Fortunately this shift in portfolio emphasis and performance typically coincides with a reduction in the client's other personal financial responsibilities. The client might have finished funding his or her children's education and largely paid off homes and personal assets. These reduced demands make available savings that can be used to supplement amounts already being set aside for retirement.

Other Investment-Related Issues

Many clients in this phase of their retirement accumulation planning and investing are nearing the peak years of their earning power. Therefore their employers' contributions (or their own contributions if self-employed) to a qualified pension plan approach the largest amounts that will be set aside on their behalf. As a consequence, the importance of integrating pension plan accumulation with personal retirement accumulation becomes more crucial. Each client needs to assess his or her situation and then make the necessary allocations in the personal plan segment to most effectively combine the two components to achieve the final phases of accumulation and to provide the appropriate sources, stability, level, and growth of income during the retirement years. For example, if it is a defined-benefit pension plan and a lump-sum distribution from the plan is not permissible, then the retirement income will take the form of a fixed-pension income. With this constraint the client could certainly consider placing a portion of the personal assets, both before and during retirement, into investments having some opportunity for growth to supplement the fixed pension plan income and provide inflation protection. However, if a defined-contribution plan or profit-sharing plan is the employer's primary retirement plan and if the funds being set aside are placed primarily in the employer's stock, then a more conservative investment policy may be needed to provide the appropriate balance and diversification during the later years of retirement asset accumulation. No single solution or mix of portfolio assets can be prescribed as the only one acceptable, but guidelines such as those shown in figure 24-2 that are adjusted to fit the particular client provide the starting point for making the portfolio selections.

A second issue arises for clients who are at or near the peak of their earning power. Their accumulation objective would be achieved more easily if the setting aside of investments outside of qualified plans could be done in a tax-advantageous manner. Ideally the annual funding contributions would be deductible, and the income earnings of the fund would have tax-deferred status. Unfortunately recent changes in the income tax laws reduced the tax-advantaged opportunities and eliminated most of the opportunities to deduct contributions. Some tax-deferral opportunities still remain and planners should use them when appropriate for the client's accumulation objectives. For example, both fixed and variable-deferred annuities retain their tax deferral on income earned during the accumulation period. Thus these investment vehicles can fit the needs of either a low- or medium-risk portfolio. Even if a tax-deductible contribution cannot be converted to an IRA, the opportunity to accumulate earnings on a tax-deferred basis until the monies are withdrawn without penalties also provides a meaningful tax saving during the accumulation period. Of course, seeking the capital appreciation with medium- or high-risk investment provides additional tax deferral since gain is not taxed until the securities are sold. Unless these contributions can be made directly to a qualified plan, as discussed earlier in this chapter, this avenue of tax-deductible investment contributions is essentially extinct.

A third common factor that will affect many clients in this accumulation period is the reinvestment. Reinvestment is a recurring event for personally managed portfolios. In addition, clients who take a lump-sum distribution from a qualified pension plan will have to reinvest a large amount at one time. If such distributions are likely, the client should be developing plans for their eventual reinvestment at the time of their distribution or maturity. In addition to developing the primary plan for investing these funds, contingent alternatives must be developed should investment conditions change drastically just prior to the receipt of the plan distribution. Consider for a moment the dilemma of a client who received a plan distribution on October 19, 1987, the day the market lost more than 20 percent of its value. Without contingent plans a faulty investment program might have been instituted.

PRESERVATION AND CURRENT INCOME PERIOD

This period encompasses the time that begins just prior to the retirement date and continues throughout the retirement period. The portfolio design now focuses on preserving the assets. The opportunity to rebuild the stock of assets no longer exists since retirement is at hand. The client wants to keep what he or she has and utilize these investment assets as one source of planned retirement income. Therefore some further restructuring of the portfolio will take place as the client seeks to both reduce the portfolio's risk profile and provide the desired current income to supplement social security and pension plan benefits. However, a portion of the invested assets must be devoted to protecting the client from the effects of inflation during the retirement years. The relative size of this portfolio portion will be influenced by factors such as the client's risk profile, health of self and spouse, financial obligations other than personal maintenance, and expected stability of pension plan income.

Portfolio shifting can generate income tax gains and losses. A successful buy-and-hold strategy generally produces significant gains over a long period of years. Careful planning and scheduling can reduce the tax consequences of the portfolio repositioning. Obviously using losses to offset gains is one effective technique to reduce tax consequences. Another strategy involves carefully assessing, prior to the end of the year, one's income level and tax liability for the year. Then carefully shift enough assets to realize an amount of gain from the sale of assets that will not push the client into a higher tax bracket. Clients who are at the maximum taxable income level for the 33 percent bracket could consider realizing additional capital gains at this time, since the gains will then be taxed at the lower 28 percent rate rather than at next year's 33 percent rate. Further, the taking of capital losses to offset gains made earlier in the year can reduce the tax burden as well as prune the portfolio of problem investments.

(*Planning Note:* Clients often seek additional income but are reluctant to incur the tax liabilities that arise from repositioning portfolio assets. This is particularly so when the client owns Series EE bonds and has deferred any recognition of the interest income earned on these bonds. Some clients could have had the maturity dates of their bonds extended several times. Consequently considerable untaxed interest income is invested in these EE bonds. If the bonds are redeemed, taxes must be paid on the accumulated interest and only the after-tax proceeds would be available for repositioning. A little known income tax deferral technique permits individual owners of Series EE bonds to roll the full redemption amount of the EE bonds into Series HH bonds, continue to defer the recognition of the accumulated EE bond interest until the HH bonds are redeemed, and also receive semiannual interest payments from the HH bonds. When the HH bonds mature, they can be further extended without having to recognize the deferred interest transferred from the EE bonds. Only when the bonds either are redeemed or are passed into the estate of the deceased owner will that untaxed, accumulated Series EE interest be subject to income taxation.)

Common Elements

In addition to shifting the portfolio to meet the retirement objectives, a common consideration among clients is how to manage the portfolio with minimum care and effort. The design of the portfolio should include such factors as an easy system of record keeping for personal and tax purposes and relative stability of the income flow among the months (or perhaps quarters) of the year. For clients who travel extensively or spend extended periods at a vacation home, the ability to have direct deposit of income into income-earning accounts prevents the accumulation of idle, non-income-producing money. (*Planning Note:* More likely than not, the flow of retirement income, particularly if a large portion is portfolio income, will not be level during the year. The use of a money market account or mutual fund provides an easily accessible repository for temporarily accumulated funds and will earn a competitive short-term interest rate.)

Frequently only one spouse actively manages the family finances. If this spouse is the first to die or become disabled, the surviving spouse faces what may appear to be insurmountable problems. Many advisers suggest that the financially inexperienced spouse be given the opportunity to manage the family finances in case the task later becomes his or her responsibility.

Lastly, the potential for a major expenditure such as buying into a retirement life-care community is a common concern for many retirees and spouses. Often the financing for this expenditure comes from the sale of the residence. The current prices of these life-care facilities and the average prices of residences indicate that a transaction of this form may generate some additional investable assets for income-producing purposes. Retirees can always find uses for any additional income, such as increasing their standard of living or making gifts to relatives.

PAY NOW OR PAY LATER

The last item we will discuss in the context of investing for retirement is the concept of deferring income for retirement.

When considering investing in a retirement plan, many accountants and other tax professionals often ask whether it's better to defer income or to pay taxes at current, comparatively lower rates. After all, they reason, wouldn't it be more advantageous to pay taxes at current rates rather than to pay taxes at the increased rates of the future?

Your answer to their question will vary depending on

- the tax rate when funds are distributed
- the timing of the tax increase
- the length of the deferral
- the interest rate that deferred funds earn

These factors come into play because the central issue is whether the deferral of current taxation (that is, the present value of the use of dollars that otherwise would be payable in current income tax) will offset the probable increase in tax rates. In other words, if an employee uses a retirement plan today, he or she is able to invest one dollar for every dollar put aside. If, on the other hand, the money is paid out currently, the employee only has 72 cents out of every dollar to invest, since 28 cents is paid in taxes. The 28 cents per dollar (or the amount of the tax rate) that is deferred under a retirement plan can be likened to an interest-free loan from the government. At what point, then will the interest earned on a certain interest-free loan be enough to offset the *probable* increase in the tax rate? Figure 24-3 shows the amount of time it will take to break even, taking into account various future tax rates, projected after-tax interest rates, and the timing of the tax change.

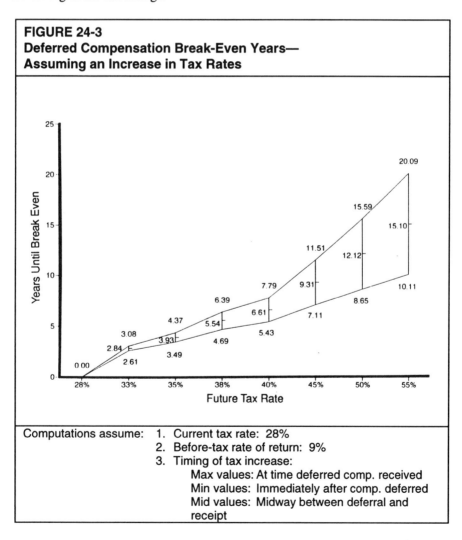

FIGURE 24-3
Deferred Compensation Break-Even Years—
Assuming an Increase in Tax Rates

Computations assume: 1. Current tax rate: 28%
                                      2. Before-tax rate of return: 9%
                                      3. Timing of tax increase:
                                            Max values: At time deferred comp. received
                                            Min values: Immediately after comp. deferred
                                            Mid values: Midway between deferral and
                                            receipt

Example: Dan DiAngelo currently pays taxes at the 28 percent rate and is 10 years away from retirement. Dan expects tax rates to change in 5 years (the mid values) to earn 9 percent on his investment and to pay a tax of 40 percent when he retires. Dan would like to know if he is better off taking his bonus as taxable income or deferring it in his 401(k) plan. According to the table Dan will be better off after 6.61 years by using a deferred compensation plan (go to the 40 percent future tax rate on the bottom and look up to the mid-point, 6.61).

25

Distributions from Retirement Plans—Part 1

Chapter Outline

Planning for the distribution of funds from employer-sponsored retirement plans and IRAs can be one of the most challenging aspects of retirement planning. Any strategy selected must account for the following factors:

- the client's needs and goals

- the variety of distribution options that are available in your client's particular situation
- the implications of choosing one option over another from a tax perspective
- the implications of choosing one option over another from a cash-flow perspective
- the implications of choosing one option over another from a death benefit and estate tax perspective
- the ability to delay the receipt and taxation of a distribution by rolling the distribution over into an IRA or another qualified plan

This chapter and chapter 26 will examine the issues and choices associated with taking distributions from retirement plans, with emphasis on the extensive and complicated tax laws that apply to distributions. There are two caveats before we start. First, all too often planners feel that reducing the taxation on a client's retirement distribution is the only consideration when making a distribution decision. Tax planning is only part of the process. The ultimate goal is to maximize wealth while meeting the client's cash-flow and other needs, not merely to save taxes. Second, rollovers to an IRA or to another qualified plan are not considered taxable distributions from a plan. In fact, the use of rollovers helps to delay taxation.

DISTRIBUTIONS PRIOR TO RETIREMENT

Clients should be discouraged from taking distributions from retirement plans prior to retirement. These distributions may reduce retirement resources to unacceptable levels by undermining the objective of maximizing retirement savings on a tax-advantaged basis. Nevertheless, distributions prior to retirement are common, and planners must know the rules and tax ramifications involved so that they can provide comprehensive financial services for their clients. Let's look at an overview of these rules and their tax ramifications.

In-Service Distributions

Whether or not an individual can obtain a distribution while still employed depends on the type of plan involved. Pension plans prohibit these so-called in-service withdrawals altogether. If a pension plan (defined-benefit plan, cash-balance plan, target-benefit plan, or money-purchase plan) permits an employee to receive a distribution while employed, the plan will lose its tax- sheltered status. Profit-sharing plans, stock bonus plans, and employee stock ownership plans (ESOPs), however, may be designed to permit employees to receive in-service withdrawals after funds have been in the client's account for 2 years or after 5 years of participation. In addition, 401(k) plans and 403(b) plans may be designed to allow in-service withdrawals if the employee has a financial hardship. Finally, IRAs and simplified employee pension plans (SEPs) allow withdrawals with absolutely no plan impediments. (*Planning Note:* Plans may distribute funds to former employees who become disabled or distribute funds to the beneficiary of a deceased employee.)

Distributions When Changing Employers

When an employee leaves employment prior to retirement for reasons other than death or disability, the provisions of the plan will dictate whether a distribution of retirement funds can occur. Many plans have adopted a cash-out provision and will permit employees to take funds in a lump-sum payout when they terminate employment prior to retirement. If the plan has such a provision, an employer is entitled to cash out the former employee's retirement account (or accrued benefit) if the employee's balance or accrued benefit is $3,500 or less, regardless of the employee's decision to the contrary. If the employee's account balance or accrued benefit is over $3,500, however, an employee can opt to have his or her funds remain in the former employer's plan until retirement. This option is seldom chosen because most clients do not want to deal with a former employer. (*Planning Note:* Clients should compare the investment performance of plan funds when making distribution decisions. If the former employer's plan earns a better rate of return than the new employer's plan, your client should consider leaving his or her plan assets in the former employer's plan.) Also remember that clients may roll balances over to IRAs where they may have considerable flexibility in how the balances are invested. However, they also lose some tax advantages and flexibility in other regards (as will be discussed later).

Some employers do not provide a cash-out provision. These employers decide to play hardball with an employee who leaves their company, and they design a plan to hold a former employee's funds until retirement time. (*Planning Note:* Regardless of your client's situation, advise him or her not to squander a distribution at termination. According to one study, over 90 percent of those currently taking distributions prior to retirement use their distribution for current consumption. Funds should be rolled over into an IRA or, if permitted, into the new employer's plan.)

Taxation of Distributions Prior to Retirement

In the case of a plan that allows for preretirement distributions, it is not atypical for a participant to receive an in-service distribution on a portion of his or her benefit in order to meet financial hardships or to pay for other expenses. If the participant's entire benefit consists of pretax contributions, any distribution will be included in the participant's taxable income. However, if a portion of the benefit is attributable to amounts that have already been taxed (referred to as the investment in the contract), some or all of such distribution will not be taxed. Investment in the contract includes employee after-tax contributions and PS 58 costs as well as other amounts.

Prior to 1987, an amount up to the participant's investment could be withdrawn prior to the annuity starting date (the time retirement benefits begin) without income tax consequences. The Tax Reform Act of 1986 changed this rule significantly. A grandfather provision still allows a participant to withdraw an amount equal to the pre-1987 investment in the contract without tax as long as the plan provided for in-service distributions on May 5, 1986. Post-86 amounts attributable to the investment in the contract, however, are now subject to a pro rata rule. The general rule is that the amount of the distribution that is excluded from tax is based on a ratio, with the numerator being the investment in the contract and the denominator being the total account balance at the time of the distribution. However, when determining the ratio, an individual may treat employee after-tax contributions and the investment experience thereon separately from the rest of the participant's benefit. This rule still allows a participant to withdraw after-tax contributions with limited tax liability. This principle can be best illustrated with an example.

Example: Joe has an account balance of $1,000, $200 of which is attributable to post-1986 employee contributions and $50 of which is attributable to investment earnings on $200. Joe takes an in-service distribution of $100. The exclusion ratio is $200/$250 or 80 percent. Therefore Joe will receive $80 income tax free and will owe tax on $20.

Early-Distribution Penalty

Despite the fact that clients may legally be allowed to obtain their retirement funds prior to retirement, the government imposes penalties on those who do. A 10 percent penalty will be imposed on the taxable amount of a preretirement distribution in most cases (commonly referred to as the Sec. 72(t) penalty). In addition, taxpayers must include the appropriate amount of the distribution in their taxable income.

The 10 percent tax applies only to the "taxable portion" of the distribution. If a distribution includes amounts that have been previously subject to tax, such as after-tax employee contributions, the nontaxable portion of the distribution is exempt from the 10 percent penalty tax.

The 10 percent penalty applies to distributions that are made from a qualified plan, a Sec. 403(b) plan, an individual retirement account, and a SEP. The rule is stated in such a way that the penalty is supposed to apply to all preretirement distributions. However, a distribution can escape the 10 percent penalty if it qualifies under one of several exceptions. To escape the 10 percent penalty the distributions must be made

- on or after attainment of age 59 1/2
- to a beneficiary or to an employee's estate on or after the employee's death
- attributable to disability

- as part of a series of substantially equal periodic payments made at least annually over the life or life expectancy of the employee or the joint lives or life expectancies of the employee and beneficiary. (If the distribution is from a qualified plan, the employee must separate from service.)
- after a separation from service for early retirement after age 55 (not applicable to IRAs)
- to the extent of medical expenses deductible for the year under Code Sec. 213 whether or not actually deductible (not applicable to IRAs)

The following examples should help to illustrate when the 10 percent penalty applies and when it does not.

Example: ,Greg Murphy, aged 55, takes a $50,000 lump-sum distribution from his profit-sharing plan. The $50,000 lump-sum distribution will be subject to a $5,000 penalty unless Greg has taken early retirement pursuant to an early retirement provision in his plan.

Example: Jane Goodall, aged 45, takes a life annuity from Biological Researchers, Inc., when she quits and goes to work for The Primate Institute. Jane's distribution is not subject to penalty because of the periodic payments exception.

Example: Ed Miller, aged 35, takes a distribution from his 401(k) plan to meet an extreme financial hardship. Ed's distribution is subject to the 10 percent penalty.

RETIREMENT DISTRIBUTIONS: AN OVERVIEW

Choosing the best distribution at retirement can be a rather complex decision. This decision involves personal preferences, financial considerations, and an interplay between tax incentives and tax penalties. Planners must keep in mind a myriad of factors in order to render effective advice.

For example, typical considerations include

- whether the periodic distribution will be used to provide income necessary for sustaining the retiree or whether the distribution will supplement already adequate sources of retirement income
- whether the client has properly coordinated distributions from several different qualified plans and IRAs
- whether the retiree will have satisfactory diversification of his or her retirement resources after the distribution occurs
- whether the client has complied with the rules for minimum distributions from a qualified plan

- whether the client is receiving "too much" from the retirement plan, thereby subjecting his or her distributions to a success tax (the 15 percent excise tax on excess distributions and excess accumulations, which is discussed later in this chapter)

Qualified retirement plans typically stipulate the type of distribution that your client will receive. In pension language this is referred to as the normal form of benefit. The normal form of benefit from a qualified plan for a married individual is a joint and survivor benefit of not less than 50 percent or greater than 100 percent. For a single individual the normal form of benefit is typically a life annuity (or in a contributory plan a modified cash-refund annuity). Regardless of the plan's normal-form-of-benefit payment, participants frequently elect out of the normal form in order to choose a different type of distribution (a married individual needs his or her spouse's written consent to elect out). Options for distributions include

- annuity payments
- installment payments
- lump-sum distributions

The remainder of this chapter deals with the two forms of periodic distributions—annuities and installment payments. The advantage of a client taking a periodic distribution as opposed to a lump-sum distribution is the continuance of deferral of taxation afforded retirement assets until the assets are actually distributed. Let's take a closer look at these distributions now and at lump-sum distributions in chapter 26.

Annuity Distributions

Annuity contracts provide for the payment of income on a monthly basis as if part of the client's salary was being paid during retirement. These contracts are basically the distribution or liquidation of a sum of money (the plan's benefit) on an actuarial basis. The amount of the benefit that is payable depends on several factors. These factors include

- the amount used to fund the annuity called the annuity's purchase price (which is a function of the plan's contribution or benefit formula)
- the age of your client
- the number of lives covered by the annuity (if the annuity covers two lives, the amount of the benefit is dependent on the ages of both people)
- any minimum guarantees that are offered
- the interest assumption used

Each annuity payment is composed of part payback of the annuity purchase price, part investment earnings on the purchase price, and some benefit of survivorship to surviving annuitants from other annuitants who died before receiving a full return of their purchase price. In addition, part of the forfeited funds will be pooled with funds from other annuitants to provide extended benefits for those annuitants who live beyond their life expectancy.

There are several types of annuity forms from which the planner can choose. Let's take a closer look. (See table 25-1.)

Life Annuity

A life annuity provides monthly payments to your client during his or her lifetime. Payments from a life annuity completely stop when your client dies and no other benefit is paid to any beneficiary. Since all of the annuity funds are being applied toward providing the monthly benefit and none of the annuity funds toward providing a survivor benefit or a refund of premium (as is the case in any other type of annuity), a life annuity provides the largest monthly benefit for a given amount of money (table 25-1).

A life annuity is an ideal choice for persons trying to stretch their assets as far as possible while still guaranteeing a lifetime income because a life annuity maximizes the amount of the monthly benefit. Typically individuals who are not concerned about providing retirement income to a spouse or other dependent choose a life-annuity option. Caution is advised, however, because even if an annuitant receives just one payment under the contract before he or she dies, all the remaining value in this contract is forfeited. If your client is seeking a minimum payback guarantee to be provided for a beneficiary and does not need to squeeze the maximum benefit out of his or her annuity, he or she should be advised to reject the straight life annuity because of the possibility of forfeiture.

Life Annuity with Guaranteed Payments

A life annuity with guaranteed payments (sometimes referred to as a life annuity with a period-certain guarantee) provides monthly benefit payments to your client during his or her lifetime. Similar to a life annuity, payments stop when your client dies. Unlike a life annuity, however, if an agreed-upon minimum amount of guaranteed payments has not been paid to the annuitant, these payments (or their lump-sum commuted value) will be paid out to your client's beneficiary. Any length of guarantee is available. Typical guarantee periods are for 5 years or 10 years. The longer the payout that is guaranteed means the lower the monthly benefit that your client will receive (table 25-1). This decrease occurs because the underwriter must allocate part of the annuity funds toward the guarantee feature, and the larger the guarantee the more assets that must be shifted away from the pooled assets providing current monthly benefits.

For retirement-planning purposes clients who have no need to provide retirement income to a spouse or other dependent will choose a life annuity. If, however, there is a need to provide for the continuation of retirement income, a joint and survivor annuity is typically used. If your client falls between these polar positions, then a life annuity with minimum guarantees may be appropriate. A life annuity with guaranteed payments is often used by clients who would like to make sure that a portion of the annuity premium will be recovered either as a benefit to themselves or to a beneficiary.

Life annuities with guaranteed payments are also used to provide a limited survivor benefit to an unhealthy spouse. For example, if a retiring husband expects to outlive his wife who is in relatively poor health, then a life annuity with a minimum guarantee might be purchased to protect against the unlikely case of the husband predeceasing the wife. The period chosen should reflect to some extent the planner's best estimate of the wife's maximum life expectancy and, if applicable, the client's desire to pass on wealth. A client can pass on wealth because minimum guaranteed payments will be made to any beneficiary until the guarantee is completed. (*Planning Note:* If a client outlives the guarantee period, he or she has, in effect, gambled and lost because lower monthly benefits will be paid under a life annuity with guaranteed payments than under a straight life annuity.)

Modified Cash-Refund Annuity

A modified cash-refund annuity (MCR) is the typical normal form of benefit for single individuals in a contributory pension plan. An MCR annuity provides monthly payments to your client during his or her lifetime and stops at your client's death (similar to a life annuity). Under this contract, however, the amount that is refunded is not the participant's benefit for a specified number of years but for a specified amount of minimum benefits (typically the client's contributions to the plan with interest). This type of annuity ensures that the client's contributions to the pension plan will not be lost because of premature death. As with the life annuity with guaranteed payments the refund feature costs the participant in the form of lower monthly benefits. The reduction in monthly benefits depends upon the size of the refund in that the larger the refund that is chosen, the smaller the amount of monthly benefits and vice versa. In addition, as with a life annuity with guaranteed payments, if the client recovers the amount of the cash refund in benefit payments, the client has gambled and lost because monthly payments will be lower.

Joint and Survivor Annuity

As previously mentioned, the normal form of benefit paid to a married individual from a qualified plan is a joint and survivor annuity. A joint and survivor annuity provides monthly payments to your client during his or her lifetime. The retirement income continues after your client's death with payments made to your client's spouse (*the survivor*). The amount of the survivor payment can be

- the same amount that was being paid out to your client (J&S 100)
- two-thirds of the amount that was being paid out to your client (J&S 66 2/3)
- one-half of the amount that was being paid out to your client (J&S 50)

Annuity payments will cease upon the surviving spouse's death, and no death benefit or refund of premiums will be paid. The beneficiary under a joint and survivor annuity does not have to be the spouse. If the client is married, however, the spouse must consent not to be the beneficiary. When recommending a joint and survivor annuity, the planner should consider the following:

- In general, the younger the beneficiary is, the lower the monthly benefit that will be paid (because of the increased "survivor portion" of the annuity). For example, a joint and survivor annuity where the spouse is much younger than the plan participant will provide a lower monthly payment.
- As a general rule when the survivor benefit ratio is higher (that is, 100, 66 2/3, or 50 percent), the monthly benefit will be lower. For example, a joint and survivor annuity with 100 percent survivor benefits will be more costly in a given case (that is, provide lower monthly payments) than a joint and survivor annuity that provides a two-thirds survivor annuity.
- The life expectancy, based on the health of your client and his or her spouse, must be strongly considered. For example, if there is a great likelihood that the spouse will outlive the plan participant, a 100 percent joint and survivor annuity may be appropriate.
- Any life insurance coverage that is in force on the life of the participant should be considered when determining the need for a survivor option. Depending on the circumstances, a better benefit package may sometimes be created by combining the single life annuity option with the purchase of life insurance on the participant's life to provide the survivor benefit rather than by electing the J&S annuity from the plan.
- The amount of income needed by the surviving spouse will help to determine the percentage of the survivorship benefit that will be chosen. For example, retirement income needs may drop radically if one party dies (for example, in the case where one party was disabled or sickly and required expensive medical attention).

Other Annuities

In addition to the typical forms of annuities, your client's plan may contain one or more of the following less frequently used annuity forms.

Full Cash Refund. A full-cash-refund annuity pays back the full purchase price as a guaranteed minimum benefit. Under this annuity, if the client dies prior to receiving monthly benefits equal to the annuity purchase price, the difference between the purchase price and aggregate monthly payments already received is refunded to the client's beneficiary.

Temporary Annuity. A temporary annuity is a life annuity that expires after a given period of time. A temporary annuity can be elected by those participants who retire prior to age 65 and wish to provide a level benefit from the combination of social security and pension payments. Under a temporary annuity an amount equal to what will be received as a social security benefit will be provided until the earlier of the social security starting date or the client's death.

Annuity Certain. This annuity provides you with a specified amount of monthly guaranteed payments after which time all payments stop (for example, payments for 20 years). An annuity certain continues to be paid whether your client survives the annuity period or not. If the client dies prior to 20 years, payments will be made to the client's beneficiary. This can also be used as a pre-social security benefit supplement.

TABLE 25-1 Comparison of Annuity Forms ($200,000 purchase price at client aged 65, spouse aged 65)	
Annuity Form	Monthly Benefit
Life	$1,565
Life Annuity/10-year guarantee	1,494
Life Annuity/20-year guarantee	1,360
Joint and Survivor (50 percent)	1,418
Joint and Survivor (66 2/3 percent)	1,375
Joint and Survivor (100 percent)	1,296

Case Studies

Ralph and Dora Archer. Ralph Archer, aged 65, is nearing retirement and must choose the form of his retirement distribution. His wife, Dora, is independently wealthy, and both Ralph and Dora have families from previous marriages. Essentially all Dora's wealth will be directed to her children upon her death. Ralph earns a modest income and is concerned about outliving his own financial resources if he survives Dora. The marriage is very solid and Ralph will have no financial difficulties as long as Dora is alive.

Ralph's two main objectives are to maximize his retirement benefits and to guarantee that his benefits will be lifelong. Ralph may be well advised to delay the inception of his retirement benefits until the earlier of legally required distributions at age 70 1/2 or Dora's death. When Ralph does start receiving his benefits, he would be wise to select a life annuity since he does not need to provide survivor benefits for Dora and is not bothered by the prospect of forfeiting unpaid benefits at death. Ralph's $200,000 fund balance can provide him with $1,565 per month for the rest of his life starting at age 65. This payment is 20 percent more than he would receive if he were to elect a joint survivor annuity benefit providing equal payments to Dora after his death.

Jerry and Joan Davenport. Jerry and Joan Davenport have no children and have been completely dependent on Jerry's modest income for their financial support. They are both aged 65 and Jerry must now select the form of his retirement distribution. Joan has been fighting cancer for the last year and the doctors do not expect her to live more than 8 months. Jerry is in extremely good health and comes from a very long-lived family. He is concerned about having an adequate income and wants to make sure that he does not exhaust his resources before his death. Jerry can maximize his guaranteed lifetime income by selecting a life-annuity option. In addition, Jerry might consider buying term insurance as a hedge against his predeceasing his wife.

Larry and Sheila Richardson. Larry and Sheila Richardson are preparing for Larry's retirement at age 65. They have no children and are both in good health. Because Sheila is only 50 years old, selection of a survivorship annuity will significantly decrease the monthly benefit available from the pension plan. They are wondering whether they should take the joint and survivor benefit or elect out of the survivorship benefit and apply the difference to the purchase of life insurance on Larry with the benefits payable to Sheila. This decision depends on Larry's insurability and the cost of coverage relative to the benefit it provides. If the death benefit provided is greater than the cost of the life annuity for Sheila, the purchase of life insurance is a viable alternative.

Variable Annuities

Some employer plans offer variable-annuity contracts as well as the fixed-dollar annuity contracts just discussed. The variable-annuity contracts are designed to provide fluctuating benefit payments over the payout period that may provide increasing benefits during periods of inflation. Insurance companies do this by investing the assets backing these contracts in higher-risk investments than are used for fixed-dollar annuity contracts and by allowing your client to participate in the investment performance. (*Planning Note:* Variable annuities have historically enabled clients to maintain some degree of the purchasing power of their benefits. Clients who can undertake the additional risk should seriously consider a variable annuity.)

The types of benefit arrangements available under variable-annuity contracts are the same as those available under fixed-dollar annuities. The only thing that changes is the fluctuating nature of the actual benefit payments.

Operation of a Variable Annuity

Under a variable-annuity contract your client will have a given number of annuity units as of the date the contract is annuitized, and that number of units will not change during the benefit payout period. However, the value of any one annuity unit does change. That value fluctuates in direct relationship to the net asset value of the annuity assets managed by the insurance company. As the value of the invested assets increases, the value of the annuity units will also increase. Likewise, decreases in the investment portfolio for the contracts will lead to decreases in the value of annuity units. The actual benefit payment each month will depend on the current value of the annuity unit multiplied by the number of units owned.

Under most variable-annuity contracts there is an assumed investment rate (AIR) that the investment portfolio must earn in order for benefit payments to remain level. If the investment performance exceeds that AIR, then the level of benefit payments will increase. On the other hand, if the investment performance falls below the AIR, then the level of benefit payments will decrease.

> *Example:* Your client, Frank Jackson, has purchased a variable-annuity contract that was issued with a 6 percent AIR and a beginning unit value of $20. Frank owns 100 units. The investment yield during the first month in Frank's contract was 12 percent, and the investment yield during the second month was 4 percent. Frank can calculate his monthly benefit by monitoring the changes in the unit value and by comparing the actual performance with the assumed 6 percent interest rate. During the first month the 12 percent return on portfolio doubles the assumed 6 percent AIR and leads to a 6 percent increase in the $20 unit value. The new unit value is now $21.20 ($2,120 per month). During the subsequent month because the actual return is only 4 percent, which is 2 percent less than the AIR, there will be a 2 percent reduction in the unit value and a new unit value of $20.77 ($2,077 per month) is produced. The unit value could actually drop below the beginning $20 value ($2,000 per month) if investment performance remains below the assumed 6 percent level for an extended period of time.

Under some contracts the purchaser is able to select the AIR from a narrow range of possible rates. It is much easier to receive an increasing stream of benefit payments by selecting a lower AIR even though it is initially more expensive. The effect of choosing a different AIR can be demonstrated by returning to the Frank Jackson example.

Example: The effect of choosing a different AIR can be demonstrated by returning to the Frank Jackson example. If Frank Jackson had chosen an AIR of 8 percent rather than 6 percent (necessitating a lower premium), the benefit increase in the first month would have been only 4 percent instead of 6 percent. The unit value would have changed to $20.80 instead of $21.20. The next month's decrease in benefits would have been a more drastic 4 percent reduction rather than the 2 percent reduction. The unit value would have decreased to $19.96 instead of $20.77 from the lower AIR. By choosing the less costly higher AIR, the client increases the likelihood that benefit payments will increase less rapidly and decrease more rapidly.

YOUR FINANCIAL SERVICES PRACTICE:
VARIABLE ANNUITIES

Variable annuities can only be sold by agents licensed as both securities dealers and life insurance agents. This dual qualification is needed because the sales of these products are regulated by both the Securities and Exchange Commission (SEC) and the state insurance departments. The reason for both SEC and state insurance department involvement is that the risk involved with these products is greater than with most other insurance products.

If your client has a variable annuity, keep in mind that although variable-annuity contracts are intended to provide a hedge against inflation and protect the purchasing power of the benefits, these increases have not always occurred with price increases. Often prices go up significantly before the level of benefits increase. These temporary mismatches between price increases and benefit increases are inevitable and can lead to a temporary loss of purchasing power.

TAXATION OF PERIODIC DISTRIBUTIONS

Periodic payments (annuity or installment payments) made from qualified plans, IRA accounts, and 403(b) annuities are generally taxable as ordinary income. However, if some of the participant's benefit under the plan is attributable to dollars in the plan that have already been subject to taxation, such as employee contributions and amounts attributable to term insurance premiums (PS 58 costs), then a portion of each annuity payment will be exempt from tax until the total nontaxable amount has been distributed.

Different rules apply depending upon whether the recipient has begun to receive periodic payments as a retirement benefit or whether an in-service preretirement distribution is being made. The rules applicable to preretirement in-service distributions have already been discussed. This section will review the rules applicable to retirement distributions.

In a qualified plan or 403(b) annuity, when the plan pays out an annuity, the exclusive method for determining how much of each distribution which will be excluded from tax is determined by dividing the investment in the contract by the number of expected monthly annuity payments (as determined by an IRS table; see table 25-2).

The investment in the contract is the aggregate amount of after-tax contributions to the plan (plus other after-tax amounts such as PS 58 costs and repayments of loans previously taxed as distributions) minus the aggregate amount received before the annuity starting date that was excluded from income.

TABLE 25-2 Number of Months for Exclusion Method	
Age of Distributee	Number of Payments
55 and under	360
56–60	310
61–65	260
66–70	210
71 and over	160

The distributee recovers his or her investment in the contract in level amounts over the number of monthly payments determined in the table above. The amount excluded from each payment is calculated by dividing the investment by the set number of monthly payments determined as follows:

$$\frac{\text{Investment}}{\text{Number of monthly payments}} = \frac{\text{Tax - free portion}}{\text{of monthly annuity}}$$

The dollar amount determined will be excluded from each monthly annuity payment, even where the amount of the annuity payments changes. For example, the amount to be excluded as determined at the annuity starting date remains constant, even if the amount of the annuity payments rises due to cost-of-living increases or decreases (in the case of a reduced survivor benefit annuity). If the amount to be excluded from each monthly payment is greater than the amount of the monthly annuity (as might be the case with decreased survivor payments), then each monthly annuity payment will be completely excluded from gross income until the entire investment is recovered. Once the entire investment is recovered, each monthly payment is fully taxable.

Example: John Thomas is about to begin a retirement benefit in the form of a life annuity. His investment in the contract is $40,000. John is aged 65 at the time benefit payments begin. The set number of months used to compute the exclusion amount is 260 (for age 65 from table 25-2). Since his investment in the contract is $40,000, the amount excluded from each payment is $154 ($40,000/260).

MINIMUM DISTRIBUTION RULES

Some clients are in the enviable position of being so financially well off that they would prefer to minimize distributions from their qualified plans, IRAs, 403(b) annuities, SIMPLEs, and SEPs during their lifetime to defer taxes on the distributions and enhance wealth. To ensure that these plans are used for their legislatively intended purpose—to provide *retirement income* for the participant—the tax law requires that certain minimum distributions be made to participants beginning at a specified age. To make sure that taxpayers comply with this purpose a 50 percent excise tax is imposed on the amount by which a distribution in a given year falls short of the minimum required distribution. In addition, if money is not withdrawn on schedule from an IRA, the IRA could lose its tax-exempt status.

If a plan so provides, a participant can defer distributions until the "required beginning date." The required beginning date for minimum distributions is generally April 1 of the year following the year in which the covered individual attained age 70 1/2. Subsequent distributions must be made by December 31 of each year thereafter. An exception to the required beginning date applies to distributions from qualified plans and 403(b) plans. Under these plans the required beginning date (for anyone other than a 5 percent owner) is the later of April 1 following the year in which the individual attained age 70 1/2 or retired. This exception does not apply to IRAs—meaning that it also does not apply to SEPs and SIMPLEs.

If your client is interested in taking the minimum possible amount of distribution each year, he or she should elect to take the minimum required distribution under either the installment or account plan rules instead of electing an annuity distribution. If, as is often the case, the employer plan does not offer an installment payout option, plan benefits may often be rolled out to an IRA, where the owner has complete discretion as to the distribution schedule.

The amount that must be distributed each year to satisfy the requirements is fairly involved and depends on several factors, such as (1) whether the covered individual's beneficiary is a spouse or not, (2) whether payments are received in the form of an annuity or discretionary payments, and (3) whether the life expectancy of the participant and/or the beneficiary (if a spouse) is recalculated each year. (Life expectancies are typically recalculated to compute the minimum possible distribution.)

General Rules for Determining Minimum Distributions

In general, the minimum distribution rules provide two alternative tests that are used to determine the required minimum distribution. The first test, which is defined here as the Applicable Life Expectancy (ALE) method, applies in all cases. The second test, called the Minimum Distribution Incidental Benefit (MDIB) requirement, applies in any case where the participant's beneficiary is not a spouse. When the beneficiary is not the spouse, the required minimum distribution is determined using the method (ALE method or MDIB requirement) that provides the *greater* distribution.

The ALE Method

To determine the minimum required distribution the participant's aggregate benefit balance is divided each year by the ALE for the distribution year. In the first distribution year (the year the participant reaches age 70 1/2) the ALE is equal to the joint and last survivor life expectancy at the participant's and beneficiary's attained ages in the distribution year as determined using table VI of IRS Reg. 1.72-9 (appendix 5). If the participant has no beneficiary, the ALE is equal to the single-life expectancy from table V of IRS Reg. 1.72-9 (appendix 5).

> *Example:* Bob Ericson, aged 71, is in the first distribution year. His wife, Betty, is aged 59. Bob's aggregate benefit balances are equal to $1,500,000. The ALE (joint and survivor expectancy) from table VI (appendix 5) is 26.7 years. Therefore the required minimum distribution is $56,180 ($1,500,000/26.7).

In subsequent years the ALE is recomputed depending on whether life expectancies are recalculated each year. If neither life expectancy is recalculated each year, the ALE in each year subsequent to the initial distribution year is determined by subtracting 1 from the initial ALE (which was 26.7) for each year since the required beginning date.

> *Example:* If life expectancies are not recalculated for either Bob or Betty, the ALE in the second distribution year is 25.7 (initial ALE of 26.7 minus 1). If the aggregate benefits are now $1,560,000 (assuming the benefit balance remaining after the first year distribution grew at 8 percent), the required minimum distribution is $60,700 ($1,560,000) 25.7). The ALE in the third distribution year would be 24.7; in the fourth year, 23.7; and so on until the 27th year when the remaining benefit balances would be distributed.

However, using the ALE without a recalculation is not the most typical case. Unless a plan specifies otherwise or the participant elects otherwise, life expectancies will be recalculated annually. In the case where the beneficiary is a spouse, both the participant's and the spouse's life expectancies may be recalculated annually. In the case of a nonspousal beneficiary, only the participant's life expectancy may be recalculated.

When both a participant and a spousal beneficiary recalculate life expectancies, the ALE is computed each year (while both are alive) by finding the joint and survivor life expectancy at their attained ages in table VI in the same manner as when determining the initial ALE.

Example: If Bob and Betty's life expectancies are both recalculated in the second year, when Bob is aged 72 and Betty is aged 60, the ALE is 25.8 (table VI) as compared to 25.7 when life expectancies are not recalculated. Consequently, the required minimum distribution in the second distribution year is $60,465 as compared to $60,700 without recalculation. The difference between the ALE with recalculation and the ALE without recalculation increases each year. When Bob is aged 86 and Betty is aged 74, the ALE with recalculation is 14.1, as compared to 11.7 (26.7 minus 15) without recalculation, which translates into more than an 11 percent smaller distribution for a given fund balance.

Although recalculating life expectancies will reduce the required minimum distributions while the parties whose life expectancies are being recalculated live, recalculating does have one serious drawback. When a person whose life expectancy is being recalculated dies, the ALE for calculating minimum distributions in subsequent years is determined using only the survivor's life expectancy, not the joint and survivor life expectancy. Consequently, in the years after the death of a person whose life expectancy was being recalculated, the required minimum distribution may be significantly higher than it would have been otherwise if the life expectancy had not been recalculated.

Example: Bob's and Betty's life expectancies are both recalculated each year. In the second distribution year, at age 60, Betty dies. The required distribution in the second year is based on their attained ages as if Betty had not died (see prior example), but in the year after Betty's death—the third distribution year—the required minimum distribution is based solely on Bob's attained age, 73. The ALE is 13.9 (from the single-life expectancy table V of IRS Reg. 1.72-9) as compared to 24.9 had Betty lived. Furthermore, if Bob and Betty had elected not to recalculate regardless of which spouse died first, the ALE would have remained 24.7.

Because there is the penalty of larger required distributions after the death of either the participant or spouse whose life expectancy is being recalculated, it may sometimes be advisable to not recalculate life expectancies or to recalculate the life expectancy of only one partner. This would be especially true if either is in poor health.

If the participant elects to have only one of the two life expectancies recalculated, the ALE is computed using a complicated formula. The ALE so computed for each distribution year will fall between the ALE when both spouses recalculate life expectancies and the ALE when neither spouse recalculates life expectancy. Consequently the required distribution while both participant and beneficiary live will be greater than those required when both recalculate and less than those required if neither recalculates.

Minimum Distribution Incidental Benefit Requirement (MDIB)

The Minimum Distribution Incidental Benefit requirement (MDIB) applies only when the beneficiary is *not* a spouse. This added restriction ensures that required distributions are not reduced below a given level by selecting a beneficiary, such as a grandchild, whose age is substantially less than the participant's age. The required minimum distribution under the MDIB requirement is determined by dividing the participant's benefit balances by a factor from a table given in IRS regulations based on the participant's age (appendix 6). The values in the table are essentially the same as the joint and survivor life expectancy at the participant's attained age for a beneficiary assumed to be 10 years younger than the participant. In other words, if the participant's beneficiary is not the spouse, the factor used to determine the required minimum distribution is the ALE (as described above) if the beneficiary is less than 10 years younger than the participant. If the beneficiary is more than 10 years younger than the participant, the values from the MDIB table are used (based on a 10-year spread in ages).

Minimum Distribution Rules with Annuities

If your client's plan does not allow the flexibility to use installment payout distributions, there are similar rules for annuity forms of payments. As with the rules for discretionary installments from qualified plans, these rules also prevent participants from manipulating the plan distribution to reduce payments below certain required minimums.

Essentially an annuity contract will meet the minimum distribution requirements if, at all times after the required beginning date, payments are at least equal to what would be required under the rules applicable to discretionary installment payments. For a participant with a spousal beneficiary, a joint and survivor life annuity or a period-certain annuity (that is not in excess of the applicable joint and survivor life expectancy under table VI) will usually meet the minimum distribution requirements. When the beneficiary is not the spouse of the participant, the annuity payment method is subject to the MDIB requirements that may require payments in excess of those computed using joint and survivor life expectancies.

The annuity payments must always be nonincreasing unless any increase is determined under a specified cost-of-living index, paid as a refund of employee contributions upon the participant's death or paid pursuant to a variable annuity according to the investment performance of the annuity assets.

In applying the MDIB requirements to annuity payments for a participant and a nonspousal beneficiary, the regulations use two tables. The first table (appendix 6) is used to determine the maximum period certain under the MDIB requirements. If benefits are received in the form of a period-certain annuity without a life contingency (an annuity that pays out for a given number of periods regardless of whether the beneficiaries live or die), the table provides a maximum allowable period certain corresponding to the attained age of the participant at the time the annuity commences. These values are identical to those used for computing the MDIB requirement for discretionary installment payments.

If the participant chooses a period-certain annuity that is in excess of the maximum period certain under the table, the MDIB requirement will not be satisfied. Therefore it is important for the participant to be sure that a period-certain annuity does not exceed the maximum period certain under the table.

If the annuity is in the form of a life annuity, the MDIB requirement is determined by reference to a different table (appendix 7). This table is used to determine the applicable percentage. The applicable percentage is applied to the amount payable to the participant, and the resulting amount is the maximum amount that may be payable to the survivor upon the death of the participant. To qualify under the MDIB requirements the amount payable to a nonspousal survivor must be equal to or less than the applicable percentage given in the table. This means that the amount payable to the survivor will be less than the amount payable to the participant if the participant is more than 10 years older than the survivor.

The minimum distribution rules apply to each plan in which a person participates. In general, a person is required to take the minimum distributions from each of the plans in which he or she participates. However, under proposed regulations that have been recently released, persons with more than one individual retirement account may determine their aggregate minimum required distributions from each of their plans and then take the distribution from one or more of the plans, as desired, as long as the total distribution equals the aggregate required minimums from each of the plans. Similar rules apply for tax-sheltered annuities. However, these rules apply separately to IRAs and tax-sheltered annuities in that the owner is required to take at least one distribution from his or her IRAs and at least one distribution from his or her tax-sheltered annuities.

TAX ON EXCESS DISTRIBUTIONS AND EXCESS ACCUMULATIONS

The Tax Reform Act of 1986 (TRA '86) created a 15 percent excise tax on excess retirement distributions and excess retirement accumulations. This "success" tax applies to benefits from qualified retirement plans, IRAs, SEPs, Keogh plans, and 403(b) tax-deferred annuities.

Excess Lifetime Distributions

Briefly, excess distributions are defined separately for regular and lump-sum distributions. The 15 percent excise tax is imposed on regular lifetime (non-lump-sum) distributions, with certain limited exclusions, to the extent that the total of such distributions received in any year exceeds the applicable annual exemption (the annual threshold amount). The applicable annual exemption is $160,000 (as indexed in 1997).

The applicable annual exemption for lump-sum distributions where 5-year or 10-year averaging is elected is equal to 5 times the applicable annual exemption for regular distributions. For example, in 1997 the lump-sum exemption is $800,000 (5 times the $160,000 annual exemption for regular distributions).

Another exception to the $160,000 limit is for individuals who elected a special irrevocable grandfather provision on a tax return for a tax year beginning before January 1, 1989. In this case the threshold is the greater of the annual exemption or the grandfather recovery amount for the year (until the grandfather recovery amount is used up).

Finally note that the Small Business Job Protection Act of 1997 provided temporary relief from this tax by indicating that distributions in 1997, 1998, and 1999 would not be subject to the excess distributions tax. The moratorium is discussed further below.

Grandfather Recovery Methods

As mentioned above, certain individuals made a grandfather election on their 1988 tax return to protect future distributions from the excise tax. Although the election period has ended, financial advisers need to understand these rules for those clients who made the election and who have yet to receive all their pension distributions.

The grandfather recovery amount depends on the amount grandfathered and the method chosen for making the calculation. Briefly, the amount that could be grandfathered was the total taxable balance in all qualified plans, IRAs, SEPs, and 403(b) tax-deferred annuities as of August 1, 1986. Only those individuals who had more than $562,500 in total as of that date could have made the election. The law allowed two methods for computing the grandfather recovery amount, the *discretionary method* and the *attained-age method*. However, the attained-age method provided no advantage over the discretionary method and virtually all individuals elected the discretionary method.

If a person elects the *discretionary method,* 10 percent of each distribution is considered a recovery of the remaining grandfather amount. For example, if a person receives a regular distribution of $140,000, then 10 percent of this amount ($14,000) would be considered a recovery of any remaining grandfather amount. The amount protected from the excise tax is the greater of the indexed annual limit ($160,000 in 1997) or the recovered grandfathered amount (in this example, $14,000). Since 10 percent of each distribution will rarely exceed the indexed limit, the 10 percent method will virtually never provide any tax shelter for lifetime distributions.

A person who elects the discretionary recovery method may in any year choose to increase the recovery rate to 100 percent. Once the accelerated rate is chosen, however, the accelerated rate applies to all future years until the entire grandfather amount is used up. For example, if the person described above elected to increase the recovery rate to 100 percent, the entire $140,000 distribution would be sheltered from the excise tax, assuming the grandfather amount had not already been used up. Consequently, the accelerated discretionary recovery method will generally provide tax shelter for lifetime distributions that would otherwise be subject to the excise tax, but the grandfather amount is used up more quickly.

(*Planning Note:* While these rules seem complex, the decision making is quite straight forward. First, the election period has ended and no new grandfather elections may be made. If your client had a large pension and/or IRA amounts in 1986, ask whether he or she made the election. If the answer is yes, then look at the election form to determine whether the individual elected the 10 percent or the accelerated 100 percent method. Assuming the 10 percent method was elected, at the time distributions begin the decision must be made whether or not to accelerate to 100 percent. If the amount of the distribution is less than the annual exemption ($160,000 in 1997) the acceleration election should not be made. Remember to reduce the grandfathered amount by 10 percent of the distributed amount. If the distribution exceeds the annual exemption, the accelerated election must be considered. If the entire benefit is distributed, make the acceleration elect to protect the distribution from the excise tax. If the distribution is slightly higher than the annual exemption ($160,000 in 1997), the decision is more difficult. Accelerating protects the current distribution from the excise tax but uses up the grandfathered amount quickly. Furthermore, since the remaining grandfather amount is used when determining the excise tax on excess retirement accumulations at death, choosing to accelerate the recovery rate to shelter lifetime distributions may increase a person's exposure to the tax at death.

Excess Retirement Accumulations

Since a person could obviously avoid the excise tax by minimizing lifetime distributions (within the limits imposed by the uniform minimum distribution rules), the law provides that excess retirement accumulations at death are also subject to a 15 percent excise tax. This death excise tax is deductible when computing the federal estate tax. Also, if virtually all of the decedent's retirement balances (defined by committee reports as at least 99 percent) go to the surviving spouse, the surviving spouse may elect to treat the balances as his or her own for purposes of the excise tax. In this case the excise tax is not imposed on the excess retirement accumulations at the first death.

Briefly, excess retirement accumulations are defined as the amount by which the value of a person's plan balances (less any nontaxable portions such as after-tax employee contributions or life insurance proceeds in excess of cash values) exceed the present value of a hypothetical single life annuity in the amount of the applicable annual exemption in the year of death for the decedent's attained age, in whole years, using the interest rate and mortality assumptions for valuing life annuities as provided in IRS Regs. 20-2031-7. For example, assuming a discount rate of 12 percent and an age of 60 at the time of death, the hypothetical annuity for a person who has not made the grandfather election is $1,017,195.

(*Planning Note:* Since the life expectancy factors decline at advancing ages, the hypothetical annuity is smaller for older persons. Therefore for any given retirement balances, the excess accumulation and potential death excise tax will be greater as age increases.)

If a person has made the grandfather election and the remaining grandfather amount is greater than the hypothetical annuity, the remaining grandfather amount is used to determine the excess retirement accumulation at death. Therefore a person with a sizable grandfather amount who has preserved as much of the grandfather amount as possible by electing to use the 10 percent discretionary recovery method and by minimizing lifetime distributions may shelter more of his or her retirement accumulations at death than would otherwise be exempt based on the hypothetical annuity.

Clearly, planning for this tax is involved and many factors must be considered. Every technique employed to reduce exposure to the excise tax must take into account the client's overall financial situation as well as relevant income and estate tax considerations.

Moratorium on the Excess Distributions Excise Tax

The Small Business Jobs Protection Act of 1996 placed a moratorium on the excess distributions excise tax for distributions made in 1997, 1998, and 1999. The moratorium does not apply to the 15 percent estate tax on excess accumulations. This unusual provision seems to be an attempt by Congress to encourage distributions from tax-advantaged plans, thus accelerating tax receipts. The strategy of taking large distributions during these years may be appropriate for the individual who needs a large sum or someone with a large account balance and a short life expectancy. Otherwise, proceed with caution; the ability to defer the payment of income taxes might easily offset the savings due to the moratorium on the excise tax.

Strategies for Reducing the Excise Tax on Lifetime Distributions

Your clients who are likely to pay the excise tax on excess distributions should consider the following strategies to manipulate the timing of distributions and to minimize the effect of the tax.

Extend the Period over Which Distributions Are Received

Extending the payout period will reduce exposure to the life excise tax in two ways. First, extending the payout period reduces the annual payments for a given benefit balance.

Second, extending the payout period allows inflation to push the annual exemption amount higher and thus to reduce the excess amount subject to tax.

This strategy will be especially effective for persons who have made the grandfather election.

Inflation alone is no panacea. Without significant withdrawals plan balances can be expected to grow faster than the rate of inflation, and exposure to the tax can only be expected to increase over time. However, by employing the following strategies to extend the period over which distributions are received and thereby to reduce annual payments, a person may have a fighting chance against this onerous "success" tax.

1. Elect to receive payments in the form of one of the life annuity options, preferably based on two, rather than just one life.

    Annual payments will always be less and, therefore, exposure to the 15 percent life excise tax on excess distributions will be reduced when payments are determined and paid based on life expectancy rather than on a period-certain shorter than life expectancy. The expected payout period will always be longer and annual payments lower when they are based on two lives rather than one.

2. Elect the maximum-permitted survivor benefit under joint and survivor annuity options. The amount paid while both annuitants live will be smaller compared to the larger benefit amount payable to the survivor beneficiary after the participant's death.

3. Elect to receive guaranteed payments on life annuity payout options. Since guaranteed payments extend the payout period when the annuitant dies before the end of the guaranteed period, the annual amount paid with the guarantee will be less than the amount paid without the guarantee.

4. Elect to receive distributions under the installment minimum required distribution rules rather than in the form of an annuity.

    Since the minimum required annual distributions are always less under the minimum distribution rules than the amount that would be paid under an annuity form of payment (at least for the first several years of payout), a person will substantially reduce exposure to the life excise tax. In addition, in later years when payouts increase under the minimum distribution rules, the annual exemption for the life excise tax will have increased as a result of indexing for inflation.

5. Defer distributions as long as possible to allow the indexing of the inflation-adjusted annual exemption to increase.

    As mentioned above, taking the minimum required distributions is one method for both deferring distributions, at least until age 70 1/2, and minimizing the exposure to the excise tax on lifetime distributions. In addition, when a person is eligible for distributions because of plan termination or separation from service, he or she should consider rolling plan benefits over to IRAs or, if possible, to other qualified plans. When permitted, a person who is separating from service should consider leaving plan benefits with the employer until normal retirement age or until age 70 1/2, if permitted.

Combine Lump-sum Distributions with Installment Payouts

A second major strategy to reduce the effect of the life excise tax is to take both a lump-sum distribution with a 5- or 10-year-averaging election from one plan and installment payouts from other plans. Since the lump-sum exemption and the regular exemption apply separately, a person may potentially shelter up to $960,000 in a single year with a proper combination of regular and lump-sum distributions.

Shift the Benefit Mix from Qualified Retirement Plans to Nonqualified Deferred-Compensation Plans

Distributions from nonqualified deferred-compensation plans are not taken into account for purposes of the 15 percent excise tax. From the perspective of the employee whose qualified plan benefits are large enough to trigger the 15 percent excise tax, nonqualified plans appear attractive.

Reduce Contributions to Qualified Plans and IRAs and Make Future Investments in Other Tax-advantaged Vehicles

A certain level of annual contributions is generally required for pension plans unless a plan is amended or terminated. However, voluntary after-tax contributions and contributions to profit-sharing and stock bonus plans, IRAs, and some forms of Keogh plans and SEPs are more-or-less discretionary. When discretion is allowed, a person who is likely to have a problem with the 15 percent excise tax should consider investing in tax-favored vehicles such as municipal bonds, commercial annuity contracts, life insurance policies, and even Series EE savings bonds, rather than making additional contributions to the qualified plans.

Transfer Portions of Qualified Plan Benefits to a Spouse under a Qualified Domestic Relations Order in the Case of Divorce

If a divorce is pending, the participant can negotiate to receive assets outside the qualified plans and to transfer to the spouse a portion of the retirement accumulation under a qualified domestic relations order (QDRO). Distributions and accumulations subject to a QDRO are not subject to the income and excise taxes of the original participant. Instead, taxes on the amount subject to a QDRO are determined with regard to the alternative payee if the alternative payee is a former spouse.

Strategies to Reduce the Estate Excise Tax

Many strategies that minimize the 15 percent life excise tax on lifetime distributions may increase a person's exposure to the estate excise tax at death. Specifically, strategies that defer or reduce lifetime distributions (such as receiving distributions over life expectancy rather than over a period certain shorter than life expectancy, having annual payments determined and paid on the basis of two lives rather than one, electing to receive payments under the uniform minimum distribution rules, and maintaining a TEFRA 242(b) election) will tend to preserve benefit balances. In addition, naming a person other than the spouse as the primary beneficiary may cause the 15 percent estate excise tax to be imposed when it could otherwise be avoided with a special election by the spouse.

Preserving qualified plan benefit balances may often be a desirable strategy, despite greater exposure to the 15 percent estate excise tax. First, the benefit of the tax-deferred compounding, given a sufficient period of deferral, will outweigh the cost of the additional tax. Second, preserving qualified plan benefit balances may make tax and economic sense because of the estate tax deductibility of the estate excise tax. A person whose estate will be taxed at the maximum 55 percent rate will pay an effective estate excise tax of only 6.75 percent ($[1 - 0.55]$ x 15 percent) as compared with the 15 percent excise tax on lifetime distributions.

Some of the strategies for reducing the excise tax on lifetime distributions also help to reduce the likelihood of paying the estate excise tax at death. Specifically electing the maximum survivor benefit under joint and survivor annuity options and maximum period-certain guarantees (if a person lives beyond the guarantee period) will reduce the accumulations at death relative to what they would have been without such elections. Taking early withdrawals, combining a lump-sum distribution from one plan with installment payments from other plans, shifting the benefit mix from qualified plans to nonqualified deferred-compensation plans, reducing contributions to qualified plans and IRAs, terminating qualified plans, and transferring a portion of the retirement accumulation under a qualified domestic relations order in the event of a divorce settlement either deplete the retirement benefits or reduce the rate of growth of accumulations.

The following strategies will also reduce the estate excise tax on excess retirement accumulations at death and in some cases help to reduce the potential excise tax on lifetime distributions.

Use Life Insurance in Qualified Plans

The value of any death benefits payable immediately after death with respect to the decedent are exempt from the estate excise tax to the extent that the sum of such death benefits plus other benefits payable with respect to the decedent exceeds the total value of benefits payable with respect to the decedent immediately prior to death. Consequently life insurance benefits within a plan that are payable at death are not subject to the estate excise tax to the extent that the death benefits exceed the amount the decedent could have received just prior to death if he or she had terminated or redeemed the policies. This means that only policy cash values are subject to the estate excise tax, and the *net amount at risk* (the pure protection element of the policies) is excludable.

Make the Special Spousal Election

A surviving spouse is now permitted in certain cases to elect not to have the 15 percent estate excise tax apply to the deceased spouse's benefit balances. In return, the deceased spouse's plans and IRAs are treated as the surviving spouse's for purposes of computing the survivor's own excess distributions and excess accumulation. The election is available only if the spouse is the beneficiary of at least 99 percent of all the deceased's interests.

Take a Distribution of a Nontransferable Annuity

If a participant receives an annuity contract representing an irrevocable commitment under the plan to provide benefits, the value of this policy is disregarded when calculating the life excise tax on excess distributions in the year the policy is distributed. However, amounts paid from the policy, both in the year the policy is transferred and in future years, are subject to the life excise tax.

Although the regulations are not absolutely clear on this point, the principal benefit of this technique is that when the participant dies, the beneficiary's benefit from the annuity policy should not be treated as a part of the participant's excess retirement accumulations. Since nothing is received from the plan at the time of the participant's death, the value of the annuity contract to the beneficiary should not be subject to the estate excise tax. However, payments to the beneficiary after the participant's death will presumably continue to be subject to the life excise tax as determined with respect to the beneficiary's overall qualified plan distributions.

26

Distributions from Retirement Plans—Part 2

Chapter Outline

In addition to taking periodic payments from a qualified plan, employees are sometimes able to receive their retirement benefit in a lump-sum distribution. Historically, employees receiving lump-sum distributions from qualified plans have had the opportunity to elect from one of several options available under special tax rules. Today, many of these tax advantages have been taken away, meaning that in most cases, distributions are treated as ordinary income when calculating income tax for the year. Therefore most individuals receiving a lump-sum distribution choose to receive installment payments from the plan or to roll the distribution over into an IRA, where the taxes on the distribution will be delayed until proceeds are received.

What's confusing about the special distribution rules today is that some of the rules have been grandfathered and are still available in some circumstances. For this reason the financial services professional still needs to learn about the opportunity to select either 5- or 10-year income averaging, the grandfathered capital gains treatment for distributions attributable to pre-1974 participation, and the rules that allow deferral of taxation when employees receive employer securities from the plan.

From a planning standpoint, several key questions arise when clients are considering taking a lump-sum distribution. These questions include

- Should clients who qualify for 10-year averaging (that is, clients born on or before January 1, 1936) choose to use 5-year or 10-year averaging for lump-sum distributions?
- Should eligible clients use the existing capital-gains provision election for pre-1974 accruals?
- Should clients elect one of the averaging provisions or receive installment payments from the plan or from an IRA rollover account?

LUMP-SUM DISTRIBUTION DEFINED

Before evaluating the above questions, let's define what qualifies as a lump-sum distribution, discuss the potential tax advantages of lump-sum distributions, and indicate what conditions are necessary to make an averaging election.

Qualifying Distributions

A lump-sum distribution must meet the following conditions for your client to qualify for favorable tax treatment:

- The client must have been a plan participant for at least 5 years.
- The funds must be distributed to your client within one taxable year.
- The distribution must represent your client's entire account balance or benefit.
- The amount distributed must be payable only if the client dies, attains at least age 59 1/2, separates from service, or is disabled.

Remember that only distributions from qualified plans are eligible for lump-sum distribution tax treatment. Distributions from SEPs, SIMPLEs, IRAs, and 403(b) annuities do not qualify. In addition, the election of favorable tax treatment can be made only once in a lifetime. (*Planning Note:* Clients can aggregate distributions from one or more employers made in a single year.)

Tax Advantages

The tax advantages available on a lump-sum distribution vary depending on the age of your client. Clients born before January 1, 1936, have the most options. Two special rules have been grandfathered for this group: 10-year averaging and a special capital-gains provision for distributions attributable to pre-1974 plan participation.

5-year averaging was recently eliminated by the Small Business Job Protection Act of 1996. Instead of a traditional grandfathering provision, Congress used a "sunsetting" provision with 5-year averaging. Clients who receive a qualifying lump-sum distribution before the year 2000 can still elect 5-year averaging. The group of individuals eligible for 5-year averaging is quite small. Only individuals aged 59 1/2 or older who receive the qualifying distribution before 2000 will be eligible. After December 31, 1999 *no one* will be eligible for 5-year averaging.

One rule that hasn't gone away is the deferral of unrealized appreciation. Whenever a recipient receives a lump-sum distribution, he or she may elect to defer paying tax on the net unrealized appreciation in employer securities. If the distribution is not a lump-sum distribution, unrealized appreciation is excludable only to the extent that the appreciation is attributable to nondeductible employee contributions.

Computing the 5-Year or 10-Year Forward-Averaging Tax on Lump-Sum Distributions

Under both 5-year and 10-year averaging, the tax rate that applies to the distribution is not the same as if the distribution were treated as ordinary income. Under either of the averaging rules, the applicable tax rate is determined by treating the income as if it is earned by a separate, single taxpayer. The rate of tax is then determined by dividing the lump sum by 5 or 10, and then looking at the applicable rate for such amount. Tax rates are determined under 5-year averaging with the current year's tax rates, while 10-year averaging uses 1986 tax rates. Once the tax rate is determined, it is then applied to the whole distribution. All taxes are paid in the year of the distribution.

Form 4972, Tax on Lump-Sum Distributions, must be used to compute the forward-averaging tax. However, planners do not need to perform the entire computation each time a client desires tax planning advice concerning distributions from a qualified plan. The initial separate tax for any distribution amounts can be found by using table 26-1 or 26-2. Table 26-1 shows the 5-year averaging tax table assuming 1995 tax rates. Table 26-2 shows the 10-year forward-averaging tax table using 1986 tax rates.

To compute the 5- or 10-year tax on a lump-sum distribution using these tables, the planner must first compute the *adjusted total taxable amount*. The adjusted total taxable amount is equal to the total amount of the distribution less several items including

- any nontaxable portions (such as portions that are attributable to nondeductible employee contributions or PS 58 costs)
- the amount subject to tax at the capital-gains rate if the capital-gains provision is elected.

TABLE 26-1
5-Year Averaging
(Lump-sum distributions received in 1995)*

If the adjusted total taxable amount is		the separate tax is	plus this %	of the excess over
at least	but not over			
. . .	$ 20,000	0	7.5	0
$ 20,000	70,000	$ 1,500	18.0	$ 20,000
70,000	116,750	10,500	15.0	70,000
116,750	282,750	17,512.50	28.0	116,750
282,750	589,750	63,992.50	31.0	282,750
589,750	1,282,500	159,162.50	36.0	589,750
1,282,500	. . .	408,552.50	39.6	1,282,500

*Based on the 1995 single tax rate schedule. In future years these numbers will shift slightly upward, corresponding to the indexation of tax rates for inflation.

The best way to explain how to use these tables would be to use an example. Assume your client receives a lump-sum distribution of $150,000. For simplicity, assume that the entire distribution is taxable and that there are no plan accumulations attributable to pre-1974 service. The 5-year averaging tax is found in table 26-1 by finding the range of values into which the adjusted total taxable amount falls. In this case the $150,000 distribution falls in the range between $116,750 and $282,750. Therefore the tax on this distribution is equal to $17,512.50 plus 28 percent of the amount of the distribution in excess of $116,750. The amount of the distribution in excess of $116,750 is $33,250; 28 percent of $33,250 is $9,310. Thus the entire tax on the distribution is equal to $17,512.50 plus $9,310, or $26,822.50 (an effective tax rate of 17.9 percent). Note that your client would have to pay $42,000, or $15,177.50 more in tax on this distribution if he or she was in the 28 percent tax bracket and did not elect to use 5-year averaging.

If your client was born before 1936, he or she would qualify for 10-year averaging. The 10-year averaging tax on the $150,000 distribution is found using table 26-2 in the same way that we used table 26-1 to calculate the 5-year averaging tax. The $150,000 distribution falls in the range between $137,100 and $171,600 in table 26-2. Therefore the tax on the $150,000 distribution is equal to $21,603 plus 23 percent of the excess over $137,100. The excess over $137,100 is $12,900; 23 percent of $12,900 is $2,967. Thus the total 10-year averaging tax on a $150,000 distribution is equal to $21,603 plus $2,967, or $24,570 (an effective tax rate of 16.38 percent). Clearly, if your client qualifies, he or she should use 10-year averaging rather than 5-year averaging since he or she would save $2,252.50.

TABLE 26-2
10-Year Averaging
(1986 tax rates)

If the adjusted total taxable amount is

at least	but not over	the separate tax is	plus this %	of the excess over
. . .	$ 20,000	$ 70	5.5	0
$ 20,000	21,583	1,100	13.2	$ 20,000
21,583	30,583	1,309	14.4	21,583
30,583	49,417	2,605	16.8	30,583
49,417	67,417	5,769	18.0	49,417
67,417	70,000	9,009	19.2	67,417
70,000	91,700	9,505	16.0	70,000
91,700	114,400	12,977	18.0	91,700
114,400	137,100	17,063	20.0	114,400
137,100	171,600	21,603	23.0	137,100
171,600	228,800	29,538	26.0	171,600
228,800	286,000	44,410	30.0	228,800
286,000	343,200	61,570	34.0	286,600
343,200	423,000	81,018	38.0	343,200
423,000	571,900	111,342	42.0	423,000
571,900	857,900	173,880	48.0	571,900
857,900	. . .	311,160	50.0	857,900

WHEN QUALIFYING TAXPAYERS SHOULD ELECT 10-YEAR RATHER THAN 5-YEAR AVERAGING

In 1995 10-year averaging was more favorable than 5-year averaging when the adjusted total taxable amount was less than or equal to $367,687 (assuming no portion qualified for capital-gains treatment). If some portion of the distribution qualifies for capital-gains treatment (taxed at a 20 percent rate), 10-year averaging would be more favorable than 5-year averaging for even larger distributions. Table 26-3 shows the tax differentials under 5-year and 10-year averaging for 1995. This table clearly demonstrates the superiority of 10-year averaging for smaller distribution amounts and the superiority of 5-year averaging for larger distribution amounts. In future years the crossover point at which 5-year averaging is more favorable than 10-year averaging will fall as the tax rate schedule used when computing 5-year averaging is adjusted upwards for inflation. Remember that 5-year averaging will no longer be available after 1999.

TABLE 26-3
**Differences in Tax under 5-Year and 10-Year Forward Averaging
(No capital gain)**

Taxable Distribution Amount	Tax Using 5-Year Forward Averaging (1995 tax rates used)	Tax Using 10-Year Forward Averaging (1986 tax rates used)	Differential (5-year minus 10-year averaging)	% of Increase or Decrease
$ 100,000	$ 15,000	$ 14,471	$ 529	37.0
150,000	26,822	24,570	2,252	9.2
200,000	40,822	36,922	3,900	10.6
250,000	54,822	50,770	4,052	7.9
300,000	69,340	66,330	3,010	4.5
350,000	84,840	83,602	1,238	1.4
367,687	90,323	90,323	(0)	0.0
400,000	100,340	102,602	(2,262)	-2.3
450,000	115,840	122,682	(6,842)	-5.9
500,000	131,340	143,682	(12,342)	-9.4
550,000	146,840	164,682	(17,842)	-12.2
600,000	162,852	187,368	(24,515)	-15.1
750,000	216,852	259,368	(42,515)	-19.6
1,000,000	306,852	382,210	(75,357)	-24.5
1,500,000	507,552	632,210	(124,658)	-24.6

**YOUR FINANCIAL SERVICES PRACTICE:
MITIGATING THE EFFECT OF THE SUCCESS TAX**

Another tax advantage may come from electing to average. The 15 percent excise tax on excess distributions applies to lump-sum distributions as well as to periodic distributions. When a taxpayer elects 5- or 10-year averaging for a lump-sum distribution, the exemption from the 15 percent excise tax for the lump-sum distribution is equal to 5 times the applicable annual exemption for regular distributions where averaging is not elected ($800,000 as indexed in 1997). Note, however, that this is not a concern for distributions made in 1997, 1998, or 1999 **due to** the moratorium on the success tax for distributions made in these years.

The Existing Capital-Gains Provision

Clients born before January 1, 1936, may also elect to treat the portion of a lump-sum distribution that is attributable to pre-1974 participation in a plan as capital gains. If a person elects capital-gains treatment, the existing capital gains, that is, the pre-1974 plan accruals, are taxed at a flat 20 percent rate. If the capital-gains provision is elected, the existing capital-gains portion of a lump-sum distribution is then excluded when the person calculates either the 5- or 10-

year averaging tax. Therefore the total tax payable on a lump-sum distribution when a person elects capital-gains treatment for pre-1974 plan accruals is equal to 20 percent of the portion of the distribution attributable to the pre-1974 plan accruals plus the averaging tax on the remainder as computed by using either table 26-1 or 26-2.

The portion of a lump-sum distribution attributable to pre-1974 plan accruals is determined by finding the ratio of the person's months of plan participation before 1974 to the total months of plan participation. However, participation for any part of a calendar year prior to 1974 counts as 12 months of participation.

For example, if your client began his or her participation in the plan on July 1, 1970, and retired on June 30, 1988, with continuous service, the number of months of plan participation before 1974 is 48 (participation in 4 calendar years prior to 1974), and the total months of participation were 222 (48 months pre-74 and 174 months post-73). Therefore the capital-gains portion is calculated as follows:

$$\text{Capital - gains portion} = \frac{\text{Months of pre - 1974 participation}}{\text{Total months of participation}}$$

$$= \frac{48}{222}$$

$$= (22\%)$$

Assuming that the lump-sum distribution is equal to $150,000, the capital-gains portion would be $33,000. If your client elects capital-gains treatment, only the portion of the distribution not attributable to the capital-gains portion (in this case $117,000) is included in the adjusted total taxable amount when computing the averaging tax.

When Should a Person Born before January 1, 1936, Elect the Capital-Gains Provision?

Clearly a client born before January 1, 1936, should elect to use the capital-gains provision for pre-1974 plan accruals whenever the adjusted total taxable amount after subtracting the capital-gains portion is taxed at an effective rate of more than 20 percent. In table 26-1, for example, we can see that in 1995 a person would always benefit by electing the capital-gains treatment for pre-1974 plan accruals if the adjusted total taxable amount after subtracting the capital-gains portion equals or exceeds $116,750. (This amount will increase in future years as a result of the inflation adjustment to the tax rate schedule.) At that level all additional amounts are taxed at 28 percent or more. Since the capital-gains portion is taxed at a flat 20 percent rate, a person in these circumstances would pay less tax by electing the capital-gains treatment.

If we look at table 26-2, we can see that a person who elects 10-year averaging would always benefit by electing the capital-gains treatment for pre-1974 plan accruals if the adjusted total taxable amount after subtracting the capital-gains portion is equal to or greater than $137,100. At that level each additional dollar of adjusted total taxable amount is taxed at a rate of 23 percent or higher.

For example, suppose your client receives a taxable distribution of $170,000, of which $30,000 may be treated as capital gain. Your client is eligible for 10-year averaging. Since under the applicable averaging formula any amount over $137,100 is taxed at a rate of 23 percent or higher, your client should elect capital-gains treatment. With capital-gains treatment the last $30,000 of the distribution—the capital-gains amount—will be taxed at a rate of only 20 percent instead of 23 percent or more.

NET UNREALIZED APPRECIATION

The net unrealized appreciation in the employer's stock that is included in a lump-sum distribution is excluded when computing the income tax on the distribution. (The appreciation is included, however, when computing the 15 percent excess distributions tax.) The net unrealized appreciation is the difference between the value of the stock when credited to the participant's account and its fair market value on the date of distribution. This unrealized appreciation is taxable as long-term capital gain to the recipient when the shares are sold, even if sold immediately. If the recipient holds the shares for a period of time after distribution, any additional gain (above the net unrealized appreciation) is taxed as long- or short-term capital gain, depending on the holding period.

The participant may elect at the time of the distribution to pay tax on the net unrealized appreciation (versus taking advantage of the opportunity to defer taxes). Since the long-term capital-gains tax rate (28 percent) may be substantially higher than the rates under special averaging, this is a viable choice for the individual who anticipates selling the stock soon after the distribution. Deferring taxes under the unrealized appreciation rules means forgoing the opportunity to have the distribution taxed under the averaging rules or at the special 20 percent capital-gains rate.

Example: Randi receives a distribution including $1,000 of net unrealized appreciation, and she is eligible for 10-year averaging treatment. The marginal tax rate under the 10-year averaging rules (based on the amount of her total distribution) is 18 percent. In the following year she sells the stock and pays 28 percent capital-gains tax on the unrealized appreciation. Randi paid $280 in tax instead of the $180 she would have paid if she had included the amount in income at the time of the distribution.

In contrast, if the recipient plans to hold the stock for a period of time, the tax deferral on the unrealized appreciation of the distributed stock may provide a significant benefit. In fact, if the stock is held until death, any gain on the stock subsequent to the distribution will escape tax altogether because of a step-up in basis.

LUMP-SUM DISTRIBUTIONS VERSUS PERIODIC PAYOUTS

One critical question remains to be answered: When should your clients elect to receive lump-sum distributions, where they may enjoy the tax benefits of averaging and capital-gains treatment, rather than periodic payouts from their plans (or from IRA rollover accounts), where the tax is deferred? This decision involves a number of variables unique to each client. Because of this circumstance, it is difficult to come up with a mathematical model that takes into consideration all the appropriate factors. Also such models involve so many assumptions that in the end, the comparisons are not that meaningful. The financial services professional will need, instead, to have a feeling for both the rules and the situation of the individual client.

The reality is that for clients with distributions over $500,000, the effective tax rates are not going to be that much different from the tax rate applicable to ordinary income. Therefore, generally, lump-sum averaging is considered only for distributions less than this amount. Consider the following factors when helping clients with this decision:

- *Length of the payout period*—The longer the period of tax deferral, the more likely that deferring taxes and taking a stream of payments from the plan over time will result in a larger total payout than paying lump-sum taxes currently. The length of the payout period can be affected by a number of factors. If the benefit is being paid out over the life expectancies of the participant and a beneficiary, the individuals' ages will affect the length of the payout period. The client's need may also affect the length of the payout period. For example, a client might know that he or she will need the money over a short period of time in order to make a particular investment or because of other special needs. On the other end of the scale is the individual who has other assets to live on and has the option to defer distributions as long as necessary to ensure proper tax planning.

- *Amount of the lump-sum averaging tax*—Of course, when determining whether to pay taxes now or defer, the amount of taxes paid under the lump-sum tax rules is crucial. As described above, for larger distributions the amount of tax savings for lump-sum averaging is almost nil. Also eligibility for 10-year averaging will result in lower taxes when the distribution is $367,687 or less. In addition, if a portion of the distribution is treated as capital gain, the special grandfathered 20 percent tax rate may reduce the total tax due. All factors that act to reduce taxes will favor paying taxes now versus deferring taxes.

- *Amount of outside income*—When pension assets are paid out over time, they are taxed as ordinary income—meaning that they will be taxed at the individual's marginal (top) tax rate. This means that as an individual's taxable income from sources outside of the plan (and, along with it, the marginal tax rate) rises, the more attractive special averaging tax treatment becomes.

- *Interest rate assumptions*—Paying taxes now under the lump-sum tax rates looks less attractive the higher the available rate of investment return. This is because the participant loses the ability to earn a return on the amount of taxes paid. For example, if the distribution is $100,000 and the individual pays $22,000 in taxes, now only $78,000 remains to be invested versus the original $100,000.

- *Changes in the tax rates*—Whether an individual wants to elect special averaging will also depend on his or her outlook regarding tax rates. If the individual expects tax rates to go up, then the results of averaging will look even better. On the other hand, if the client expects tax rates to go down, deferral will be favorable. However, be aware that the advantages of tax deferral can be powerful, and even a substantial increase in the tax rate in the future may not offset the advantages of deferring taxes.

Appendix 1

Post-ERISA Legislation

Below is description, law by law, of legislation affecting the pension field. Following that is a table identifying the laws for those interested in researching them further.

In 1981 the ***Economic Recovery Tax Act*** expanded the retirement market by breathing new life into old retirement products. ERTA lifted the prohibition against employees who were active participants in employer-sponsored plans having an individual retirement account (IRA) and opened the door for widespread sales of IRAs. The public response was tremendous as millions flocked to save for retirement. ERTA also contributed to the success of stock option plans by liberalizing the rules for deducting leveraged employee stock ownership plans (ESOPs) and creating payroll-based stock option plans (PAYSOPs). PAYSOPs, phased out in 1987, allowed for an income tax credit that benefited certain corporations. Finally, ERTA started the trend of making the rules for retirement plans for the self-employed (Keogh plans) similar to those for corporate plans.

The Tax Equity and Fiscal Responsibility Act of 1982 created plan parity between Keogh plans and corporate plans, finishing the job started by ERTA. The major emphasis of TEFRA, however, was on stopping tax abuses, primarily loopholes used by small-employer plans. TEFRA created special rules for plans that unduly benefit key employees—if a plan inordinately favors the privileged few, restrictive "top-heavy" rules take effect. The top-heavy rules guarantee minimum benefits for rank-and-file employees and restrict benefits available for key employees. Other loopholes were closed by TEFRA: it stopped plan loan abuses, limited contributions to the plan and distributions from the plan by reducing the maximum contributions or distributions allowed, and forced plan distributions to be used for retirement purposes, as opposed to sheltering the money for the beneficiary.

The Retirement Equity Act of 1984 shifted Congress's focus from tax abuses by small employers to the perceived mistreatment of women under the pension rules. REA helps people (male or female) who do not fit the standard work pattern, especially those who interrupt or stop their career for children, by reducing the age required to participate in a retirement plan. In addition, REA makes it harder to lose pension benefits because of career interruptions. REA also protects the rights of the spouse or ex-spouse of a plan participant by assuring that the spouse has some say in how retirement money is distributed and by allowing retirement funds to be part of a divorce settlement.

The Tax Reform Act of 1986 represented the biggest shake-up since ERISA. A need for revenue was the motivation for TRA '86 rules that cut back salary reduction contributions previously allowed under some types of plans (401(k), tax-sheltered annuities) and restricted the deductibility of contributions made to individual retirement accounts. A second target of TRA '86 was the discrimination in favor of officers and key employees. Existing discrimination restrictions were tightened, and some plans that had previously escaped nondiscrimination coverage were brought under a new, tougher nondiscrimination umbrella. Other tax reform changes were also included:

- modifications to the profit-sharing rules, which permit profit-sharing contributions when the employer has no profits (this was a response to the trend of using profit-sharing plans as a major source of pension benefits)
- amendments liberalizing ERISA's vesting schedules
- creation of a 10 percent premature distribution penalty tax for most plan distributions prior to age 59 1/2
- minimum distribution requirements and restrictive changes in the taxation of retirement distributions

The Omnibus Budget Reconciliation Act of 1987 (OBRA '87)) focused on yet another legislative target—the underfunded pension plan. OBRA '87 tightened ERISA's funding requirements in an effort to prevent plans from being inadequately funded and consequently reneging on the pension-benefit promises that they have made. OBRA '87 took away some of the leeway actuaries had concerning the amount and timing of plan contributions and forced employers to meet stricter funding requirements. In addition to tightening funding standards the Revenue Act of 1987 also increased insurance premiums that are owed the PBGC from $8.50 to $16 per participant per year. Under the higher premium schedules that were imposed underfunded plans were subject to a variable rate greater than $16, depending on the amount they were underfunded.

The Revenue Reconciliation Act of 1989 represented yet another legislative change to pension law. This act focused on, among other things, restructuring the rules governing employee stock ownership plans (ESOPs). Specifically the act abolished many of the special tax advantages that an ESOP had, such as the estate tax reduction brought about by selling employer stock back to the ESOP after an employee's death.

The Revenue Reconciliation Act of 1990 dramatically changed the rules governing an employer's ability to acquire an asset reversion from a terminating defined-benefit plan (see chapter 13). In addition, the new law enhanced an employer's ability to prefund retiree health benefits in a so-called 401(h) account by allowing excess pension assets to be transferred to the 401(h) account without the employer having to pay either regular income tax or a pension reversion excise tax on the amount transferred. Finally, the new law increased annual PBGC premiums for covered defined-benefit plans from $16 to $19 per participant.

The Emergency Unemployment Act of 1992 changed several of the rules governing distributions from qualified plans. Apparently the policy behind the changes was to encourage employees to save preretirement distributions for their retirement needs. The new rules, effective for distributions after December 31, 1992, liberalize the rollover rules (allowing most preretirement distributions to be rolled into a tax-sheltered IRA or qualified plan); require mandatory 20 percent federal income tax withholding on most distributions made directly to participants; and require qualified plans to allow participants the option to have distributions transferred directly to another tax-sheltered vehicle. (Transferred amounts are not subject to the 20 percent withholding requirements.)

The Omnibus Budget Reconciliation Act of 1993 targeted the benefits of the highly compensated by capping the amount of compensation that could be taken into account for determining contributions or benefits to $150,000.

The Retirement Protection Act of 1994 (RPA '94) made significant changes in the funding rules for single-employer defined-benefit plans, the cash-out provisions for lump sums, and the PBGC premium structure for underfunded defined-benefit plans. The primary focus of the legislation was to give employers added incentive to fund underfunded defined-benefit plans and to put the PBGC in a better financial position.

The Small Business Job Opportunities Act of 1996 is the most sweeping legislation in the pension area in years. Believe it or not, the new law actually simplifies the pension rules. For example, the law creates a less complicated definition of highly compensated employees, simplifies the nondiscrimination testing in a 401(k) plan, and even eliminates nondiscrimination testing in 401(k) plans that comply with certain safe harbors. In the distribution area, the law simplifies the annuity taxation rules and eliminates special 5-year averaging. To provide a 401(k) look-alike savings plan for small employers, the law establishes a "SIMPLE."

TABLE Appendix 1-1
Major Legislation Affecting Qualified Retirement Plans

Act	Enactment Date	Reference*
Employee Retirement Income Security Act	Sept. 2, 1974	P.L. 93-406
Social Security Amendments of 1977	April 12, 1977	P.L. 95-216
Revenue Act of 1978	Nov. 6, 1978	P.L. 95-600
Technical Corrections Act of 1979	April 1, 1980	P.L. 96-222
Multiemployer Pension Plan Amendments Act of 1980	Sept. 26, 1980	P.L. 96-364
Economic Recovery Tax Act of 1981	August 13, 1981	P.L. 97-34
Tax Equity and Fiscal Responsibility Act of 1982	Sept. 3, 1982	P.L. 97-248
Technical Corrections Act of 1982	Jan. 12, 1983	P.L. 97-448
Social Security Act of 1983	April 20, 1983	P.L. 98-21
Tax Reform Act of 1984 (dubbed DEFRA)	July 18, 1984	P.L. 98-369
Retirement Equity Act of 1984	August 23, 1984	P.L. 98-397
Consolidated Omnibus Budget Reconciliation Act	April 7, 1986	P.L. 99-272
Single Employer Pension Plan Amendments Act of 1986	April 7, 1986	P.L. 99-272
Omnibus Budget Reconciliation Act of 1986	Oct. 21, 1986	P.L. 99-509
Tax Reform Act of 1986	Oct. 22, 1986	P.L. 99-514
Age Discrimination in Employment Amendments	Oct. 31, 1986	P.L. 99-592
Omnibus Budget Reconciliation Act of 1987	Dec. 22, 1987	P.L. 100-203
Technical and Miscellaneous Revenue Act of 1988	Nov. 10, 1988	P.L. 100-647
Revenue Reconciliation Act of 1989	Dec. 19, 1989	P.L. 101-239
Revenue Reconciliation Act of 1990	Nov. 5, 1990	P.L. 101-508
The Emergency Unemployment Act of 1992	July 3, 1992	P.L. 102-318
Omnibus Budget Reconciliation Act of 1993	Aug. 10, 1993	P.L. 103-66
Retirement Protection Act of 1994	Dec. 8, 1994	H.R. 5110
Small Business Job Protection Act of 1996	Aug. 8, 1996	H.R. 3448

*Pension legislation is usually codified in the Internal Revenue Code. The P.L. number given to an act frequently appears under the specific provision of the Internal Revenue Code that the act affected.

Appendix 2

Pension Acronyms

ADP test	actual deferral percentage test
AGI	adjusted gross income
AIR	assumed investment return
Automatic J & S	automatic joint and survivor annuity
CODA	cash or deferred arrangement
COLA	cost-of-living adjustment
DA contract	deposit-administration contract
DAM contract	discretionary asset management contract
DB	defined benefit
DBO Plan	death benefit only plan
DC	defined contribution
DOL	Department of Labor
ERIC	ERISA Industry Committee
ERISA	Employee Retirement Income Security Act of 1974
ESOP	employee stock ownership plan
FASB	Financial Accounting Standards Board
FSA	flexible spending account
GIC	guaranteed-investment contract

IG contract	investment-guarantee contract
IPG contract	immediate-participation-guarantee contract
IRA	individual retirement account
IRC	Internal Revenue Code
IRD	income in respect of a decedent
IRS	Internal Revenue Service
ISO	incentive stock option
LSD	lump-sum distribution
MPPAA	Multiemployer Pension Plan Amendments Act
NRA	normal retirement age
NRD	normal retirement date
PAYSOP	payroll-based stock option plan
PBGC	Pension Benefit Guaranty Corporation
PC	professional corporation
PLR	private-letter ruling
PTE	prohibited-transaction exemption
QDRO	qualified domestic relations order
QPAM	qualified professional asset manager
QPSA	qualified preretirement survivor annuity
QVEC	qualified voluntary employee contribution
SAR	summary of annual reports
SARSEP	salary reduction simplified employee pension
SEP	simplified employee pension plan

SERP	supplemental executive retirement plan
SIMPLE	savings incentive match plan for employees
SMM	summary of material modifications
SPAC	single-premium annuity contract
SPD	summary plan description
TDA	tax-deferred annuity
TPA	third-party administrator
TSA	tax-sheltered annuity
VDEC	voluntary deductible employee contribution
VEBA	Voluntary Employee's Beneficiary Association
401(a)(4)	discrimination rule
401(k) plan	cash or deferred arrangement
403(b) plan	tax-deferred annuity
410(b)(1)	discrimination rule
457 plan	state or local government plan
501(c)(3)	charitable organizations
5500s	pension forms filed with IRS

Appendix 3

Average Life Expectancies

1983 Individual Annuity Table (1971–1976)*				
	Male		Female	
Age	Deaths per 1,000	Expectation of Life (Years)	Deaths per 1,000	Expectation of Life (Years)
30	.76	49.83	.44	54.75
31	.79	48.87	.46	53.77
32	.81	47.91	.48	52.80
33	.84	46.95	.50	51.82
34	.88	45.99	.52	50.85
35	.92	45.03	.55	49.87
36	.97	44.07	.57	48.90
37	1.03	43.11	.61	47.93
38	1.11	42.15	.65	46.96
39	1.22	41.20	.69	45.99
40	1.34	40.25	.74	45.02
41	1.49	39.30	.80	44.05
42	1.67	38.36	.87	43.09
43	1.89	37.43	.94	42.12
44	2.13	36.50	1.03	41.16
45	2.40	35.57	1.12	40.20
46	2.69	34.66	1.23	39.25
47	3.01	33.75	1.36	38.30
48	3.34	32.85	1.50	37.35
49	3.69	31.96	1.66	36.40
50	4.06	31.07	1.83	35.46
51	4.43	30.20	2.02	34.53
52	4.81	29.33	2.22	33.59
53	5.20	28.47	2.43	32.67
54	5.59	27.62	2.65	31.75
55	5.99	26.77	2.89	30.83
56	6.41	25.93	3.15	29.92
57	6.84	25.09	3.43	29.01
58	7.29	24.26	3.74	28.11
59	7.78	23.44	4.08	27.21
60	8.34	22.62	4.47	26.32

1983 Individual Annuity Table (1971–1976) (Continued)*				
	Male		Female	
Age	Deaths per 1,000	Expectation of Life (Years)	Deaths per 1,000	Expectation of Life (Years)
61	8.98	21.80	4.91	25.44
62	9.74	20.99	5.41	24.56
63	10.63	20.20	5.99	23.69
64	11.66	19.41	6.63	22.83
65	12.85	18.63	7.34	21.98
66	14.20	17.87	8.09	21.14
67	15.72	17.12	8.89	20.31
68	17.41	16.38	9.73	19.49
69	19.30	15.66	10.65	18.67
70	21.37	14.96	11.70	17.87
71	23.65	14.28	12.91	17.07
72	26.13	13.61	14.32	16.29
73	28.84	12.96	15.98	15.52
74	31.79	12.33	17.91	14.76
75	35.05	11.72	20.13	14.02
76	38.63	11.13	22.65	13.30
77	42.59	10.56	25.51	12.60
78	46.95	10.00	28.72	11.91
79	51.76	9.47	32.33	11.25
80	57.03	8.96	36.40	10.61
81	62.79	8.47	40.98	9.99
82	69.08	8.01	46.12	9.40
83	75.91	7.57	51.89	8.83
84	83.23	7.15	58.34	8.28
85	90.99	6.75	65.52	7.77
86	99.12	6.37	73.49	7.28
87	107.58	6.02	82.32	6.81
88	116.32	5.69	92.02	6.38
89	125.39	5.37	102.49	5.98
90	134.89	5.07	113.61	5.60
91	144.87	4.78	125.23	5.26
92	155.43	4.50	137.22	4.94
93	166.63	4.24	149.46	4.64
94	178.54	3.99	161.83	4.37
95	191.21	3.75	174.23	4.12
96	204.72	3.51	186.54	3.88
97	219.12	3.29	198.65	3.65
98	234.74	3.07	211.10	3.44
99	251.89	2.86	224.45	3.22
100	270.91	2.66	239.22	3.01

1983 Individual Annuity Table (1971–1976) (Continued)*				
	Male		Female	
Age	Deaths per 1,000	Expectation of Life (Years)	Deaths per 1,000	Expectation of Life (Years)
101	292.11	2.46	255.95	2.80
102	315.83	2.26	275.20	2.59
103	342.38	2.08	297.50	2.38
104	372.09	1.90	323.39	2.18
105	405.28	1.73	353.41	1.98
106	442.28	1.57	388.11	1.79
107	483.41	1.41	428.02	1.60
108	528.99	1.27	473.69	1.43
109	579.35	1.13	525.66	1.26
110	634.81	1.01	584.46	1.11
111	695.70	.89	650.65	.97
112	762.34	.78	724.75	.83
113	835.06	.70	807.32	.71
114	914.17	.67	898.89	.60
115	1,000.00	.50	1,000.00	.50

*These figures come from annuity tables which typically assume a longer life expectancy than other tables that can be used.

REQUEST FOR SOCIAL SECURITY EARNINGS INFORMATION

● **Use This Form If You Need**

1. **Yearly Totals of Earnings**   **OR**   2. **More Detailed Earnings Information**

Includes total earnings for each year but does not in-   Includes periods of employment or self-employment
clude the names and addresses of employers.   and the names and addresses of employers.

PRIVACY ACT NOTICE: We are authorized to collect this information under section 205 of the Social Security Act, and the Federal Records Act of 1950 (64 Stat. 583). It is needed so we can identify your records and prepare the statement you request. You do not have to furnish the information, but failure to do so may prevent your request from being processed.

INFORMATION ABOUT YOUR REQUEST

● **How Do I Get This Information?**

You need to complete the attached form to tell us what information you want.

● **Can I Get This Information For Someone Else?**

Yes, if you have their written permission. For more information, see page 2.

● **Who Can Sign On Behalf Of The Individual?**

The parent of a minor child, or the legal guardian of an individual who has been declared legally incompetent, may sign, if he/she is acting on behalf of the individual.

● **Is There A Fee For This Information?**

1. **Yearly Totals of Earnings**

No, there is no charge for providing yearly totals. In most cases, this is all the information you will need.

2. **Detailed Earnings Information**

Yes, we usually charge a fee for detailed information. In most cases, this information is used for purposes NOT directly related to Social Security such as for a private pension plan or personal injury suit. The fee chart on page 2 gives the amount of the charge.

Sometimes, there is no charge for detailed information. If you have reason to believe your earnings are not correct (for example, you have previously received earnings information from us and it does not agree with your records), we will supply you with more detail for the period in question. Occasionally, earnings amounts are wrong because an employer did not correctly report earnings or earnings are credited to the wrong person. In situations like these, we will send you detailed information, at no charge, so we can correct your record.

Be sure to show the year(s) involved on the request form and explain why you need detailed earnings information. If you do not tell us why you need the information, we will charge a fee.

● **Can The Fee Be Waived Or Reduced?**

Yes, if you show that giving the information to you will benefit the general public. Send your explanation with the attached form to the Freedom of Information Officer, Social Security Administration, Baltimore, Maryland 21235.

● **Can This Information Be Certified?**

Yes, we will certify the information for an additional fee of $15.00. Certification is usually not necessary unless you plan to use the information in court.

FORM **SSA-7050-F3**

455

● **How Much Do I Have to Pay?**

1. Count the number of years for which you need detailed earnings information. Be sure to add in both the first and last year requested. However, do not add in the current calendar year since this information is not yet available.

2. Use the chart below to determine the correct fee.

Number of Years Requested	Fee	Number of Years Requested	Fee	Number of Years Requested	Fee
1	$15.00	19	$50.75	37	$76.25
2	17.50	20	52.50	38	77.50
3	20.00	21	54.00	39	78.75
4	22.50	22	55.50	40	80.00
5	25.00	23	57.00	41	81.00
6	27.00	24	58.50	42	82.00
7	29.00	25	60.00	43	83.00
8	31.00	26	61.50	44	84.00
9	33.00	27	63.00	45	85.00
10	35.00	28	64.50	46	86.00
11	36.75	29	66.00	47	87.00
12	38.50	30	67.50	48	88.00
13	40.25	31	68.75	49	89.00
14	42.00	32	70.00	50	90.00
15	43.75	33	71.25	51	91.00
16	45.50	34	72.50	52	92.00
17	47.25	35	73.75		
18	49.00	36	75.00		

● **Whose Earnings Can Be Requested?**

1. Your Earnings

You can request earnings information from your own record by completing the attached form; we need your handwritten signature. If you sign with an "X", your mark must be witnessed by two disinterested persons who must sign their name and address.

2. Someone Else's Earnings

You can request earnings information from the record of someone else if that person tells us in writing to give the information to you. This writing or "authorization" must be presented to us within 60 days of the date it was signed by that person.

3. A Deceased Person's Earnings

You can request earnings information from the record of a deceased person if you are the legal representative of the estate, a survivor (that is, the spouse, parent, child, divorced spouse or divorced parent), or an individual with a material interest (example - financial) who is an heir at law, next of kin, beneficiary under the will or donee of property of the decedent.

Proof of death must be included with your request. Proof of appointment as representative or proof of your relationship to the deceased must also be included.

FORM **SSA-7050-F3**

REQUEST FOR SOCIAL SECURITY EARNINGS INFORMATION

1. From whose record do you need the earnings information?

Your Reference Number

Print the Name, Social Security number, and date of birth below.

Name _____

Social Security
Number _____

Other Name(s) Used
(Include Maiden Name) _____

Date of Birth
(Mo/Day/Yr) _____

2. What kind of information do you need?

☐ Total earnings for each year.
(This information is free.)

For the year(s): _____

☐ Detailed Earnings Information
(If you check this block, tell us below
why you need this information.)

For the period(s): _____

_____

_____

3. Do you owe us a fee for this detailed earnings information?   ☐ Yes   ☐ No

If yes, enter the amount due from the Chart on page 2 .... **A.** $ _____

Do you want us to certify the information?   ☐ Yes   ☐ No

If yes, enter $15.00 .... **B.** $ _____

ADD the amounts on lines A and B, and
enter the TOTAL amount .... **C.** $ _____

- Send your check or money order for the amount on line C with the request.
- **DO NOT SEND CASH OR STAMPS.**
- Make check or money order payable to "Social Security Administration."

4. I am the individual to whom the record pertains (or a person who is authorized to sign on behalf of that individual). I understand that any false representation to knowingly and willfully obtain information from Social Security records is punishable by a fine of not more than $5,000 or one year in prison.

SIGN your name here
(Do not print)   ▶ _____   Date _____

5. Tell us where you want the information sent. (Please print)

Name _____
Address _____
City _____
State _____
and
ZIP Code _____

6. Tear off completed form and mail to:

Social Security Administration
Office of Central Records Operations
300 North Greene Street
Baltimore, Maryland 21201

FORM **SSA-7050-F3**

☆U.S. Government Printing Office: 1987—181-370/40100

	FOR SSA USE ONLY
REQUEST FOR STATEMENT OF EARNINGS (PLEASE PRINT IN INK OR USE TYPEWRITER)	**AX**
	SP

I REQUEST A SUMMARY STATEMENT OF EARNINGS FROM MY SOCIAL SECURITY RECORD

NH | Full name you use in work or business
First | Middle Initial | Last

SN | Social Security number shown on your card | **DB** Your date of birth — Month | Day | Year **A**

MA | Other Social Security number(s) you have used | **SX** Your Sex — ☐ Male ☐ Female

AK | Other name(s) you have used (Include your maiden name)

FOLD HERE

- -

PRIVACY STATEMENT

The Social Security Administration (SSA) is authorized to collect information asked on this form under section 205 of the Social Security Act. It is needed so SSA can quickly identify your record and prepare the earnings statement you requested. While you are not required to furnish the information, failure to do so may prevent your request from being processed. The information will be used primarily for issuing your earnings statement.

I am the individual to whom the record pertains. I understand that if I knowingly and willingly request or receive a record about an individual under false pretenses I would be guilty of a Federal crime and could be fined up to $5000.

Sign your name here: (Do not print)	TELEPHONE NO. (Area Code)	DATE

SEND THE STATEMENT TO: (to be completed in ALL cases.)

PN | Name

AD | Address (Number and Street. Apt. No., P.O. Box, or Rural Route)

City and state	**ZP** Zip Code

Form **SSA-7004-PC-OP1**

Appendix 5

Annuity Tables

TABLE V
Ordinary Life Annuities
One Life-Expected Return Multiples

Age	Multiple	Age	Multiple	Age	Multiple
5	76.6	42	40.6	79	10.0
6	75.6	43	39.6	80	9.5
7	74.7	44	38.7	81	8.9
8	73.7	45	37.7	82	8.4
9	72.7	46	36.8	83	7.9
10	71.7	47	35.9	84	7.4
11	70.7	48	34.9	85	6.9
12	69.7	49	34.0	86	6.5
13	68.8	50	33.1	87	6.1
14	67.8	51	32.2	88	5.7
15	66.8	52	31.3	89	5.3
16	65.8	53	30.4	90	5.0
17	64.8	54	29.5	91	4.7
18	63.9	55	28.6	92	4.4
19	62.9	56	27.7	93	4.1
20	61.9	57	26.8	94	3.9
21	60.9	58	25.9	95	3.7
22	59.9	59	25.0	96	3.4
23	59.0	60	24.2	97	3.2
24	58.0	61	23.3	98	3.0
25	57.0	62	22.5	99	2.8
26	56.0	63	21.6	100	2.7
27	55.1	64	20.8	101	2.5
28	54.1	65	20.0	102	2.3
29	53.1	66	19.2	103	2.1
30	52.2	67	18.4	104	1.9
31	51.2	68	17.6	105	1.8
32	50.2	69	16.8	106	1.6
33	49.3	70	16.0	107	1.4
34	48.3	71	14.3	108	1.3
35	47.3	72	14.6	109	1.1
36	46.4	73	13.9	110	1.0
37	45.4	74	13.2	111	.9
38	44.4	75	12.5	112	.8
39	43.5	76	11.9	113	.7
40	42.5	77	11.2	114	.6
41	41.5	78	10.6	115	.5

Table VI — Ordinary Joint Life and Last Survivor Annuities — Two Lives — Expected Return Multiples

AGES	51	52	53	54	55	56	57	58	59	60	61	62	63	64	65	66
51	38.2	...	...	...	...	...	...	...	...	...	...	...	...	...	...	...
52	37.8	37.3	...	...	...	...	...	...	...	...	...	...	...	...	...	...
53	37.3	36.8	36.3	...	...	...	...	...	...	...	...	...	...	...	...	...
54	36.9	36.4	35.8	35.3	...	...	...	...	...	...	...	...	...	...	...	...
55	36.5	35.9	35.4	34.9	34.4	...	...	...	...	...	...	...	...	...	...	...
56	36.1	35.6	35.0	34.4	33.9	33.4	...	...	...	...	...	...	...	...	...	...
57	35.8	35.2	34.6	34.0	33.5	33.0	32.5	...	...	...	...	...	...	...	...	...
58	35.5	34.8	34.2	33.6	33.1	32.5	32.0	31.5	...	...	...	...	...	...	...	...
59	35.2	34.5	33.9	33.3	32.7	32.1	31.6	31.1	30.6	...	...	...	...	...	...	...
60	34.9	34.2	33.6	32.9	32.3	31.7	31.2	30.6	30.1	29.7	...	...	...	...	...	...
61	34.6	33.9	33.3	32.6	32.0	31.4	30.8	30.2	29.7	29.2	28.7	...	...	...	...	...
62	34.4	33.7	33.0	32.3	31.7	31.0	30.4	29.9	29.3	28.8	28.3	27.8	...	...	...	...
63	34.2	33.5	32.7	32.0	31.4	30.7	30.1	29.5	28.9	28.4	27.8	27.3	26.9	...	...	...
64	34.0	33.2	32.5	31.8	31.1	30.4	29.8	29.2	28.6	28.0	27.4	26.9	26.4	25.9	...	...
65	33.8	33.0	32.3	31.6	30.9	30.2	29.5	28.9	28.2	27.6	27.1	26.5	26.0	25.5	25.0	...
66	33.6	32.9	32.1	31.4	30.6	29.9	29.2	28.6	27.9	27.3	26.7	26.1	25.6	25.1	24.6	24.1
67	33.5	32.7	31.9	31.2	30.4	29.7	29.0	28.3	27.6	27.0	26.4	25.8	25.2	24.7	24.2	23.7
68	33.4	32.5	31.8	31.0	30.2	29.5	28.8	28.1	27.4	26.7	26.1	25.5	24.9	24.3	23.8	23.3
69	33.2	32.4	31.6	30.8	30.1	29.3	28.6	27.8	27.1	26.5	25.8	25.2	24.6	24.0	23.4	22.9
70	33.1	32.3	31.5	30.7	29.9	29.1	28.4	27.6	26.9	26.2	25.6	24.9	24.3	23.7	23.1	22.5
71	33.0	32.2	31.4	30.5	29.7	29.0	28.2	27.5	26.7	26.0	25.3	24.7	24.0	23.4	22.8	22.2
72	32.9	32.1	31.2	30.4	29.6	28.8	28.1	27.3	26.5	25.8	25.1	24.4	23.8	23.1	22.5	21.9
73	32.8	32.0	31.1	30.3	29.5	28.7	27.9	27.1	26.4	25.6	24.9	24.2	23.5	22.9	22.2	21.6
74	32.8	31.9	31.1	30.2	29.4	28.6	27.8	27.0	26.2	25.5	24.7	24.0	23.3	22.7	22.0	21.4
75	32.7	31.8	31.0	30.1	29.3	28.5	27.7	26.9	26.1	25.3	24.6	23.8	23.1	22.4	21.8	21.1
76	32.6	31.8	30.9	30.1	29.2	28.4	27.6	26.8	26.0	25.2	24.4	23.7	23.0	22.3	21.6	20.9
77	32.6	31.7	30.8	30.0	29.1	28.3	27.5	26.7	25.9	25.1	24.3	23.6	22.8	22.1	21.4	20.7
78	32.5	31.7	30.8	29.9	29.1	28.2	27.4	26.6	25.8	25.0	24.2	23.4	22.7	21.9	21.2	20.5
79	32.5	31.6	30.7	29.9	29.0	28.2	27.3	26.5	25.7	24.9	24.1	23.3	22.6	21.8	21.1	20.4
80	32.5	31.6	30.7	29.8	29.0	28.1	27.3	26.4	25.6	24.8	24.0	23.2	22.4	21.7	21.0	20.2
81	32.4	31.5	30.7	29.8	28.9	28.1	27.2	26.4	25.5	24.7	23.9	23.1	22.3	21.6	20.8	20.1
82	32.4	31.5	30.6	29.7	28.9	28.0	27.2	26.3	25.5	24.6	23.8	23.0	22.3	21.5	20.7	20.0
83	32.4	31.5	30.6	29.7	28.8	28.0	27.1	26.3	25.4	24.6	23.8	23.0	22.2	21.4	20.6	19.9
84	32.3	31.4	30.6	29.7	28.8	27.9	27.1	26.2	25.4	24.5	23.7	22.9	22.1	21.3	20.5	19.8
85	32.3	31.4	30.5	29.6	28.8	27.9	27.0	26.2	25.3	24.5	23.7	22.8	22.0	21.3	20.5	19.7
86	32.3	31.4	30.5	29.6	28.7	27.9	27.0	26.1	25.3	24.5	23.6	22.8	22.0	21.2	20.4	19.6
87	32.3	31.4	30.5	29.6	28.7	27.8	27.0	26.1	25.3	24.4	23.6	22.8	21.9	21.1	20.4	19.6
88	32.3	31.4	30.5	29.6	28.7	27.8	27.0	26.1	25.2	24.4	23.5	22.7	21.9	21.1	20.3	19.5
89	32.3	31.4	30.5	29.6	28.7	27.8	26.9	26.1	25.2	24.4	23.5	22.7	21.9	21.1	20.3	19.5
90	32.3	31.3	30.5	29.5	28.7	27.8	26.9	26.1	25.2	24.3	23.5	22.7	21.8	21.0	20.2	19.4

Table VI — Ordinary Joint Life and Last Survivor Annuities — Two Lives — Expected Return Multiples

AGES	67	68	69	70	71	72	73	74	75	76	77	78	79	80	81	82
67	23.2	...	...	...	...	...	...	...	...	...	...	...	...	...	...	...
68	22.8	22.3	...	...	...	...	...	...	...	...	...	...	...	...	...	...
69	22.4	21.9	21.5	...	...	...	...	...	...	...	...	...	...	...	...	...
70	22.0	21.5	21.1	20.6	...	...	...	...	...	...	...	...	...	...	...	...
71	21.7	21.2	20.7	20.2	19.8	...	...	...	...	...	...	...	...	...	...	...
72	21.3	20.8	20.3	19.8	19.4	18.9	...	...	...	...	...	...	...	...	...	...
73	21.0	20.5	20.0	19.4	19.0	18.5	18.1	...	...	...	...	...	...	...	...	...
74	20.8	20.2	19.6	19.1	18.6	18.2	17.7	17.3	...	...	...	...	...	...	...	...
75	20.5	19.9	19.3	18.8	18.3	17.8	17.3	16.9	16.5	...	...	...	...	...	...	...
76	20.3	19.7	19.1	18.5	18.0	17.5	17.0	16.5	16.1	15.7	...	...	...	...	...	...
77	20.1	19.4	18.8	18.3	17.7	17.2	16.7	16.2	15.8	15.4	15.0	...	...	...	...	...
78	19.9	19.2	18.6	18.0	17.5	16.9	16.4	15.9	15.4	15.0	14.6	14.2	...	...	...	...
79	19.7	19.0	18.4	17.8	17.2	16.7	16.1	15.6	15.1	14.7	14.3	13.9	13.5	...	...	...
80	19.5	18.9	18.2	17.6	17.0	16.4	15.9	15.4	14.9	14.4	14.0	13.5	13.2	12.8	...	...
81	19.4	18.7	18.1	17.4	16.8	16.2	15.7	15.1	14.6	14.1	13.7	13.2	12.8	12.5	12.1	...
82	19.3	18.6	17.9	17.3	16.6	16.0	15.5	14.9	14.4	13.9	13.4	13.0	12.5	12.2	11.8	11.5
83	19.2	18.5	17.8	17.1	16.5	15.9	15.3	14.7	14.2	13.7	13.2	12.7	12.3	11.9	11.5	11.1
84	19.1	18.4	17.7	17.0	16.3	15.7	15.1	14.5	14.0	13.5	13.0	12.5	12.0	11.6	11.2	10.9
85	19.0	18.3	17.6	16.9	16.2	15.6	15.0	14.4	13.8	13.3	12.8	12.3	11.8	11.4	11.0	10.6
86	18.9	18.2	17.5	16.8	16.1	15.5	14.8	14.2	13.7	13.1	12.6	12.1	11.6	11.2	10.8	10.4
87	18.8	18.1	17.4	16.7	16.0	15.4	14.7	14.1	13.5	13.0	12.4	11.9	11.4	11.0	10.6	10.1
88	18.8	18.0	17.3	16.6	15.9	15.3	14.6	14.0	13.4	12.8	12.3	11.8	11.3	10.8	10.4	10.0
89	18.7	18.0	17.2	16.5	15.8	15.2	14.5	13.9	13.3	12.7	12.2	11.6	11.1	10.7	10.2	9.8
90	18.7	17.9	17.2	16.5	15.8	15.1	14.5	13.8	13.2	12.6	12.1	11.5	11.0	10.5	10.1	9.6

AGES	83	84	85	86	87	88	89	90
83	10.8	...	...	...	...	...	...	...
84	10.5	10.2	...	...	...	...	...	...
85	10.2	9.9	9.6	...	...	...	...	...
86	10.0	9.7	9.3	9.1	...	...	...	...
87	9.8	9.4	9.1	8.8	8.5	...	...	...
88	9.6	9.2	8.9	8.6	8.3	8.0	...	...
89	9.4	9.0	8.7	8.3	8.1	7.8	7.5	...
90	9.2	8.8	8.5	8.2	7.9	7.6	7.3	7.1

AGES	51	52	53	54	55	56	57	58	59	60	61	62	63	64	65	66
Table VI — Annuities for Joint Life Only — Two Lives — Expected Return Multiples																
51	26.1	...	...	...	...	...	...	...	...	...	...	...	...	...	...	...
52	25.7	25.3	...	...	...	...	...	...	...	...	...	...	...	...	...	...
53	25.2	24.8	24.4	...	...	...	...	...	...	...	...	...	...	...	...	...
54	24.7	24.4	24.0	23.6	...	...	...	...	...	...	...	...	...	...	...	...
55	24.2	23.9	23.5	23.2	22.7	...	...	...	...	...	...	...	...	...	...	...
56	23.7	23.4	23.1	22.7	22.3	21.9	...	...	...	...	...	...	...	...	...	...
57	23.2	22.9	22.6	22.2	21.9	21.5	21.1	...	...	...	...	...	...	...	...	...
58	22.6	22.4	22.1	21.7	21.4	21.1	20.7	20.3	...	...	...	...	...	...	...	...
59	22.1	21.8	21.5	21.2	20.9	20.6	20.3	19.9	19.5	...	...	...	...	...	...	...
60	21.5	21.2	21.0	20.7	20.4	20.1	19.8	19.5	19.1	18.7	...	...	...	...	...	...
61	20.9	20.6	20.4	20.2	19.9	19.6	19.3	19.0	18.7	18.3	17.9	...	...	...	...	...
62	20.2	20.0	19.8	19.6	19.4	19.1	18.8	18.5	18.2	17.9	17.5	17.1	...	...	...	...
63	19.6	19.4	19.2	19.0	18.8	18.6	18.3	18.0	17.7	17.4	17.1	16.8	16.4	...	...	...
64	19.0	18.8	18.6	18.5	18.3	18.0	17.8	17.5	17.3	17.0	16.7	16.3	16.0	15.6	...	...
65	18.3	18.2	18.0	17.9	17.7	17.5	17.3	17.0	16.8	16.5	16.2	15.9	15.6	15.3	14.9	...
66	17.7	17.6	17.4	17.3	17.1	16.9	16.7	16.5	16.3	16.0	15.8	15.5	15.2	14.9	14.5	14.2
67	17.1	16.9	16.8	16.7	16.5	16.3	16.2	16.0	15.8	15.5	15.3	15.0	14.7	14.5	14.1	13.8
68	16.4	16.3	16.2	16.1	15.9	15.8	15.6	15.4	15.2	15.0	14.8	14.6	14.3	14.0	13.7	13.4
69	15.8	15.7	15.6	15.4	15.3	15.2	15.0	14.9	14.7	14.5	14.3	14.1	13.9	13.6	13.3	13.1
70	15.1	15.0	14.9	14.8	14.7	14.6	14.5	14.3	14.2	14.0	13.8	13.6	13.4	13.2	12.9	12.6
71	14.5	14.4	14.3	14.2	14.1	14.0	13.9	13.8	13.6	13.5	13.3	13.1	12.9	12.7	12.5	12.2
72	13.8	13.8	13.7	13.6	13.5	13.4	13.3	13.2	13.1	12.9	12.8	12.6	12.4	12.3	12.0	11.8
73	13.2	13.2	13.1	13.0	13.0	12.9	12.8	12.7	12.5	12.4	12.3	12.1	12.0	11.8	11.6	11.4
74	12.6	12.6	12.5	12.4	12.4	12.3	12.2	12.1	12.0	11.9	11.8	11.6	11.5	11.3	11.2	11.0
75	12.0	12.0	11.9	11.9	11.8	11.7	11.7	11.6	11.5	11.4	11.3	11.1	11.0	10.9	10.7	10.5
76	11.4	11.4	11.3	11.3	11.2	11.2	11.1	11.1	11.0	10.9	10.8	10.6	10.5	10.4	10.3	10.1
77	10.8	10.8	10.8	10.7	10.7	10.6	10.6	10.5	10.4	10.3	10.3	10.2	10.0	9.9	9.8	9.7
78	10.3	10.2	10.2	10.1	10.1	10.1	10.0	10.0	9.9	9.8	9.8	9.7	9.6	9.5	9.4	9.2
79	9.7	9.7	9.7	9.6	9.6	9.6	9.5	9.5	9.4	9.3	9.3	9.2	9.1	9.0	8.9	8.8
80	9.2	9.2	9.1	9.1	9.1	9.0	9.0	9.0	8.9	8.9	8.8	8.7	8.7	8.6	8.5	8.4
81	8.7	8.7	8.6	8.6	8.6	8.5	8.5	8.5	8.4	8.4	8.3	8.3	8.2	8.1	8.0	8.0
82	8.2	8.2	8.1	8.1	8.1	8.1	8.0	8.0	8.0	7.9	7.9	7.8	7.8	7.7	7.6	7.5
83	7.7	7.7	7.7	7.6	7.6	7.6	7.6	7.5	7.5	7.5	7.4	7.4	7.3	7.3	7.2	7.1
84	7.2	7.2	7.2	7.2	7.2	7.1	7.1	7.1	7.1	7.0	7.0	7.0	6.9	6.9	6.8	6.7
85	6.8	6.8	6.8	6.7	6.7	6.7	6.7	6.7	6.6	6.6	6.6	6.5	6.5	6.5	6.4	6.4
86	6.4	6.4	6.3	6.3	6.3	6.3	6.3	6.3	6.2	6.2	6.2	6.2	6.1	6.1	6.0	6.0
87	6.0	6.0	6.0	5.9	5.9	5.9	5.9	5.9	5.9	5.9	5.8	5.8	5.8	5.7	5.7	5.6
88	5.6	5.6	5.6	5.6	5.6	5.5	5.5	5.5	5.5	5.5	5.5	5.4	5.4	5.3	5.3	5.3
89	5.2	5.2	5.2	5.2	5.2	5.2	5.2	5.2	5.2	5.1	5.1	5.1	5.1	5.1	5.0	5.0
90	4.9	4.9	4.9	4.9	4.9	4.9	4.9	4.9	4.9	4.9	4.8	4.8	4.8	4.8	4.7	4.7

AGES	67	68	69	70	71	72	73	74	75	76	77	78	79	80	81	82
Table VI — Annuities for Joint Life Only — Two Lives — Expected Return Multiples																
67	13.5	...	...	...	...	...	...	...	...	...	...	...	...	...	...	...
68	13.1	12.8	...	...	...	...	...	...	...	...	...	...	...	...	...	...
69	12.8	12.5	12.1	...	...	...	...	...	...	...	...	...	...	...	...	...
70	12.4	12.1	11.8	11.5	...	...	...	...	...	...	...	...	...	...	...	...
71	12.0	11.7	11.4	11.2	10.9	...	...	...	...	...	...	...	...	...	...	...
72	11.6	11.4	11.1	10.8	10.5	10.2	...	...	...	...	...	...	...	...	...	...
73	11.2	11.0	10.7	10.5	10.2	9.9	9.7	...	...	...	...	...	...	...	...	...
74	10.8	10.6	10.4	10.1	9.9	9.6	9.4	9.1	...	...	...	...	...	...	...	...
75	10.4	10.2	10.0	9.8	9.5	9.3	9.1	8.8	8.6	...	...	...	...	...	...	...
76	9.9	9.8	9.6	9.4	9.2	9.0	8.8	8.5	8.3	8.0	...	...	...	...	...	...
77	9.5	9.4	9.2	9.0	8.8	8.6	8.4	8.2	8.0	7.8	7.5	...	...	...	...	...
78	9.1	9.0	8.8	8.7	8.5	8.3	8.1	7.9	7.7	7.5	7.3	7.0	...	...	...	...
79	8.7	8.6	8.4	8.3	8.1	8.0	7.8	7.6	7.4	7.2	7.0	6.8	6.6	...	...	...
80	8.3	8.2	8.0	7.9	7.8	7.6	7.5	7.3	7.1	6.9	6.8	6.6	6.3	6.1	...	...
81	7.9	7.9	7.7	7.5	7.4	7.3	7.1	7.0	6.8	6.7	6.5	6.3	6.1	5.9	5.7	...
82	7.5	7.4	7.3	7.2	7.1	6.9	6.6	6.7	6.5	6.4	6.2	6.0	5.9	5.7	5.5	5.3
83	7.1	7.0	6.9	6.8	6.7	6.6	6.5	6.4	6.2	6.1	5.9	5.8	5.6	5.5	5.3	5.1
84	6.7	6.6	6.5	6.4	6.4	6.3	6.2	6.0	5.9	5.8	5.7	5.5	5.4	5.2	5.1	4.9
85	6.3	6.2	6.2	6.1	6.0	5.9	5.8	5.7	5.6	5.5	5.4	5.3	5.2	5.0	4.9	4.7
86	5.9	5.9	5.8	5.8	5.7	5.6	5.5	5.4	5.4	5.3	5.1	5.0	4.9	4.8	4.7	4.5
87	5.6	5.6	5.5	5.4	5.4	5.3	5.2	5.2	5.1	5.0	4.9	4.8	4.7	4.6	4.4	4.3
88	5.3	5.2	5.2	5.1	5.1	5.0	5.0	4.9	4.8	4.7	4.6	4.5	4.4	4.3	4.2	4.1
89	5.0	4.9	4.9	4.8	4.8	4.7	4.7	4.6	4.5	4.5	4.4	4.3	4.2	4.1	4.0	3.9
90	4.7	4.6	4.6	4.6	4.5	4.5	4.4	4.4	4.3	4.2	4.2	4.1	4.0	3.9	3.8	3.8

AGES	83	84	85	86	87	88	89	90
83	4.9	...	...	...	...	...	...	...
84	4.7	4.6	...	...	...	...	...	...
85	4.6	4.4	4.2	...	...	...	...	...
86	4.4	4.2	4.1	3.9	...	...	...	...
87	4.2	4.1	3.9	3.8	3.6	...	...	...
88	4.0	3.9	3.8	3.6	3.5	3.4	...	...
89	3.8	3.7	3.6	3.5	3.4	3.2	3.1	...
90	3.7	3.5	3.4	3.3	3.2	3.1	3.0	2.9

Appendix 6
Determining the Applicable Divisor for Installment Payments and Maximum Period Certain for Term Annuities

Determining the Applicable Divisor for Installment Payments and Maximum Period Certain for Term Annuities			
Age of the Employee	Applicable Divisor	Age of the Employee	Applicable Divisor
70	26.2	93	8.8
71	25.3	94	8.3
72	24.4	95	7.8
73	23.5	96	7.3
74	22.7	97	6.9
75	21.8	98	6.5
76	20.9	99	6.1
77	20.1	100	5.7
78	19.2	101	5.3
79	18.4	102	5.0
80	17.8	103	4.7
81	16.8	104	4.4
82	16.0	105	4.1
83	15.3	106	3.8
84	14.5	107	3.6
85	13.8	108	3.3
86	13.1	109	3.1
87	12.4	110	2.8
88	11.8	111	2.6
89	11.1	112	2.4
90	10.5	113	2.2
91	9.9	114	2.0
92	9.4	115 and older	1.8

Appendix 7
Determining the Applicable Percentage for Joint and Survivor Annuities

Determining the Applicable Percentage for Joint and Survivor Annuities	
Excess of Age of Employee over Age of Beneficiary	Applicable Percentage
10 years or less	100
11	96
12	93
13	90
14	87
15	84
16	82
17	79
18	77
19	75
20	73
21	72
22	70
23	68
24	67
25	66
26	64
27	63
28	62
29	61
30	60
31	59
32	59
33	58
34	57
35	56
36	56
37	55
38	55
39	54
40	54
41	53
42	53
43	53
44 and greater	52

Glossary

accrued benefit • the amount of benefit earned as of a given date. In a defined-benefit plan special accrued-benefit rules require that the plan benefit must be earned over an employee's entire period of employment rather than in the waning years of employment.

accumulated earnings tax • a penalty tax for C corporations that attempt to reduce shareholders' tax burden by accumulating earnings instead of paying them out to shareholders

active participant • an individual who is covered by an employer plan and actually receives a benefit or contribution from the employer under the plan. An active participant cannot have a deductible IRA unless he or she has an adjusted gross income below prescribed limits.

actual deferral percentage (ADP) test • a test applied to salary reduction 401(k) plans that ensures that salary reductions taken by highly compensated employees are in line with salary reductions taken by other employees. In order to pass the ADP test one of two requirements must be satisfied:

- *the 1.25 requirement*—The actual deferral percentage for highly compensated employees for the current year cannot be more than 125 percent of the actual deferral percentage for nonhighly compensated employees for the previous year.
- *the 200 percent/2 percent difference requirement*—The actual deferral percentage for highly compensated employees for the current year cannot be more than 200 percent of the actual deferral percentage for nonhighly compensated employees for the previous year, and the spread between the two cannot be more than 2 percent.

actuarial assumptions • assumptions that are made about investment return, mortality, turnover, and other factors concerning the employee group to determine the annual funding required in a defined-benefit plan

actuarial cost methods • methods used to determine the annual employer contribution to a defined-benefit plan

adoption agreement • the vehicle used for choosing among the various optional provisions provided in a master or prototype plan. The adoption agreement lists the various design choices that are available, and employers then pick from the menu of provided options.

advance-determination letter • a letter from the IRS stating that a plan meets the qualification standards. A request for an advance-determination letter is made on IRS Form 5300 (defined-benefit plan), 5301 (defined-contribution plan), or 5307 (master or prototype plan).

advisory opinion • an opinion, issued by the Department of Labor, regarding the legality of a given situation. An advisory opinion can be sought before a client enters a transaction in which the ERISA consequences are unknown.

affiliated service group • two or more organizations that are aggregated for purposes of the qualified plan requirements. There are actually several different affiliation rules; all were promulgated to ensure that employees who worked together to produce a single product could not be divided into separate entities to avoid the qualified plan coverage requirements.

after-tax contribution • the portion of a person's income that has already been taxed by the IRS. Contributions to a qualified plan with after-tax income are not as tax efficient as contributions made to a qualified plan with before-tax income. After-tax contributions make up part or all of the "basis" when an exclusion ratio is calculated.

age-weighted plan • a defined-contribution plan that allocates contributions to participants in such a way that when contributions are converted to equivalent benefit accruals (stated as a percentage of compensation), each participant receives the same rate of benefit accrual

aggregation rules • rules that determine whether affiliated companies will be considered the same entity for purposes of conducting qualified pension plan tests such as the nondiscrimination test

allocated funding • a method by which contributions are assigned to provide benefits for specific employees, such as individual insurance or annuity contracts

allocation formula • a formula used to determine the amount of profits distributed to each participant in a profit-sharing plan. Allocation formulas can divide the profit-sharing "pie" to favor employees with higher salaries and longer service.

annuity • the distribution or liquidation of a sum of money on an actuarial basis. The amount paid to an annuitant is typically paid monthly and is determined by such factors as the annuity purchase price, the client's age, the number of lives covered by the annuity, the number of guarantees that are offered, and the interest assumption used.

annuity certain • provides an annuitant or his or her beneficiary with a specified number of monthly guaranteed payments after which time all payments stop

anticutback rules • rules that state that once a participant has accrued a benefit or has received a contribution, the benefit or contribution cannot be reduced. Future reductions in accruals or contributions (prospective reductions), however, can be made.

applicable life expectancy (ALE) method • the principal method for determining a person's minimum distribution under the minimum distribution rules. Under the ALE method the taxpayer's benefit is divided by the average life expectancy (found in tables V and VI of Reg. 1.72-9). Alternative methods are available for taxpayers who wish to recalculate each year and for those who do not. Different planning implications apply in both situations.

assumed investment rate • the rate assumed in a variable annuity that the investment portfolio must earn in order for benefit payments to remain level. If the experience rate or actual investment rate is higher than the assumed investment rate, then annuity payouts will be higher. Conversely, if the experience or actual investment rate is lower than the assumed rate, annuity payouts will be lower.

average benefit percentage test • one of the nondiscrimination rules set out under Code Sec. 410(b). The average benefit of nonhighly compensated employees must be 70 percent of the average benefit of highly compensated employees, and a fair cross section of employees must be covered.

backloading • the prohibited practice of excessively accruing benefits in later years. The accrued-benefit rules make backloading impossible in a qualified plan.

before-tax contributions • contributions or prefunded benefits that are set aside for an employee and are not subject to taxation until retirement. When the nontaxable contribution is made to a qualified plan, the employer can take a tax deduction, which is not the case for other retirement vehicles.

break in service • an employee will be considered to have a break in service if he or she was employed by the employer and left service for any reason. In order for a break in service to occur under which the employee will forfeit rights, the employee must be gone the greater of 5 years or the amount of time he or she had worked prior to the break in service.

buy-and-hold strategy • a retirement planning strategy under which the client buys securities, bonds, mutual funds, etc. and holds them until restructuring is required—the opposite of market timing

cafeteria plan • a plan that provides flexible benefit dollars that an employee can allocate to pay for certain benefits from a menu of benefit choices (such as life insurance, health insurance, or child care) and/or place in a 401(k) plan

capital-gains election • a portion of a participant's benefit earned prior to 1974 that may be entitled to capital-gains treatment. The amount subject to capital-gains tax is determined by dividing the amount of months prior to 1974 into the total months that the participant worked under the plan. The subsequent ratio is then multiplied by the amount of distribution to determine the portion that is subject to the favorable capital-gains tax rate.

career-average benefit formula • a defined-benefit formula that bases the retirement benefit on the employee's entire earnings record with the employer. This formula typically provides a lower benefit than a final-average salary formula because it fails to account for preretirement inflation.

cash-balance plan • a defined-benefit plan that promises a benefit based on a hypothetical account balance versus a traditional plan, which promises a monthly retirement benefit for life

catch-up provision • a provision that allows employees covered by a 403(b) plan to make larger than typically permitted contributions to the plan

cliff vesting • a vesting schedule under which an employee is not entitled to any percentage of his or her retirement benefit until he or she is fully vested after the attainment of a specific amount of years of service. The maximum amount of years of service that an employee can be forced to wait in a qualified plan is 5 years.

collectibles • items such as antique cars, precious metals, stamps, coins, and Persian rugs. Individual retirement accounts cannot invest in collectibles.

conduit IRA • a parking place for funds in transition between two qualified plans. Any IRA used as a conduit must not contain funds other than the qualified plan distribution.

contribution carryover • contributions made by an organization to a profit-sharing trust that are not deductible but can be carried forward and used as a deduction in future years as long as the maximum 15 percent deduction is not exceeded

contributory plan • a plan that requires employees to make contributions of their own to be eligible for plan participation

controlled group rules • rules that require companies with a sufficient amount of common control to be tested as a single employer for purposes of the qualified plan requirements

covered compensation • the average of the maximum social security wage bases for the number of years of earnings used to calculate the social security benefit for the 35-year period ending with the year the employee reaches the social security retirement age. Covered compensation is the integration level used in most defined-benefit plans.

cross-tested plan • a qualified plan of the defined-contribution type that tests whether its contribution formula discriminates in favor of the highly compensated employees by converting contributions made for each participant into equivalent benefit accruals.

deferred compensation • an agreement that states that compensation for services rendered is postponed until sometime after the services in question have been performed

deferred retirement age • any retirement age beyond the normal retirement age. In a defined-contribution plan, contributions will continue to be made after the normal retirement age until the deferred retirement age. In a defined-benefit plan, unless there's a years-of-service cap on the benefit formula, benefit accruals will continue until the deferred retirement age.

defined-benefit plan • a retirement plan that specifies the benefits that each employee receives at retirement. The maximum yearly benefit allowed is the lesser of 100 percent of the high 3-year average compensation or $125,000 (1997 indexed number).

defined-contribution plan • a retirement plan that specifies the contributions that each employee receives. The maximum contribution allowed (called an annual addition) is the lesser of 25 percent of salary or $30,000 (as indexed in 1997) for each year of employment. These contributions are made to an individual's account during the employment years.

distress termination • a plan termination that is allowed because the employer is experiencing financial difficulties

diversification requirement • a requirement that fiduciaries diversify the investments of the plan to minimize the risk of large losses

dividend reinvestment plan • a shareholder's option to have cash dividends automatically reinvested in additional shares of the company's common stock

dollar-cost averaging • a system for timing investment transactions that has a fixed dollar amount being invested in a particular security in each time period

early-retirement age • the age at which, if the plan permits, employees are permitted to retire and receive benefits prior to the normal retirement age. Typical early-retirement ages are 55, 60, and 62.

elapsed time method • the computation of credit for plan service that is measured from date of employment to date of severance

Employee Retirement Income Security Act (ERISA) • the act that laid the foundation for modern pension law. ERISA established the nondiscrimination requirements, reporting and disclosure requirements, plan funding standards, vesting and participation requirements, and fiduciary responsibilities.

ERISA 404(c) individual account plan exception • provision of ERISA that relieves fiduciaries from liability for the investment decisions of plan participants

employee stock ownership plan (ESOP) • a profit-sharing plan that invests primarily in employer stock. ESOPs are usually leveraged by borrowing from a bank to fund the plan.

enrollment meeting • a meeting during which employees may sign up to be covered by the employer's plan. An enrollment meeting is typically held to get proper enrollments in salary reduction plans, such as 401(k) and 403(b) plans, and also to get the adequate participation in a contributory plan.

entry date • a sign-up time at which an employee becomes a participant under the plan. An employee must first satisfy the plan's eligibility requirements to be admitted as a participant on the next plan entry date.

excess distributions • annual distributions from qualified plans, 403(b) plans, SEPs, SIMPLEs, and IRAs that exceed $160,000 (as indexed for 1997) for a periodic distribution, or five times the $160,000 for lump-sum distributions) are subject to a 15 percent excise tax. Note the moratorium on this tax for distributions made in 1997, 1998, and 1999.

exclusive-benefit rule • a rule that prevents misuse of the retirement plan. A fiduciary is required to discharge all duties solely in the interest of plan participants and their beneficiaries.

fiduciary • a person or corporation that exercises any discretionary authority or control over the management of the plan or plan assets, renders investment advice for a fee, or has any discretionary authority or responsibility in the administration of the plan

filing-status floor • the level of adjusted gross income under which a person is entitled to a full IRA deduction. For marrieds filing jointly the filing-status floor is $40,000; for single taxpayers the filing-status floor is $25,000.

final-average benefit formula • a defined-benefit formula that bases the retirement benefit on salary levels in the last few years preceding retirement. This formula typically provides an adequate benefit because it accounts for preretirement inflation.

final regulations • regulations that explain and interpret the various sections of the Internal Revenue Code. Final regulations are legally enforceable, and the Internal Revenue Service is bound by them.

501(c)(3) organizations • certain tax-exempt organizations as specified in the Internal Revenue Code section that can have a 403(b) plan. A corporation, community chest, fund, or foundation that is organized and operated exclusively for religious, charitable, scientific, testing for public safety, literary, or educational purposes; for fostering national or international amateur sports competition; or for the prevention of cruelty to children or animals will probably qualify for 501(c)(3) status.

flat-amount formula • a formula for determining benefits that does not take into account an employee's service or salary

flat-amount-per-year-of-service formula • a benefit formula that relates the pension benefit solely to service and does not reflect an employee's salary

flat-percentage-of-earnings formula • a benefit formula that is related solely to salary and does not reflect an employee's service

forfeiture • the amount that is lost when a participant terminates employment before being fully vested under the plan's vesting schedule

forward averaging • a preferential method for computing the tax on a qualifying lump-sum distribution from a qualified plan (but not SEPs, IRAs, or 403(b) TDAs). A person born after January 1, 1936, may elect 5-year averaging. A person born on or before January 1, 1936, may elect either 5-year or 10-year averaging. Note that 5-year averaging will no longer be available for distributions made after December 31, 1999.

401(a)(4) rule • a rule that forbids disparity in the amount of contributions or benefits that can be provided for highly compensated employees as compared with those provided for the rank-and-file employees

401(k) plan • a defined-contribution profit-sharing plan that gives participants the option of reducing their taxable salary and contributing the salary reduction on a tax-deferred basis to an individual account for retirement purposes

403(b) plan • a retirement plan similar to a 401(k) plan that is available to certain tax-exempt organizations and to public schools

fractional rule • a method for determining a person's accrued benefit as follows:

$$\frac{\text{years of participation}}{\begin{array}{c}\text{years of participation to}\\ \text{normal retirement age}\end{array}} \times \begin{array}{c}\text{projected monthly}\\ \text{benefit at normal}\\ \text{retirement age}\end{array} = \text{accrued benefit}$$

frozen plan • a qualified plan that does not permit continued accruals of benefits or additional contributions for existing employees and does not recognize new plan participants

full cash-refund annuity • an annuity under which payments are made to the annuitant until the annuitant's death. If, however, at the time of the annuitant's death the full amount of the annuity purchase price has not been returned to the annuitant, then any remainder will be returned to the annuitant's beneficiary.

funding standard account • the account used to determine if the minimum funding standards are being satisfied

general-counsel memorandum • a legal memorandum that is relied on by IRS personnel in deciding disputes with taxpayers

golden handshakes • additional benefits paid to employees to induce early retirement

golden parachutes • substantial payments made to corporate executives who are terminated upon change of ownership or corporate control

graded vesting • a vesting schedule under which the participant gradually becomes fully vested over time. The statutory maximum 3-through-7 graded schedule requires no vesting until the third year of service has been completed, and at that point the benefit increases 20 percent for each year served.

hardship • a withdrawal permitted under a 401(k) plan or 403(b) plan if the participant has a hardship and has no other resources available to meet the financial hardship. Under regulations a hardship has been described as payments for a college education, for a residence, and for medical bills.

highly compensated employee • any person who is a more-than-5-percent owner of the business in the previous or current year, and any person who earned over $80,000 (as indexed for 1997) in the previous year. The employer can elect to limit the second category to only those individuals in the top 20 percent of the employer pay group.

hour of service • any hour for which a participant is paid or entitled to be paid

hours-worked-excluding-overtime method • a method for counting hours of service that looks only at actual hours worked excluding overtime, vacations, holidays, and sick time. If this method is used, an employee needs to work only 750 hours to earn a year of service.

hours-worked-including-overtime method • a method for counting hours of service that looks at actual hours worked including overtime but excluding nonworked hours such as vacation, holidays, and sick time. If this method is used, an employee needs to work only 870 hours to earn a year of service.

incentive stock options • options that allow executives to acquire stock at a bargain without incurring a taxable interest when the stock is acquired

incidental-death-benefit rules • ERISA rules that limit the amount of life insurance that can be used in a qualified plan

income-replacement ratio • the amount of gross income that is replaced by the retirement plan

individual retirement account • a trust or custodial agreement that allows savings for retirement in a tax-advantaged manner

individual retirement annuity • an individual retirement account that is funded with an annuity contract

inflation • an increase in the general (average) level of prices

in-service withdrawals • withdrawals taken from the qualified plan while the participant is still employed. No in-service withdrawals are permitted from a pension plan.

installment payout • the periodic payout of funds from a qualified plan

integration • a method of dovetailing a qualified plan with social security benefits. Because social security discriminates in favor of low-paid employees, an integrated plan is allowed to discriminate in favor of highly paid employees to the extent permitted under the integration rules.

integration level • the dividing line between the base and excess percentages in an integrated plan. The integration level for a defined-benefit plan is typically covered compensation; the integration level for a defined-contribution plan is typically the taxable wage base.

involuntary termination • termination that is called for by the PBGC when a plan is seriously unfunded and the PBGC would be liable for continuation of unfunded benefits. An involuntary termination can also be called for by the IRS if plan contributions cease and no provision is made for plan continuance.

IRS news releases • announcements about forthcoming regulations and information about statistical and survey results

IRS publications • general reviews of retirement topics provided by the IRS to aid individuals in filing their tax returns

joint and survivor annuity • an annuity for a participant's life that terminates at the participant's death. If, however, at the participant's death his or her spouse is still alive, annuity payments in a predetermined amount will continue for the life of the surviving spouse. A joint and survivor annuity is the normal form of benefit for married individuals in a qualified plan.

Keogh plan • a qualified plan for unincorporated businesses

key employee • an employee who owns more than 5 percent of the business, an officer who earns over one-half of the 415 defined-benefit limit, an employee who owns one of the 10 largest shares of the company, or a one percent owner who earns over $150,000

leased employee • a term of art under the pension rules that describes an individual who is leased on a full-time, ongoing basis. The rules require that such leased employees be generally treated as employees for purposes of the qualified plan coverage requirements.

level annual funding • a schedule to save funds for a specific dollar retirement goal where the same level investment is made each year until retirement age

life annuity • an annuity that pays income for the participant's life and stops payments at the participant's death. No survivor or additional death benefits are payable. It will yield the largest monthly payment per given purchase price of all the annuity types, since there are no residual benefits.

life annuity with guaranteed paymcnts • an annuity that pays benefits for a participant's life and stops when a participant dies. If, however, a participant dies before the guaranteed payments are made, payments are made to the participant's beneficiary for the remainder of that period. The longer the stipulation or guaranteed period, the smaller the monthly amount for a given dollar figure. Conversely, the shorter the stipulated or guaranteed period, the larger the monthly amount for a given dollar figure.

long-term accumulation period • the stage in an individual's investment program that begins when funds are first accumulated for retirement and is phased out with the onset of the portfolio restructuring period

loose-leaf services • publications that describe the legal and administrative framework of pensions in an up-to-date manner

lump-sum distribution • a distribution from the plan that represents the participant's entire account balance. (See also qualified lump-sum distribution.)

mandatory contributions • contributions required as a condition for plan participation

master or prototype plans • standardized plans approved and qualified in concept by the Internal Revenue Service that the insurance companies make available for their agents. Although these plans must go through qualification procedures, a favorable result is more predictable. The master or prototype plan offers an employer fewer choices in plan design and thus can be installed very easily.

maximum insured benefits • the maximum amount that the PBGC will insure. This amount is $2,642 per month (as indexed in 1996).

Medicare, Part A • the hospital portion of medicare. It provides benefits for expenses incurred in hospitals, skilled nursing facilities, and hospices with various limits and restrictions, and for home health care for a condition treated in a hospital or skilled nursing facility. It is available at no monthly cost to any person aged 65 or older who is entitled to monthly retirement benefits under social security.

Medicare, Part B • the supplementary medical insurance portion of medicare. It provides benefits for physicians' and surgeons' fees, diagnostic tests, certain drugs and medical supplies, rental of certain medical equipment, and home health service when prior hospitalization has not occurred. With some exceptions, part B pays 80 percent of the approved charges for covered medical expenses after the satisfaction of an annual deductible. Any person eligible for part A is eligible for part B and is automatically enrolled. A monthly premium is charged for part B which is adjusted annually to reflect the cost of the benefits provided.

minimum distribution incidental benefit (MDIB) method • the secondary method for determining a person's minimum distribution under the minimum distribution rules. Under the MDIB method the IRS is assured that payouts of retirement funds will reasonably occur during the taxpayer's lifetime by limiting the amount of benefits that may be provided for a nonspouse beneficiary.

minimum distribution rules • set out procedures for determining the minimum required distributions from qualified plans, 403(b) plans, SEPs, and IRAs once a person reaches age 70 1/2

modified cash-refund annuity • an annuity that provides payments for a person's life and stops payment at a person's death. If, however, a stipulated amount of the annuity purchase price has not been received by the annuitant, then that portion will be refunded to the annuitant's beneficiary. It is typically the normal form of benefit for single individuals in a contributory pension plan, thus returning any contributions they made to the plan.

money-purchase pension plan • a defined-contribution plan that specifies a level of contribution (for example, 10 percent of salary) to each participant's account each year

new-money method • a method used by insurance companies that credits each contribution with the rate of return equal to the current investment rate at which it is invested. This makes insurance company rates competitive in times of rising interest rates.

nonqualified plan • a retirement plan that can discriminate in favor of executives but is not eligible for the special tax benefits available for qualified or other tax-advantaged retirement plans

normal form of benefit • a distribution from a qualified plan that for a married individual is a joint and survivor annuity of at least 50 percent. For a single individual the normal form of benefit is typically a life annuity, or in a contributory plan, a modified cash-refund annuity.

normal retirement age • the age at which a participant can retire and receive the full, specified retirement benefit

notice to interested parties • a letter sent out to affected employees when a qualified plan is instituted. The notice informs participants and those excluded from participation that they can make comments concerning the plan to the Department of Labor.

Office of Pension and Welfare Benefit Plans (OPWBP) • the branch of the Department of Labor responsible for overseeing retirement plans

offset integration • a method of integrating defined-benefit plans by subtracting out a specified amount from the benefit formula that represents a percentage of the participant's social security benefits

1-and-21 rule • a rule that states that to be eligible for participation in the plan an employee must have one year of service and be at least age 21

133 1/3 percent rule • a method for determining a person's accrued benefit. The accrued benefit is the employee's actual benefit earned to date under the plan, provided that any future rate of benefit accrual is not more than 133 1/3 percent of the current benefit accrual rate.

$125,000 exclusion for the sale of a home • a one-time exclusion from federal income taxation of up to $125,000 of any capital gain realized from the sale of an individual's primary residence that applies to individuals at least 55 years of age

partial termination • a termination in which part of the plan continues for a smaller group of participants and part of the plan ceases to exist

party-in-interest • a person who has a relationship to the qualified plan. Parties-in-interest include plan fiduciaries, plan counsels, persons providing services to the plan, employers connected with the plan, employees in the plan, employee organizations whose members are covered by the plan, relatives of any of the above, and shareholders, officers, and directors who have a 10-percent-or-more ownership interest in any of the above.

past service • service prior to the inception of the plan. In a defined-benefit plan the employer has the option of funding for past service.

Pension Benefit Guaranty Corporation (PBGC) • an organization that oversees defined-benefit plans and provides insureds protection in case a defined-benefit plan cannot pay promised benefits to participants

pension plan • a qualified plan structured to provide a pension at retirement. Characteristics include an annual funding commitment by employers, an inability to access retirement funds through preretirement withdrawals by employees, and a limitation on investments to 10 percent of employer stock.

percentage match • a situation in which the employee can contribute up to a specified percent of pay per year, and the employer will match up to a specified percent of the employee's contribution

percentage test • one of the nondiscrimination tests set out under Code Sec. 410(b). Under this test the plan must benefit at least 70 percent of employees who are not highly compensated employees.

permanency requirement • a requirement that all qualified plans must be intended to be permanent

piggybacking • a method that combines a money-purchase and profit-sharing plan. Piggybacking is also used when referring to combining a qualified and nonqualified plan.

plan administrator • the person who administrates the plan

plan termination • the means by which the employer may discontinue his or her obligation to make contributions to participant accounts in a defined-contribution plan or to fund a promised benefit in a defined-benefit plan

portfolio restructuring period • the investment stage during which an individual's portfolio composition shifts from growth orientation to income orientation prior to retirement

preservation and current income period • the retirement period when portfolio management objectives focus most heavily on the preservation of capital and high current income and only to a limited degree on long-term growth

private-letter ruling • an IRS interpretation of the law in light of a specific set of circumstances that face a taxpayer. A method by which a taxpayer can inquire about the acceptability of a specific transaction in which he or she is engaged.

profit-sharing plan • a defined-contribution plan structured to offer an employee participation in company profits that he or she may use for retirement purposes

prohibited transaction • a prohibited dealing between the plan and a party-in-interest

prohibited-transaction exemption • an exemption from the prohibited-transaction rules that allows a transaction that would otherwise be prohibited

proposed regulations • regulations issued right after major legislation so that practitioners can receive guidance on complex provisions of new laws. Unlike final regulations, proposed regulations have no legal force or effect.

prudent-fiduciary rule • a rule that states a plan fiduciary must perform his or her functions as a prudent person would perform them under like circumstances or else legal liability will be incurred. A prudent fiduciary must use the care, skill, prudence, and diligence under the circumstances then prevailing that a prudent fiduciary acting in like capacity would use.

PS 58 costs • a present benefit received by a participant in the form of current life insurance protection that must be included in taxable gross income for that year. The cost attributable to this pure life protection will be the lower of the actual cost as provided by the carrier or the rates supplied by the so-called PS 58 table.

qualified domestic relations order • a decree under state law that assigns a participant's plan benefits to a spouse or other designated party

qualified joint and survivor annuity • the normal form of benefit distribution offered to a married participant at retirement

qualified lump-sum distribution • a distribution that is entitled to favorable tax treatment under the 5-year and 10-year averaging rules. In order to be considered a qualified lump-sum distribution, the distribution must meet the following conditions:

- The client must have been a plan participant for at least 5 years.
- The funds must be distributed to the client within one taxable year.
- The distribution must represent the entire account balance or benefit.
- The amount distributed must be payable only upon death, attainment of age 59 1/2, separation from service, or disability.
- The distribution must be from a qualified plan. Individual retirement accounts, simplified employee pensions, and 403(b) tax-sheltered annuities are not considered qualified plans for this purpose.

qualified plan • a retirement plan that is rewarded with favorable tax status for meeting Internal Revenue Code restrictions such as eligibility and coverage, funding and vesting, and nondiscrimination in benefits and contributions

qualified preretirement survivor annuity (QPSA) • death benefit given to a surviving spouse following the death of a participant prior to retirement. For a defined-benefit plan, the amount of the survivor annuity is basically equal to the amount that would have been paid under the qualified joint and survivor annuity. To determine this amount, the plan administrator assumes the participant had retired the day before death. Or, if the participant was not yet able to retire, he or she had left the company the day prior to death, survived until the plan's earliest retirement age, and then retired with an immediate joint and survivor annuity. For a defined-contribution plan, the qualified preretirement survivor annuity is an annuity for the life of the surviving spouse that is at least actuarially equivalent to 50 percent of the vested account balance of the participant as of the date of death.

rabbi trust • a trust established and funded by the employer that is subject to the claims of the employer's creditors (thus avoiding current taxation for the employee), but the funds in the trust cannot be used by, or revert back to, the employer

ratio test • one of the nondiscrimination tests set out under Code Sec. 410(b). A plan must benefit a percentage of nonhighly compensated employees that is at least 70 percent of the percentage of highly compensated employees benefited under the plan.

reallocated • amounts forfeited by employees leaving prior to fully vesting that are distributed to the remaining plan participants

replacement ratio • the percentage of preretirement income replaced in the postretirement period. For example, a qualified defined-benefit plan will typically replace between 40 and 60 percent of a person's final-average salary.

required beginning date • the date when distributions from qualified plans, 403(b) TDAs, SEPs, and IRAs must commence under the uniform minimum distribution rules. In most cases, this date is April 1 of the year after a person becomes aged 70 1/2.

revenue procedures • statements concerning the internal practices and procedures of the IRS

revenue rulings • the IRS's interpretations of the provisions of the Internal Revenue Code and regulations as they apply to factual situations presented by taxpayers. Revenue rulings may be used as precedents.

reverse annuity mortgage • a life or term annuity in the form of a loan, paid to an individual and secured by the individual's ownership of his or her residence

risk tolerance • the degree to which an investor can accept risk and uncertainty in either the performance and/or the value of his or her investments

rollover • a way to delay taxation by transferring funds from one IRA or qualified plan to a second IRA or qualified plan

salary reduction agreement • the form that authorizes the employer to reduce an employee's salary and make plan contributions to a 401(k) or a 403(b) plan in the amount of the reduction

sale-leaseback agreement • the sale of a property ownership interest in real estate (or other asset) and the immediate leasing of the property by the seller for either a specified or an indefinite term

Section 72(t) penalty • Section 72(t) imposes a 10 percent penalty tax on premature withdrawals from qualified plans, 403(b) TDAs, SEPs, and IRAs. All distributions will incur these penalties except distributions that are

- made on or after the attainment of age 59 1/2, or, if made from a qualified plan, after separation from service for early retirement after age 55
- made to a beneficiary or to an employee's estate on or after the employee's death
- attributable to disability
- part of a series of substantially equal periodic payments made at least annually over the life or life expectancy of the employee or the joint lives or life expectancies of the employee and beneficiary. (If the distribution is from a qualified plan, the employee must also be separated from service.)
- made to cover medical expenses deductible for the year under Code Sec. 213 whether or not actually deductible (not applicable to distributions from IRAs)
- from certain tax-credit ESOP payments

separate lines of business • a term used under the minimum coverage rules that allows a company that operates a separate line of business and has at least 50 employees to treat that entity as a separate company under the qualified plan rules.

simplified employee pension (SEP) • a retirement plan that uses an individual retirement account (IRA) as the receptacle for contributions. A SEP is a simplified alternative to a profit-sharing or 401(k) plan.

savings incentive match plan for employees (SIMPLE) • a simplified retirement plan that allows employees to save on a pretax basis, with limited employer contributions.

single-premium annuity contract (SPAC) • a product sold when a plan terminates that transfers the employer's liability under the plan to an insurer. SPACs require the payment of a single premium by the employer in return for which the life insurance company issues paid-up annuities to all former participants.

split-interest purchase • the acquisition of property by two parties whereby one party owns certain rights to the property such as lifetime use and the other party owns the remaining rights such as full ownership upon the death of the lifetime-use owner

spousal consent • the protection generally afforded by qualified plans for a spouse's interest in a participant's qualified plans by automatic provision of a qualified preretirement survivor annuity (QPSA) in the event the participant dies before retirement and a qualified joint and survivor annuity (QJSA) as the normal benefit when the participant retires. Elections to waive QPSA or QJSA benefits and to elect some other form of benefit or to designate some other beneficiary are not valid unless the spouse of the participant consents in writing in the election.

spousal IRA • an IRA for a nonworking spouse that can be up to $2,000 in any given year

standard-hours counting method • a way to compute the hours of service an employee has for plan purposes by counting each hour the employee works and each hour for which the employee is entitled to be paid

standard termination • a voluntary termination of a qualified defined-benefit plan in which the plan sponsor has sufficient assets to pay its benefit commitments

stepped-up annual funding • a schedule to save funds for a specific dollar retirement goal in which lower annual contributions are made in earlier years and the amount invested is increased every year

stipulated annuity • see life annuity with guaranteed payments

stock bonus plan • a defined-contribution profit-sharing plan in which all employer contributions are in the form of employer stock and distributions to participants can be made in the form of employer stock

summary annual report • a summary of the 5500 forms filed with the IRS that is provided to plan participants every year

summary of material modification • an explanation given to plan participants that informs them about major changes in their plan

summary plan description • an easy-to-read booklet that explains the retirement plan to participants

superannuated employee • an older employee whose productivity level is lower than his or her salary level

target-benefit pension plan • a hybrid retirement plan that uses a benefit formula like that of a defined-benefit plan and the individual accounts like that of a defined-contribution plan. The contribution is derived from the benefit formula in a target-benefit plan, but once determined, the plan resembles a money-purchase plan in all other ways.

tax-advantaged retirement plans • employer-sponsored retirement plans that are eligible for special tax treatment. These plans include qualified plans, SEPs, SIMPLEs, and 403(b) plans.

technical-advice memorandum • a private ruling on a completed transaction issued by the national office of the IRS

temporary annuity • a life annuity that expires after a given period of time

temporary regulations • regulations issued right after major legislation so that practitioners can receive guidance on complex provisions of new laws. Temporary regulations have legal force and effect until withdrawn.

third-party administrator • an organization that offers design consulting, record-keeping, legal, and actuarial services to support the plan administrator

3 percent method • a way to determine the amount a participant could accrue under the plan

thrift plan • a plan under which employees contribute a fixed percentage of salary to the plan and the employer makes a contribution in the same amount or in a reduced amount

title IV plan • a plan that is covered by PBGC insurance

top-heavy plan • a plan that unduly favors key employees by providing 60 percent or more of the benefits or contributions to these employees. These plans are subject to additional restrictions.

unallocated funding • a method by which contributions are assigned to a general pool and specifically allocated to employees only at retirement—for example, deposit-administration contracts and immediate-participation-guarantee contracts

unit-benefit formula • a formula that accounts for both service and salary in determining the participant's benefit in a defined-benefit plan

valuation date • the date when investment earnings, gains, and losses are allocated to participant's accounts

variable annuity • an annuity with an equity-based component to it. It is designed to provide fluctuating benefit payments over the payout period that may provide increasing benefits during periods of inflation.

vesting • the acquisition by an employee of his or her right to receive a present or future pension benefit

voluntary nondeductible employee contributions • contributions that do not result in matching employer contributions

wasting trust • the trust that holds plan funds when a qualified plan is frozen. Under a wasting trust, payouts are made to plan participants when called for under the terminated plan, but no new contributions are received by the trust.

year of service • a 12-month period in which the participant has 1,000 hours of service

Index